101
QUESTIONS & ANSWERS
SERIES

LAW OF CONTRACT

101
QUESTIONS & ANSWERS
SERIES

LAW OF CONTRACT

JACQUELINE WILKINSON
BA, PhD

OLD BAILEY PRESS

OLD BAILEY PRESS
200 Greyhound Road, London W14 9RY

First Printed 1998
Reprinted 1999

© The HLT Group Ltd 1998

All Old Bailey Press publications enjoy copyright protection and the copyright belongs to the HLT Group Ltd.

All rights reserved. No part of this publication may be reproduced or transmitted in any form or by any means, electronic, mechanical, photocopying, recording or otherwise, or stored in any retrieval system of any nature without either the written permission of the copyright holder, application for which should be made to the Old Bailey Press, or a licence permitting restricted copying in the United Kingdom issued by the Copyright Licensing Agency.

Any person who infringes the above in relation to this publication may be liable to criminal prosecution and civil claims for damages.

ISBN 1 85836 089 7

British Library Cataloguing-in-Publication Data

A catalogue record for this book is available from the British Library.

Printed and bound in Great Britain

Contents

Foreword *vii*

Acknowledgement *ix*

Table of Cases *xi*

1. Offer and Acceptance *1*
2. Consideration and Intention to Create Legal Relations *21*
3. Form and Contents of Contract *39*
4. Misrepresentation, Duress and Undue Influence *64*
5. Exclusion Clauses *80*
6. Capacity *99*
7. Mistake *113*
8. Duress and Undue Influence *139*
9. Privity of Contract and Assignment of Contractual Rights *148*
10. Illegality *166*
11. Frustration, Discharge and Breach *184*
12. Remedies and Quasi-Contract *199*
13. Agency and Sale of Goods *215*

Foreword

This book is part of a series designed specifically for those students studying at undergraduate level. Coverage is not restricted to any one syllabus but embraces the main examination topics found in a typical examination paper.

This book is concerned with contract law in the context of examinations. Each chapter contains an Introduction setting out the scope of the topic, important recent cases and articles, and other helpful advice as to likely examination questions on that topic.

Additionally, in each chapter there are Interrograms and Examination Questions. The Interrograms are designed as short questions testing knowledge of the fundamentals of the topic being covered. The Examination Questions are a selection of actual questions taken mainly from papers set by a university, and have been selected because they represent the most typical examples of how knowledge of the syllabus is tested. It is intended that students should work through the Interrograms and Examination Questions before checking their knowledge (and presentation style) against the suggested answers contained in each chapter. The answers state the law as at 1 August 1998.

Acknowledgement

Examination questions are the copyright of the University of London (where specified).

The questions are taken or adapted mainly from past University of London LLB Degree for external students examination papers. Our thanks are extended to the University of London for their kind permission to use and publish the questions.

Caveat

The answers given are not approved, sanctioned or endorsed by the University of London and are entirely the Publishers' responsibility.

Table of Cases

A-Z Bazaars (Pty) Ltd v Minister of Agriculture [1974] (4) SA 392 (c)   7, 8, 9
Adams v Lindsell (1818) B & Ald 681   5, 6, 7, 8, 10, 12, 16, 17, 136, 137
Addis v Gramophone Co Ltd [1909] AC 488   204, 206
Adler v Dickson [1955] 1 QB 158   87, 89
Aerial Advertising v Batchelors Peas Ltd [1938] 2 All ER 788   53, 54
Ailsa Craig Fishing Co Ltd v Malvern Fishing Co [1983] 1 WLR 964; [1983] 1 All ER 101   93, 95
Ajayi (F A) v R T Briscoe (Nigeria) Ltd [1964] 1 WLR 1326   27, 28, 29, 30, 31, 32, 35, 36
Alan (W J) & Co Ltd v El Nasr Export and Import Co [1972] 2 QB 189   27, 28, 30, 32, 35, 37
Alderslade v Hendon Laundry Ltd [1945] KB 189   87, 88, 225, 226
Alec Lobb (Garages) Ltd v Total Oil (Great Britain) Ltd [1985] 1 All ER 303   141, 145, 147, 171
Alev, The see Vantage Navigation Corporation v Suhail and Saud Bahwan Building Materials LLC
Alexander v Rayson [1936] 1 KB 169   169, 180, 181
Allen v Pink (1838) 4 M & W 140   56, 57
Alpenstow Ltd v Regalian Properties Ltd [1985] 2 All ER 545   45
Amalgamated Investment and Property Co Ltd v John Walker & Sons Ltd [1977] 1 WLR 164; [1976] 3 All ER 509   119, 120, 122, 124, 133, 135
Amoco v Rocca Bros [1975] AC 561   171
Andre et Cie SA v Ets Michel Blanc [1977] 2 Lloyd's Rep 166   68, 70
Andrews v Hopkinson [1957] 1 QB 229   227, 229
Anglia Television Ltd v Reed [1972] 1 QB 60   201
Appleby v Myers (1867) LR 2 CP 651   188, 189
Appleton v Campbell (1826) 2 C & P 347   169, 181, 183

Archbolds (Freightage Ltd) v S Spanglett Ltd [1961] 1 QB 374; [1961] 1 All ER 417   172, 176, 177, 178, 179, 181, 182
Archer v Stone (1898) 78 LT 34   220, 221, 223
Armstrong v Jackson [1917] 2 KB 822   77, 78
Ashbury Railway Carriage and Iron Co v Riche (1875) LR 7 HL 653   101
Ashmore, Benson, Pease & Co Ltd v A V Dawson Ltd [1973] 1 WLR 828   172, 178, 179, 181, 182
Associated Japanese Bank (International) Ltd v Credit du Nord SA [1988] 3 All ER 902   121, 122, 123, 125, 127, 128, 129, 130, 131, 133, 134, 135
Atlantic Baron, The see North Ocean Shipping v Hyundai Construction
Atlas Express Ltd v Kafco (Importers and Distributors) Ltd [1989] 1 All ER 641   30, 31, 146, 192, 194
Attorney-General for Australia v Adelaide Steamship Co [1913] AC 781   173, 175
Attwood v Lamont [1920] 3 KB 571   171
Attwood v Small (1838) 6 Cl & F 232   66

B & S Contracts and Design v Victor Green Publications Ltd [1984] ICR 419   29-30, 31, 146
Balfour v Balfour [1919] 2 KB 571   23, 24, 25
Bank of Credit and Commerce International SA v Aboody and Another [1990] 1 QB 923   142, 143
Barclays Bank plc v O'Brien [1993] 3 WLR 786   142, 143, 144
Bartlett v Sydney Marcus [1965] 1 WLR 1013   225, 226, 227, 228
Barton v Armstrong [1976] AC 104   141
Beattie v Lord Ebury (1872) LR 7 Ch App 777   68, 69
Bell v Lever Brothers Ltd [1932] AC 161   119, 120, 121, 122, 123, 124, 125, 126, 127, 128, 129, 130, 131, 132, 133, 134, 135
Belvoir Finance Co v Stapleton [1971] 1 QB 210   176, 178

Tables of Cases

Bendall v McWhirter [1952] 2 QB 466   *150, 153, 154*
Bensten v Taylor Sons & Co [1893] 2 QB 274   *45, 46, 53, 53-54*
Beswick v Beswick [1968] AC 58   *153, 155, 156, 157, 158, 159, 160, 161, 162, 164, 165*
Bettini v Gye (1876) 1 QBD 183   *51, 52, 53, 54, 195, 196*
Bigg v Boyd Gibbins Ltd [1971] 1 WLR 913; [1971] 2 All ER 183   *10, 136, 137*
Bigos v Bousted [1951] 1 All ER 92   *176, 177*
Birmingham and District Land Co v London & NW Railway (1888) 40 Ch D 268   *35, 36*
Bisset v Wilkinson [1927] AC 177   *66, 71, 72, 75, 76*
Blackburn Bobbin & Co Ltd v T W Allen & Sons Ltd [1918] 2 KB 467   *190, 191*
Blackstone (David) Ltd v Burnetts (West End) Ltd [1973] 1 WLR 1487   *197*
Bliss v South East Thames Regional Health Authority [1987] ICR 700   *105, 107, 153, 154*
Bloxsome v Williams (1824) 3 B & C 232   *178, 180*
Boulton v Jones (1857) 2 H & N 564   *126, 128, 130*
Bowmakers Ltd v Barnet Instruments Ltd [1945] KB 65   *176, 178*
Brett v J S (1600) Cro Eliz 756   *33, 34*
Bridge v Deacons [1984] AC 705   *171*
Brikom Investments Ltd v Carr [1979] QB 467; [1979] 2 All ER 753   *35, 37, 197, 198*
Brimnes, The [1975] QB 929   *10, 11, 12, 13*
Brinkibon Ltd v Stahag Stahl [1983] 2 AC 34; [1982] 1 All ER 293   *5, 8, 10, 11, 16, 18*
British Bank for Foreign Trade v Novinex [1949] 1 KB 623   *44*
British Motor Trade Association v Salvadori [1949] Ch 556   *150, 153, 154*
BP Exploration v Hunt (No 2) [1982] 1 All ER 925   *187, 188, 189, 190*
British Westinghouse Electric Co Ltd v Underground Electric Railways [1912] AC 673   *203, 205*
Brogden v Metropolitan Railway Co (1877) 2 App Cas 666   *5, 83, 85*
Brown v Raphael [1958] Ch 636   *68, 69*
Bruce v Warwick (1815) 6 Taunt 341   *105, 107*
Bunge Corporation v Tradax Export SA [1981] 1 WLR 711; [1981] 2 All ER 513   *45, 47, 51, 52, 53, 54, 59, 60*

Burgess' Policy, Re (1915) 113 LT 443   *159*
Burmah Oil v Bank of England (1981) The Times 4 July   *141*
Burnard v Haggis (1863) 14 CB (NS) 45   *103, 105*
Butler Machine Tool Co Ltd v Ex-cell-o Corporation (England) Ltd [1979] 1 WLR 401   *6, 9, 10, 11, 83, 85*
Byrne v Van Tienhoven (1880) 5 CPD 344   *8, 9, 10, 11, 12, 14, 15, 18, 19*

C & P Haulage v Middleton [1983] 1 WLR 1461   *201*
CCC Films (London) Ltd v Impact Quadrant Films Ltd [1984] 3 WLR 245   *188, 189, 201*
CIBC Mortgages v Pitt [1993] 3 WLR 802   *142, 144, 145*
Campbell v Edwards [1976] 1 WLR 403 CA   *44*
Car and Universal Finance Co Ltd v Caldwell [1965] 1 QB 525   *77, 78*
Carlill v Carbolic Smoke Ball Co Ltd [1893] 1 QB 256   *4, 5, 10, 14, 18, 19*
Casey's Patents, Re [1892] 1 Ch 104   *25*
Castle v Wilkinson (1870) LR 5 Ch App 534   *17, 18*
Cehave v Bremer Handelsgesellschaft mbH (The Hansa Nord) [1976] QB 44   *45, 46, 51, 52, 59*
Central London Property Trust Ltd v High Trees House Ltd [1947] 1 KB 130   *27, 28, 29, 30, 31, 35, 36, 37, 197, 198*
Chapleton v Barry Urban District Council [1940] 1 KB 532   *5, 82*
Chaplin v Hicks [1911] 2 KB 786   *202, 213*
Chaplin v Leslie Frewin (Publishers) Ltd [1966] Ch 71   *102, 104*
Chappell & Co Ltd v Nestlé Co Ltd [1960] AC 87   *24, 33, 34*
Chapple v Cooper (1844) 13 M & W 252   *108, 109*
Charter v Sullivan [1957] 2 QB 117   *219*
Chelini v Nieri (1948) 196 P 2d 915   *48, 50*
Chesneau v Interhome Ltd (1983) The Times 9 June   *68, 70*
Chichester v Cobb (1866) 14 LT 433   *25, 26, 27, 28*
Chikuma, The [1981] 1 WLR 314   *51, 53*
Citibank NA v Brown Shipley & Co Ltd [1991] 2 All ER 690   *132, 134*
City and Westminster Properties (1934) Ltd v Mudd [1959] Ch 129   *56, 57*

Clarke v Dickson (1858) EB & B 148   77, 78
Clarke v Dunraven (The Satanita) [1897] AC 59   159, 162
Clements v L & NW Railway [1894] 2 QB 482   102, 104, 110, 112
Cleveland Petroleum Co Ltd v Dartstone Ltd [1969] 1 WLR 116   171, 174, 176
Clifford Davis Management Ltd v WEA Records Ltd [1975] 1 WLR 61   140, 145, 147
Clifton v Palumbo [1944] 2 All ER 497   12
Clyde Cycle Co v Hargreaves (1898) 78 LT 296   110, 112
Cohen v Nessdale [1982] 2 All ER 97   45
Cohen v Roche [1927] 1 KB 169   210, 212
Colgate v Bachelor (1569) Cro Eliz 872   173, 174
Collins v Associated Greyhound Racecourses Ltd [1930] 1 Ch 1   220, 221, 223
Collins v Godefroy (1831) 1 B & Ad 950   19, 20
Combe v Combe [1951] 2 KB 215   11, 12, 13, 35, 36
Condor v The Barron Knights [1966] 1 WLR 87   193, 194
Cooper v Phibbs (1867) LR 2 HL 149   68, 69, 119, 120, 121, 122, 133, 134
Coral Leisure Group v Barnet [1981] ICR 503   225, 227
Corpe v Overston (1833) 10 Bing 252   107, 108, 110, 112, 143, 145
Couchman v Hill [1947] KB 54   56, 57
Couturier v Hastie (1856) 5 HL Cas 673   119, 120, 121, 122, 133, 134
Cox v Phillips Industries [1976] 1 WLR 638   204, 206
Craven-Ellis v Canons Ltd [1936] 2 KB 403   203, 209
Crowther v Shannon Motor Co [1975] 1 All ER 139   225, 226
Cundy v Lindsay (1878) 3 App Cas 459   116, 117, 118, 125, 132, 134
Currie v Misa (1875) LR 10 Exch 153   33
Curtis v Chemical Cleaning and Dyeing Co [1951] 1 KB 805   48, 50

D & C Builders Ltd v Rees [1966] 2 QB 617   27, 29, 30, 32, 35, 37, 141, 197, 198, 209
Darby v Boucher (1694) 1 Salk 279   108, 109
Daulia Ltd v Four Millbank Nominees Ltd [1978] Ch 231; [1978] 2 All ER 557   5, 14, 15, 18, 19

Davis Contractors Ltd v Fareham Urban District Council [1956] AC 696   186, 187, 188, 189, 190, 191, 193, 194
De Francesco v Barnum (1890) 45 Ch D 430   102, 104, 110, 112
Dearle v Hall (1828) 3 Russ 1   152
Denmark Productions v Boscobel Productions Ltd [1969] 1 QB 699   102, 104
Denny v Denny [1919] 1 KB 583   169
Denny, Mott & Dickson Ltd v James B Fraser & Co Ltd [1944] AC 265   190, 192
Derry v Peek (1889) 14 App Cas 337   66, 68, 70, 71, 72, 73, 75, 76, 77
Dick Bentley Productions Ltd v Harold Smith (Motors) Ltd [1965] 1 WLR 623   68, 71, 75, 92, 93
Dickinson v Dodds (1876) 2 Ch D 463   10, 11
Dimmock v Hallett (1866) 2 Ch App 21   68, 69, 71, 72, 75
Dimskal Shipping Co SA v International Transport Workers' Federation (The Evia Luck) [1991] 4 All ER 871   142, 192, 194
Dixon v Sadler (1839)   48, 49
Doyle v Olby (Ironmongers) Ltd [1969] 2 QB 158   76, 77, 79
Doyle v White City Stadium Ltd [1935] 1 KB 110   110, 112
Drive Yourself Hire Co (London) Ltd v Strutt [1954] 1 QB 250   159
Drughorn (F) v Rederiaktiebolaget Transatlantic [1919] AC 203   220, 221, 223
Dunlop Pneumatic Tyre Co Ltd v Selfridge & Co Ltd [1915] AC 847   152, 153, 154, 156, 159, 162, 163
Dyster v Randall & Sons [1926] Ch 932   221, 223

East v Maurer [1991] 2 All ER 733   77, 79
Eastham v Newcastle United Football Club [1964] Ch 413   171, 174, 176
Edgington v Fitzmaurice (1885) 29 Ch D 459   66, 68, 69, 71, 72
Edler v Auerbach [1950] 1 KB 359   172
Edwards v Aberayron Insurance Society Ltd (1876) 1 QBD 563   56, 57
Edwards v Skyways Ltd [1964] 1 WLR 349   24
Ellis v Barker (1871) LR 7 Ch App 104   140
Entores v Miles Far East Corporation [1955] 2 QB 327   5, 10, 12, 13, 16, 18

xiv Tables of Cases

Erlanger v New Sombrero Phosphate Co (1878) 3 App Cas 1218   *68, 70*
Errington v Errington and Woods [1952] 1 KB 290   *5, 14, 15*
Esso Petroleum Co Ltd v Harper's Garage (Stourport) Ltd [1968] AC 269   *170, 171, 173, 175*
Esso Petroleum Co Ltd v Mardon [1976] QB 801   *71, 72, 75, 76, 92, 93*
Eugenia, The see Ocean Tramp Tankers Corporation v V O Sovfracht
European Asian Bank v Punjab & Sind Bank [1983] 1 WLR 642   *217, 221, 222*
Eurymedon, The see New Zealand Shipping Co Ltd v A M Satterthwaite & Co Ltd
Evans v Merzario Ltd [1976] 1 WLR 1078   *23*
Evia Luck, The see Dimskal Shipping Co SA v International Transport Workers' Federation

Faccenda Chicken v Fowler [1986] 3 WLR 288   *170, 173, 175*
Fairline Shipping Corporation v Adamson [1975] QB 180   *136, 138*
Falck v Williams [1900] AC 176   *132, 134*
Federal Commerce & Navigation Co Ltd v Molena Alpha Inc [1979] AC 757   *193, 194*
Felthouse v Bindley (1862) 11 CBNS 869   *136, 137*
Fercometal Sarl v Mediterranean Shipping Co SA [1988] 2 All ER 742   *193, 194*
Financings Ltd v Baldock [1963] 2 QB 104   *53, 54*
Financings Ltd v Stimson [1962] 1 WLR 1184; [1962] 3 All ER 386   *6*
Firstpost Homes Ltd v Johnson [1995] 1 WLR 1567   *45*
Fisher v Bell [1961] 1 QB 394   *4*
Fitch v Dewes [1921] 2 AC 158   *171, 173, 175*
Flavell, Re (1883) 25 Ch D 89   *156, 158*
Flight v Bolland (1824) 4 Russ 298   *108, 109*
Flint v Brandon (1803) 3 Ves 159   *202*
Foakes v Beer (1884) 9 App Cas 605   *27, 28, 30, 31, 35, 36, 197, 198*
Forster v Silvermere Golf and Equestrian Centre (1981) 125 Sol Jo 397   *150–151, 152, 153, 156, 157, 159, 160, 163, 165*
Forster & Sons Ltd v Suggett (1918) 35 TLR 87   *171, 173, 175*
Foster v Mackinnon (1869) LR 4 CP 704   *116*
Freeman & Lockyer v Buckhurst Park Properties Ltd [1964] 2 QB 480   *218*

Fulham Football Club Ltd v Cabra Estates plc (1992) The Times 11 September   *168*

Gallie v Lee [1971] AC 1004 (sub nom Saunders v Anglia Building Society)   *116, 126*
Galloway v Galloway (1914) 30 TLR 531   *121, 123, 133, 134*
George Mitchell (Chesterhall) Ltd v Finney Lock Seeds Ltd [1983] 2 AC 803; [1983] 2 All ER 737   *83, 84, 85, 86, 87, 88, 90, 91, 225, 226*
Gibbons v Proctor (1891) 64 LT 594   *5, 18, 19*
Gibson v Manchester City Council [1979] 1 All ER 972; [1979] 1 WLR 294 HL; [1978] 2 All ER 583 CA   *9, 16, 17*
Gillespie Bros & Co Ltd v Roy Bowles Transport Ltd [1973] QB 400   *87, 88*
Glencoe Grain Rotterdam BV v Lebanese Organisation for International Commerce [1997] 4 All ER 54   *55*
Glolite v Jasper Conran (1998) The Times 28 January   *45, 46*
Goldsoll v Goldman [1915] 1 Ch 292   *171*
Goldsworthy v Brickell [1987] 1 All ER 853   *30, 32, 35, 37*
Gompertz v Bartlett (1853) 2 E & B 849   *119, 120*
Gould v Gould [1970] 1 QB 275   *23*
Grainger & Son v Gough [1896] AC 325   *4, 5, 6*
Graves v Legg (1857) 2 H & N 210   *217, 221, 222*
Greaves & Co (Contractors) Ltd v Baynham Meikle and Partners [1975] 1 WLR 1095; [1975] 3 All ER 99   *45, 47*
Greer v Downs Supply Co [1927] 2 KB 28   *220, 221, 223*
Green (R W) Ltd v Cade Bros Farms [1978] 1 Lloyd's Rep 602   *84, 86*
Gregory and Parker v Williams (1817) 3 Mer 582   *159, 160*
Greig v Insole [1978] 1 WLR 302   *171, 174, 176*
Griffiths v Brymer (1903) 19 TLR 434   *121, 123, 133, 134*
Griffiths v Young [1970] Ch 675   *45*
Grist v Bailey [1967] Ch 532   *119, 120, 121, 122, 124, 125, 127, 130, 131, 135*

Hadley v Baxendale (1854) 9 Exch 341   *50, 93, 95, 105, 107, 201, 203, 204, 205, 206, 210, 212, 213*

Hamzeh Malas & Sons *v* British Imex Industries Ltd [1958] 2 QB 127   *156, 158*
Hansa Nord, The *see* Cehave *v* Bremer Handelsgesellschaft mbH
Harbutt's Plasticene Ltd *v* Wayne Tank and Pumps Co Ltd [1970] 1 QB 447   *83*
Hardwick *v* Johnson [1978] 1 WLR 683   *23*
Harling *v* Eddy [1951] 2 KB 739   *56, 57*
Harlingdon & Leinster Enterprises Ltd *v* Christopher Hull Fine Art Ltd [1990] 3 WLR 13   *128, 129*
Harrison & Jones Ltd *v* Bunten and Lancaster Ltd [1953] 1 QB 646   *121, 123, 125, 127, 128, 130, 131, 133, 135*
Harse *v* Pearl Assurance Co [1904] 1 KB 558   *176, 177*
Hartley *v* Ponsonby (1857) 7 E & B 872   *25, 26, 27, 29, 30, 33*
Hartog *v* Colin and Shields [1939] 3 All ER 566   *118, 132, 134*
Harvey *v* Facey [1893] AC 552   *10, 11, 16, 17*
Hayes *v* James and Charles Dodd (1988) The Times 14 July   *14, 15, 153, 155*
Heard *v* Pilley (1869) LR 4 Ch App 548   *220, 221*
Hebb's Case (1867) LR 4 Eq 9   *8*
Hedley Byrne & Co Ltd *v* Heller and Partners Ltd [1964] AC 465; [1963] 2 All ER 575   *66, 67, 70, 73, 74, 75, 77*
Heilbut, Symons & Co *v* Buckleton [1913] AC 30   *68, 71, 75, 92, 93*
Henthorn *v* Fraser [1892] 2 Ch 27   *8, 10, 12, 136, 137*
Herbert Morris Ltd *v* Saxelby [1916] AC 688   *173, 175*
Hermann *v* Charlesworth [1905] 2 KB 123   *169*
Herne Bay Steamboat Company *v* Hutton [1903] 2 KB 683   *190, 192*
Heron II, The [1969] 1 AC 350   *15, 16, 93, 95, 202, 203, 205, 213*
Heywood *v* Wellers [1976] 1 QB 446   *204, 206*
Hillas & Co *v* Arcos (1932) 147 LT 503   *44*
Hirji Mulji *v* Cheong Yue SS [1926] AC 497   *188, 189*
Hitchcock *v* Giddings (1817) 4 Price 135   *119, 120*
Hivac Ltd *v* Park Royal Scientific Instruments [1946] Ch 169   *61, 62*
Hollier *v* Rambler Motors [1972] 2 QB 71   *87, 87-88*

Holwell Securities Ltd *v* Hughes [1974] 1 WLR 155   *8, 9, 10, 11, 12, 16, 17*
Hong Kong Fir Shipping *v* Kawasaki Kisen Kaisha Ltd [1962] 2 QB 26   *45, 46, 48, 50, 51, 52, 53, 54, 59*
Household Fire Insurance Co Ltd *v* Grant (1879) 4 Ex D 216   *7, 8, 10, 12, 16, 17, 136, 137*
Howard *v* Millar's Timber and Trading Co (1917)   *169*
Howard *v* Patent Ivory Manufacturing (1888)   *151*
Howard *v* Shirlstar Container Transport Ltd [1990] 1 WLR 1292   *169, 172, 180, 181*
Howard Marine & Dredging Co Ltd *v* A Ogden & Sons (Excavations) Ltd [1978] QB 574   *71, 73, 92, 94*
Howatson *v* Webb [1907] 1 Ch 537; affirmed [1908] 1 Ch 1   *116*
Hughes *v* Liverpool Victoria Legal Friendly Society [1916] 2 KB 482   *176, 177, 178, 180*
Hughes *v* Metropolitan Railway Co (1877) 2 App Cas 439   *30, 31, 35, 36*
Humble *v* Hunter (1848) 12 QB 310   *220, 221, 223*
Hutton *v* Watling [1948] Ch 398   *48, 56, 57*
Hyde *v* Wrench (1840) 3 Beav 334   *10, 11, 12, 13, 136, 137*
Hybart *v* Parker (1858) 4 CB (NS) 209   *159, 162*

IBA *v* EMI Electronics (1980) 14 Building LR 1   *159, 162*
Inche Noriah *v* Shaik Allie Bin Omar [1929] AC 127   *142, 144*
Ingram *v* Little [1961] 1 QB 31   *117, 118, 125, 126, 128, 130, 132, 134*
Introductions Ltd, Re [1970] Ch 199   *101*

Jackson *v* Horizon Holidays [1975] 1 WLR 1468   *48, 50, 150, 153, 154, 155, 156, 157, 159, 161, 163, 164, 202, 204, 206*
Jackson *v* Union Marine Insurance Co (1873) LR 10 CP 125   *187, 190, 192*
Jacobs *v* Batavia and General Plantations Trust [1924] 1 Ch 287   *56*
Jarvis *v* Swans Tours [1973] 2 QB 233   *48, 50, 153, 154, 163, 164, 202, 204, 206*
JEB Fasteners Ltd *v* Marks, Bloom & Co [1983] 1 All ER 583   *92, 93*
Jennings *v* Rundall (1799) 8 Term R 335   *103, 104*

Jerome v Bentley & Co [1952] 2 All ER 114
  217, 221, 222
Johnson v Shrewsbury and Birmingham
  Railway (1853) 3 DM & G 358   210, 211
Jones v Padavatton [1969] 1 WLR 328   24,
  25
Jones v Vernons Pools [1938] 2 All ER 626
  23
Jorden v Money (1854) 5 HL Cas 185   30, 31,
  35, 36
Joseph Travers & Sons Ltd v Cooper [1915] 1
  KB 73   93, 85, 87, 88

Kasumu v Baba-Egbe [1956] AC 539   176,
  177
Kearley v Thomson (1890) 24 QBD 742
  176, 177
Kendall (Henry) & Sons v William Lillico &
  Sons [1969] 2 AC 31; [1968] 3 WLR 110
  87
Kennedy v Brown (1863) 13 CB 677   25
Kennedy v Panama Royal Mail Co (1867) LR 2
  QB 580   121, 123, 125, 129, 133, 135
King's Norton Metal Co Ltd v Edridge, Merrett
  & Co Ltd (1897) 14 TLR 98   116, 118,
  125, 126
Kiriri Cotton Co Ltd v Dewani [1960] AC 192
  176, 177
Konski v Peet (1915)   170
Krell v Henry [1903] 2 KB 740   187, 188,
  189, 190, 192

Laconia, The see Mardorf Peach & Co v Attica
  Sea Carriers Corp of Liberia
Lake v Simmons [1927] AC 487   118, 128,
  130, 132, 134
Lambert v HTV Cymru (Wales) Ltd (1998) The
  Times 17 March   44
Lampleigh v Braithwait (1615) Hob 105   25,
  33
Laurence v Lexcourt Holdings Ltd [1978] 2 All
  ER 810   119, 120, 124
Law v Jones [1974] Ch 112   45
Leaf v International Galleries [1950] 2 KB 86
  77, 78, 121, 123, 125, 127, 128, 129, 130,
  131, 133, 135, 136
Lee v York Coach & Marine [1977] RTR 35
  227, 228
Les Affreteurs Reunis Société Anonyme v
  Leopold Walford (London) Ltd [1919] AC
  801   156, 157, 159, 160
L'Estrange v Graucob Ltd [1934] 2 KB 394
  83, 85, 89, 90

Levison v Patent Steam Carpet Cleaning Co
  [1978] QB 69; [1977] 3 All ER 498   140,
  145, 147
Lewis v Averay [1972] 1 QB 198   117, 118,
  125, 126, 130, 132, 134
Lewis v Clay (1898) 67 LJQB 224   116
Linden Gardens Trust v Lenesta Sludge
  Disposals Ltd [1993] 3 WLR 408   159,
  161, 163, 164
Lipkin Gorman v Karpnale Ltd [1991] AC 548
  24, 33, 34, 209
Lloyds v Harper (1880) 16 Ch D 270   156,
  157
Lloyds Bank Ltd v Bundy [1975] QB 326
  140, 142, 143, 145, 147
Lombard North Central v Butterworth [1987] 1
  All ER 267   51, 53, 55
Long v Lloyd [1958] 1 WLR 753   77, 78
Lord Strathcona Steamship Co v Dominion Coal
  Co [1926] AC 108   150, 153, 154
Lowe v Peers (1768) 4 Burr 2225   169
Lumley v Gye (1853) 2 E & B 216   150, 153,
  154
Lumley v Wagner (1852) 1 De GM & G 604
  210, 211

M & S Drapers v Reynolds [1957] 1 WLR 9
  171, 173, 175
McArdle, Re [1951] Ch 669   25
McCutcheon v David MacBrayne Ltd [1964] 1
  WLR 125   87
McRae v Commonwealth Disposals
  Commission (1950) 84 CLR 377   14, 15,
  121, 122, 124, 134
Magee v Pennine Insurance Co Ltd [1969] 2 QB
  507   119, 120, 121, 125, 127, 129, 130,
  131, 133, 134, 135
Mahmoud and Ispahani, Re [1921] 2 KB 716;
  [1921] All ER Rep 217   172, 176, 177,
  178, 180, 181, 182
Malins v Freeman (1837) 2 Keen 25   133,
  135
Manchester Diocesan Council for Education v
  Commercial & General Investments [1970]
  1 WLR 241   6, 7
Mardorf Peach & Co v Attica Sea Carriers Corp
  of Liberia (The Laconia) [1977] AC 850
  197
Maritime National Fish Ltd v Ocean Trawlers
  Ltd [1935] AC 524   188, 189, 190, 192
Marlow v Pitfield (1719) 1 P Wms 558   102,
  103, 108, 109
Martell v Consett Iron Co Ltd [1955] Ch 363
  168

Maskell v Horner [1915] 3 KB 106   *141*
Mason v Provident Clothing & Supply Co Ltd [1913] AC 724   *171, 173, 175*
Mathew v Bobbins (1980) 256 EG 603   *140*
May and Butcher v R [1934] 2 KB 17   *44*
Meritt v Meritt [1970] 1 WLR 1211   *23*
Mersey Steel and Iron Co v Naylor Benzon & Co (1884) 9 App Cas 434   *192-193, 194*
Metropolitan Water Board v Dick, Kerr & Co Ltd [1918] AC 119   *190, 192*
Michael v Hart & Co [1902] 1 KB 482   *210, 211*
Midland Bank v Shephard [1988] 3 All ER 17   *140*
Mihalis Angelos, The [1971] 1 QB 164   *45, 46, 51, 53, 54*
Mitchell v Homfray (1881) 8 QBD 587   *140*
Moorcock, The (1889) 14 PD 64   *48, 49, 56, 58*
Morgan v Fry [1968] 2 QB 710   *141*
Museprime Properties Ltd v Adhill Properties Ltd [1990] 36 EG 114   *92, 93*
Mynn v Joliffe (1834) 1 M & Rob 326   *217, 221, 222*

Nagle v Fielden [1966] 2 QB 633   *174, 176*
Nash v Inman [1908] 2 KB 1   *101, 102, 103, 106, 108, 109, 110, 111*
Nash v Dix (1898) 78 LT 445   *221, 223*
Nash v Stevenson Transport Ltd [1936] 2 KB 128   *172, 181, 182*
National Carriers v Panalpina (Northern) Ltd [1981] AC 675   *186, 188, 189, 190, 191*
National Permanent Benefit Building Society, Re (1869) LR 5 Ch App 309   *108, 109*
National Westminster Bank plc v Morgan [1985] 1 All ER 821 HL   *141, 142, 144, 145, 147*
Neilson v Stewart 1991 SLT 523 HL; 1990 SLT 346   *44*
Nema, The see Pioneer Shipping Ltd v BTP Tioxide Ltd
New York Star, The see Port Jackson Stevedoring Ltd v Salmond and Spraggon Ltd
New Zealand Shipping Co Ltd v A M Satterthwaite & Co Ltd (The Eurymedon) [1975] AC 154; [1974] 1 All ER 1015   *14, 18, 19, 25, 26, 27, 28, 87, 89*
Newell v Radford (1867) LR 3 CP 52   *56, 58*
Nicholson and Venn v Smith-Marriott (1947) 177 LT 189   *121, 123, 125, 127, 133, 135*

Nicolene v Simmonds [1953] 1 QB 543   *44*
Nordenfelt v Maxim Nordenfelt Guns & Ammunition Co Ltd [1894] AC 535   *170, 171, 173, 174*
North Ocean Shipping Co v Hyundai Construction Co (The Atlantic Baron) [1979] QB 705; [1978] 3 All ER 1170   *27, 28, 29, 30, 31, 141, 145, 146, 192, 193*
North West Salt Co v Electrolytic Alkali Co Ltd [1914] AC 461   *173, 174*
Norwich & Peterborough Building Society v Steed [1992] 3 WLR 669   *116*
Norwich Union Fire Insurance Society v Price [1934] AC 455   *133, 134*

Occidental Worldwide Investment Corp v Skibs A/S Avanti (The Siboen and The Sibotre) [1976] 1 Lloyd's Rep 293   *29, 31, 141, 145, 146, 192, 193*
Ocean Tramp Tankers Corporation v V O Sovfracht (The Eugenia) [1964] 2 QB 226   *188, 189, 190, 191*
Olley v Marlborough Court [1949] 1 KB 532   *87*
Oom v Bruce (1810) 12 East 225   *176, 177*
Orion Insurance Co v Sphere Drake Insurance [1992] 1 Lloyd's Rep 239   *23*
Oscar Chess Ltd v Williams [1957] 1 WLR 370   *68, 71, 75*

P v P [1957] NZLR 854   *35, 37*
Paal Wilson v Blumenthal [1983] AC 854   *190, 192*
Page One Records Ltd v Britton [1968] 1 WLR 157   *210, 211*
Panorama Developments (Guildford) Ltd v Fidelis Furnishing Fabrics [1971] 2 QB 711   *218*
Pao On v Lau Yiu Long [1980] AC 614; [1979] AC 614; [1979] 3 All ER 65 PC   *25, 26, 27, 28, 30, 31, 141, 145, 146, 192, 193*
Paradine v Jane (1647) Aleyn 26   *186, 190*
Parker v South Eastern Railway (1877) 2 CPD 416   *83, 85*
Parkinson v Royal College of Ambulance [1925] 2 KB 1   *169*
Parkinson (Sir Lindsay) & Co Ltd v Commissioners of Works [1949] 2 KB 632   *203, 209*
Parsons (H) (Livestock) Ltd v Uttley Ingham & Co Ltd [1978] QB 791   *14, 16, 105, 107, 202, 203, 205, 212, 213, 214*
Partridge v Crittenden [1968] 2 All ER 421   *4, 10, 83, 85*

Pearce v Brain [1929] 2 KB 310   103, 104
Pearce v Brooks (1866) LR 1 Ex 213   169, 172, 178, 179, 180, 181, 183
Peco Arts Inc v Hazlitt Gallery Ltd [1983] 3 All ER 193   121-122, 123, 125, 127, 128, 129, 130, 135
Perry v Barnett (1885) 15 QBD 388   217, 221, 222
Perry v Sidney Phillips & Son [1982] 1 WLR 1297   204, 206
Peters v Fleming (1840) 6 M & W 42   101, 102, 103, 105, 106, 108, 109, 110, 111
Petrofina (Great Britain) Ltd v Martin [1966] Ch 146   169, 173, 174
Pettit v Pettit [1970] AC 777   23
Peyman v Lanjani [1985] Ch 457   77, 78, 197
Pharmaceutical Society of Great Britain v Boots Cash Chemists (Southern) Ltd [1953] 1 All ER 482; [1952] 2 All ER 456   4
Pharmaceutical Society of Great Britain v Dickson [1970] AC 403; [1968] 2 All ER 686   174, 176
Phillips v Brooks [1919] 2 KB 243   77, 78, 117, 118, 125, 126, 128, 130, 132, 134
Phoenix General Insurance Co of Green SA v Adas [1988] QB 216   173, 176, 177, 178, 180, 181, 182
Phonographic Performance Ltd v Maitra [1997] 3 All ER 560   208
Photo Production Ltd v Securicor Transport Ltd [1980] AC 827   83, 85, 87, 88, 89, 90, 225
Picton Jones & Co v Arcadia Developments [1989] 3 EG 85   168
Pinnel's Case (1602) 5 Co Rep 117a   27, 28, 30, 31, 35, 36, 197, 198
Pioneer Shipping Ltd v BTP Tioxide Ltd (The Nema) [1982] AC 724   186, 188, 189, 190, 191
Plowman v Ash [1964] 1 WLR 568   170
Port Jackson Stevedoring Ltd v Salmond and Spraggon Ltd (The New York Star) [1981] 1 WLR 138   87, 89
Port Line Ltd v Ben Line Steamers Ltd [1958] 2 QB 146   150, 153, 154
Post Chaser, The see Société Italo-Belge v Palm and Vegetable Oils
Poussard v Spiers & Pond (1876) 1 QBD 410   53, 54, 195, 196
Printers & Finishers v Holloway [1965] RPC 77   170
Produce Brokers Co Ltd v Olympia Oil and Cake Co Ltd (1916)   56, 58

Punjab National Bank v De Boinville [1992] 1 WLR 1138   44
Pym v Campbell (1856) 6 E & B 370   56, 58

R & B Customs Brokers Co Ltd v United Dominions Trust Ltd [1988] 1 All ER 847   89, 90
R Leslie Ltd v Sheill [1914] 3 KB 607   108, 110
R v Clarke (1927) 40 CLR 227   18, 19
R W Green Ltd v Cade Bros Farms [1978] 1 Lloyd's Rep 602   225, 226
Rabin v Gerson Berger Association Ltd [1986] 1 WLR 526   56, 57
Raffles v Wichelhaus (1864) H & C 906   117, 132, 134, 136
Reardon Smith Line v Hansen-Tangen [1976] 1 WLR 989; [1976] 3 All ER 570   45, 46, 51, 52, 59
Redgrave v Hurd (1881) 20 Ch D 1   68, 69, 71, 72
Reed v Dean [1949] 1 KB 188   48, 49
Regazzoni v KC Sethia [1958] AC 301   169
Reigate v Union Manufacturing Co (Ramsbottom) [1918] 1 KB 592   48, 49, 61, 63
Riverlate Properties Ltd v Paul [1975] Ch 133   128, 130, 131, 132, 133, 135
Roberts v Gray [1913] 1 KB 520   102, 105, 106, 108, 109
Robinson v Harman (1848) 18 LJ Ex 202   48, 50
Roche v Sherrington [1982] 1 WLR 599   140
Rolled Steel Products v BSC [1984] BCLC 466   101
Roscorla v Thomas (1842) 3 QB 234   25
Rose (F E) (London) Ltd v W H Pim, Junior & Co Ltd [1953] 2 QB 450   125, 127
Rose & Frank Co v J R Crompton Bros [1925] AC 445   24
Routledge v Grant (1828) 4 Bing 653   10, 11, 18, 19
Routledge v McKay [1954] 1 WLR 615   56, 57, 75, 92, 93
Rowland v Divall [1923] 2 KB 500   209
Royscott Trust Ltd v Rogerson [1991] 3 WLR 57   77, 79, 93, 94
Ryan v Mutual Tontine Association [1893] 1 Ch 116   202, 203
Ryder v Wombwell (1869) LR 4 Ex 32   101, 102, 103, 110, 111

Said v Butt [1920] 3 KB 497   221, 223

St John Shipping Corporation *v* Joseph Rank Ltd [1957] 1 QB 267   *172, 178, 179, 180, 181, 182, 183*
St Marylebone Property Co Ltd v Payne (1994) 45 EG 156   *66*
Samuels *v* Davis [1943] 1 KB 526; [1943] 2 All ER 3   *45, 47*
Satanita, The *see* Clarke *v* Dunraven
Scammel & Nephew *v* Ouston [1941] AC 251   *44*
Scarfe *v* Adams [1981] 1 All ER 843   *56, 58*
Schebsman, Re [1944] Ch 83   *156, 158, 159, 160*
Schroeder Music Publishing Co Ltd *v* Macaulay [1974] 1 WLR 1308   *141, 145, 147, 171, 173, 174*
Schuler AG *v* Wickman Machine Tool Sales Ltd [1974] AC 235 HL   *46, 51, 52, 53, 55, 59, 60*
Scotson *v* Pegg (1861) 6 H & N 295   *25, 26, 27, 28*
Scott *v* Coulson [1903] 2 Ch 249   *121, 123, 133, 134*
Scriven Bros & Co *v* Hindley & Co [1913] 3 KB 564   *118, 132, 134, 136*
Scruttons Ltd *v* Midland Silicones Ltd [1962] AC 446   *87, 89, 156, 158, 159*
Shadwell *v* Shadwell (1860) 9 CBNS 159   *25, 26, 27, 28*
Shanklin Pier Ltd *v* Detel Products Ltd [1951] 2 KB 854   *156, 158, 159, 162, 163, 164, 227, 229*
Sharneyford Supplies Ltd *v* Edge [1987] 1 All ER 588; [1985] 1 All ER 976   *68, 70, 71, 73, 75, 77*
Shearson Lehman Hutton Inc *v* Maclaine Watson & Co [1989] 1 All ER 1056   *56, 57*
Sheikh Brothers Ltd *v* Ochsner [1957] AC 136   *121, 123, 133, 134*
Shelley *v* Paddock [1980] QB 348   *173, 178, 180*
Shirlaw *v* Southern Foundries (1926) Ltd [1940] AC 701 HL; [1939] 2 KB 206   *48, 49, 56, 58, 61, 63*
Shuey *v* United States 92 US 73 (1875)   *14, 15, 18, 19*
Siboen, The and The Sibotre *see* Occidental Worldwide Investment Corp *v* Skibs A/S Avanti
Simpkins *v* Pays [1955] 1 WLR 975   *23*
Simpson *v* Simpson (1988) The Times 11 June   *140*

Siu Yin Kwan *v* Eastern Insurance Co [1994] 2 AC 199   *220, 221, 223*
Skeate *v* Beale (1840) 11 Ad & El 983   *141*
Smith *v* Cuff (1817) 6 M & S 160   *176, 177*
Smith *v* Eric S Bush [1990] 1 AC 831   *90, 91, 92, 94, 162, 229*
Smith *v* Hughes (1871) LR 6 QB 597   *118, 121, 123, 125, 127, 128, 129, 131, 132, 133*
Smith *v* Land and House Property Corporation (1884) 28 Ch D 7   *66, 68, 69, 71, 72, 75, 76*
Smith *v* South Wales Switchgear [1978] 1 All ER 18   *225, 226*
Smith *v* Wilson (1832) 3 B & Ad 728   *56, 58*
Smith and Snipes Hall Farm *v* River Douglas Catchment Board [1949] 2 KB 500   *159*
Société Italo-Belge *v* Palm and Vegetable Oils (The Post Chaser) [1982] 1 All ER 19   *27, 29, 30, 32, 35, 37*
Solle *v* Butcher [1950] 1 KB 671   *119, 120, 121, 122, 124, 125, 127, 129, 130, 131, 133, 135*
Southern Water Authority *v* Carey [1985] 2 All ER 1077   *87, 89*
Southwell *v* Bowditch (1876)   *223*
Spencer *v* Harding (1870) LR 5 CP 561   *56*
Spurling *v* Bradshaw [1956] 2 All ER 121   *87*
Stag Line Ltd *v* Tyne Shiprepair Group Ltd [1984] 2 Lloyd's Rep 211   *87, 89*
State Trading Corp of India *v* M Golodetz Ltd [1989] 2 Lloyd's Rep 277   *193, 194*
Steinberg *v* Scala (Leeds) Ltd [1923] 2 Ch 452   *103, 104*
Stevenson Jacques & Co *v* McLean (1880) 5 QBD 346   *136, 137*
Stilk *v* Myrick (1809) 2 Camp 317; (1809) 6 Esp 129   *27, 29, 30, 33*
Stocks *v* Wilson [1913] 2 KB 235   *103, 104, 105*
Stocznia Gdanska SA *v* Latvian Shipping Co [1998] 1 WLR 574   *208*
Strongman (1945) Ltd *v* Sincock [1955] 3 All ER 90   *173, 178, 180*
Suisse Atlantique Société d'Armament Maritime *v* Rotterdamsche Kolen Centrale [1967] 1 AC 361   *83, 89, 90, 225*
Summers *v* Solomon (1857) 7 E & B 879   *218, 221, 224*
Swain *v* Law Society [1983] AC 598   *159, 160*

Taddy *v* Sterious [1904] 1 Ch 354   *150*

Tables of Cases

Tamplin v James (1880) 15 Ch D 215   *133, 135*
Tanner v Tanner [1975] 1 WLR 1346   *169*
Taylor, ex parte (1856) 8 DM & G 254   *110, 112*
Taylor v Bowers (1876) 1 QBD 291   *176, 177*
Taylor v Caldwell (1863) 3 B & S 826   *186, 188, 190, 190-191, 192, 193, 194*
Taylor v Chester (1869) LR 4 QB 308   *176, 178*
Texaco v Mulberry Filling Station [1972] 1 WLR 814   *171*
Thomas v Thomas (1842) 11 LJ QB 104   *33, 34*
Thompson v London Midland & Scottish Railway Co [1930] 1 KB 41   *83*
Thompson (W L) Ltd v Robinson (Gunmakers) Ltd [1955] Ch 177   *219*
Thornton v Shoe Lane Parking Ltd [1971] 2 QB 163   *5, 82*
Thorp v Thorp (1701) 12 Mod 445   *33*
Tinn v Hoffman & Co (1873) 29 LT 271   *12*
Tinsley v Milligan [1994] 1 AC 340   *172*
Tiverton Estates Ltd v Wearwell Ltd [1975] Ch 146   *45*
Tomlinson v Gill (1756) Amb 330   *156, 157, 159, 160*
Tool Metal Manufacturing Co Ltd v Tungsten Electric Co Ltd [1955] 1 WLR 761   *27, 29, 30, 35, 37*
Torkington v Magee [1902] 2 KB 427   *151*
Tsakiroglou & Co Ltd v Noblee Thorl GmbH [1962] AC 93; [1961] 2 All ER 179   *187, 188, 189, 190, 192*
Tulk v Moxhay (1848) 2 Ph 774   *150, 153, 154*
Turner v Forwood [1951] 1 All ER 746   *56, 58*
Tweddle v Atkinson (1861) 1 B & S 393   *153, 155, 156, 157, 158, 159, 162, 163*
Tyrer & Co v Hessler & Co (1902) 7 Com Cas 166   *197*

Union Eagle Ltd v Golden Achievement Ltd [1997] AC 514   *203*
United Scientific Holdings v Burnley Borough Council [1978] AC 904   *51, 53*
Universe Tankships of Monrovia v International Transport Workers' Federation (The Universe Sentinel) [1983] AC 366; [1982] 2 WLR 803   *142, 143, 144, 145, 146, 147, 192, 193*

Valentini v Canali (1889) 24 QBD 166   *103, 104*
Vancouver Malt v Vancouver Breweries [1934] AC 181   *171*
Vantage Navigation Corporation v Suhail and Saud Bahwan Building Materials LLC (The Alev) [1989] 1 Lloyd's Rep 138   *146, 192, 194*
Victoria Laundry (Windsor) Ltd v Newman Industries Ltd [1949] 2 KB 528   *14, 15, 48, 50, 93, 95, 201, 203, 204, 210, 212, 213, 214*

W F Trustees v Expo Safety Systems Ltd (1993) The Times 24 May   *56, 57*
Walker v Boyle [1982] 1 WLR 495   *92, 94*
Walton Stores (Interstate) Ltd v Maher (1988) 164 CLR 387   *12, 13, 35, 36*
Ward v Byham [1956] 1 WLR 496   *19, 20, 27, 28*
Warner Bros Pictures Inc v Nelson [1937] 1 KB 209   *210, 211*
Watteau v Fenwick [1893] 1 QB 346   *217, 221, 222*
Watts v Spence [1976] Ch 165   *152, 154*
Weigall v Runciman (1916) 85 LJKB 1187   *217, 220-221, 222*
Wenkheim v Arndt (NZ) IJR (1873)   *6, 7, 8, 9*
White v Blackmore [1972] 2 QB 651   *87, 88*
White v Bluett (1853) 23 LJ Ex 36   *24, 33, 34*
Whittington v Seale-Hayne (1900) 82 LT 49   *68, 70, 77, 79*
Whitwood Chemical Co v Hardman [1926] Ch 609   *210, 211*
Whywall v Campion (1738) 2 Str 1083   *102, 104*
Williams v Carwardine (1833) 5 Car & P 566   *18, 20*
Williams v Roffey Bros & Nicholls (Contractors) Ltd [1991] 1 QB 1   *19, 20, 33, 192, 194*
Williams v Travel Promotions Ltd (1998) The Times 9 March   *163, 164*
Williams v Williams [1957] 1 WLR 158   *19, 20, 27, 28*
Wilson v Kearse (1800) Peake Add Cas   *110, 112*
With v O'Flanagan [1936] Ch 575   *66, 71, 72*
Woodar Investment Development Ltd v Wimpey Construction (UK) Ltd [1980] 1 WLR 277; [1980] 1 All ER 571   *150, 151, 152, 153, 155, 156, 157, 158, 159, 160, 161, 163, 164, 165, 193, 194*

Woodhouse AC Israel Cocoa Ltd v Nigerian
  Produce Marketing Co Ltd [1972] AC 741
  27, 28, 30, 31
Wright v Carter [1903] 1 Ch 27   *140*

Wright v Vanderplank (1855) 2 K & J 1   *140*
Wroth v Tyler [1974] Ch 30   *204, 205*
Wyatt v Kreglinger & Fernau [1933] 1 KB 793
  25, 26

1

Offer and Acceptance

Introduction

Offer and acceptance are the traditional foundations of the Law of Contract. It is not therefore surprising to see a question on this topic appearing on virtually every examination paper – and very often the question is compulsory. A good student will be expected to demonstrate a clear understanding of the principles relevant to this area.

While there may have been some movement in the courts away from a traditional analysis of a contract in terms of offer and acceptance, it is clear these are exceptional cases. The student (while naturally showing awareness of these cases) is thus expected to perform the traditional analysis on problem questions. This usually requires a detailed consideration of the rules as to acceptance and withdrawal of an offer. From time to time, however, a question will be set on unilateral rather than bilateral contracts and here the student will be required to demonstrate knowledge of the very different set of rules, especially relating to acceptance and withdrawal of the offer.

The consolation for the student is that questions on this topic follow a very similar basic pattern and someone who has learned how to apply the rules should have no difficulty in obtaining a good mark.

Questions

INTERROGRAMS

1   Explain why it is so important to distinguish between an offer and an invitation to treat and how the courts proceed to do so.
2   What is meant by a unilateral contract?
3   Olivia, in England, sends a fax message to Anna in Germany, accepting her contractual offer. Where is the contract made? Would there be a contract if the fax had been sent to the wrong number?

QUESTION ONE

Alan, a wholesaler, wrote to Ben and other retailers that he had just taken delivery of some high quality video tapes and was offering them for sale at £495 per hundred. On 1 April Ben sent a written order for two hundred tapes 'to be delivered by 30 April' and asked Alan to send 'written confirmation as soon as possible'.

Ben heard nothing further from Alan and on 22 April he telephoned to find out whether Alan had received the order. Alan told him that everything was fine and that the confirmation would be on its way soon.

On the morning of 2 May Alan posted a confirmation of Ben's order, but during the afternoon he discovered that a number of the video tapes were defective and that he no longer had enough to satisfy all the orders which had been placed. He immediately sent a telex to Ben, 'Cannot accept your order, as tapes sold out.' Ben received the written confirmation the next morning. No tapes have been delivered.

Advise Ben.

London University LLB Examination
(for external students) Elements of the Law of Contract June 1985 Q1

QUESTION TWO

On Wednesday, 1 May an announcement appears in the morning newspapers to the effect that shares in Natoil, an oil exploration company, may be subscribed for at £1 each.

That day Slick sees the announcement and fills in the application form in the newspaper requesting 1,000 shares. He posts the application on the same day together with a cheque for £1,000. His application is received by the company the following day and the Secretary promptly sends the share certificates to Slick by that morning's post. However, Slick changes his mind and on the same afternoon (ie Thursday) he posts a letter to that effect to the company.

During the day a rich oil source is discovered by the company in the North Sea and the Secretary telephones Slick informing him that they do not wish to accept his application and would like him to return the certificates when they arrive.

By now Slick has heard of the oil discovery and wishes to buy the shares after all.

Advise Slick.

London University LLB Examination
(for external students) Elements of the Law of Contract June 1986 Q1

QUESTION THREE

Bob owns a stamp shop in Muncaster High Street. On Monday he places an item in the advertisement column of the *Muncaster Evening Gazette*: 'Utopian Penny Red Stamp, one only, £750 or nearest offer.'

Later that day, Alan, a stamp collector, telephones Bob and says, 'The Utopian Red for sale, I'll take it for £700.' Bob replies, 'I cannot accept less than £725 but I will not sell it to anyone else before Saturday. Let me have a reply by Friday if you want it.' Alan says 'That is kind of you. Remind me to buy you a drink when I see you.'

On Wednesday Alan telephones Bob and leaves a message on his answering machine stating 'I accept your offer.' Unfortunately Bob's infant son later presses a button on the machine which erases the message before Bob listens to the recording. Later that day Bob sells the stamp to Cedric for £750.

On Thursday Alan meets Cedric's aged mother who tells him that she has seen Cedric's nine year old son who told her that his father was very excited at having acquired a Utopian Penny Red from a High Street dealer.

Alan rushes home and posts a letter to Bob confirming the message which he has left on the machine. On the same day Bob writes to Alan withdrawing his offer.

On Friday morning Alan receives Bob's letter and at lunchtime Bob receives Alan's letter.

Advise Alan.

London University LLB Examination
(for external students) Elements of the Law of Contract June 1987 Q1

QUESTION FOUR

On Monday, A telephoned B offering to sell A's Greenacre field to B for £18,000. B said, 'I'll think about it and let you know.' A replied, 'Don't leave it too long.' On Tuesday, B decided not to buy the field and posted a letter to A telling him that he was not interested. B later changed his mind and telephoned A, leaving a message on A's answerphone stating, 'I would like to buy it.' Because of the failure of A's answering machine it never played back the message. On Friday, the value of Greenacre field doubled. B telephoned A and said, 'When will I be hearing from your solicitor?' A believed that B was referring to another matter between them and said, 'It is all right – no need for concern.'

Advise the parties.

London University LLB Examination
(for external students) Elements of the Law of Contract June 1992 Q3

QUESTION FIVE

K advertised in a local newspaper that he offered a reward of £2,000 for the return of his lost cat of which K was inordinately fond. K had lost the cat when he had moved house. L realised that the cat may have tried to return to its former home and took a train ticket costing £76 return to K's former home. Eventually, when L had spent five days at a local hotel, the cat arrived. Two days earlier K had put a notice in a local shop window withdrawing his offer of reward because he had been given a new kitten by his girlfriend. L paid his hotel bill of £45 a day and after a return trip by train he took the cat to K's address. K refused to pay L and L refused to let him have the cat. L fed the cat for 10 days (costing £4 a day) before K snatched the cat from L's garden.

Advise L.

University of London LLB Examination
(for external students) Elements of the Law of Contract June 1993 Q4

QUESTION SIX

A wrote to B stating, 'I hear you have a Morris Mini 1969 special model for sale. I would be interested in buying it for £1,200 if it is in good condition.' B wrote to A, 'I agree to sell the car to you but there are still a few things which need doing to it before it is fully restored.' However the letter was lost in the post. A wrote a week later stating, 'As I have not heard from you I assume that the price was not enough. Will you accept £2,000?' B replied by telephone leaving a message on A's answerphone stating, 'I accept the amended offer.' Unfortunately, A was away and three weeks later returned to hear the message. Meanwhile B having heard nothing sold the car to C for £1,500.

Advise A.

London University LLB Examination
(for external students) Elements of the Law of Contract June 1994 Q1

QUESTION SEVEN

On Monday, M advertised in a local newspaper, the Trecynon Mail, that he was offering a reward of £5,000 to anyone finding and recovering a rare breed of dog, answering to the name of 'Gin'. M had lost the animal while exercising it on a nearby mountain. The dog was estimated to be worth £25,000. On Wednesday, N saw the advertisement and bought special equipment costing £1,500 which he used to try to find the dog. On Tuesday, P, a shepherd, found the dog attacking his sheep. He caught the dog and on Friday brought it down to the town of Trecynon where he was told about the reward. He went immediately to M to claim it. On Thursday, M had placed a notice in the Trecynon shop saying that the reward was no longer on offer.

Advise M. What difference, if any, would it make to your advice if (a) P, who had found the dog, was a local constable, or (b) Q, P's son, had seen the notice in the village shop but had not told P about it?

London University LLB Examination
(for external students) Elements of the Law of Contract June 1995 Q7

Answers

ANSWERS TO INTERROGRAMS

1   An offer may be accepted, turning it into a contract. An invitation to treat may not. Invitations to treat are merely steps in the negotiation of a contract. They may be an invitation to make an offer but they are not the offer itself. So far as the courts are concerned, it is a question of what was intended. Presumptions of intention are, however, made in certain circumstances. A display of goods in a shop, in a window or on shelves, is an invitation to treat: *Pharmaceutical Society of Great Britain* v *Boots Cash Chemists (Southern) Ltd* (1952); *Fisher* v *Bell* (1961). A newspaper advertisement of goods for sale is also usually presumed to be an invitation to treat (*Partridge* v *Crittenden* (1968)), although not if the contract advertised is unilateral: *Carlill* v *Carbolic Smoke Ball Co Ltd* (1893). Similarly, catalogues, price lists, brochures and other advertising material are usually presumed to be invitations to treat unless there is a clear contrary intention: *Grainger & Son* v *Gough* (1896).

The question of whether there was an invitation to treat or an offer is important not only in deciding whether there was a contract between the parties but also when the contract was concluded. This has proved to be an important issue in a number of cases where a defendant has sought to rely on an exclusion clause printed on a ticket. If the ticket is a contractual document, the exclusion clauses are incorporated, but if it is a mere receipt they are not. The question is therefore whether the defendant by holding himself out as ready to trade is making an offer or an invitation to treat: *Chapleton* v *Barry UDC* (1940); *Thornton* v *Shoe Lane Parking Ltd* (1971).

2   A unilateral contract is an offer to the world at large which is accepted by someone who performs the conditions of the offer. The offeror is then bound to make good his promise. An example is *Carlill* v *Carbolic Smoke Ball Co Ltd* (1893) where the defendants offered in a newspaper advertisement to make a payment to anyone who wore the smoke ball as instructed and nevertheless contracted influenza. The plaintiff performed this condition and was held entitled to the payment. A common example is the offer of a reward for performing some act such as finding a lost pet or giving information leading to a conviction: *Gibbons* v *Proctor* (1891).

   Unilateral contracts differ from bilateral contracts in some ways. First, as noted above, acceptance is by embarking on performance of the condition. The acceptor does not need to communicate acceptance to the offeror. The offeror is bound, even though he does not know that the acceptor has embarked on performance. Acceptance is, however, not complete until performance is complete. Thus, if a number of people embark on performance, the first to complete will have accepted the offer. Second, the offer can only be withdrawn by giving the withdrawal at least as much publicity as the original offer. Third, there is an implied condition that the offer cannot be revoked once performance has commenced: *Errington* v *Errington and Woods* (1952); *Daulia Ltd* v *Four Millbank Nominees Ltd* (1978).

3   The general rule is that acceptance must be communicated to the offeror: *Brogden* v *Metropolitan Railway Co* (1877). That is to say that it must be brought to his attention (*Entores* v *Miles Far East Corporation* (1955)). The only exception to this is the 'postal rule' which states that acceptance sent by post is effective when posted: *Adams* v *Lindsell* (1818). A telex is a form of instantaneous communication and therefore the normal rules apply to it (*Brinkibon Ltd* v *Stahag Stahl* (1982)), as is the telephone. By analogy (although there appears to be no reported decision on this question), a fax is also an instantaneous means of communicating acceptance. Acceptance is effective when and where received. The acceptance was received in Germany and the contract was therefore made in Germany.

   Had the fax not been received by Anna, there would have been no contract unless acceptance was communicated by some other means.

SUGGESTED ANSWER TO QUESTION ONE

General Comment

This question requires an analysis of a series of actions in order to establish whether a contract exists between the parties. The main object of the question is to ascertain whether the candidate has grasped the differences between acceptance and counter-offer and between the normal rules relating to acceptance and the so-called 'postal rule'.

Key Points

- Is there an offer or merely an invitation to treat? - *Spencer* v *Harding* (1870); *Grainger & Sons* v *Gough* (1896)

- What is the effect of introducing a new term? – *Butler Machine Tool Co Ltd* v *Ex-cell-o Corp* (1979)
- The effect of prescribing a mode of acceptance – *Manchester Diocesan Council for Education* v *Commercial & General Investments Ltd* (1970)
- Where written acceptance has been requested oral acceptance is not binding – *Financings Ltd* v *Stimson* (1962)
- The effect of the postal rule of acceptance – *Adams* v *Lindsell* (1818)
- Withdrawal of acceptance – *Wenkheim* v *Arndt* (1873); *A to Z Bazaars* v *Minister of Agriculture* (1974)

Suggested Answer

It is necessary to consider whether a contract for the sale of video tapes was concluded between Ben and Alan in the course of the various communications between them; if it was, then Ben will have an action for damages against Alan for non-delivery.

The first communication was Alan's letter to Ben 'offering' tapes for sale at £495 per hundred. On the facts there seems no reason for not attributing to the letter the ordinary meaning of the language used, namely that it is a contractual offer, not merely an invitation to treat. The distinction is that an offer may be accepted so as to become a contract while an invitation to treat may not. Nevertheless, the use of the word 'offer' is not conclusive (*Spencer* v *Harding* (1870)) and it has sometimes been held that an 'offer' of goods at a particular price was a mere invitation to treat since further bargaining may be contemplated: eg *Grainger & Son* v *Gough* (1896).

Ben's response was a written order dated 1 April. Rather than acceptance, this is probably a counter-offer, since it appears to be introducing a new term, ie delivery by 30 April (*Butler Machine Tool Co Ltd* v *Ex-cell-o Corporation (England) Ltd* (1979)), Alan's letter having been wholly silent as to delivery dates. Further, it appears that Ben so regarded it, because he asked for Alan's 'written confirmation'. Such a request may be a prescription of the mode of acceptance (*Manchester Diocesan Council for Education* v *Commercial & General Investments Ltd* (1970)), or the fixing of a time for acceptance. By requiring delivery by 30 April, Ben stipulates that Alan must accept his counter-offer within that time scale and by asking for acceptance in writing he will not be bound by oral acceptance: *Financings Ltd* v *Stimson* (1962).

The next communication is the telephone conversation on 22 April. The difficulty here is to determine whether what Alan said amounted to an acceptance of Ben's counter-offer. On balance, it is likely that a court would conclude that the language used was too ambiguous on both sides. Ben did not clearly dispense with the requirement of written confirmation (ie acceptance) and Alan did not unequivocally commit himself to honour Ben's order. Both parties seem to have regarded the counter-offer as open for acceptance but Alan had not at that time accepted in the prescribed form.

On the other hand it is possible that the telephone conversation was not wholly without legal effect. It could be construed as an indication by Ben that his counter-offer was still open for acceptance by Alan and, moreover, by not making any reference to the 30 April delivery date, Ben may have impliedly waived that date or extended the duration of his offer. A not dissimilar situation arose in the *Manchester Diocesan Council* case in which Buckley J held that by implication an offer remained open for acceptance where the offeree had manifested an intention to accept without having done so in law.

Thus by 2 May, Ben's counter-offer was probably still open for Alan to accept and had not lapsed. By posting his acceptance on 2 May, therefore, Alan will have been regarded as having accepted the counter-offer at the moment of posting: *Adams* v *Lindsell* (1818).

The postal rule of acceptance will normally apply where it is reasonable for the offeree to accept by post, where the letter of acceptance is properly stamped and addressed and where the offeror has not otherwise stipulated. Whereas the first two conditions are satisfied here, it is at least possible that Ben has, perhaps inadvertently, excluded the operation of the rule by his request for 'written confirmation'.

This is important since, if the postal rule does not apply, acceptance is only effective when received by the offeree. If this is the case, no contract is formed because Alan's subsequent rejection by telex overtakes his letter and is thus effective. If the postal rule does apply, however, the effect of the telex is less certain. The difficulty, which has not yet been resolved by the courts, is whether the offeree can withdraw a posted letter of acceptance by means of a speedier mode of communication which overtakes it.

An orthodox application of the postal rule would say that it cannot. Ordinarily, once an acceptance is effective the offeree has no right unilaterally to retire from it, and it would seem unjust that the offeror should be bound once the letter is posted, yet the offeree retain the right to withdraw at any time before receipt of the letter by the offeror. In two Commonwealth cases, *Wenkheim* v *Arndt* (1873) (New Zealand) and *A-Z Bazaars (Pty) Ltd* v *Minister of Agriculture* (1974) (South Africa), the courts refused to allow withdrawal though without considering in detail the policy reasons one way or the other, and textbook writers too generally oppose allowing withdrawal, eg Cheshire and Fifoot and Treitel.

The most vehement proponent of the argument in favour of withdrawal is Professor Hudson. He argues that the postal rule is one of convenience not logic and ought not to be inflexibly applied. He says that the offeror is not prejudiced by allowing the offeree to withdraw, since until he receives the letter, he is unaware of the 'acceptance'; that the offeror should be considered to take the risk of withdrawal, as he takes the risk of the letter being lost or delayed (*Grant's Case*); and that is is open to the offeror to protect himself against withdrawal by framing his offer appropriately. Further, in *Dick* v *US* (1949) an American court held a withdrawal to be effective, though the authority of the case is somewhat diminished by the fact that the state in question allowed posted letters to be retrieved by the sender (unlike England).

Whilst Professor Hudson's arguments are cogent and persuasive, it is submitted that the English courts would decide against allowing withdrawal, following their brethren in *Wenkheim* and *A-Z Bazaars (Pty) Ltd* v *Minister of Agriculture*, and hold that Alan is bound by his letter and that his subsequent telex is of no effect in law. On this footing, Ben would have a claim for damages against Alan for his failure to deliver the tapes.

101 Questions and Answers – Law of Contract

SUGGESTED ANSWER TO QUESTION TWO

General Comment

Here the examinee must be aware of the effect of an 'offer' of company shares to the public. A successful answer will demonstrate a clear understanding of the legal position with respect to the 'postal rule' concerning acceptance of an offer and the effect of withdrawing both offers and acceptance.

Key Points

- 'Offer' of shares to the public is an invitation to treat – *Hebb's Case* (1867)
- Actual offer is the application for shares
- Offer is accepted when the share certificates are posted – *Adams* v *Lindsell* (1818); *Household Fire Insurance Co Ltd* v *Grant* (1879); *Henthorn* v *Fraser* (1892); *Brinkibon Ltd* v *Stahag Stahl* (1983); *Holwell Securities* v *Hughes* (1974)
- Revocation of offer must be communicated before acceptance – *Byrne* v *Van Tienhoven* (1880)
- Withdrawal of acceptance – *Wenkheim* v *Arndt* (1873); *A-Z Bazaars* v *Minister of Agriculture* (1974)

Suggested Answer

In advising Slick it is necessary to consider whether or not there has been a concluded contract for the sale of the shares between himself and the company. It is well settled that a company which makes an 'offer' of its shares to the public is, in law, merely inviting the public to subscribe and the offer in contractual terms is made by members of the public applying for shares (*Hebb's Case* (1867)). Thus the newspaper advertisement constitutes an invitation to treat not an offer and Slick's application is the offer to purchase the shares. Since he has completed the prescribed form and paid the required sum, Slick's actions amount to a firm offer.

The next point to consider is whether Slick's offer has been accepted. The sending of the share certificates to Slick is an act of acceptance of his offer. What has to be considered is whether and when this acceptance has been communicated to Slick, in the light of the rule relating to acceptances through the post. The rule, established in *Adams* v *Lindsell* (1818), is that, where there has been communication through the post, the acceptance is complete as soon as it has been posted. This rule has been consistently affirmed: see for example *Household Fire Insurance Co Ltd* v *Grant* (1879), *Henthorn* v *Fraser* (1892), *Brinkibon Ltd* v *Stahag Stahl* (1982). There is, at this stage, no suggestion that the normal postal rule has been displaced, as where the offeror prescribes that he should receive actual notice of the acceptance, as in *Holwell Securities Ltd* v *Hughes* (1974). Accordingly the application of the postal rule would mean that the contract is concluded when the secretary posts the share certificates to Slick on the morning of Thursday, 2 May.

Slick has, however, purported to revoke his offer. Whilst an offer may be revoked at any time before acceptance, there must be actual communication of the revocation to the offeree before it has been accepted. The application of the ratio in *Byrne* v *Van Tienhoven* (1880) requires the answer here that, the revocation of the offer having been communicated after acceptance, this purported revocation must be deemed to be ineffective.

It appears further that the Company has attempted to withdraw its acceptance after it has been posted, but before it has come to the notice of Slick. There is no clear authority in English Law on whether an offeree can withdraw his acceptance after it has been posted, by a swifter method of communication. The strict application of the postal rule would suggest that withdrawal is not allowed. There are decisions to this effect in new Zealand in *Wenkheim* v *Arndt* (1873) and South Africa in *A-Z Bazaars (Pty) Ltd* v *Minister of Agriculture* (1974). It does seem contrary to the principle, too, to hold the offeror bound as soon as the acceptance has been posted and yet to permit the offeree to withdraw.

The contrary view is forcibly argued by Professor Hudson. He holds that the postal rule is merely one of convenience and ought not to be inflexibly applied. He says that, if the offeror takes 'the risks of delay and accident in the post, it would not seem to strain matters to say that he also assumes the risk of a letter being overtaken by a speedier means of communication.'

Although there is merit in Professor Hudson's argument, it might apply where the offeror has chosen the post as a means of communication and not to the present situation where it is arguably the Company which has elected to receive offers through the post and should therefore be bound by the postal rule in all its rigour.

The strict application of *Byrne* v *Van Tienhoven* and the postal rule would, therefore, lead to the conclusion that there is a binding contract for the sale of the shares which would afford Slick an action for specific performance, or alternatively, a claim in damages. However, in *Holwell Securities Ltd* v *Hughes,* Lawton LJ observed that the postal rule does not apply if its application would produce manifest inconvenience and absurdity. It may well be that the court would find that such inconvenience and absurdity resulted from its application where, as in the present instance, both parties clearly showed their intention of withdrawing from the contract. Moreover the traditional analysis of offer and acceptance has been criticised by Lord Denning MR in *Gibson* v *Manchester City Council* (1979) and *Butler Machine Tool Co Ltd* v *Ex-cell-o Corporation (England) Ltd* (1979). His Lordship stated that in many cases the traditional analysis was out of date and that the better approach was to look at the correspondence as a whole in order to determine whether the parties had reached an agreement.

Whilst it cannot be said with certainty that the flexible approach urged by Professor Hudson, Lawton LJ and Lord Denning would necessarily be adopted by the court in the present case, it is submitted that it would be more realistic for the court to do so.

In conclusion, therefore, it appears that the conduct of the parties will have precluded the formation of a binding contract.

SUGGESTED ANSWER TO QUESTION THREE

General Comment

This variation on the offer/acceptance analysis theme examines the student's knowledge of acceptance, counter-offer and revocation. However, the mode of acceptance provides an interesting modern complication: acceptance is by a message left on an answering machine and subsequently erased. It thus tests the student's ability to extend by analogy the legal rules to facts which have never been considered by the court.

Key Points

- An advertisement can be an offer – *Carlill* v *Carbolic Smoke Ball Co* (1893) – but, if bilateral, is likely to be an invitation to treat – *Partridge* v *Crittenden* (1968)
- An offer can be couched as acceptance – *Biggs* v *Boyd Gibbins Ltd* (1971)
- The effect of a counter-offer as compared with a statement as to price – *Butler Machine Tool Co Ltd* v *Ex-cell-o Corp* (1979); *Hyde* v *Wrench* (1840); *Harvey* v *Facey* (1893)
- A gratuitous promise to keep an offer open for a fixed time is not binding – *Routledge* v *Grant* (1828)
- Communication of acceptance – do the 'postal' or normal rules apply to an answering machine? – *Holwell Securities* v *Hughes* (1974); *Entores* v *Miles Far East Corp* (1955); *Brinkibon Ltd* v *Stahag Stahl* (1982)
- Effect of failure to receive acceptance due to default – *The Brimnes* (1975)
- Revocation of offer must be communicated before acceptance – *Byrne* v *van Tienhoven* (1880)
- Revocation may be communicated by a reliable third party – *Dickinson* v *Dodds* (1876)
- Application of the postal rule – *Adams* v *Lindsell* (1818); *Household Fire Insurance Co Ltd* v *Grant* (1879); *Henthorn* v *Fraser* (1892); *Holwell Securities* v *Hughes* (1974)

Suggested Answer

In advising Alan it is necessary to analyse the various actions of and communications passing between the parties to determine whether at any stage Alan entered into a contract with Bob to buy the stamp in question.

The first material event was Bob placing an advertisement in the *Gazette*. Although there is no reason in principle why an advertisement should not constitute a contractual offer, this will normally only be the case if there is a unilateral contract, as in *Carlill* v *Carbolic Smoke Ball Co* (1893). Since the envisaged contract here is bilateral, a court would be likely to construe the advertisement as an invitation to treat and not capable of being converted into a contract by acceptance: *Partridge* v *Crittenden* (1968).

Alan's telephone reply, although couched in terms of an acceptance, can thus only be an offer, as there was no prior offer capable of acceptance. A statement can be an offer although it is expressed as acceptance: *Biggs* v *Boyd Gibbins Ltd* (1971).

Alan's offer is not accepted by Bob. The latter's reply, however, gives rise to a problem of construction: it could be regarded as a rejection and counter offer (*Hyde* v *Wrench* (1840) and *Butler Machine Tool* v *Ex-cell-o Corporation (England) Ltd* (1979)) or a rejection together with a statement as to price (similar to *Harvey* v *Facey* (1893)). It is submitted that the last part of Bob's reply, giving Alan until Friday to respond, indicates that the first construction is correct.

Bob has promised to keep his counter offer open until Friday. It is to be noted that he is under no obligation so to do. A gratuitous promise to keep an offer open for a fixed period of time is not binding on the offeror (*Routledge* v *Grant* (1828)), and he can revoke the offer at any time. The only way an offer may be irrevocable for a fixed time is if the offeree furnishes consideration for the offeror's promise not to revoke, but Alan has not done so. Alan's promise to buy Bob a drink is a consequence of Bob's promise to keep the offer open; it was not requested by him nor was it given in return for Bob's promise in the contractual sense: *Combe* v *Combe* (1951).

Next, Alan dictates a message of acceptance on Bob's answering machine on Wednesday. The general rule is that an acceptance is ineffective unless and until communicated to the offeror: *Holwell Securities Ltd* v *Hughes* (1974). Although different principles apply to acceptance by letter or telegram (to be dealt with below), in *Entores* v *Miles Far East Corp* (1955), approved in *Brinkibon* v *Stahag Stahl* (1982), the Court of Appeal held that an acceptance by telephone or telex is only effective when received.

The principle was formulated on the proposition that telephones and telexes are instantaneous means of communication. That is obviously not the case where an acceptance is left on an answering machine. Trietel has suggested that the reason that the postal rule does not apply to telexes and telephones is because a letter may go astray and the acceptor will not know of the loss until too late. A telemessage dictated on the telephone should, he argues, take effect when it is dictated. That argument could also be applied here. However, Winfield argues to the contrary.

Due to the activities of Bob's son he never heard it. Although reference may be made to dicta in *Entores* and also in *The Brimnes* (1975), as indicating that where one party's failure to receive communication is due to his own default, he is to be treated as having received it, it is doubtful whether the infant's activities can be placed in this class.

Thus when Bob sells the stamps to Cedric, and also when Alan hears news of Cedric's excitement, Alan has not accepted Bob's offer. Equally, though, Bob has not revoked it, since revocation of an offer must be communicated: *Byrne* v *Van Tienhoven* (1880).

In *Dickinson* v *Dodds* (1876) it appears to have been held either that sale of the subject matter of the offer, or at any rate communication of the fact of the sale by a third party to the offeree, operates to revoke the offer. Whatever the true ratio of that case, which has been much criticised, it is very unlikely that a court would hold that the information given to Alan by Cedric's mother acquired from Cedric's son constituted revocation of Bob's offer. Although Alan may have suspected it was the same stamp, he could not have known it was, nor even that the information was strictly correct.

Bob's offer is thus still capable of acceptance when Alan posts his letter. The key issue now is whether the postal acceptance rule applies. If it does, a contract was concluded when Alan posted his letter: *Adams* v *Lindsell* (1818), *Household Fire Insurance* v *Grant* (1879) and *Henthorn* v *Fraser* (1892). Conversely it is settled law that Bob's letter of revocation is effective only when received by Alan: *Byrne* v *Van Tienhoven*.

The postal acceptance rule does not invariably apply. It is a rule of convenience which may (inter alia) be ousted by contrary stipulation: *Holwell* v *Hughes*. Although the language used by Bob was not totally clear, the words 'Let me have a reply by Friday' suggest that to be effective the acceptance must be received by him.

On this interpretation, as Alan's letter of acceptance arrived after Bob's letter of revocation, it is submitted that no contract was concluded and Alan has no claim.

SUGGESTED ANSWER TO QUESTION FOUR

General Comment

The focus of this question is on the ambiguity and informality of the statements made by the parties which, together with the need to know the court's attitude to negotiations for the sale of land and the doubt concerning acceptance by answering machine, creates an interesting problem.

Key Points

- In regard to sale of land, the court assumes the offeror does not intend to be bound by an informal offer - *Clifton* v *Palumbo* (1944)
- Rejection of an offer terminates it if communicated - *Tinn* v *Hoffman* (1873)
- Acceptance must be communicated - *Entores* v *Miles Far East Corporation* (1955)
- A party may not be able to take advantage of his own default - *The Brimnes* (1975)
- A terminated offer cannot be revived by subsequent acceptance - *Hyde* v *Wrench* (1840)
- Promissory estoppel probably does not apply - *Combe* v *Combe* (1951); *Walton Stores (Interstate) Ltd* v *Maher* (1988)
- Contracts for the sale of land must comply with s2 Law of Property (Miscellaneous Provisions) Act 1989

Suggested Answer

It must be assumed that A's telephone call to B constitutes a firm offer to sell Greenacre field, although *Clifton* v *Palumbo* (1944) suggests that the court may consider that A did not intend to be bound to a transaction concerning real property in such an informal way.

B requires time to consider the offer, and it appears that A requires a reasonably swift response.

When B sends the letter on Tuesday he is rejecting A's offer. It is clear that the rejection of an offer terminates the offer: *Tinn* v *Hoffman & Co* (1873). But the rejection of an offer has no effect until it is communicated to the offeror. Unlike acceptances through the post there is no rule of convenience requiring the rejection to be deemed to be communicated when the letter of rejection is posted. If B accepts the offer, and this acceptance is communicated before the letter of rejection reaches A, a contract will have been concluded.

Later on the Tuesday B purports to accept the offer; the question is, however, whether that acceptance has been communicated. There is no clear authority regarding the leaving of a message on an answering machine. In discussing instantaneous communications in *Entores Ltd* v *Miles Far East Corporation* (1955) Denning LJ said:

> 'But if there should be a case where the offeror without any fault on his part does not receive the message of acceptance - yet the sender of it believes it has got home when it has not - then I think there is no contract.'

B apparently believes that his message has got home. Can it be assumed that A is at fault because of the failure of his answering machine? A's demand for a swift response to his offer suggests that he does, or should, expect a telephone call from B. If the failure of the machine is due to the fault of A it might be possible to argue that the message of acceptance was deemed to be communicated when A should have heard it. Perhaps some slender support for this suggestion could be gleaned from *The Brimnes* (1975) though that case concerned the termination of a contract, not its formation, and dealt with the communication of a telex message during normal office hours. That case is, therefore, not authority for the view that, even if A were at fault, he could be deemed to have received B's message. Moreover, there is nothing to suggest that A was at fault.

At this stage, therefore, the offer has not been effectively rejected, nor has it been accepted.

On the Friday, when B enquires as to when he will be hearing from A's solicitor, it is clear that he believes that his message of acceptance has been received. We are not told whether or not A has received the letter rejecting his offer. If he has, then the rejection will have been communicated before the acceptance, and the offer would have been terminated and cannot be revived by subsequent acceptance: *Hyde* v *Wrench* (1840).

But the possibility must be considered that when this telephone call was made A was still unaware of the letter of rejection. In this event it becomes necessary to examine the import of Friday's telephone conversation. Clearly the parties had a different understanding of it. For B to succeed in a contention that a contract had been concluded he would have to convince a court that, in the light of the circumstances, A should have known that he (B) was referring to the purchase of Greenacre field and must be deemed to have known that his offer had been accepted. B would then argue that A's conduct had led him to believe that a contract had been concluded and that he had relied on this. The basis of B's contention would be that A was estopped from denying that a contract had been concluded. Whatever the limits of promissory estoppel, it is submitted that the doctrine cannot be stretched this far. *Combe* v *Combe* (1951) is still authority for the rule that promissory estopped does not create a cause of action where none existed before, and the decision in the contrasting Australian case of *Walton Stores (Interstate) Ltd* v *Maher* (1988) could not be applied here. There is, furthermore, nothing to indicate that B has acted to his detriment so as to found a proprietory estoppel.

It is submitted, therefore, that no contract has been concluded between the parties, nor has B any other basis for a cause of action.

It remains to note the effect of the Law of Property (Miscellaneous Provisions) Act 1989. Under s2 of that Act the contract for the sale of Greenacre field would have to be in writing and all the terms agreed would have to be in a document signed by or on behalf of both parties. Clearly none of these requirements has been met.

SUGGESTED ANSWER TO QUESTION FIVE

General Comment

While the examiner here expects a traditional analysis of offer and acceptance, the candidate is also required to demonstrate an in-depth knowledge of the rules relating to unilateral contracts which differ significantly from those relating to bilateral contracts.

Key Points

- A newspaper advertisement of this nature which envisages a unilateral contract is an offer – *Carlill* v *Carbolic Smoke Ball Co* (1893); *New Zealand Shipping Co Ltd* v *A M Satterthwaite & Co Ltd (The Eurymedon)* (1975)
- Acceptance in a unilateral contract is by performance
- Revocation must be communicated before acceptance – *Byrne* v *Van Tienhoven* (1880)
- There is no clear authority on what constitutes revocation in a unilateral contract – *Shuey* v *United States* (1875)
- The offeror cannot withdraw once performance has commenced – *Errington* v *Errington & Woods* (1952)
- There is an implied obligation on the offeror not to prevent a condition of the offer being satisfied – *Daulia Ltd* v *Four Millbank Nominees Ltd* (1978)
- L's right to claim a reward depends on whether he can be said to have 'returned' the cat
- K's refusal to pay may be a breach of a fundamental term – *McRae* v *Commonwealth Disposals Commission* (1950); *Hayes* v *James and Charles Dodd* (1988)
- L can recover his expenses only so far as they were 'reasonably foreseeable', which may not include the hotel bill – *Victoria Laundry (Windsor) Ltd* v *Newman Industries Ltd* (1949); *H Parsons (Livestock) Ltd* v *Uttley Ingham & Co Ltd* (1978)

Suggested Answer

The first point for decision is whether K's advertisement constitutes an offer. It appears beyond doubt that an offer of a reward (unlike offers to buy or sell articles) is an offer in the legal sense, and that it can be made to the world at large: *Carlill* v *Carbolic Smoke Ball Co* (1893). This problem is an example of a 'unilateral' contract; an offer which matures into a contract after performance; see also *New Zealand Shipping Co Ltd* v *Satterthwaite & Co Ltd (The Eurymedon)* (1975).

In unilateral contracts, acceptance is by performance of the terms of the offer. Thus, in this case, return of the cat would constitute acceptance. An offer may be revoked at any time before acceptance but revocation must be actually communicated to the offeree before acceptance: *Byrne* v *Van Tienhoven* (1880). The question here is whether K has effectively revoked the offer before L has accepted it.

There is no clear authority in English law as to what would constitute an effective revocation of an offer contained in a newspaper advertisement. As the offeror cannot ensure that the revocation comes to the notice of the offeree, it seems that it would be sufficient if he took all reasonable steps to do so. In *Shuey* v *United States* (1875), an American court decided that a revocation published in the same newspaper as the preceding offer was deemed to be effective. It is doubtful, however, whether placing a notice in the shop window would be regarded as taking all reasonable steps to communicate revocation to the offeree.

Even if all reasonable steps had been taken, it is likely that, in a unilateral contract, the offeror cannot withdraw the offer once the offeree has commenced performance (*Errington* v *Errington and Woods* (1952)). There is an implied obligation on the offeror not to prevent a condition of the offer being satisfied and this obligation arises as soon as an offeree embarks on performance – see the judgment of Goff LJ in *Daulia Ltd* v *Four Millbank Nominees Ltd* (1978).

If L has commenced performance, therefore, K is not able to prevent him from fulfilling the condition, ie returning the cat. The question is whether L's actions constitute starting performance or are mere preparation for it. It is submitted that, since the steps taken by L were directed solely to the recovery of the cat, they constitute commencement of performance.

It is therefore submitted that the purported revocation by K is ineffective.

It appears that L, in taking the cat to K's address, has tendered performance of the contract, and K, in refusing payment of the promised reward, is in breach. What must then be considered are the remedies, if any, available to L.

Firstly, dealing with the situation before K removed the cat from L's garden: the condition on which L could claim payment was the actual return of the cat, and had he left the cat with K he would have been entitled to the reward. However, by refusing to leave the cat, L may have forfeited his right. This depends on how the court would construe the word 'return'. On the other hand, it is submitted, by refusing to pay the reward, K has committed an anticipatory breach of a fundamental term, releasing L from the obligation to further perform the contract. By accepting the breach, L would have a right of rescission without losing his claim for damages. His claim would be based on the wasted expenditure he incurred in the performance of the contract, see for example *McRae* v *Commonwealth Disposals Commission* (1950); *Hayes* v *James and Charles Dodd* (1988). This is subject to the rule that the loss is not too remote. This rule limits the loss recoverable to that which was 'reasonably foreseeable': *Victoria Laundry (Windsor) Ltd* v *Newman Industries Ltd* (1949). The House of Lords in *The Heron II* (1969) preferred the expression 'within the reasonable contemplation of the parties', this denoting a higher degree of probability.

Adopting the latter expression, it is necessary to ask whether it was within the reasonable contemplation of K that an offeree would be 'likely to' or 'liable to' (terms used by their Lordships in *The Heron II*) incur expenses in the performance of the contract. This in not beyond doubt, but in can be concluded that the incurring of some expenditure was, or should have been, within K's reasonable contemplation. Furthermore if K could have been expected to contemplate the type of loss that would be incurred, it is no answer for him to say that he could not have contemplated the extent of that loss: *H Parsons (Livestock) Ltd* v *Uttley Ingham & Co Ltd* (1978).

Applying these principles to the present facts it appears that K should have contemplated that an offeree would incur travelling expenses in recovering the cat. He might not have contemplated the extent of L's expenses – a return ticket costing £76 – but this does not avail him. In consequence, L would be entitled to recover this expenditure.

L would have difficulty, however, in recovering the amount of his hotel bill. Arguably, it would not have been within K's reasonable contemplation that an offeree would stay at a hotel. Moreover by staying at the hotel for five days, L has unnecessarily increased his loss, contrary to the rule of common law requiring him to mitigate his loss. On the other hand, L could not have been expected to know when the cat would arrive.

The remaining point to consider is the action of K in snatching the cat from L's garden and the costs L incurred in feeding the cat. By removing the cat, K has effected its return, albeit by improper means, a return which was made possible by L having found it. This can be construed as acceptance of the return by L. In this event, the condition for the payment of the reward has been fulfilled and L is entitled to payment of the £2,000. He would not then be entitled to claim the expenses discussed above. A plaintiff is entitled to reliance loss or expectation loss, but not both. It would, however appear that the costs incurred in feeding the cat were a necessary expenditure, for which L is entitled to be compensated.

SUGGESTED SOLUTION TO QUESTION SIX

General Comment

The focus in this problem on whether or not a contract has been concluded is on vague and ambiguous statements. The candidate there has to consider the effect of alternative interpretations. The two possible acts of purported acceptance also force the candidate to consider alternative possibilities depending on whether the normal or the postal rules apply.

Key Points

- Is A's letter an offer or an invitation to treat? – *Harvey* v *Facey* (1893); *Gibson* v *Manchester City Council* (1979)
- Apply postal rules to determine whether acceptance has been communicated – *Adams* v *Lindsell* (1818); *Household Fire Insurance Co* v *Grant* (1879); *Holwell Securities Ltd* v *Hughes* (1974)
- If there was no communication, apply normal rules to determine whether the answering machine message amounts to communication of acceptance – *Entores* v *Miles Far East Corporation* (1955); *Brinkibon Ltd* v *Stahag Stahl* (1983)

- A has no clear-cut cause of action but might obtain a remedy in damages.
- Order for specific performance would not be available because compliance would be impossible – *Castle* v *Wilkinson* (1870)

Suggested Answer

The initial point that falls for discussion is whether A's first letter to B can be considered to be an offer or is merely an invitation to treat. An offer is defined by Treitel as an 'expression of willingness to contract on certain terms, made with the intention that it shall become binding as soon as it is accepted by the person to whom it is addressed.' The wording of the letter suggests that it does not constitute an offer in this sense; it does not evidence the intention 'that it shall become binding', but does no more than express an interest in buying the car and, moreover, A wishes to be assured that the car is in good condition. On this analysis the letter is an invitation to treat. The decisions in *Harvey* v *Facey* (1893) and *Gibson* v *Manchester City Council* (1979) would, it is submitted, support this view.

However, it is not always easy to distinguish an offer from an invitation to treat; the wording is not necessarily conclusive. B appears to have regarded A's letter as an offer. It appears also, from A's second letter, that he regarded his first letter as making an offer. Consider the possibility, therefore, that A was making an offer which was conditional on the car being in good condition. On this assumption it is necessary to examine whether B has accepted the offer. At first sight B's letter appears to be ambiguous; it is by no means certain that B is unequivocally accepting the terms of the offer. However, B does not introduce any new terms into his letter and it is, therefore, possible to construe it as an acceptance. The next question is whether the acceptance has been communicated. The postal rule, established in *Adams* v *Lindsell* (1818), is that in the case of postal communications, the acceptance is deemed to be communicated as soon as the letter of acceptance is posted. The postal rule will apply whenever use of the post is, or is deemed to be, contemplated by the parties, and the presumption that it is so contemplated will arise when the offeror makes his offer by post: *Henthorn* v *Fraser* (1892). Here A has made the offer (on the assumption that it is an offer) by post. B's letter is lost in the post, but nevertheless, where the postal rule applies, the contract is concluded when the letter is posted and the contract cannot be 'unmade' because of a casualty in the post: *Household Fire Insurance Co Ltd* v *Grant* (1879).

On the above assumptions, therefore, it is possible to argue that a contract has been concluded for the sale of the car at £1,200. But it is at least doubtful whether there has been offer and acceptance and whether the postal rule will apply. The postal rule is not an inflexible one. In *Holwell Securities Ltd* v *Hughes* (1974) Lawton J expressed the view that the rule 'probably does not operate if its application would produce manifest inconvenience and absurdity'. The subsequent conduct of the parties, involving apparently a fresh offer and acceptance, would, it is submitted, produce 'inconvenience and absurdity' in applying the postal rule.

Proceeding on the basis that no contract had been concluded at this stage, A, in his second letter, makes a further offer to buy the car at £2,000. Although the letter is couched in the form of a query, it does however express willingness to be bound at the new price. If that is so, it is necessary to consider whether the fresh offer has been accepted. B purported to accept the fresh offer. But the question is – has this acceptance been effectively communicated? In the case of instantaneous communications the contract is only concluded when the acceptance has been actually received: *Entores* v *Miles Far East Corporation* (1955). There is no direct authority in English law on the use but it appears from the authority of *Entores* and *Brinkibon Ltd* v *Stahag Stahl* (1982) that B's acceptance is communicated not when he leaves the message on the machine, but only when it is heard by A. When A returns and hears the message the acceptance is, therefore, then communicated, and the contract would be concluded at that point. However, it appears that at that stage B has already sold the car to a third party.

A must be advised that he has no clear-cut cause of action. For the reasons set out above the formation of a contract at the initial price of £1,200 cannot be supported. Whilst there may well be a concluded contract for the sale of the car at £2,000 there is no suggestion that B effectively withdrew his acceptance. A has no satisfactory remedy. An order for specific performance would not be available to him. A court will not make such an order where compliance with it is impossible: *Castle* v *Wilkinson* (1870). A remedy in damages would be available to A, but on the information given one cannot say whether this would be worth pursuing.

SUGGESTED ANSWER TO QUESTION SEVEN

General Comment

This question on 'reward' contracts takes the frequently-met form of posing alternatives to the basic facts so that the candidate must consider how advice to the parties might be affected by different factors. The question tests in depth the candidate's understanding of the rules relating to unilateral contracts and requires a good knowledge of case law.

Key Points

- The advertising of a reward is an 'offer to all the world' – *Carlill* v *Carbolic Smoke Ball Co* (1893); *New Zealand Shipping Co Ltd* v *A M Satterthwaite & Co Ltd (The Eurymedon)* (1975)
- Acceptance of the offer is by performing the required act, ie 'finding and recovering' the dog
- Offer may be revoked at any time before acceptance but must be communicated – *Routledge* v *Grant* (1828); *Byrne* v *Van Tienhoven* (1880)
- There is some doubt as to what constitutes effective revocation – *Shuey* v *United States* (1875)
- Possibly N has accepted the offer by embarking on performance – *Daulia Ltd* v *Four Millbank Nominees* (1978)
- If P has performed the required acts in ignorance of the offer he cannot claim the reward – *R* v *Clarke* (1927); *Gibbons* v *Proctor* (1891)
- Motive for catching the dog would not be relevant – *Williams* v *Carwardine* (1833)
- As a local constable, P might be discharging a public duty but this need not deprive

him of the reward – *Collins* v *Godefroy* (1831); *Ward* v *Byham* (1956); *Williams* v *Williams* (1957); *Williams* v *Roffey Bros & Nicholls (Contractors) Ltd* (1991)
- The notice in the shop might be evidence of adequate revocation but Q's involvement would not affect the advice as he did not inform P

Suggested Answer

The advertising of the reward constitutes a unilateral offer 'made to all the world which is to ripen into a contract with anybody who comes forward and performs the conditions': *Carlill* v *Carbolic Smoke Ball Co* (1893); *New Zealand Shipping Co Ltd* v *A M Satterwhwaite & Co Ltd (The Eurymedon)* (1975).

The acceptance of the offer would be the 'finding and recovering' of the dog.

An offer can be revoked at any time before acceptance: *Routledge* v *Grant* (1828). In order, however, for a revocation to be effective, it must be communicated to the offeree before the offer has been accepted: *Byrne* v *Van Tienhoven* (1880).

M, having advertised the offer of the reward in the local newspaper, has purported to revoke the offer by a notice in the shop. It is extremely doubtful whether this constitutes an effective revocation. In *Shuey* v *United States* (1875) the offer had been made in a newspaper publication and the revocation published in the same newspaper. The Supreme Court of the United States held that the revocation of an offer of a reward was effective where:

> 'it was withdrawn through the same channel in which it was made. The same notoriety was given to the revocation that was given to the offer ...'.

This cannot be said of the purported revocation in this problem. It is submitted, therefore, that the placing of the notice in the shop did not constitute an effective revocation.

The rights of N in relation to the offer

N had bought special equipment which he used trying to find the dog. Clearly he would not be entitled to the reward until he had performed the condition required. But it could be argued that N had accepted the offer by embarking on performance. In *Daulia Ltd* v *Four Millbank Nominees Ltd* (1978) Goff J said that:

> 'there must be an implied obligation on the part of the offeror not to prevent the condition becoming satisfied, which obligation it seems to me must arise as soon as the offeree starts to perform.'

The rights of P in relation to the offer

When P found the dog he was unaware of the offer. Indeed he was unaware of the offer until after he had brought the dog down to the town. It is clear that if the offeree is unaware of the offer he is not entitled to the reward, even though he performs the required condition: *R* v *Clarke* (1927). Here, however, it appears that P informed M that he had recovered the dog after learning of the reward. It is possible that the decision in *Gibbons* v *Proctor* (1891) could be applied so as to entitle P to the reward. If this were so, and it is by no means certain that it is, P's claim for the reward would not be defeated by the fact that he caught the dog because it was attacking his sheep. This may have been the motive for his catching the dog, but this would not be relevant if he was held to have acted within the terms of the offer: *Williams v Carwardine* (1833).

If P was a local constable

In this situation P, in finding and recovering the dog, could be held to have acted in the discharge of a public duty. On the strict application of *Collins v Godefroy* (1831) P would not have furnished good consideration for the promise. But this case has come under scrutiny: see *Ward v Byham* (1956); *Williams v Williams* (1957); and *Williams v Roffey Bros & Nicholls (Contractors) Ltd* (1991). In the light of these later developments and as there would not appear to be any public policy reasons to the contrary, it seems that, as P has conferred a factual benefit on M, there is good consideration for the promise. Therefore the mere fact that P was a local constable should not disentitle him to the reward.

If Q had not told P about the notice

It is not clear what is required here. It might be suggested that P is deemed to have knowledge of the revocation because his son could have been expected to tell him of it. Alternatively, the fact that Q saw the notice implies that there was adequate notice of the revocation of the offer. But these are slender suppositions and would not affect the advice.

2

Consideration and Intention to Create Legal Relations

Introduction

The two further elements of a simple contract (one not under seal), consideration and intention to be legally bound, are no less important than offer and acceptance, since without them there is no enforceable contract. Thus, this topic is scarcely less highly-favoured by examiners.

While legal intention is generally straightforward and can be discerned from the nature of the transaction and the relationship between the parties, the concept of consideration often causes difficulty. Consideration merely means that a party who wishes to sue under a contract must have given or promised something of value in return. The main question in this area is what amounts to 'valuable' or 'good' consideration. Examples of consideration which may not be 'good' are acts performed prior to the making of the contract or the performance of an existing legal duty. Students are advised to read the cases and examples carefully in order to discuss this point, and to note the apparent recent change in attitudes of the courts.

The question of promissory estoppel also falls within this area. Promissory estoppel is the equitable principle that when a creditor has agreed to forego part of his debt, he cannot then renege on that agreement, even though there was no consideration for it. Candidates should be fully aware of the circumstances in which this principle may be invoked and the development of rules in relation to it.

Questions

INTERROGRAMS

1 Under what circumstances (if any) is the court prepared to uphold social and domestic agreements?
2 What words in commercial agreements have been deemed evidence that there was no intention to enter into a legally binding contract?
3 'Consideration must have some economic value but need not be adequate.' Explain.

QUESTION ONE

Colin made the following promises:

i to give his daughter, Diana, £500 if she will abandon her career as a photographic model and become a social worker;
ii to pay his secretary, Enid, £250 for having been willing to give up her lunch hour when necessary during the previous three months;

iii to pay Fred, who has a contract with the local newsagent to deliver the newspapers in that area, £10 if he delivers the newspaper by 8 am every day for a month and puts it through the letter-box without tearing it;
iv to give his old lawn-mower to George, a neighbour, if George collects it from the garden shed.

Advise Colin to what extent, if at all, the above promises are legally binding on him.

London University LLB Examination
(for external students) Elements of the Law of Contract June 1985 Q2

QUESTION TWO

a Consider to what extent, if any, a person provides consideration for a promise by doing or promising to do what he was already contractually bound to do.

b Albert rents a caravan from Bernard. Albert's wife, Wendy, is subsequently injured in a road accident and has to give up work. After a discussion between them Bernard promises Albert that he will accept half rent until Wendy is able to go back to work. Albert pays half rent for the next twelve months but is then advised that Wendy will never be able to work again. On learning this Bernard tells Albert that he wants full rent from now and also the balance of the past twelve month's rent.

Advise Albert. How would your advice differ, if at all, if Wendy had recently received £100,000 compensation for her injuries?

London University LLB Examination
(for external students) Elements of the Law of Contract June 1987 Q2

QUESTION THREE

Giles engaged Illtyd, a landscape gardener, to construct a patio and fish pond in his garden for a fixed price of £3,000. The contract provided that the work was to be completed by 30 April 1988 and that payment was to be made in stages as the work proceeded.

In order to pay Illtyd, Giles borrowed £3,000 from Peter, agreeing to repay this sum, together with interest of £720, in 24 equal monthly instalments.

In March, while Illtyd was excavating the ground for the pond, he uncovered an ancient cannon which he could only remove by using special lifting equipment and he informed Giles that he could only continue with the work if Giles agreed to pay an additional £500. Giles objected but agreed to pay.

Soon after this Giles was made redundant. Peter then agreed that Giles need pay only the interest of the loan until he found a new job. Although Giles is still out of work he recently received a letter from Peter demanding immediate payment of the outstanding arrears of capital and the immediate resumption of payments of instalments at the agreed rate. Illtyd is also pressing for payment of the additional £500.

Advise Giles.

London University LLB Examination
(for external students) Elements of the Law of Contract June 1988 Q7

QUESTION FOUR

'Consideration is a form as much as seal.' Discuss.
Written by the Editor June 1998

QUESTION FIVE

'The concept of so-called promissory estoppel has a dubious pedigree ... moreover, it is in practice almost totally unnecessary.'
   Discuss.
*London University LLB Examination
(for external students) Elements of the Law of Contract June 1993 Q7*

Answers

ANSWERS TO INTERROGRAMS

1 There is a presumption that the parties to social and domestic agreements do not intend them to be legally binding (*Balfour* v *Balfour* (1919)). However this is a rebuttable presumption, which is to say that it will not apply if strong evidence is shown to the contrary: *Petitt* v *Petitt* (1970).

   In *Jones* v *Padavatton* (1969) a mother induced her daughter to leave her job in America and read for the Bar in England by the promise of a monthly allowance, for which was later substituted an agreement that the daughter would live rent-free in a property of hers. The court found an intention to create legal relations in the promise to pay a monthly allowance but not in the agreement for rent-free accommodation which was deemed a family arrangement.

   The courts are, however, sometimes more ready to find intention to create legal relations where the agreement concerns the occupation of real property, even if the arrangement is between family members: *Hardwick* v *Johnson* (1978).

   Separation agreements between spouses have been held to be legally binding (*Merritt* v *Merritt* (1970); *Gould* v *Gould* (1970) but only where their terms were clear and unambiguous.

   Finally, the court may be prepared to find an intention to create legal relations where there is 'mutuality'. In *Simpkins* v *Pays* (1955) three people living together were accustomed to enter a weekly newspaper competition, sending in the entry alternately in each name. When one of them won a monetary prize, the court held that the other two were entitled to share it.

2 Where the agreement is a commercial one, the court presumes that it was intended to be legally binding. However, as with the opposite presumption in relation to social and domestic agreements, it is rebuttable by clear evidence to the contrary.

   While evidence as to a contrary intention may be drawn from the surrounding circumstances (*Orion Insurance Co* v *Sphere Drake Insurance* (1992); *Evans* v *Merzario Ltd* (1976)), more often the words of the contract itself will rebut the presumption. In *Jones* v *Vernons Pools* (1938) a football pools agreement was stated to be 'binding in honour only' and the plaintiff was therefore unable to sue. In *Rose & Frank Co* v *J R Crompton Bros* (1925), the contract itself contained the words 'This agreement is not entered into ... as a formal or legal agreement, and shall not be subject to legal jurisdiction in the law courts.' These words were held sufficiently clear and unambiguous to negative the usual presumption. A further example is provided by *Edwards* v *Skyways Ltd* (1964) where, in an agreement to make a termination payment to an employee, the payment was stated to be 'ex gratia'. These words were held to indicate that the defendants did not intend to be legally bound by their promise to pay.

3   Consideration must have some value, and it has long been established that the value must be economic: *White* v *Bluett* (1853). The consideration, however, need not be adequate. That is to say, the court refuses to act as valuer and, provided there is some consideration of economic value, will not judge whether it reflects the true value of what is promised in return.

Thus the practice has grown of giving nominal consideration: one peppercorn by way of annual rent or £1 in return for the transfer of shares or other property. This may lead to the enforcement of what are, in effect, gratuitous promises. Atiyah suggests that the nominal consideration can be regarded as a form to make the contract binding. This does not, however, accord with some of the reasons for non-enforcement of gratuitous promises, eg rashness of the promisor, or prejudice to creditors (although there may be more effective ways of dealing with these situations in modern times).

Rather than nominal, the consideration may be trivial but can nevertheless still be valuable. In *Chappell & Co Ltd* v *Nestlé Co Ltd* (1960) delivery of chocolate wrappers which were then thrown away was held to be valuable consideration. However, most recently in *Lipkin Gorman* v *Karpnale Ltd* (1991) the House of Lords held that gaming chips supplied by a club to one of its member were not consideration for the money paid to them. This decision sits uneasily beside *Chappell*, although a number of distinguishing points were noted. Perhaps, as Atiyah has suggested, the refusal to find valuable consideration was based on the context – ie the money paid by the member had been stolen, and the club was arguing against liability to the true owner – and the case may therefore be confined to its facts.

SUGGESTED ANSWER TO QUESTION ONE

General Comment

This example demonstrates the multiple question style of problem. It should be noted that, as here, this type of question is often used to combine different areas of the syllabus in one. Each part of the question is given equal weight and examines a specific point of law. The issues should be treated as separate questions.

Key Points

- Diana – there is offer, acceptance and consideration, but is there an intention to create legal relations? – *Balfour* v *Balfour* (1919); *Jones* v *Padavatton* (1969)

- Enid – the legal effect of this promise turns on the question whether past consideration can support a binding contract – *Roscorla* v *Thomas* (1842); *Re McArdle* (1951); *Lampleigh* v *Braithwait* (1615); *Kennedy* v *Brown* (1863); *Re Casey's Patents* (1892); *Pao On* v *Lau Yiu Long* (1980)
- Fred – the question here is whether doing more than performing an existing contractual obligation can furnish consideration for an additional promise – *Hartley* v *Ponsonby* (1857); *Shadwell* v *Shadwell* (1860); *Scotson* v *Pegg* (1861); *Chichester* v *Cobb* (1866); *New Zealand Shipping Co Ltd* v *A M Satterthwaite and Co Ltd* (1975); *Pao On* v *Lau Yiu Long* (1980)
- George – for there to be a binding contract, consideration must move from the promisee, otherwise there is merely a conditional gift – *Wyatt* v *Kreglinger* (1933)

Suggested Answer

i If Diana does become a social worker, then, prima facie, Colin is bound by his promise: he has made an offer to her, and by abandoning her career as a model she both accepts the offer and furnishes consideration. However, Colin may be able to avoid liability if he can persuade the court that there was no intention to create legal relations.

    The traditional approach of the courts to 'family' agreements of this nature is that there is rebuttable presumption that the parties did not intend to create legal relations: *Balfour* v *Balfour* (1919). It is perfectly possible for a parent and child to enter into a binding contract but there must be clear evidence that they intended legal consequences to flow from their agreement. Thus in *Jones* v *Padavatton* (1969) the majority of the Court of Appeal held that a mother's promise to her daughter to pay her a monthly allowance if she moved from the United States to England and read for the bar was held to be unenforceable At first sight, *Jones* would appear to be close to the present case. However, one point of distinction is that in *Jones* the court was heavily influenced by the vagueness of the agreement; here, by contrast, the agreement is precise and specific.

    Although this distinction of fact does exist, ultimately it would be likely that the court would hold, on these facts, in the context of a parent–child relationship the presumption had not been rebutted and that Colin was under no liability to Diana.

ii Colin's promise to Enid is in return for her having given up her lunch hour in the previous three months: this immediately raises the problem of past consideration. Because consideration is given in return for the promisor's promise and, once furnished, the promise becomes binding and irrevocable, acts done prior to the making of the promise cannot constitute good consideration. Past consideration, so it is said, is no consideration: *Roscorla* v *Thomas* (1842) and *Re McArdle* (1951). A simple application of this rule would mean that Enid had no claim against Colin.

    The rule is, however, subject to a number of exceptions. The relevant one here derives from the decisions in *Lampleigh* v *Braithwait* (1615), *Kennedy* v *Brown* (1863) and *Re Casey's Patents* (1892), and was recently affirmed and restated in *Pao On* v *Lau Yiu Long* (1980). The exception provides that an antecedent act can be good consideration for a subsequent promise where (a) it was done at the promisor's request, (b) it was understood that the act was to be remunerated by payment or the conferment of some other benefit, and (c) the payment or benefit, if promised in advance, would have been legally enforceable.

Accordingly, if Enid can satisfy these three conditions, Colin will be liable on his promise. If she cannot, and merely gave up her lunch hour in the hope, rather than the legal expectation, of payment, Colin is not liable. On the limited facts given it is impossible to reach a conclusion one way or the other.

iii Fred is already bound by his contract with the newsagent to deliver newspapers: the issue raised is whether by delivering the paper by 8 am and not tearing it, he furnishes consideration for Colin's promise. It is submitted that Fred does furnish consideration in one of two ways. First, unless his contract with the newsagent obliges him to deliver Colin's paper by 8 am, in doing so he is doing over and above his existing contractual duty: *Hartley* v *Ponsonby* (1857). The same cannot be said about not tearing the paper, since this must clearly be an implied if not an express term of his contract with the newsagent. Secondly, and more simply, as the law stands it matters not whether Fred is doing more than he is bound to do by his contract with the newsagent, or whether he is merely performing his existing contractual obligation. A succession of cases in the nineteenth century, namely *Shadwell* v *Shadwell* (1860), *Scotson* v *Pegg* (1861) and *Chichester* v *Cobb* (1866), affirmed and followed recently in *New Zealand Shipping Co Ltd* v *A M Satterthwaite and Co Ltd* (1974) and *Pao On* v *Lau Yiu Long* (1980) established that the performance of an existing contractual duty owed to a third party (as opposed to the promisor) is good consideration It therefore follows that Fred does furnish consideration for Colin's promise and the latter is bound to honour it.

iv It is submitted that this instance illustrates the distinction between consideration and a condition. No contract exists between Colin and George because no consideration moves from the latter to support the former's promise The true legal analysis is that Colin is promising to make a gift of the lawn-mower to George providing the latter collects it; it is a conditional gift: *Wyatt* v *Kreglinger & Fernau* (1933). At any time before George collects, Colin is at liberty to revoke his promise; once George has collected, the conditional gift becomes unconditional and complete and property in the lawn-mower will pass to George.

SUGGESTED ANSWER TO QUESTION TWO

General Comment

Two separate questions make up this question on consideration. The first requires an essay-style answer which analyses the effect of the cases on acts which the promisor is already contractually bound to do. The second is a problem-style question which requires an analysis of the rules relating to agreement of a party to accept a lesser sum in discharge of a contractual obligation and the application of promissory estoppel to the situation.

2 Consideration and Intention to Create Legal Relations – Answers

Key Points

a
- Where the contractual duty is owed to the promisor, the cases are not clear but the general rule is that performance or promise to perform an existing contractual duty is not good consideration – *Stilk* v *Myrick* (1809); *Hartley* v *Ponsonby* (1857); *The Atlantic Baron* (1979)
- Where the duty is owed to a third party, it is clear that its performance can be good consideration – *Shadwell* v *Shadwell* (1860); *Scotson* v *Pegg* (1861); *Chichester* v *Cobb* (1866); *New Zealand Shipping Co* v *A M Satterthwaite* (1974); *Pao on* v *Lau Yiu Long* (1979)
- It may be possible to argue that performance of an existing duty of whatever type should be good consideration – Lord Denning in *Ward* v *Byham* (1956) and *Williams* v *Williams* (1950)

b
- The common law rule is that payment of a lesser sum does not discharge the obligation to pay the full amount – *Pinnel's Case* (1602); *Foakes* v *Beer* (1884)
- The defence of promissory estoppel may be invoked by Albert – *Central London Property Trust Ltd* v *High Trees House Ltd* (1947); *Hughes* v *Metropolitan Railway* (1877)
- There must be a promise by the creditor intended to affect the parties' legal relations – *Central London Property Trust Ltd* v *High Trees House Ltd* (1947); *Woodhouse* v *Nigerian Produce Marketing* (1972)
- The debtor must probably act on the promise, whether or not to his detriment is doubtful – *Ajayi* v *R T Briscoe* (1964); *W J Alan & Co Ltd* v *El Nasr Export and Import Co* (1972); *Société Italo-Belge* v *Palm Oils* (1982)
- It must be inequitable for Bernard to go back on his promise – *D & C Builders Ltd* v *Rees* (1966); *Tool Metal* v *Tungsten Electric* (1955); *F A Ajayi* v *R T Briscoe (Nigeria) Ltd* (1964)
- Was it intended to be extinctive of Bernard's rights or merely suspensive?
- The usual equitable principles apply

Suggested Answer

a Two different situations must be considered here, namely: (i) where the contractual duty in question is owed to the promisor; (ii) where such duty is owed not to the promisor but to a third party.

As to (i), although there are relatively few cases on the topic and none of very high authority, the position at present is that the performance or promise of performance of an existing contractual duty owed to the promisor is not good consideration. Thus in *Stilk* v *Myrick* (1809) sailors who were promised a share of the wages of two deserters for working the ship home failed in an action brought on that promise because they were already contractually bound to work her home; they furnished no consideration for the promise. Conversely, in *Hartley* v *Ponsonby* (1857) the level of desertions was so high that the sailors would have been justified in refusing to work further. By remaining at their posts, they therefore did more than their existing contractual duty and succeeded in an action on a promise to pay them additional remuneration. This distinction between merely doing that which one is bound to do by contract with the promisor, and doing over and above one's duty, was accepted and applied more recently by Mocatta J in *The Atlantic Baron* (1979).

As to (ii), three nineteenth-century cases, *Shadwell* v *Shadwell* (1860), *Scotson* v *Pegg* (1861) and *Chichester* v *Cobb* (1866) suggested (without definitively deciding) that the performance or promise of performance of an existing contractual duty owed to a third party could be good consideration. Two recent decisions of the Privy Council, *New Zealand Shipping Co Ltd* v *A M Satterthwaite & Co Ltd* (1975) and *Pao On* v *Lau Yiu Long* (1979) have stated clearly and unequivocally that this is indeed the law. Although neither is strictly binding in England, it is almost inconceivable that the English court would not adopt this principle. In a third party case, therefore, the performance or promise of performance of the existing duty is sufficient on its own and there is no need to look for some additional element of consideration over and above the duty itself. In *Ward* v *Byham* (1956) and *Williams* v *Williams* (1950), Denning J (as he then was) suggested a more radical approach. His Lordship suggested that the performance of an existing duty (of whatever type) should be good consideration providing there was nothing in the transaction contrary to the public interest; his Lordship was perhaps thinking of duress, improper pressure or unfair bargaining being involved. Although this view has attracted academic support, it has not yet been adopted by the courts and it is thus still necessary to distinguish (in cases involving existing contractual duties) between the two and three party cases.

b In advising Albert one must consider the principles governing discharge of a debtor when he makes part payment only and whether the doctrine of promissory estoppel may afford him a defence as to all or part of Bernard's claim.

The general rule is that a creditor who promises to accept a lesser sum in satisfaction of a larger debt can subsequently insist on the balance being paid unless the debtor has furnished consideration for that promise: *Pinnel's Case* (1602) and *Foakes* v *Beer* (1884). Prima facie, Bernard can therefore recover the balance of the past twelve months' rent and insist on the full amount thereafter.

However the doctrine of promissory estoppel can provide a good defence to a debtor in Albert's position in certain cases. This doctrine, which owes its existence to certain obiter remarks of Denning J (as he then was) in *Central London Property Trust Ltd* v *High Trees House Ltd* (1947), relying on the decision of the House of Lords in *Hughes* v *Metropolitan Railway Co* (1877), is an important exception to the general rule above stated. For this to apply, a number of conditions must be satisfied.

First, there must be a promise by the creditor (Bernard) which is intended to affect the parties' legal relations and which is not a mere concession or indulgence: *High Trees* and *Woodhouse AC Israel Cocoa Ltd* v *Nigerian Produce Marketing Co Ltd* (1972). It is submitted that this condition is satisfied.

Second, the debtor (Albert) must act on the promise. Although certain cases, eg *FA Ajayi* v *R T Briscoe (Nigeria) Ltd* (1964), suggest that the debtor must alter his position to his detriment (the classic equitable requirement for estoppel), the preponderance of authority indicates that this is not necessary here. There was no detriment present in *High Trees* and in *W J Alan & Co Ltd* v *El Nasr Export and Import Co* (1972). Lord Denning disclaimed it as an element of promissory estoppel, saying it was sufficient if the debtor acted on the promise by paying the lesser sum. Robert Goff J (as he then was) adopted the same view in *Société Italo-Belge* v *Palm and Vegetable Oils (The Post Chaser)* (1982). Thus by paying the lower rent, Albert did act on Bernard's promise.

Third, it must be inequitable for the creditor (Bernard) to go back on his promise. There are two aspects to this third condition. In the first place, the creditor's promise must not have been extracted by threats or coercion by the debtor, as happened in *D & C Builders Ltd* v *Rees* (1966). There is no evidence of that here. Next, it must be borne in mind that in certain cases the courts have allowed a debtor to resile from his promise and to insist on his full contractual rights in future: *Tool Metal Manufacturing Co Ltd* v *Tungsten Electric Co Ltd* (1955) and *Ajayi F A* v *R T Briscoe (Nigeria) Ltd* (1964).

As to the balance of the rent over the last twelve months, it is submitted (for the reasons given in *High Trees*) that it would be inequitable for Bernard to go back on his promise. There is no reason for believing that he intended to suspend payment of the balance; he intended to forego it altogether.

As to the future payments, however, Albert's case is less strong. Bernard agreed to accept half rent until Wendy was able to go back to work, both sides believing that at some stage she would be able to return. That belief was unfounded. It would be a harsh conclusion to draw that as a result of that mistaken belief, Bernard is bound to accept half rent for the remainder of the lease. A court would be likely to hold that he would insist on being paid the full rent on giving reasonable notice.

If Wendy received £100,000 compensation, this would obviously make Bernard's claim to the balance of the past rent more difficult to resist. It was a promise induced by Albert and Wendy's poor financial circumstances. If their financial position were to be improved so dramatically a court might well conclude that it would not be inequitable for Bernard to insist on both the full rent henceforth and to recover the balance of past payments.

SUGGESTED ANSWER TO QUESTION THREE

General Comment

This question involves a number of issues: the rules relating to sufficiency of consideration; duress and promissory estoppel. There are two contracts in the question, one between Giles and Illtyd and the other between Giles and Peter. A sensible approach would be to take the two contracts separately to avoid confusion in the answer.

Key Points

The contract between Giles and Illtyd
- Was there consideration for the promise to make the additional payment? – *Stilk* v *Myrick* (1809); *North Ocean Shipping Co* v *Hyundai Construction Co (The Atlantic Baron)* (1979); *Hartley* v *Ponsonby* (1857)
- Was the promise obtained by duress? – *Occidental Worldwide Investment Corp* v *Skibs A/S Avanti (The Sibeon and The Sibotre)* (1976); *North Ocean Shipping Co* v *Hyundai Construction Co (The Atlantic Baron)* (1979); *B & S Contracts and Design*

v *Victor Green Publications Ltd* (1984); *Pao On* v *Lau Yiu Long* (1979); *Atlas Express Ltd* v *Kafco (Importers and Distributors) Ltd* (1989)

The contract between Giles and Peter
- At common law Peter's promise to suspend his contractual rights is unenforceable because there has been no consideration for it – *Pinnel's Case* (1602); *Foakes* v *Beer* (1884); *Jorden* v *Money* (1854)
- The doctrine of promissory estoppel may apply – *Hughes* v *Metropolitan Railway Co* (1877); *Central London Property Trust Ltd* v *High Trees House Ltd* (1947); *Tool Metal Manufacturing Co Ltd* v *Tungsten Electric Co Ltd* (1955); *F A Ajayi* v *R T Briscoe (Nigeria) Ltd* (1964)
- For the doctrine to apply, Peter must have made an unequivocal promise, Giles must have acted upon it, and the promise must not have been extracted by duress – *Woodhouse A C Israel Cocoa Ltd* v *Nigerian Produce Marketing Co Ltd* (1972); *W J Alan & Co Ltd* v *El Nasr Export and Import Co* (1972); *Société Italo-Belge* v *Palm and Vegetable Oils (The Post Chaser)* (1982); *Goldsworthy* v *Brickell* (1987); *D & C Builders Ltd* v *Rees* (1966)
- Is Peter's promise extinctive or suspensive of his rights? – *F A Ajayi* v *R T Briscoe (Nigeria) Ltd* (1964)

Suggested Answer

This question involves discussion of a number of issues: the rules relating to sufficiency of consideration; duress; and promissory estoppel. There are two contracts in question, one between Giles and Ilityd, the other between Giles and Peter. These two contracts will be discussed in turn.

The contract between Giles and Illtyd
The contract between Giles and Illtyd is for the latter to perform the construction work for the fixed price of £3,000. Illtyd then discovers that certain additional work is necessary and Giles has agreed to pay an additional £500. Two matters arise: whether there was any consideration for the promise to make the additional payment, and whether the promise to pay was exacted by duress. The question here is whether, in continuing the work, Illtyd was performing no more than an existing contractual duty, or whether he was now performing something over and above his original contractual obligations. It may well be that Illtyd undertook, in constructing the patio and fish pond, to do whatever was necessary to complete that task, and that if the removal of the cannon was necessary, it was part of his original obligation. If Illtyd is performing no more than his existing contractual duty, there is authority for the view that this is not sufficient consideration: *Stilk* v *Myrick* (1809); *North Ocean Shipping Co* v *Hyundai Construction Co (The Atlantic Baron)* (1979). If the removal of the cannon was within Illtyd's existing contractual obligations, then no fresh consideration has been furnished for Giles' promise to pay the additional £500. That promise would, therefore, be unenforceable.

It is, however, possible that Illtyd is now performing some extra task, in which case there has been fresh consideration for the promise to pay the £500: *Hartley* v *Ponsonby*

(1857). Proceeding on that assumption, if there has been fresh consideration, the further question remains as to whether the promise to pay the additional amount was obtained by duress. Illtyd threatens to break his contract with Giles unless Giles pays the additional amount. There is now substantial authority for the proposition that a threat to break a contract constitutes economic duress: *Occidental Worldwide Investment Corp* v *Skibs A/S Avanti (The Sibeon and The Sibotre)* (1976); *North Ocean Shipping Co* (above); *B & S Contracts and Design* v *Victor Green Publications Ltd* (1984).

In *Pao On* v *Lau Yiu Long* (1979), Lord Scarman stated that four criteria would have to be considered in order to decide whether or not there had been economic duress. These criteria were: i) whether the victim had protested, ii) whether the victim had an alternative legal remedy, iii) whether the victim had had independent legal advice, and iv) whether he took steps to avoid the transaction, after the duress had ceased.

The effect of economic duress is that the victim can have the contract set aside and may be entitled to claim damages in tort. It is not clear, on the facts presented, whether or not Giles could establish that he had been induced to make the promise to pay the additional amount by virtue of economic duress, having regard to the criteria set out above. However, the courts have shown increasing readiness to recognise the concept of economic duress, and if Giles can establish, in particular, that he had no choice but to submit to Illtyd's demand, then he may well succeed in establishing economic duress. See the recent case of *Atlas Express Ltd* v *Kafco (Importers and Distributors) Ltd* (1989).

The contract between Giles and Peter
In agreeing that Giles need only pay the interest on the loan and not the instalments, Peter has promised to suspend his contractual rights. At common law Peter's promise to suspend his contractual rights is unenforceable because there has been no consideration for that promise. This common law principle laid down in *Pinnel's Case* (1602) was affirmed by the House of Lords in *Foakes* v *Beer* (1884). The common law rule has, however, been modified by the equitable doctrine of promissory estoppel. This doctrine derives from the decision of the House of Lords in *Huges* v *Metropolitan Railway Co* (1877). It was developed further by Denning J (as he then was) in obiter dicta in *Central London Property Trust Ltd* v *High Trees House Ltd* (1947). Although the doctrine of promissory estoppel has been criticised as being inconsistent with *Foakes* v *Beer* (above) and with *Jorden* v *Money* (1854), it has become established. It has been recognised by the House of Lords in *Tool Metal Manufacturing Co Ltd* v *Tungsten Electric Co Ltd* (1955) and by the Privy Council in *F A Ajayi* v *R T Briscoe (Nigeria) Ltd* (1964). The essence of the doctrine is that when one party to a contract promises, in the absence of fresh consideration, not to enforce his rights, an equity will be raised in favour of the other party, which will estop the party who made the promise from going back on it.

In order to determine whether the equity operates in Giles' favour certain aspects have to be considered.

1   In order for the doctrine to operate Peter must have made an unequivocal promise: *Woodhouse AC Israel Cocoa Ltd* v *Nigerian Produce Marketing Co Ltd* (1972). He appears to have done so.

2   The further requirement is that Giles has acted on Peter's promise. It has to be shown that there has been reliance on the promise. The balance of authority suggests that it is not necessary to show that Giles has acted to his detriment: *W J Alan & Co Ltd v El Nasr Export and Import Co* (1972); *Société Italo-Belge v Palm and Vegetable Oils (The Post Chaser)* (1982). (There is a suggestion to the contrary in the obiter dicta of Nourse J in *Goldsworthy v Brickell* (1987)). It is, however, necessary for Giles to show that as a result of Peter's promise he was led to act differently from the way he would otherwise have done. It is not clear, from the present facts, whether this is so.

3   It does not appear that Peter's promise was exacted by any form of pressure as in *D & C Builders Ltd v Rees* (1966). It could not be suggested, therefore, that it would not be inequitable to allow Peter to resile from his promise.

4   The further aspect that has to be examined is whether Peter's promise is extinctive or merely suspensive of his rights. In *F A Ajayi v R T Briscoe (Nigeria) Ltd* (above) Lord Hodson stated that the promisor can resile from his promise on giving the promisee a reasonable opportunity of resuming his position. It is only when the promisee cannot resume his former position that the promise becomes irrevocable. This suggests that when Giles finds a new job Peter can demand the resumption of the payments of the agreed instalments, on giving Giles reasonable notice to do so. There is no direct authority as to whether or not Peter would be entitled to demand immediate payment of the outstanding arrears of capital. Lord Denning has stated extra-judicially that the rights to the arrear payments in *High Trees* had been extinguished. This does not mean that Peter has abandoned any portion of the capital sum due to him, but that he has promised to extend the period of repayment. He might not be able to resile from this promise.

The difficulty for Giles is to establish that he relied on Peter's promise. If he cannot do so the doctrine of promissory estoppel cannot operate in his favour. If Giles can establish reliance, he is advised that Peter cannot resile from his promise until he (Giles) has found a new job. When Giles obtains a new job Peter can demand resumption of payment of the agreed instalments until the full capital sum has been paid off. Peter would not be able to claim immediate payment of the outstanding arrears of capital.

SUGGESTED ANSWER TO QUESTION FOUR

General Comment

The question is short but it concerns a fundamental issue: it is not always clear why the courts insist on consideration before they will enforce a contract. The decisions which the courts have made concerning consideration and the often fine distinctions make this a rather difficult topic to grasp. Considering the answer to this question may lead to an understanding of why the courts appear at some times to have applied the rule harshly and at others leniently.

Key Points

- Original reason for the doctrine – protection for the defendant

- The idea of reciprocity - *Thorp* v *Thorp* (1701); *Currie* v *Misa* (1875)
- Apparent changes in the court's attitude - *Lampleigh* v *Braithwait* (1615); *Pao On* v *Lau Yiu Long* (1980); *Stilk* v *Myrick* (1809); *Hartley* v *Ponsonby* (1857); *Williams* v *Roffey Bros & Nicholls (Contractors) Ltd* (1991)
- The adequacy of the consideration - *Brett* v *J S* (1600); *Thomas* v *Thomas* (1842); *White* v *Bluett* (1853); *Chappell & Co* v *Nestlé Co Ltd* (1960); *Lipkin Gorman* v *Karpnale Ltd* (1991)

Suggested Answer

It has long been a fundamental principle of English law that a contract is unenforceable without consideration unless it is under seal. The main reason is that the law once believed that people must be protected from the rashness with which they might make promises. The formality required of a contract under seal provided some pause for thought and showed, furthermore, that the parties had a strong intention to be legally bound. Thus, even if a promise is gratuitous, if it has been made under seal the courts will enforce it.

The requirement for consideration is based on a similar view. The requirement for consideration at least provides some protection for the defendant who will not be held to his promise unless he has been given something in return. This may be an act or a promise:

> 'Where the doing a thing will be a good consideration, a promise to do that thing will be so too': Holt CJ in *Thorpe* v *Thorpe* (1701).

An accepted definition of consideration is to be found in *Currie* v *Misa* (1875):

> 'A valuable consideration, in the sense of the law, may consist in some right, interest, profit or benefit accruing to one party or some forebearance, detriment, loss or responsibility, given, suffered or undertaken by the other.'

This definition embodies the idea of reciprocity: a promise will only be enforceable if it is given in return for a promise or act. Thus the promise is not gratuitous.

However, over the centuries which have seen the development of the doctrine of consideration, the courts have evolved fine distinctions which have given rise to much criticism. Certain acts which would not in the past have been regarded as constituting consideration have been in more recent times subject to exceptions. The first example is past acts or promises, ie made prior to the promise on which the action is brought. These were held in *Lampleigh* v *Braithwait* (1615) not to be good consideration, but in the more recent case of *Pao On* v *Lau Yiu Long* (1980), an earlier promise not to break a contract was held to be good consideration. Similarly, acts which the promisor was already legally bound to do were not good consideration: *Stilk* v *Myrick* (1809). However, an inroad was made into this principle as early as 1857 (*Hartley* v *Ponsonby*), where it was held that something over and above what the promisor was legally bound to do would provide good consideration, and it has had doubt cast upon it recently in *Williams* v *Roffey Bros & Nicholls (Contractors) Ltd* (1991) where consideration for additional payments to a builder was provided by the work he had already contracted for on the basis that his client had reason to believe the builder might not complete the work in time because of financial difficulties.

The best support for the view put forward by the question, however, comes from that line of cases where the court has consistently refused to act as valuer of consideration. It was clearly established by the mid-nineteenth century that consideration must have some economic value. Feelings of natural love and affection (*Brett* v *J S* (1600)), the natural desire to benefit someone (*Thomas* v *Thomas* (1842)), and a promise not to complain (*White* v *Bluett* (1853)) are all examples of consideration which has no economic value and therefore cannot be 'good' or 'valuable' consideration sufficient to support a contract. However, once a value has been established, the courts will not concern themselves with whether or not it was adequate in relation to what was being promised in return.

The consideration may therefore be quite trivial. In *Chappell & Co Ltd* v *Nestlé Co Ltd* (1960) chocolate wrappers were held to be consideration, even though they were only to be thrown away by the company, for a special offer to purchase records. Lord Somervill said in that case:

> 'It is said that, when received, the wrappers are of no value to the respondents, the Nestle Co Ltd. This I would have thought to be irrelevant. A contracting party can stipulate for what consideration he chooses. A peppercorn does not cease to be good consideration if it is established that the promisee does not like pepper and will thrown away the corn.'

A peppercorn has, of course, long been considered good consideration for the grant of a lease. More recently perhaps, it has become the practice for valuable shares in a business to be transferred for £1. The practical reason for this is that a deed takes more time and cost to prepare and it is easier to draw up a simple agreement, and the use of such 'nominal' consideration is now quite widespread. In such cases, gratuitous promises are in effect being enforced and the consideration is merely the formality which seals the bargain.

Certainly, recent cases have shown a trend in the courts to find valuable consideration more readily in cases where they might not previously have done so. The modern view seems to be that the technical absence of this formality will not permit a fully consenting adult to renege on his promises. The reason may be that the courts no longer feel the need to protect a defendant from the consequences of his own rashness and consider that there are sufficiently adequate means of dealing with preferment of creditors and duress without bringing consideration into the matter.

However, one should not assume that the courts will always find consideration when asked to do so. In the case of *Lipkin Gorman* v *Karpnale Ltd* (1991) the House of Lords refused to accept that gaming chips supplied to a club member could be consideration for the money paid for them. Atiyah points out that, while Lord Goff states that where a department store provides tokens in exchange for cash the store 'does not for the present purposes give valuable consideration for it', he also accepts that a contract is made when the customer obtains them at the cash desk. The question to be decided 'for present purposes' was not breach of contract, but the ownership of stolen money. Atiyah concludes that:

'The question whether a party has provided consideration may thus receive one answer when it arises for the purpose of determining the enforceability of a promise, and a different and narrower one when it arises for the purpose of determining whether a transaction has adversely affected the rights of a third party.'

The purposes for which the question is being decided ought to be irrelevant, however, and, if they are not then this would support the view that consideration is no more than a mere formality which will be found in those bargains which the courts wish to enforce.

SUGGESTED ANSWER TO QUESTION FIVE

General Comment

Perhaps because examiners recognise the difficulty of the concept of consideration, discussion questions abound in this area. This one concerns the usefulness of the doctrine of promissory estoppel. It necessitates a good grasp of the doctrine of consideration which gave rise to this equitable relief and also an understanding of the rules which have developed concerning the award of the relief since its inception in 1947.

Key Points

- The common law rule against which equitable relief is awarded – *Pinnel's Case* (1602); *Foakes v Beer* (1884); *Jorden v Money* (1854)
- The equitable doctrine – *Hughes v Metropolitan Railway Co* (1877); *Birmingham and District Land Co v London & NW Railway* (1888); *Central London Property Trust Ltd v High Trees House Ltd* (1947); *D & C Builders Ltd v Rees* (1964)
- Limitation of the doctrine – *Combe v Combe* (1951); *Walton Stores (Interstate) Ltd v Maher* (1988); *F A Ajayi v R T Briscoe (Nigeria) Ltd* (1964); *W J Alan & Co Ltd v El Nasr Export and Import Co* (1972); *Société Italo-Belge v Palm and Vegetable Oils (The Post Chaser)* (1982); *Goldsworthy v Brickell* (1987)
- Is the doctrine suspensive or extinctive? – *P v P* (1957); *Central London Property Trust Ltd v High Trees House Ltd* (1947); *D & C Builders Ltd v Rees* (1964); *F A Ajayi v R T Briscoe (Nigeria) Ltd* (1964); *W J Alan & Co Ltd v El Nasr Export and Import Co* (1972); *Tool Metal Manufacturing Co Ltd v Tungsten Electric Co Ltd* (1955)
- Is the doctrine necessary? – *Brikom Investments Ltd v Carr* (1979)

Suggested Answer

The common law rule is that payment of a lesser sum is no discharge of a greater sum: *Pinnel's Case* (1602); *Foakes v Beer* (1884). The reason behind this rule is that a promise to accept the lesser sum is unenforceable unless it is supported by fresh consideration. But, it was the view of Lord Denning MR in *D & C Builders Ltd v Rees* (1964) that:

'The harshness of the common law has been relieved. Equity has stretched out a merciful hand to help the debtor.'

Lord Denning was referring to the mitigation of the common law rule by the equitable doctrine of promissory estoppel. The doctrine derives from the statement of the equitable principle by Lord Cairns LC in the House of Lords in *Hughes* v *Metropolitan Railway Co* (1877) that where the parties have entered into a course of negotiations, which has the effect of leading one of the parties to believe that the strict rights arising under the contract will not be enforced, or will be suspended, the person who might otherwise have enforced those rights will not be allowed to enforce them where it would be inequitable to allow him to do so. Lord Cairns did not cite any authority in support of this principle. *Hughes* v *Metropolitan Railway* was decided in the context of a landlord and tenant relationship in connection with the forfeiture of a lease. The principle there enunciated was extended beyond this context in *Birmingham and District Land Co* v *London & NW Railway* (1888). In both these cases the effect of this principle of equitable estoppel was held to be merely suspensive of rights, and no mention was made of promissory estoppel. The decision in *Jorden* v *Money* (1854), below, was not quoted.

The principle was developed by Denning J (as he then was) in *Central London Property Trust Ltd* v *High Trees House Ltd* (1947) into the modern doctrine of promissory estoppel. The effect of this development was to establish the principle that if a creditor promised to accept a lesser sum in satisfaction of a larger sum, this promise would suspend, or even extinguish, the creditor's rights to claim the balance. This principle appeared to be in conflict with *Foakes* v *Beer* (above) and with the earlier House of Lords decision in *Jorden* v *Money*. In the latter case Mrs Jorden had promised not to enforce a claim against Money. This promise was not supported by consideration, but it was argued that, having made this representation, she could not, in equity, resile from it. Lord Cranworth LC held that the equitable principle applied to representations of existing fact, and not to representations of future conduct. Denning J in *High Trees* overcame these authorities by finding that the House of Lords in *Foakes* v *Beer* had not considered the equitable principle and that Mrs Jorden had not clearly promised not to enforce the claim.

Despite this perhaps 'dubious pedigree' the doctrine of promissory estoppel has received a measure of recognition by the courts, though with limited effect and with remaining areas of uncertainty.

The effect of the doctrine was limited in *Combe* v *Combe* (1951) where the Court of Appeal, which included Denning LJ, held that the principle of promissory estoppel did not create new causes of action where none existed before: it only served to prevent a party from enforcing his legal rights where it would be inequitable to allow him to do so. What is implicit in this decision is that for the doctrine to operate there must be a pre-existing legal relationship between the parties: this view has been challenged by the High Court of Australia in *Walton Stores (Interstate) Ltd* v *Maher* (1988).

At the risk of repetition it is useful at this point to formulate the principle in precise terms. In the words of Lord Hodson in *F A Ajayi* v *R T Briscoe (Nigeria) Ltd* (1964):

'The principle, which has been described as quasi estoppel and perhaps more aptly as promissory estoppel, is that when one party to a contract in the absence of fresh consideration agrees not to enforce his rights, an equity will be raised in favour of the

2 Consideration and Intention to Create Legal Relations – Answers

other party. This equity is, however, subject to the qualification (a) that the other party has altered his position, (b) that the promisor can resile from his promise on giving reasonable notice, which need not be formal notice, giving the promisee a reasonable opportunity of resuming his position, and (c) the promise only becomes final and irrevocable if the promisee cannot resume his position.'

The first qualification is that 'the other party has altered his position'. It is not beyond doubt what this entails. There are obiter statements to the effect that all that is required is that the promisee acts on the promise in the sense that he does something he would not otherwise have done; it is not necessary for him to have acted to his detriment: Lord Denning in *W J Alan & Co Ltd* v *El Nasr Export and Import Co* (1972); Robert Goff J in *Société Italo-Belge* v *Palm and Vegetable Oils etc (The Post Chaser)* (1982). In *Goldsworthy* v *Brickell* (1987), however, Nourse J expressed the view, also obiter, that for promissory estoppel to operate the promisee must be shown to have acted to his detriment.

This, then, is one area of uncertainty. Another relates to the effect of promissory estoppel having in mind the further qualifications in Lord Hodson's formulation: Does the promise merely suspend the promisor's rights or can it extinguish them? It seems clear from *Hughes* v *Metropolitan Railway* that the effect of the estoppel there being considered was merely to suspend the landlord's rights. There is no decisive authority in our law that the effect can be extinctive. It was held to be so by a New Zealand court in *P* v *P* (1957). Lord Denning held that the landlord's rights to the arrear rentals had been permanently extinguished in *High Trees*, but this finding was not necessary for the actual decision in that case. Lord Denning has also expressed the view that the estoppel could be final and permanent in *D & C Builders Ltd* v *Rees* and *Alan* v *El Nasr*, but these findings were again obiter.

Whilst the doctrine of promissory estoppel has been recognised in a number of cases there is no clear case in which it has been unequivocally applied. In the Court of Appeal in *Tool Metal Manufacturing Co Ltd* v *Tungsten Electric Co Ltd* (1955) it was applied only to the extent of holding that the promisor could resile from the particular promise on giving reasonable notice. The decision in the House of Lords subsequently was confined to the question of whether the delivery of a counterclaim constituted reasonable notice. Their Lordships did not consider the correctness of the Court of Appeal's decision.

In the other cases previously mentioned in this answer the doctrine has been held either not to apply or, where Lord Denning has applied it, the other members of the Court of Appeal have based their decision on different grounds. The view that the concept of promissory estoppel 'is in practice almost totally unnecessary' is further supported by a consideration of the judgments in the Court of Appeal in *Brikom Investments Ltd* v *Carr* (1979). The landlords in that case had made oral representations to the tenants that they would repair the roofs at their own expense. The leases which were subsequently signed provided that the tenants would contribute to these costs. All three members of the Court of Appeal held that the landlords' representations amounted to a collateral contract. But the main ground on which Lord Denning based his judgment was that the tenants could rely on promissory estoppel. Roskill LJ, with whom Cumming-

Bruce LJ agreed, refused to decide the case on promissory estoppel. He held that in addition to the collateral contract the tenants were protected by 'a plain waiver by the landlords of their right to claim the cost of these repairs from these tenants'.

It can be argued therefore that, not only is the concept of promissory estoppel questionable as to its origin, but that it is uncertain in its operation and the desired result can be attained by the application of other, less controversial, legal concepts.

3

Form and Contents of Contracts

Introduction

This chapter covers the diverse areas connected with the terms of a contract, other than excluding and limiting clauses, which are dealt with in Chapter 5.

A question on terms may appear in a number of different forms. First, there is the question of formalities required for a contract. When must the terms – or at least a memorandum of them – be in writing? What contracts must be made by deed? Such a question merely requires a candidate to summarise factual knowledge, but in such a way as to show a clear understanding.

Second, when the terms of a contract have been written down, to what extent will the courts allow in other evidence to add to, vary or contradict those terms? Again factual knowledge is required, together with examples which must, of course, be supported by case law.

The third area, which lends itself most readily to problem questions, but may also form the topic of a discussion question, is categorisation of terms. This naturally leads to a discussion of breach and remedies (see further, Chapter 12, where combined questions of this nature may also be found). Implied terms have sufficient scope to appear as a lone topic but may also be combined with a question which primarily concerns exemption clauses (see Chapter 5). Candidates should be aware of terms implied by statute and the circumstances under which a court would be likely to imply a term. Additionally, it is necessary to be able to categorise terms into conditions, warranties and intermediate terms in such a way as to reflect an understanding of the consequences of a breach of each.

Questions

INTERROGRAMS

1   'Form is not a necessary requirement under English Law.' Explain, giving examples.
2   How do the courts apply the rule that an agreement must be certain?
3   How has the Law of Property (Miscellaneous Provisions) Act 1989 affected the law relating to contracts for the sale of land?

QUESTION ONE

J made a contract with K, a builder, for K to build an extension to J's house for a price of £8,000 to be paid on completion. The contract stated: 'It is a condition of this contract that all work will be performed with proper skill and care and that the house will remain habitable throughout the period of the work.'

The work was estimated to take six weeks to complete. Two weeks after work started J learned that other local builders would have done the same job for £6,000. A week after that L, a labourer employed by K, carelessly fractured a water pipe; the house was flooded and J and his family were forced to leave it for three days. J thereupon informed K that he regarded the contract as cancelled, but K wishes to complete the job. Advise K.

London University LLB Examination
(for external students) Elements of the Law of Contract June 1986 Q3

QUESTION TWO

Jeremy Fisher read a newspaper advertisement which said: 'Enjoy the perfect holiday, messing about in boats! Only £50 per week. Food provided. Water Rat Boating Holidays.' He went to the boatyard and spoke to the owner of Water Rat Boating, Ronald Rat. Ronald told him they had one small river launch available and Jeremy would have to pay a deposit of £200 as well as £100 for a two-week hire. Jeremy handed over £300 in return for the keys to the boat and was asked to sign a 'receipt' on which the following was printed:

> 'The hirer agrees to look after the boat and bring it back in good condition. This is all the terms of the contract of hire.'

Before signing the receipt, Jeremy asked Ronald to confirm that the boat was safe and that food was provided on board. Ronald replied that the boat was 'safe as you would expect and has lifesaving equipment in case of accident' and that the on-board refrigerator contained 'all the food a normal boater would need.' He added that Jeremy could take a look before parting with his money but Jeremy said he would take Ronald's word and signed the receipt.

Jeremy drove the boat out of the boatyard and proceeded along the river. Some hours later, he discovered that the on-board refrigerator contained only a pound of cheese, a stale loaf of bread and a pint of milk. He had to stop off at a waterside restaurant to buy an evening meal. On the second day, Jeremy managed to run the boat aground. He got it back into the water but due to its being excessively rusty, a hole was rubbed in the bottom. The boat began to sink. Jeremy, having discovered that the life-saving equipment consisted of a single life-jacket put it on and jumped overboard. The jacket, however, quickly deflated and Jeremy was unable to swim. He almost drowned and, after being pulled out of the water by a passer-by spent several days in hospital.

He wants to sue Water Rat Boating for the return of the £300, together with compensation for distress caused by near-drowning. Ronald Rat claims that he is entitled to keep the £300 as Jeremy had hired the boat for two weeks and had damaged it. He also says he was entitled to assume that Jeremy could swim.

Discuss the issues raised by this problem.

Written by the Editor June 1998

QUESTION THREE

'The nineteenth-century distinction between "conditions" and "warranties" has given way to a more flexible test.' (Anson's Law of Contract).

Consider in the light of the existing case law.

London University LLB Examination
(for external students) Elements of the Law of Contract June 1987 Q3

QUESTION FOUR

Xavier manufactures photocopying machines designed for customers with special requirements. It is his practice not to sell the machines but to lease them to the customers. His standard leasing contract contains the following provisions:

> '1 Punctual payment of the agreed monthly rent is deemed to be of the essence of the contract.
> 2 It is a condition of the contract that the lessee will disconnect the power supply to the machine at the close of business each day.
> 3 The lessee will notify Xavier immediately of any fault in the machine and will not permit repairs to be carried out by any other person other than Xavier's authorised representative.'

In March 1989 Linus leased a photocopier from Xavier for three years on the above terms at a monthly rental of £200. Xavier recently discovered that Linus sometimes allows the power supply to remain connected overnight and has repaired minor faults himself on a few occasions. Linus was also two days late in paying last month's rent.

Advise Xavier, who could now charge £300 a month rent if the same photocopier were leased to a new customer.

London University LLB Examination
(for external students) Elements of the Law of Contract June 1990 Q2

QUESTION FIVE

'When a contract is reduced to writing, the courts assume that this includes all the terms the parties intended to agree.' Discuss.

Written by the Editor June 1998

QUESTION SIX

Peter runs his own accounting business. He recently entered into a contract with Efficient Business Equipment for the hire of a computer. His brother, Geoff, had offered to loan him a printer so Peter stipulated for a clause to be written into the contract of hire as follows:

> 'It is a condition of this contract that the computer will be compatible with a SmartPrint 11X printer and be able to run the SuperAccounts software package.'

Otherwise the contract is Efficient Business Equipment's standard terms and conditions of hire which provide that the hire is for a fixed period of three years at a rental of £50 per month.

Peter took delivery of the computer two months ago. It proved to be incompatible with Geoff's printer and Peter had to buy a new printer at a cost of £500. It has also now run into difficulties with the SuperAccounts package, which it ran quite well at first, but now that Peter has transferred all his records to it, frequently produces errors of a very serious nature. Peter has been told that he was badly advised. He could have bought a better quality computer which would have run his software and been compatible with the printer for only £1,000. On informing Efficient Business Equipment of this, he has been told that they only deal on their standard conditions which do not include the additional condition and that they will only release him from the contract on payment of the entire balance of the hire fee, ie £1,700.

Written by the Editor June 1998

QUESTION SEVEN

At the end of November, Anthony decided he needed a holiday as he had not taken any holiday that year. There is a custom in Anthony's trade that an employee is entitled to four weeks' holiday a year, although his contract of employment is silent on the subject of holidays, and so Anthony told his manager he would be away for the last four weeks in December. His manager was displeased by this as he said Anthony had too much work to do, and said he was forbidding Anthony to go.

Nevertheless, Anthony went to Buckett's Travel Agents and told them he wanted to go somewhere hot and sunny for four weeks. They booked him onto a package holiday in Tenerife, having shown him a picture in their brochure of the hotel at which they said he would be staying, which showed a fully-built hotel with a swimming pool. Anthony was pleased because his favourite hobby was swimming. Anthony then went to his local department store and bought a suitcase, having told the salesman he was flying to Tenerife.

Anthony's holiday turned out a disaster. The hotel at which he had expected to stay was fully booked and he was located in a hotel which had not been fully built. There was no swimming pool and Anthony was awoken at 6 o'clock every morning by the sound of bulldozers and other heavy machinery. His hotel room looked out over the building site. The weather was cold and it poured with rain every day. Anthony came home after a week. On the flight home, Anthony's suitcase proved not to be up to the baggage handling and split, losing most of the clothing and personal effects it contained. When he returned to work at the beginning of January, his employers claimed he had broken his duty of good faith to them and they intended to withhold his salary and sue him for extra fees they had to pay to an agency to provide a substitute for him.

Advise Anthony.

Written by the Editor June 1998

Answers

ANSWERS TO INTERROGRAMS

1   English law does not generally require contracts to be in a particular form or for any particular formalities to be observed in their execution. This is in contrast to other jurisdictions, where writing or notarisation may be a requirement. A contract may be made in writing, orally or by conduct or by any combination of these. Even though writing or a deed may be required Equity regards 'that as done which ought to be done' and will perfect the transaction where a contract has been made.

There are, however, a number of exceptions to the general rule. This is where there is a need for certainty, or to create a written record or to avoid recklessness on the part of one or other of the parties. The exceptions may conveniently be divided into three categories: contracts required to be made by deed, contracts required to be in writing and contracts required to be evidenced in writing.

Contracts required to be made by deed
The execution of a deed – a contract under seal – is very rarely required, although any contract may be made under seal if the parties wish. The courts will not enforce gratuitous transactions and so any contract for which there is no consideration (ie something of value – an act, forbearance or promise – given in return for the promise on which the action is brought) will be unenforcable unless under seal. The formality prevents parties from entering into transactions rashly and evidences an intention to be legally bound.

There is one category of contract which the law specifically requires to be made by deed and that is a lease for a term of more than three years.

Contracts required to be in writing
While many people believe that a contract may not be made orally, this is not the case. Contracts may be oral or in writing or partly oral and partly in writing. Even where a contract is in writing, the court may agree to admit oral evidence to add to, vary or contradict its terms. Contracts of employment are often thought to be required to be in writing, but the law merely provides that the employer should, within a certain period, give the employee written notification of its terms.

The contracts for which the law requires writing are surprisingly few. Bills of exchange and promissory notes under the Bills of Exchange Act 1882 and bills of sale under the Bills of Sale Act (1878) Amendment Act (1882) have long been required to be in writing. In 1974 these were joined by consumer credit agreements subject to the Consumer Credit Act 1974. These agreements are required to be in writing for the consumer's protection, and the Act also contains detailed rules about the provision of copies, method of execution and a 'cooling off' period to permit the debtor to reconsider what might be a rash decision.

In 1989, the Law of Property (Miscellaneous Provisions) Act reformed the law relating to the sale of land and interests in land. It redefined the requirements for the execution of a deed – which was no longer required to be under seal. It also provided that a contract for the sale of land or any interest in land must incorporate express terms expressly or by reference.

Contracts required to be evidenced in writing

While there is no other requirement for contracts to be in writing, there may be a requirement for a memorandum. A memorandum is not intended to contain all the terms of a contract, merely to provide evidence that a contract was made and of its main terms.

The Statute of Frauds 1677 was originally conceived as a protective measure but it was discovered that the less scrupulous would hide behind the lack of written evidence to avoid their contractual obligations. Now the Statute applies only to guarantees (note, it does not apply to indemnities). A guarantee is where a third party promises to pay a debt owed by the debtor should that debtor fail to perform his obligation. There are some provisos to the requirement for writing: the guarantee must be a stand-alone contract and not part of a larger transaction and it must not be for the protection of some proprietory interest of the guarantor.

The contents of a memorandum required by the Statute are the identity and capacity of the parties, all material terms (except consideration) and the signature of the party to be charged (ie the guarantor).

In conclusion, therefore, while formality is not an absolute requirement, there are certain circumstances where formality must be observed.

2   The general rule is that the court will not enforce a contract which is vague or ambiguous: *Scammel & Nephew* v *Ouston* (1941). However, judges are always loath to defeat the parties' contractual intentions and will try to find a meaning wherever possible. In *Hillas & Co* v *Arcos* (1932) the court resorted to the general meaning in the trade to affix the definition of timber 'of fair specification'. In the recent case of *Lambert* v *HTV Cymru (Wales) Ltd* (1998), the defendant undertook to use all reasonable endeavours to obtain first rights of negotiation of book publishing for the plaintiff, who held the copyright in certain cartoon characters. They failed to do so and were held liable for breach.

Another possibility, illustrated by the case of *Nicolene* v *Simmonds* (1953), is to delete a meaningless phrase if this would give efficacy to the contract.

Often the court will glean the meaning of the phrase from other documents (*Punjab National Bank* v *De Boinville* (1992)), or the surrounding circumstances, or will enforce the agreement which it thinks to be reasonable in the circumstances (*Neilson* v *Stewart* (1991)).

It may be that the words are not ambiguous but that there is an essential term which has not been agreed. The courts will not enforce such a contract unless there is some provision for a solution: *British Bank for Foreign Trade* v *Novinex* (1949); *May and Butcher* v *R* (1934). However, if there is a provision for solution, eg a means of fixing an omitted price, the court will enforce the contract: *Campbell* v *Edwards* (1976).

3   Prior to the passing of the Act, contracts for the sale or disposition of land or an interest in land had to be evidenced in writing: s40 Law of Property Act 1925.

Generally speaking, however, such sales or dispositions were made by deed (a contract executed under seal) and the parties and their agents would avoid any contract inadvertently being made during negotiations by including in their letters and other documents the words 'subject to contract'. Generally this was thought to be sufficient to avoid the operation of s40: *Tiverton Estates Ltd* v *Wearwell Ltd* (1975); *Cohen* v *Nessdale* (1982); *Alpenstow Ltd* v *Regalian Properties Ltd* (1985). However, there were decisions which cast doubt upon this principle at least where there appeared to be a contrary intention: *Law* v *Jones* (1974); *Griffiths* v *Young* (1970).

Section 2 of the Law of Property (Miscellaneous Provisions) Act 1989 provides that a contract for the sale or disposition of land or an interest in land must be in writing, signed by each party and must contain all the agreed terms, otherwise it is unenforceable. Section 2 is to be construed restrictively: *Firstpost Homes Ltd* v *Johnson* (1995). Section 1 of the same Act abolishes the requirement for a deed to be sealed by individuals and, instead, it is required to be signed and attested by a witness. It must also be clear on the face of the document that it is intended to be a deed.

Contracts which were made before 27 September 1989 are still subject to the provisions of s40.

SUGGESTED ANSWER TO QUESTION ONE

General Comment

The central theme of this problem question is types of contractual term. The candidate is required to analyse the elements of the transaction to determine the relative importance of the terms which, of course, determines in turn the effect of the breach and the remedies available to the injured party. The candidate must demonstrate an in-depth knowledge of the leading cases and judicial dicta concerning the effect of categorisation.

Key Points

- Types of term – warranty, condition and innominate or intermediate – *Hong Kong Fir Shipping* v *Kawasaki Kisen Kaisha Ltd* (1962); *Cehave* v *Bremer* (1976); *Reardon Smith Line* v *Hansen-Tangen* (1976)
- Importance of the intention of the parties – *Bentsen* v *Taylor Sons & Co* (1893); *The Mihalis Angelos* (1971); *Bunge Corporation* v *Tradax* (1981)
- Use of the word 'condition' is not conclusive – *Schuler* v *Wickman Machine Tool Sales Ltd* (1974)
- Whether a breach justifies rescission must be judged in the context of the agreement as a whole – *Glolite* v *Jasper Conran* (1998)
- Whether or not a term is a condition is to be determined at the time of contracting – Lord Wilberforce in *Bunge Corporation* v *Tradax Export SA* (1981)
- Term as to care and skill may also be implied – *Samuels* v *Davis* (1943); *Greaves & Co (Contractors) Ltd* v *Baynham Meikle and Partners* (1975); s13 Supply of Goods and Services Act 1982

Suggested Answer

It is clear in this problem that the action of K's employee constitutes a breach by K of an express term of his contract with J. The question for determination is the importance of that term, that is whether the breach entitles J to treat the contract as repudiated, or whether it merely entitles J to a claim for damages.

It is therefore necessary to analyse the relative importance of contractual terms. Traditionally, terms were classified as conditions and warranties, a condition being a term of such importance that any breach of it, no matter how trivial, entitled the innocent party to accept the breach and treat the contract as terminated; a warranty being a term collateral to the main purposes of the contract, the breach of which entitles the innocent party to a claim for damages but not to treat the contract as repudiated. Comparatively recently a third category of terms has been recognised by the courts – innominate or intermediate term. In *Hong Kong Fir Shipping* v *Kawasaki Kisen Kaisha Ltd* (1962) the Court of Appeal, particularly in the judgment of Diplock J, characterised certain contractual undertakings as being of a complex nature, which did not fit into the conventional categories of conditions and warranties. All that could be predicted of such contractual undertakings was that some breaches would and others would not deprive the innocent party of the substantial benefit of the contract. In these circumstances, in the absence of express provision in the contract, the legal consequences of the breach had to be examined in the light of the event to which the breach gave rise. The notion of the innominate term was accepted by a later Court of Appeal in *Cehave* v *Bremer* (1976) and by the House of Lords in *Reardon Smith Line* v *Hansen-Tangen* (1976).

What is paramount is the intention of the parties. If the parties clearly intend to classify the term as a condition the Court will give effect to that intention. What has to be examined is the contract in the light of the surrounding circumstances (*Bentsen* v *Taylor Sons & Co* (1893)), and the intention is to be ascertained at the time the parties entered into the agreement: *The Mihalis Angelos* (1971). In the recent case of *Glolite* v *Jasper Conran* (1998), clauses in an exclusive licensing agreement between the defendant and plaintiff stated that matters relating to marketing should be the subject of prior mutual agreement and that the defendant's trade mark would only be used by the plaintiffs in accordance with the agreement. The court held that, while allowing a local football club to use the defendant's logo on their shirts was a clear breach, whether or not it justified rescission had to be judged in the context of the agreement as a whole. In this case the defendants' determination of the licence was invalid.

Reverting to the present problem, we are told that the contract describes the relevant term as a 'condition'. The use of this word is, however, not necessarily conclusive. The court will have to be satisfied that the parties intended to use the word 'condition' in the technical sense; if not the court may disregard the label and examine the substance of the clause in order to determine its true nature. In *Schuler AG* v *Wickman Machine Tool Sales Ltd* (1974) one clause of the agreement was described as a 'condition' and was the only clause bearing this description. By a 4 to 1 majority the House of Lords held that in the context of the agreement as a whole the clause could not be construed as a condition. The contract as a whole between J and K is not before us so it cannot be stated categorically that the parties intended to use the word 'condition' in its technical sense. It is arguable that they did not, as the clause in question is capable of breach in a minor or trivial manner which the parties could not have envisaged as entitling J to treat the contract as repudiated.

In *Bunge Corporation* v *Tradax Export SA* (1981) Lord Wilberforce made it clear that the time for determining whether a particular term was to be treated as a condition was at the time of contracting. His Lordship also recognised that the courts should not be too ready to interpret contractual clauses as conditions, but should not be reluctant to do so if the intentions of the parties, as shown by the contract, so indicated.

It is submitted that there are two provisions contained in the clause under discussion. The first is the obligation on K to perform the work with proper skill and care, and the second is the obligation to ensure that the house remains habitable throughout the period of the works. It may be difficult to attribute the force of a condition to the first obligation in view of the possibility of breaches of this obligation being of a trivial nature. It should be observed that even if the obligation to perform with proper skill and care were not expressly provided for in the contract, such a term would be implied. This implied term in contracts for the supply of services was recognised by the common law, see for example *Samuels* v *Davis* (1943), *Greaves & Co (Contractors) Ltd* v *Baynham Meikle and Partners* (1975). This common law implied term has been enshrined in s13 Supply of Goods and Services Act 1982. It is to be noted that this statute does not specify whether this implied term is a condition or a warranty.

Whilst, for the reasons given, the court may be reluctant to construe the first obligation as a condition, it can be argued with some confidence that the requirement to maintain the house in a habitable state throughout the works was intended to be a condition, and that this intention was made manifest at the time the contract was concluded. Therefore, J's later discovery that the work could have been done cheaper, whilst possibly a motivating factor in his seeking to rely on the clause, is, it is submitted, not relevant to the question of intention.

K should therefore be advised that J is entitled to accept his (K's) breach as a repudiation of the contract which J is accordingly entitled to terminate.

SUGGESTED ANSWER TO QUESTION TWO

General Comment

The problem here seeks to examine the candidate's knowledge and understanding of the various ways in which terms may be implied into a contract. First, it is necessary to determine whether the existence of a written contract which purports to contain all the terms precludes the implication of other terms. Then one must spot the potential terms which could be implied into the contract, and assess the likelihood of their being implied and the interpretation to be given them. The good candidate will also spot the possibility of an action for misrepresentation. Finally, the probable effect in terms of liability and the recovery of compensation must be ascertained according to the importance to be given to the terms in question.

Key Points

- The well-established parol evidence rule which states that once a contract has been reduced to writing no extrinsic evidence may be admitted to prove its terms
- The receipt is a memorandum rather than a true record so the parol evidence rule may be discounted - *Hutton v Watling* (1948)
- Possible implied term as to reasonable safety for usual purposes - *Dixon v Sadler* (1839); *Reed v Dean* (1949); *The Moorcock* (1889)
- The court will only imply a term to give business efficacy to the contract - *The Moorcock* (1889); *Reigate v Union Manufacturing Co (Ramsbottom)* (1918)
- The officious bystander test - *Shirlaw v Southern Foundries (1926) Ltd* (1939)
- A term as to fitness for purpose may be implied by the Sale of Goods Act 1979 (as amended)
- Possible action for misrepresentation (an untrue statement of fact by one party to a contract which induced the other to enter into it) - *Curtis v Chemical Cleaning and Dyeing Co* (1951)
- Distinction between warranties, conditions and innominate or intermediate terms - *Hong Kong Fir Shipping Co Ltd v Kawasaki Kisen Kaisha Ltd* (1930)
- Assessment of damages - *Robinson v Harman* (1848); *Victoria Laundry (Windsor) Ltd v Newman Industries Ltd* (1949)
- Compensation for injured feelings - *Chelini v Nieri* (1948); *Jarvis v Swans Tours* (1973); *Jackson v Horizon Holidays* (1975)

Suggested Answer

The parol evidence rule states that where the parties to a contract have reduced their contract to writing, no extrinsic evidence will be admitted to prove its terms. Doubtless Water Rat Boating would argue that the document signed by Jeremy contained, as it says, all the terms of the agreement and no further evidence of terms could be admitted. There are, however, a number of exceptions to the parol evidence rule. The first is where the written terms are not the whole agreement. A distinction must be drawn between a memorandum and a true record of the contract: *Hutton v Watling* (1948). There are indications that the writing in this case was not intended, despite the wording, to be a true record. Firstly, it is termed a 'receipt'. Secondly, it makes no mention of the price of hire or of the deposit paid. As these are clearly important elements of the contract, the receipt cannot truly be said to contain all the material terms of the contract. Water Rat could argue that the receipt had to be taken with the newspaper advertisement which states the price, but again there is no mention of the deposit. Extrinsic evidence of the oral statements would therefore be likely to be allowed.

Nevertheless, this does not greatly assist Jeremy. There was life saving equipment on board and food in the refrigerator even though these were inadequate to his needs. Moreover, the statement that the boat was 'as safe as you would expect' is a vague term and might be difficult to enforce.

However, the courts might be prepared to imply a term into the contract to the effect that the boat would be reasonably safe for usual purposes. It was established long ago in marine insurance cases that there was an implied term that a vessel would be seaworthy:

> '... it is clearly established that there is an implied warranty that the vessel shall be seaworthy, by which it is meant that she shall be in a fit state as to repairs, equipment and crew, and in all other respects, to encounter the ordinary perils of the voyage insured at the time of sailing upon it': Baron Parke, *Dixon* v *Sadler* (1839).

This principle might be translated to the present situation. Indeed in *Reed* v *Dean* (1949) the plaintiff hired the defendant's motor launch for a holiday. The launch caught fire, the firefighting equipment was out of order and the plaintiff suffered personal injuries and lost all his belongings. The defendant was liable for failing to make the launch as fit for the purpose of hiring as reasonable care could make it. This is surely analogous to the present situation, as is another case, *The Moorcock,* decided in 1889. Here the plaintiff was a shipowner who had been allowed by the defendant to discharge his cargo at a jetty owned by the defendant. At low water the vessel grounded and settled on a ridge of hard ground which damaged it. The plaintiff was allowed to sue for the damage on the ground that there was an implied undertaking that the river bottom was, so far as reasonable care could provide, in such a condition as not to endanger the vessel.

The situation in which the court is prepared to imply terms into a contract was explained by Scrutton LJ in *Reigate* v *Union Manufacturing Co (Ramsbottom)* (1918):

> 'A term can only be implied if it is necessary in the business sense to give efficacy to the contract, ie if it is such a term that it can confidently be said that if at the time the contract was being negotiated someone had said to the parties: "What will happen in such a case?" they would both have replied: "Of course so and so will happen; we did not trouble to say that; it is too clear."'

This is sometimes referred to as the 'officious bystander' test from the words of McKinnon LJ in *Shirlaw* v *Southern Foundries (1926) Ltd* (1939):

> '... if while the parties were making their bargain an officious bystander were to suggest some express provision for it in their agreement, they would testily suppress him with a common, "Oh, of course."'

Jeremy might not need to rely on a term being implied by the courts. Section 14 of the Sale of Goods Act 1979, as amended by s1 of the Sale and Supply of Goods Act 1994, implies a term that goods supplied should be fit for the purpose for which they were supplied.

Arguably, however, the purpose for which the launch was supplied did not include being run aground by the hirer, although perhaps this should have been anticipated, since hirers are very often inadequately experienced boaters. It might be a question of degree as to how badly damaged the boat already was.

The question of the food and life jacket are more difficult. On balance, it is likely that a term would be implied that the lifejacket would be fit for its purpose but that no particular terms would be implied as to the adequacy of the food on board.

A further possibility is an action for misrepresentation. A misrepresentation is an untrue statement of fact by one party to another which induced the other to enter the contract. The statements made by Ronald to Jeremy were not strictly untrue. However they could be deemed half-truths which were, and perhaps were intended to be, misleading. Such statements are also misrepresentations: *Curtis* v *Chemical Cleaning and Dyeing Co* (1951). As to whether the misrepresentations induced the contract, this may depend on how likely Jeremy would have been to part with his money had he known the truth. Arguably he would not have entered the contract had he known of the boat's true condition. He was offered the opportunity of inspecting the facilities but was prepared to rely on Ronald's statements. How far these can be said to have induced the contract is debatable, but the misrepresentation does not have to be the only thing which induced the contract.

It is submitted therefore that Jeremy has actions for both breach of contract and misrepresentation. It is therefore necessary to consider the remedies available.

The remedy for a breach of contract is damages if the term breached was a warranty; rescission if the term breached was a condition. An implied term as to the safety of the boat is more likely to be a condition, given its fundamental nature. Any term implied as to the lifesaving equipment is probably a warranty. However, these terms could equally be held to be 'innominate' or 'intermediate' terms. These are terms which cannot be labelled until the consequences of breach are known: *Hong Kong Fir Shipping Co Ltd* v *Kawasaki Kisen Kaisha Ltd* (1930). It is submitted that Jeremy is entitled to rescind the contract as a consequence of the seriousness of the breach and to a full refund of his money.

Damages are a common law remedy designed to compensate the plaintiff for the loss of his bargain – ie what he would have obtained had the contract been performed: *Robinson* v *Harman* (1848). The plaintiff is entitled to damages for such things as:

> 'may fairly and reasonably be considered either arising naturally, ie according to the usual course of things, from such breach of contract itself, or such as may reasonably be supposed to have been in the contemplation of both parties at the time they made the contract as a probable result of the breach': Alderson B, in *Hadley* v *Baxendale* (1854),

or, as reformulated in *Victoria Laundry (Windsor) Ltd* v *Newman Industries Ltd* (1949):

> 'reasonably foreseeable as liable to result from the breach': (Asquith LJ).

It is submitted that Ronald Rat had no justification for assuming that Jeremy could swim and that the injury Jeremy suffered was reasonably foreseeable as a result of the existing damage to the boat and the inadequacy of the life jacket.

Despite the fact that the principal damage is to Jeremy's feelings, he may be able to recover compensation for this. Damages have been awarded for distress consequent upon physical injury in eg *Chelini* v *Nieri* (1948) and damages have also been awarded for injured feelings where at least one object of the contract was to provide enjoyment, security, comfort or sentimental benefits. In particular damages have been awarded for a spoiled holiday in *Jarvis* v *Swans Tours* (1973), *Jackson* v *Horizon Holidays* (1975) and a number of other cases.

It is therefore likely that Jeremy could sue for the return of the monies paid and for compensation for additional distress caused to him.

SUGGESTED ANSWER TO QUESTION THREE

General Comment

An essay question on types of term, while appearing deceptively simple, should not be tackled unless the candidate has full command of the case law. The successful candidate should not only be familiar with the three categories of term and be able to explain the effect of each but should also demonstrate an understanding of why it is necessary for the courts to classify terms in this way. A complete answer will explain why earlier in this century the courts chose to depart from the rigidity of a dual ab initio classification and consider whether it was in fact as rigid as is often supposed.

Key Points

- The nineteenth-century classification into conditions and warranties
- The consequences of the classification – breach of a condition entitles the innocent party to repudiate the contract – *Hong Kong Fir Shipping* v *Kawaskai Kisen Kaisha Ltd* (1962); *Bunge* v *Tradax* (1981); *Lombard North Central* v *Butterworth* (1987)
- The consequences of classification – breach of a warranty only entitles the injured party to recover damages – *Bettini* v *Gye* (1876)
- The introduction of a third classification – the innominate or intermediate term the importance of which is only to be ascertained when it is breached – *Hong Kong Fir Shipping* v *Kawaskai Kisen Kaisha Ltd* (1962); *Cehave* v *Bremer* (1976); *Schuler* v *Wickman Machine Tool Sales Ltd* (1974); *Reardon Smith* v *Hansen-Tangen* (1976)
- The possibility that the third classification was known to English law before 1962
- Express designation as a condition or warranty – Sale of Goods Act 1979
- Judicial classification – *The Mihalis Angelos* (1971)
- Express classification – *The Chikuma* (1981); *Lombard North Central* v *Butterworth* (1987); *United Scientific Holdings* v *Burnley BC* (1978); *Bunge* v *Tradax* (1981)

Suggested Answer

First, it is necessary to define the subject matter of this answer. The distinction referred to between conditions and warranties is the apparent approach of nineteenth-century contract lawyers to the classification of contractual terms. They appear generally (the reason for their qualification is given later in this answer) to have regarded the categories of conditions and warranties as being exhaustive: a contractual term had to be either one or the other. It is clear now, however, that English law recognises not two but three different types of term: conditions, warranties and innominate terms (sometimes called intermediate stipulations).

A condition may be defined as a term, any breach of which entitles the innocent party not only to recover damages but also to terminate the contract if he so chooses, irrespective of the consequences of the breach. The right to terminate, which is an option not an obligation, arises because of the nature of the term broken, not because of the consequences which flow from the breach: *Hong Kong Fir Shipping* v *Kawasaki Kisen Kaisha Ltd* (1962); *Bunge Corporation* v *Tradax Export SA* (1981); and *Lombard North Central* v *Butterworth* (1987).

An innominate term is a term, a breach of which entitles the innocent party to recover damages and may, in addition, entitle him to terminate the contract. The right to terminate is not always available, as with a condition, but only where the actual and prospective consequences of the breach are such as to deprive the innocent party of substantially the whole of the benefit of the consideration he bargained to receive under the contract (in short, where the breach goes to the root of the contract): *Hong Kong Fir Shipping*. Thus in the case of an innominate term, the existence of the right to terminate depends upon the severity of the consequences of the breach.

A warranty is a term, any breach of which is remediable in damages only: *Bettini v Gye* (1876). It would appear that no matter how serious the breach or its consequences, if the term broken is only a warranty then there is never a right to terminate the contract. Although this may seem harsh at first sight, to hold otherwise would so blur the distinction between innominate terms and warranties as to render it unworkable. The reason for the qualifying remarks at the beginning of this answer can now be stated. Although this threefold classification of contractual terms has been accepted and applied in practice since *Hong Kong Fir* in 1962, it has been suggested in some of the cases that innominate terms were recognised in earlier decisions in the twentieth century and in the nineteenth century too. The Court of Appeal made this point very forcibly in *Cehave v Bremer Handelsgesellschaft* (1976), and in *Bunge v Tradax* the House of Lords expressed similar views. For example Lord Scarman spoke of innominate terms being 'rediscovered' in *Hong Kong Fir* but of always having been part of English law.

If these views be accepted, then Anson is wrong to suggest that a two-fold classification only existed in the last century. However it is fair to say that even if innominate terms were known to English law before 1962, they were largely (though perhaps not entirely) overlooked by both judges and academics alike.

The threefold classification is in any event now established. Taken out of context, though, Anson's proposition could be read as meaning that the classification of terms (albeit into three rather than two categories) is no longer important. It is respectfully submitted that this is not so, nor did the editor of Anson intend so to suggest.

The classification of terms is important. For the parties to know their legal rights and liabilities, the nature of the term is crucial, particularly as regards the availability or otherwise of the rights of termination. Further, the character of all terms is ascertainable at the moment the contract is concluded. Nothing that happens after its formation can alter the status of a term, although in the case of an innominate term it will determine the availability of the right of termination. To hold otherwise would lead to unacceptable uncertainty: a contract term cannot have a status capable of changing from one day to the next.

The flexibility to which Anson refers is introduced into the law by the innominate term. Instead of saying that the innocent can, in the case of a condition, always terminate, or in the case of warranty, never terminate is manifestly inflexible. Innominate terms allow the courts to permit termination where the circumstances justify it and the consequences are sufficiently serious. It is for this reason that innominate terms were regarded with obvious favour in cases such as *Hong Kong Fir*; *Cehave v Bremer*; *Schuler v Wickman Machine Tool Sales Ltd* (1974) and *Reardon Smith v Hansen-Tangen* (1976).

Nevertheless, innominate terms are only one of the three categories and the other two cannot be ignored. It may be, for example, that the term in question is expressly designated a condition as a warranty by statute, such as the Sale of Goods Act 1979, or has already been judicially classified, as was the case in *The Mihalis Angelos* (1971). Further, it is open to the parties themselves expressly to classify the term, in which case providing their intention is clear the courts will give effect to it: *The Chikuma* (1981) and *Lombard North Central*. Lastly the courts may be of the view that the parties must have intended the term to be a condition, even though they did not bother so to call it. The most obvious examples here are stipulations as to time in mercantile contracts: *United Scientific Holdings* v *Burnley Borough Council* (1978) and *Bunge* v *Tradax*. In all these cases, there is no flexibility. The right to terminate for breach (or not, in the case of warranty) follows on from the classification of the term.

In conclusion, whilst Anson is right to suggest that there is now greater flexibility in this area of the law, the distinction between the different types of contractual terms remains of considerable importance.

SUGGESTED ANSWER TO QUESTION FOUR

General Comment

Here is a problem which requires the candidate to evaluate the importance of contractual terms with a view to ascertaining what, if any, remedies may be available for breach. The successful candidate will be able to distinguish between conditions and warranties and understand the importance of innominate terms. It is then necessary to extrapolate from these distinctions practical advice to Xavier regarding the remedies available to him.

Key Points

- Classification of terms into warranties and conditions and its effect – *Bentsen* v *Taylor Sons & Co* (1893); s61(1) Sale of Goods Act 1979
- Innominate or intermediate terms – *Bettini* v *Guy* (1876); *Poussard* v *Spiers* (1876); *Aerial Advertising Co* v *Batchelors Peas Ltd* (1938); *Hong Kong Fir Shipping Co* v *Kawasaki Kishen Kaisha Ltd* (1962); *Bunge Corporation* v *Tradax* (1981)
- Effect of making time of the essence of the contract – *The Mihalis Angelos* (1971); *Financings Ltd* v *Baldock* (1963); *Lombard North Central* v *Butterworth* (1987)
- Express statement that a term is a condition is not conclusive and classification depends on the parties' intention – *Schuler AG* v *Wickman Machine Tool Sales Ltd* (1974)

Suggested Answer

The issue raised by this question is the relative importance of contractual terms. Traditionally the terms of a contract were classified as conditions or warranties. A condition has been defined as an 'essential term' of the contract, or one where 'performance of the stipulation (went) to the very root ... of the contract': *Bentsen* v

Taylor (1893). A breach of condition can be regarded by the injured party as a repudiation of the contract and entitles him to terminate it and thereby discharge himself from further obligations. A warranty is a less important term; its breach does not entitle the injured party to terminate the contract, but confines him to a remedy in damages. Warranty is defined in the Sale of Goods Act 1979 in s61(1) as a term 'collateral to the main purpose of (the) contract, the breach of which gives rise to a claim for damages, but not a right to reject the goods and treat the contract as repudiated.'

A further category has, however, been recognised. Certain terms cannot be classified as conditions or warranties, but whether they are to be treated as conditions or warranties depends on the nature of the breach. Such terms are called 'innominate terms'. This approach was adopted in the earlier cases of *Bettini* v *Gye* (1876) and *Poussard* v *Spiers* (1876). A further example is the case of *Aerial Advertising Co* v *Batchelors Peas Ltd* (1938). But the concept of the innominate term was first expressly recognised by the Court of Appeal decision in *Hong Kong Fir Shipping* v *Kawasaki Kishen Kaisha Ltd* (1962). In the course of his judgment Diplock LJ (as he then was) said that many contractual undertakings could not be classified as conditions or warranties.

> 'Of such undertakings all that can be predicted is that some breaches will and others will not give rise to an event which will deprive the party not in default of substantially the whole benefit which it was intended that he should obtain from the contract.'

In *Bunge Corporation, New York* v *Tradax Export SA, Panama* (1981) Lord Scarman said that:

> 'Unless the contract makes it clear, either by express provision or by necessary implication arising from its nature, purpose and circumstances ... that a particular stipulation is a condition or only a warranty, it is an innominate term the remedy for a breach of which depends on the nature, consequences and effect of the breach.'

A contractual term is then a condition if the parties expressly intended it to be so, or if it is classified as such by statute, or judicial decision; otherwise whether it is treated as a condition or merely as a warranty depends on the nature, extent and consequences of the breach.

In the present problem Xavier wishes to terminate the contract. Linus has clearly been in breach of the provisions set out. The question is: are any of these breaches to be regarded as a breach of condition? Each of the provisions must be considered in turn.

The provision for punctual payment
It is provided that this 'is deemed to be of the essence of the contract'. The actual breach of this provision is trivial – Linus was two days late in paying last month's rent – but if the term is a condition any breach, however trivial, would justify Xavier in treating it as a repudiatory breach, and entitle him to terminate the contract.

Time is often of the essence in commercial contracts – see, for example, *The Mihalis Angelos* (1971). But a failure to make a punctual payment would not necessarily be considered to be repudiatory in a contract such as the present one: *Financings Ltd* v *Baldock* (1963). Clearly the nature of the breach here is not one that could be regarded as depriving Xavier of the substantial benefit of the contract. However, in *Lombard North Central* v *Butterworth* (1987) where there was a similar clause, the Court of Appeal held that even though the failure to pay promptly was not repudiatory, the clause had the effect of making failure to pay on time a breach of condition. In view of that decision, whilst it is harsh, it seems inescapable that Xavier would be able to rely on the breach by Linus as constituting a breach of condition, and thus entitling him to terminate the contract. A more recent case concerning a time stipulation is *Glencoe Grain Rotterdam BV* v *Lebanese Organisation for International Commerce* (1997). Here the buyers agreed to buy 25,000 tonnes of wheat at a set price with a stipulation for additional payments if the buyer did not take this quantity. The buyers' vessel was late arriving and the seller refused to load the wheat without prepayment of the additional amount. The court held that the breach could not be put right and the seller was justified in his action from the time the buyer had broken the contract. It did not matter that the seller had claimed a different justification at the time.

The provision with regard to disconnecting the power supply
This clause is described as a 'condition'. This is not conclusive; the court would have to be satisfied that the parties intended to use the word in the technical sense. In *Schuler AG* v *Wickman Machine Tool Sales Ltd* (1974) one particular clause was called a condition and no other term in the 20 clauses was described as a condition. It was argued that because that particular clause was described as a condition any breach of it by the one party entitled the other party to terminate the contract. This argument was rejected by the House of Lords. Lord Reid held that the use of the word 'condition' was perhaps a strong indication that the parties intended the clause to be a condition in the technical sense, but it was not conclusive evidence. Their Lordships were able to come to the conclusion that the technical use of the word was not intended, by a consideration of the contract as a whole. A further clause in the contract provided for notice to be given of a 'material breach'. This enabled the House of Lords to interpret the word in a non-technical sense. Lord Reid did say, however, that, but for this further clause, he would have found difficulty in reaching this conclusion.

The question here is not without difficulty. It seems unreasonable for Xavier to be held entitled to terminate the contract because of one failure by Linus to disconnect the power supply. But this would follow if this provision is interpreted as a condition, and it is so described. There is not the escape from that conclusion by a clause similar to the one in *Schuler*. There does not appear to be any provision for notice to Linus requiring him to remedy or desist from the breach. Accordingly it is submitted that this provision too would be regarded by the court as a condition, the breach of which would entitle Xavier to terminate.

The provision regarding faults and repairs
This provision appears to be one which cannot be categorised as being a condition or a warranty. It is typically a clause which would require consideration of – in Lord Scarman's words – 'the nature, effect and consequences of the breach'. It is therefore an innominate term. The breaches of this provision that have occurred are not of sufficient gravity to justify treating them as breaches of condition. Xavier would not be able to rely on them to justify termination.

In conclusion it is submitted that although Xavier cannot rely on the third provision as entitling him to terminate he can do so by virtue of the breaches of the the first two provisions. It must be admitted that this conclusion could be regarded as over-technical, but the authorities do not appear to allow for any alternative.

SUGGESTED ANSWER TO QUESTION FIVE

General Comment

The good candidate will instantly recognise this quotation to be a statement of the parol evidence rule. The rule has a long history and, as is the case with such ancient common law rules, has over the years collected a significant number of exceptions. It is not always easy to categorise the exceptions made in individual cases and the case law contains some fine distinctions. Success in answering this question demands excellent recollection of case law together with an understanding of the historical background against which the cases were decided and the development of judicial thought.

Key Points

- The question refers to the parol evidence rule as stated in *Jacobs* v *Batavia and General Plantations Trust* (1924)
- The rule is based on certainty – *Rabin* v *Gerson Berger Association Ltd* (1986)
- The rule is still applied – *W F Trustees Ltd* v *Expo Safety Systems Ltd* (1993)
- It does not apply where the document was not designed to contain all the terms:
- Where the contract is contained in more than one document – *Shearson Lehman Hutton Inc* v *Maclaine Watson & Co* (1989); *Edwards* v *Aberayon Insurance Society Ltd* (1876)
- Where the written document is merely a memorandum and oral warranties or representations were given – *Hutton* v *Watling* (1948); *Allen* v *Pink* (1838); *Couchman* v *Hill* (1947); *Routledge* v *McKay* (1954); *Harling* v *Eddy* (1951)
- Where there is a collateral contract – *City and Westminster Properties (1934) Ltd* v *Mudd* (1959)
- Oral terms may be implied into a contract – *Produce Brokers Co Ltd* v *Olympia Oil and Cake Co Ltd* (1916); *Smith* v *Wilson* (1832); *The Moorcock* (1889); *Shirlaw* v *Southern Foundries (1926) Ltd* (1939)
- Oral evidence may be allowed to prove the contents (but not the validity) of a contract – *Pym* v *Campbell* (1856); *Newell* v *Radford* (1867); *Scarfe* v *Adams* (1981); *Turner* v *Forwood* (1951)

Suggested Answer

This presumption by the courts results from the parol evidence rule which was stated in *Jacobs* v *Batavia and General Plantations Trust* (1924) to be as follows:

> '... parol evidence cannot be admitted to add to, vary or contradict a deed or other written instrument. Accordingly it has been held that ... parol evidence will not be admitted to prove that some particular term, which had been verbally agreed upon, had been omitted

(by design or otherwise) from a written instrument constituting a valid and operative contract between the parties.'

The rule does not exclude merely oral evidence and it does not apply only to contracts and, although there are a number of exceptions (see below) it is still very much alive: *WF Trustees Ltd v Expo Safety Systems Ltd* (1993). The basis of the rule was confirmed in 1986 to be certainty: *Rabin v Gerson Berger Association Ltd* (1986).

The presumption is however, rebuttable and extrinsic evidence may be admitted in a number of situations.

Where the document was not designed to contain all the terms
The first situation under this heading is where the contract is contained in more than one document. Where the second document is incorporated by express reference, the courts will usually give effect to its terms: *Shearson Lehman Hutton Inc v Maclaine Watson & Co* (1989). Even without express reference, a further document may be admitted if it appears to have been the parties' intention that its terms should be incorporated: *Edwards v Aberayron Insurance Society Ltd* (1876).

Secondly, the written agreement may not and may not have been intended to contain all of the terms of the agreement. In *Hutton v Watling* (1948) a written document was held to be no more than a memorandum of the agreement, other terms having been agreed orally.

Examples abound where oral warranties have been given. It must be pointed out here that it was not until 1964 in *Hedley Byrne & Co Ltd v Heller & Partners Ltd* that oral representations which were not fraudulent became actionable as misrepresentations. There was therefore a greater need to find that these statements formed terms of the contract, breach of which could lead to damages or rescission. The cases of *Allen v Pink* (1838) and *Couchman v Hill* (1947) are both examples of oral warranties given in relation to the sale of animals which the court considered were actionable for breach. A more modern case, *Routledge v McKay* (1954), concerned the sale of a motor cycle.

The question is to ascertain the parties' intentions. The court must ask at what stage of the transaction the statement was made – if at the time of sale it is liable to be a term of the contract. Secondly, they must ask whether the statement was followed by a reduction of the terms to writing, for the exclusion of the oral statement suggests that it was not intended to be a contractual term. Finally, the court will ask whether the person who made the statement had special knowledge and skill: *Harling v Eddy* (1951). If so, the statement is again more likely to have been a term of the contract.

There is a third category of cases which again may be seen as remedying a deficiency prior to the actionability of oral statements as misrepresentations, where the court has found a collateral contract: a subsidiary contract which is dependent on the main contract and for which entry into the main contract may itself be consideration. An example is *City and Westminster Properties (1934) Ltd v Mudd* (1959) where the defendant accepted a term in a new lease restricting the use of the premises to 'showrooms, workrooms and offices only' on the basis of an oral assurance that he would be allowed to sleep on the premises. The oral assurance was held to be a collateral contract which protected the defendant from forfeiture for breach of covenant.

Implied Terms

Terms may be implied into oral or written contracts by statute, by custom or by the courts themselves. There are many cases of evidence being admitted to prove a custom. In *Produce Brokers Co Ltd* v *Olympia Oil and Cake Co Ltd* (1916) Lord Sumner said:

> 'The custom, if any, is part of the bargain ... If the bargain is partly expressed in ink and partly implied by the tacit incorporation of trade customs, the first function of the arbitrators is to find out what it is: to read the language, to ascertain the custom, to interpret them both and to give effect to the whole ...'

Evidence may also be admitted to prove that certain words in a contract had a customary meaning different from the usual meaning (eg *Smith* v *Wilson* (1832) where '1000 rabbits' was proved to mean '1200 rabbits').

Terms may be implied by statute, a prime example being the implied terms as to satisfactory quality and fitness of purpose under the Sale of Goods Act 1979. It is not necessary to describe these further.

The court will imply a term where it is necessary to give 'business efficacy' to the contract: *The Moorcock* (1889). A term is usually required to pass the 'officious bystander' test described by MacKinnon LJ as follows:

> 'Prima facie that which in any contract is left to be implied and need not be expressed is something so obvious that it goes without saying; so that, if while the parties were making their bargain an officious bystander were to suggest some express provision for it in their agreement, they would testily suppress him with a common, "Oh, of course." ': *Shirlaw* v *Southern Foundries (1926) Ltd* (1939).

To prove the contents of a contract

There are a number of miscellaneous cases which come under the heading of proving the contents of a contract as opposed to its validity. These included evidence allowed in to show whether the contract operated (*Pym* v *Campbell* (1856)), who the parties were (*Newell* v *Radford* (1867)), the identification of the subject matter (*Scarfe* v *Adams* (1981)) and evidence of additional consideration (*Turner* v *Forwood* (1951)) or that it was executed by the parties under a common mistake.

In conclusion, therefore, it may be stated that while the courts do still maintain the presumption that the parties intended to include all the terms of the contract in their writing, this is a rebuttable presumption, and extrinsic evidence may be admitted in many and varied situations.

SUGGESTED ANSWER TO QUESTION SIX

General Comment

The problem posed by this question is the not unusual one of an additional term negotiated at the time a contract is made but not written into the standard terms and conditions imposed by one of the contracting parties. The main focus of the question is, however, not whether the term has been incorporated into the contract but what is the effect of breaching that term. What is needed here is an analysis of the term with regard to the classifications of warranty, condition and intermediate term, and suitable advice to Peter as to his remedies (if any) based on that analysis.

Key Points

- The term has almost certainly become an express term of the contract
- Whether Peter can rescind or merely claim damages for breach depends on the importance of the term which in turn depends on its classification as a condition or warranty
- The term may in fact be an intermediate or innominate term – *Hong Kong Fir Shipping* v *Kawasaki Kisen Kaisha Ltd* (1962); *Cehave* v *Bremer* (1976); *Reardon Smith Line* v *Hansen-Tangen* (1976)
- That the term is described as a condition is not conclusive and the court will look at the substance of the agreement to determine the parties' intentions – *Schuler AG* v *Wickman Machine Tool Sales Ltd* (1974)
- The term must be evaluated at the time of contracting – *Bunge Corporation* v *Tradax Export SA* (1981)
- If the term is innominate, the court will examine the consequences of the breach
- If Peter relied on the salesman's advice, there may have been breach of an implied term of care and skill or a negligent misrepresentation on the part of Efficient Business Equipment

Suggested Answer

It is necessary first of all to dispose of Efficient Business Equipment's contention that the additional term negotiated by Peter is not included in the contract. Unless there is evidence to the contrary, it is clear that their salesman had at least apparent authority to negotiate the term and therefore it has become an express term of the contract which has been broken.

The question is whether Peter can rescind for breach of the term or whether he can only claim for damages for the losses he has suffered. This depends on the importance of the term. Terms have traditionally been classified as conditions or warranties. Breach of condition allows the injured party to rescind the contract, ie to be put back in the position he was in before the contract was made with no further liability under the contract. Breach of warranty merely allows him to sue for compensation for his loss.

In 1962, however, a third category of express term was recognised. In *Hong Kong Fir Shipping* v *Kawasaki Kisen Kaisha Ltd*, the Court of Appeal recognised that certain terms did not fit into these neat categories and that they could not effectively be classified until the effects of breach had been seen. Should the breach be so serious as fundamentally to destroy the basis of the contract, then rescission would be appropriate and the term could be classified as a condition. Otherwise it would be a warranty.

Those terms which are thus unclassifiable until breach have been termed 'intermediate' or 'innominate' terms, and this classification has been accepted both by a later Court of Appeal (*Cehave* v *Bremer Handelsgesellschaft mbH (The Hansa Nord)*) and by the House of Lords (*Reardon Smith Line* v *Hansen-Tangen*) in 1976.

How then should the term in question be classified? It is necessary to ascertain the parties' intentions. The fact that it has been termed a condition is not conclusive, since no legal advice appears to have been taken and it is unlikely that the parties intended to use the word in its technical legal sense: *Schuler AG* v *Wickman Machine Tool Sales Ltd* (1974). The court will then look at the substance of the agreement to try and ascertain the parties' intentions.

It is to be noted that there are two parts to the clause: first, that the computer be compatible with the printer and, second, that it be able to run the software. If the clause is to be either a condition or a warranty, it is to be evaluated at the time of contracting: *Bunge Corporation* v *Tradax Export SA* (1981). On the evidence in the question, the clause would be hard to evaluate as at that particular date. Evidence might be brought as to how important it was to Peter's existing business to use that software package and to what extent the Efficient Business Equipment salesman was aware of this. It is submitted that the compatibility of the printer is a lesser issue which would have been intended to be a warranty only.

If the terms are then innominate, the breach itself must be examined. The consequences of the breach of the part relating to the printer are clear. Peter has been forced to pay £500 for a new printer which he would not have had to pay had the other been compatible. This is a breach which could easily be dealt with by an award of damages and does not fundamentally affect Peter's business.

The breach of the part relating to the software is somewhat different. It would appear that the use of this particular program is fundamental to the running of Peter's business. Indeed, if this is the only piece of software which he uses, the computer may effectively be rendered useless to him. At any event, it is likely to have serious consequences for Peter's business if it is consistently producing errors. Whether or not Peter's records could be transferred without damage to another software program which the computer can run without difficulty is a factor which is likely to be taken into consideration. It seems, however, on the face of it that Peter may be able to rescind the contract on the basis of this failure. The court would have to be persuaded to see the two parts of the clause as separate clauses and not interdependent.

Finally, there is some suggestion in the question that Peter has been badly advised, although whether by Efficient Business Equipment themselves is not clear. There is too little detail about this to evaluate this part of the problem effectively, but it may be that, if Peter relied on their advice, there would be a breach of an implied condition as to the care and skill with which he was advised. If the salesman had warranted that the machine was compatible with either the printer or the software, and Peter had relied on this warranty, this would be an untrue statement of fact which might entitle Peter to rescind the contract for negligent misrepresentation.

SUGGESTED ANSWER TO QUESTION SEVEN

General Comment

The problems in this question centre almost entirely on terms which may be implied into a contract. The solution involves terms which may be implied by statute, by custom and by the court, all of which areas need to be thoroughly understood. A successful candidate will be able to demonstrate competent analytical powers, breaking down the question into its component problems and providing a coherent solution for each part.

3 Form and Contents of Contracts – Answers 61

With this type of question is is even more important than usual to organise one's thoughts into a plan before embarking on the answer.

Key Points

Holiday in Tenerife
- A duty of care and skill is implied by the Supply of Goods and Services Act 1982 as amended by the Sale and Supply of Goods Act 1994
- Anthony relied on the travel agent's advice
- Would the 'reasonable' travel agent have known it would be cold and wet in Tenerife?
- Showing Anthony the photograph may have been a negligent or fraudulent misrepresentation
- Damages may be recovered for loss of enjoyment in a holiday contract

Broken suitcase and lost effects
- Terms as to satisfactory quality and fitness for purpose implied in ss12-15 Sale of Goods Act 1979 as amended
- Suitcase was not fit for the purpose and it was not an unusual purpose
- Anthony may recover damages for the consequences of the breach

Employer's claim for breach of good faith
- A duty of good faith from the employee to the employee is implied in every contract of employment – *Hivac Ltd v Park Royal Scientific Instruments* (1946)
- A custom may be incorporated into a contract provided there are no inconsistent terms
- The right to take the holiday may be distinguished from the means of taking it, ie all at once and without reasonable notice
- Court might imply a term on behalf of the employer that the holiday should be taken with reasonable notice and at a time convenient to the employer – *Reigate v Union Manufacturing Co (Ramsbottom)* (1918); *Shirlaw v Southern Foundries (1926) Ltd* (1939)

Suggested Answer

Contracts generally contain express terms, ie those which the parties agree orally, in writing or by conduct. However, in certain situations the law will imply terms into a contract which have not expressly been agreed by the parties. Such terms can be implied by statute, by custom or by the courts themselves, and it is with these terms that the question is concerned. The problem can be broken down into three separate elements which can be dealt with separately.

Holiday in Tenerife

The contract between Anthony and the travel agency is a contract for the supply of services. Terms are implied into such contracts by the Supply of Goods and Services Act 1982 (as amended by the Sale and Supply of Goods Act 1994). In particular, duties of care and skill are implied. Anthony expressed to the travel agents his desire to holiday somewhere hot and sunny and presumably relied on their advice as to where his destination might be. Whether or not the travel agents were in breach of their duty depends on whether or not the 'reasonable' travel agent could have been expected to know the weather would be cold and wet in Tenerife at that time. If this was a normal occurrence, they should at least have warned Anthony of this and suggested another destination. If, on the other hand, it was most unusual, they could not be held liable. So far as the hotel was concerned, by double-booking and not providing equivalent substitute accommodation, the agents were clearly in breach of their duty. Additionally, showing the picture of the hotel to Anthony in the brochure may have amounted to a negligent or even (if the agents already knew that the hotel was fully booked), a fraudulent misrepresentation (an untrue statement of fact which induced the contract), which would enable Anthony to rescind the contract and recover the money paid. Anthony's damages are, however, not limited to the amount he paid. It is well settled that damages may be recovered from a tour operator for loss of enjoyment if the holiday is spoilt as a result of the operator's breach of contract. This principle should apply here.

Broken suitcase and lost effects
Sections 12-15 of the Sale of Goods Act 1979 imply terms into contracts for the sale of goods. in particular, as to the satisfactory quality of those goods and the fitness for the purpose for which they were sold. The suitcase may have been of satisfactory quality but clearly it was not reasonably fit for the purpose for which it was sold. If this was an unusual purpose, this must have been made known to the supplier. However, a foreign holiday is hardly an unusual purpose in connection with a suitcase, and in any event Anthony told the salesman he was intending to fly to Tenerife. Anthony therefore has a claim of the return for the price of the suitcase and, as he may claim damages for all the consequences of the breach within the reasonable contemplation of the parties, damages for the loss of his clothing and other effects.

Employer's claim for breach of good faith
There is no doubt that every employee owes his employer a duty of good faith (*Hivac Ltd* v *Park Royal Scientific Instruments* (1946)) and this is implied into any contract of employment and need not be expressly stated. However, it appears that there is a custom to the effect that every employee in Anthony's trade should have an annual four-week holiday. The question is whether the parties intended this custom to be incorporated into Anthony's contract of employment. The more usual situation is where a collective agreement, made with a trade union, is incorporated by implication into individual employees' contracts, but there seems no reason why a term which is customary should not be implied into the contract.

Any contract may be deemed to incorporate a relevant custom of the market, trade or locality in which it is made unless inconsistent with the terms of of the contract. The contract of employment does not appear to deal with the question of holiday and, provided there are no inconsistent terms, there is no reason to exclude the term, if proven. If the contract is silent about holiday, given that an employee would hardly have agreed to it if there was not some agreement about holiday, it will be a difficult burden on the employers to show that Anthony was not entitled to take his holiday.

The method of taking it may pose some problem, since it could be argued that it would be implied that in order to give 'business efficacy' to the agreement, the employee should give reasonable notice of his intention to take a holiday and take it at a time convenient to the employer. Other than a term which is incorporated by statute or by usage, the courts will only imply a term to give 'business efficacy' to a contract (*Reigate v Union Manufacturing Co (Ramsbottom)* (1918)) and only if the term is so obvious as to pass the 'officious bystander' test as propounded by McKinnon LJ in *Shirlaw* v *Southern Foundries (1926) Ltd* (1939):

> 'Prima facie that which in any contract is left to be implied and need not be expressed is something so obvious that it goes without saying; so that, if while the parties were making their bargain an officious bystander were to suggest some express provision for it in their agreement, they would testily suppress him with a common, "Oh, of course." '

It would be for the court to decide whether this particular proviso was so obvious that it would naturally have been implied. Further, there would be a question of fact whether Anthony had had an opportunity of taking his holiday earlier and failed to take it or whether he simply had not been allowed the opportunity.

In summary, things are not as bleak for Anthony as they might at first seem. He has an action against the travel agents or the tour operators in respect of his holiday, an action against the department store in respect of his suitcase and lost effects, and a good defence against action by his employers.

4

Misrepresentation, Duress and Undue Influence

Introduction

Further factors which may vitiate a contract are misrepresentation, duress and undue influence. Misrepresentation is such a common cause of action in the practical world that it ranks alongside mistake as one of the most popular areas for problem questions.

Misrepresentation involves an untrue statement of fact by one party to another which induces the other to enter a contract. A problem question on misrepresentation will therefore usually involve analysing pre-contractual statements with reference to the elements of this definition, illustrating the answer with suitable examples from case law. It is therefore a fairly straightforward topic to tackle. Discussion questions such as questions 3 and 7 below will usually involve consideration of the remedies available in an action for misrepresentation. Further questions on this area may be found in Chapter 12.

Questions

INTERROGRAMS

1. What is the accepted definition of 'misrepresentation'?
2. How did the Misrepresentation Act 1967 improve the position of the plaintiff in a misrepresentation action?
3. What was the significance of the decision of the House of Lords in *Hedley Byrne & Co v Heller & Partners Ltd* (1964)?

QUESTION ONE

Joanna owned a health food shop which she wished to sell. She was approached by Kate who was interested in buying the shop. Joanna told Kate that the demand for health foods would 'increase dramatically' as people became more health conscious and that since health foods were all 'natural' there was no risk of trouble from local authority health inspectors. Joanna also said that the shop made 'up to £1,000 profit a week'. She offered to show Kate the accounts, but Kate said she was happy to take Joanna's word for it.

After buying the shop for £50,000, Kate discovered that the demand for health foods was falling and that in the previous two years the weekly profit had only once reached £1,000 and was generally below £200. The health inspector has also visited the premises and required her to stop selling certain items which infringe EEC regulations.

Advise Kate.

London University LLB Examination
(for external students) Elements of the Law of Contract June 1986 Q4

4 Misrepresentation, Duress and Undue Influence – Questions

QUESTION TWO

Percy replied to Victor's advertisement for the sale of his small printing business. Victor has been ill for the last year and the business has been run by a manager. When Percy came to see him, Victor said that the business was 'in excellent order'. When Percy asked to see the books Victor said 'You can see them if you wish but I assure you that profits have regularly topped £500 per week. Demand is exceptionally high and likely to remain so for the foreseeable future.' The figure quoted was in fact correct but recent figures indicated a likely downturn in business.

Victor's accountant had recently written to the firm warning of the need to invest heavily in new technology if the business was to survive.

Percy went ahead and bought the business which is now about to collapse unless there is substantial investment.

Advise Percy.

London University LLB Examination
(for external students) Elements of the Law of Contract June 1986 Q6

QUESTION THREE

D was considering buying a rare piece of china from E (an antique dealer). C, a friend of E, said to D that the piece was genuine. This was not correct but the piece was a very good fake. D agreed to buy the china for £25,000. Subsequently, the fact that it was a fake came to light.

Advise D. What difference, if any, would it make to your advice if, alternatively, (i) the statement had been made by E; (ii) E was a private seller?

London University LLB Examination
(for external students) Elements of the Law of Contract June 1995 Q3b

QUESTION FOUR

In January 1989 X privately advertised his house for sale for £100,000. J and his wife, M, who was expecting a baby in March 1989, came to inspect the House. X informed J that the house was in 'first-class condition throughout' and that X had just installed a new gas central heating system that was safe and efficient and that J need not worry about the house being cold for his new baby. When J asked if the house was noisy X replied that it was always quiet. J agreed to buy the house.

After living in the house for only a few days J and M discovered that their neighbours were awful and fought all the time. J and M could hear these fights. Soon after J smelt gas and it was discovered that the gas central heating was dangerous and need to be replaced at a cost of £2,000. J was forced to move his family to a hotel for a week at a cost of £300 while the central heating was replaced. While at the hotel J heard that the local authority had just granted planning permission for the house next door to be used as a day centre for homeless teenagers. The value of J's house immediately fell by £30,000.

Advise J.

London University LLB Examination
(for external students) Elements of the Law of Contract June 1989 Q1

QUESTION FIVE

Does the law provide an adequate solution to the injustices that result when a person is induced to enter into a contract with another as a result of a misrepresentation of fact which does not constitute a term of the contract?

London University LLB Examination
(for external students) Elements of the Law of Contract June 1992 Q4

Answers

ANSWERS TO INTERROGRAMS

1   Untrue, of course, means a deliberate lie (*Derry* v *Peek* (1889)) but a misleading statement or half-truth may also be a misrepresentation. Further, where the statement was true at the time it was made, there will still be a misrepresentation if circumstances change before the contract is concluded in such a way as to make the statement misleading, and the maker has not informed the party to whom it was made: *With* v *O'Flanagan* (1936).

   A statement of fact need not be made in words (*St Marylebone Property Co Ltd* v *Payne* (1994)) but statements as to law are excluded by the definition. Statements of opinion only are not misrepresentations (*Bisset* v *Wilkinson* (1927)) unless the maker does not genuinely hold that opinion or could not reasonably have held that opinion: *Smith* v *Land and House Property Corporation* (1884). Similarly, genuine statements of intention are not misrepresentations unless the party making the statement did not have or could not reasonably have had that intention (*Edgington* v *Fitzmaurice* (1885)) or did not intend keeping to it: *Esso Petroleum* v *Mardon* (1976).

   The statement must be made by a party to the contract or on his behalf and it must have induced the other to enter into the contract. Where the other party did not rely on the statement but made his own investigations, the statement, even if untrue, will not be a misrepresentation: *Attwood* v *Small* (1838). However, if a statement is made, he is entitled to rely on it and is not obliged to ascertain whether it is true even if the maker offers him the opportunity of doing so: *Redgrave* v *Hurd* (1881).

2   Prior to the enactment of the Misrepresentation Act 1967, a plaintiff who had been induced to enter into a contract by a lie had only three courses of action. He could sue in the tort of deceit, prove that the statement formed part of the contract and sue for breach, or he could establish a claim for negligent misstatement.

   Each of these possibilities had their pitfalls. In order to be able to establish a claim in deceit, the plaintiff must be able to show absolute dishonesty: *Derry* v *Peek* (1889). Clearly this was very difficult for 'the devil himself knows not the mind of a man'. The court was very often prepared to hold a statement or warranty to be a term of the contract, but this resulted in some rather complex rules and fine distinctions. The third possibility arose from the judgment of the House of Lords in *Hedley Byrne & Co Ltd* v *Heller and Partners Ltd* (1964) when it was held that, in certain circumstances, an untrue statement made without actual dishonesty could form the basis for a claim in negligence. However the plaintiff was required to prove that a 'special relationship' existed between himself and the defendant.

Section 2(1) of the Misrepresentation Act provides that if the defendant would have been liable to the plaintiff in fraud on the basis of his statement, then he will be liable even without fraud unless he can prove that he believed the statement and had reasonable grounds for doing so up until the time the contract was concluded. This means that the plaintiff need not prove fraud or a special relationship, nor that the statement had become a term of the contract. Instead the burden has passed to the defendant to prove that he believed the statement and that it was reasonable for him to do so.

3 The decision in *Hedley Byrne & Co Ltd* v *Heller and Partners Ltd* (1964) was something of a landmark. The facts of the case were that the plaintiffs had sought a banker's reference against a third party who was a client of the defendant bank. The reference was couched in misleading terms and the plaintiffs, believing the third party to be credit-worthy, did work on credit and thus incurred a loss.

The actual decision in the case was that the plaintiffs' claim in negligence must fail because the reference had included a disclaimer exempting the defendants from liability. However, the case is important for the dicta of the judges which established that, had there been no disclaimer, the plaintiffs would have succeeded in their claim. Prior to that, the plaintiffs would have had to prove either that the statement as to the third party's credit-worthiness was a term of a contract between themselves and the defendants (a course not open to them in this case as there was no contract) or that the reference was given fraudulently, which clearly was not the case.

The House laid down certain conditions for the operation of negligent misstatement:

a   there must be a special relationship between the parties;
b   this must arise from one party having a special knowledge or skill;
c   the plaintiff must have relied on that knowledge or skill; and
d   the statement must have been made in the course of a business.

While this was a welcome relaxation of the law, because of the conditions imposed it was somewhat restrictive and it was rare for plaintiffs to be able to take advantage of it. The position of the plaintiff was improved subsequently when the Misrepresentation Act 1967 removed the requirement to prove fraud, thus allowing a claim for misrepresentation on the basis of a negligent misstatement even where there was no special relationship.

SUGGESTED ANSWER TO QUESTION ONE

General Comment

The subject area for this question may quickly be identified as misrepresentation and breach of contract by there being a number of statements made during negotiations for a sale. Misrepresentation is a large topic and there may be a temptation to write out all you know. What is required here is a well-structured answer which applies the law to the facts in the question.

Key Points

- The statements made by Joanna may be contractual terms – *Heilbut, Symons & Co v Buckleton* (1913); *Oscar Chess Ltd v Williams* (1957); *Dick Bentley Productions Ltd v Harold Smith (Motors) Ltd* (1965)
- Statement of opinion may be actionable if the maker implied that he knew facts to support his opinion – *Smith Land and House Property Corporation* (1884); *Brown v Raphael* (1958); *Edgington v Fitzmaurice* (1895)
- Although a statement of law is not actionable, a statement of mixed fact and law is – *Cooper v Phibbs* (1867); *Beattie v Lord Ebury* (1872)
- A misleading half-truth is actionable – *Dimmock v Hallett* (1866)
- The party to whom a representation is made has no duty to verify its accuracy – *Redgrave v Hurd* (1881)
- Damages may be recovered for fraudulent misrepresentation only if there is actual dishonesty – *Derry v Peek* (1889)
- Damages may be recovered for negligent misrepresentation if the maker of the statement did not have reasonable grounds for believing it to be true – s2(1) Misrepresentation Act 1967
- Damages under s2(1) are calculated on tortious principles – *Andre et Cie v Ets Michel Blanc* (1977); *Chesneau v Interhome Ltd* (1983); *Sharneyford Supplies Ltd v Edge* (1985)
- The court has a discretion to order rescission or damages in lieu of rescission – ss2(1)(b) and 2(2) Misrepresentation Act 1967
- The court may order an account of profits and make allowances for deterioration – *Erlanger v New Sombrero Phosphate Co* (1878)
- Rescission would include an indemnity against obligations necessarily incurred through entering the contract – *Whittington v Seale-Hayne* (1900)

Suggested Answer

One must advise Kate whether she has any claim against Joanna for (a) breach of contract and (b) misrepresentation as a result of the statements made by Joanna prior to Kate's purchase of the shop and, if so, what remedies are available to Kate.

First, as to breach of contract, Joanna made three statements to Kate: in relation to the demand for health foods, the position vis-à-vis the local authority health inspectors, and the profitability of the shop. Whether any or all of those statements can be regarded as terms of the contract of sale between Joanna and Kate depends upon the intention of the parties: *Heilbut, Symons & Co v Buckleton* (1913), *Oscar Chess Ltd v Williams* (1957) and *Dick Bentley Productions Ltd v Harold Smith (Motors) Ltd* (1965). The sort of matters to which the court will have regard are the importance of the truth of the statement, the time which elapsed between the making of the statement and the conclusion of the contract; whether, if the contract was reduced to writing, the

4 Misrepresentation, Duress and Undue Influence – Answers

statement was included or omitted; and whether the maker of the statement was in a better position to know the truth.

Whilst it is difficult to be categorical on such matters, in the present case it is likely that the court would regard the statements made by Joanna as mere representations rather than terms of the contract; having regard to their form and character they do not look like statements which could have been reasonably understood to have contractual force. The contrary is not unarguable but on balance one must advise Kate that the statements were not terms of the contract.

Next, as to misrepresentation, each statement will be considered in turn. As to Joanna's statement concerning the demand for health foods, at first sight this might appear not to be an actionable misrepresentation as it is a statement of opinion concerning the future behaviour of the market for health foods. However, it is not the case that a representation of opinion can never be an actionable misrepresentation of fact. Where the maker of a statement of opinion is in a better position to know the truth, he may be taken to have impliedly represented that he knew facts to justify his opinion: *Smith* v *Land* and *House Property Corporation* (1884) and *Brown* v *Raphael* (1958). If such facts do not exist, he is guilty of a misrepresentation. Here, it is submitted, Joanna's first statement falls within this head of liability. As the owner of the shop she was in a position to know whether demand would increase or not, and the evidence known to her was that demand was falling, not rising. Accordingly, she has made a false statement of fact addressed to Kate. Providing this statement induced Kate to purchase the shop, in the sense that it was one reason for her doing so (*Edgington* v *Fitzmaurice* (1895)), she has a claim for misrepresentation.

As to the statement concerning there being no risk of trouble from health inspectors, it is submitted that this too is an actionable misrepresentation. Clearly, it is false, as the subsequent visit from the inspector has shown, and it is a statement of mixed fact and law and accordingly actionable: *Cooper* v *Phibbs* (1867). Misrepresentations as to the general law are not actionable (*Beattie* v *Lord Ebury* (1872)), but statements applying law to a particular set of facts are capable of being actionable: *Cooper*. Again, providing the requirement of inducement is satisfied, as on the facts it almost certainly will be, the second statement is also an actionable misrepresentation.

As to the profitability of the shop, it is submitted that this also is an actionable misrepresentation. Joanna's statement that it made 'up to £1,000 profit per week' is literally true, in that any profit below that figure is covered by the statement. However, this is a case in which the statement is a misleading half-truth (*Dimmock* v *Hallett* (1866)), since it conveys the impression that the shop regularly made a profit of around £1,000 when the true figure was far less. Nor does it matter that Kate did not inspect the accounts, because a representee is under no duty to verify the accuracy of the representation made: *Redgrave* v *Hurd* (1881).

In summary, on actionability, one's advice to Kate is that all three statements constitute actionable misrepresentations.

Next we must consider the remedies available. First, damages. The availability of the remedy of damages depends upon the nature of the misrepresentation committed, namely whether it was fraudulent, negligent or innocent. On the facts there is insufficient evidence to warrant a plea of fraud. As the speech of Lord Herschell in *Derry v Peek* (1889) made clear, the essence of fraud is dishonesty and there is no proper evidence here of dishonesty on the part of Joanna.

On the other hand, there is probably a good claim for damages for negligent misrepresentation in that it is difficult to see how Joanna can establish that she had reasonable grounds for believing all three representations to be true. Certainly the first and the third appear to have been made negligently, which would enable Kate to recover damages under s2(1) of the Misrepresentation Act 1967. Section 2(1) imposes an absolute obligation on the representor not to make statements unless he has reasonable grounds for believing them to be true, and the burden of proof is on the representor to establish these reasonable grounds.

If, as seems likely, Joanna cannot discharge this burden, Kate is entitled to damages under s2(1) calculated according to tortious out of pocket principles: *Andre et Cie v Ets Michel Blanc* (1977), *Chesneau v Interhome Ltd* (1983) and *Sharneyford Supplies Ltd v Edge* (1985). Kate is entitled to the difference between the contract price and the value of the business that she actually bought.

For completeness on negligence, one must add that it is unlikely that Kate could establish that a *Hedley Byrne & Co Ltd v Heller and Partners* (1964) type special relationship existed between her and Joanna so as to enable her to recover damages in tort for negligent misstatement, but in the light of her strong claim under s2(1) of the 1967 Act this does not much matter.

In addition to damages, Kate may well wish to rescind the contract. This involves restoring the parties to their respective pre-contractual positions, and is effected by the representee giving notice thereof to the representor. The fact that the contract between Kate and Joanna has been executed is no longer a bar to rescission: s1(b) of the 1967 Act. Subject to the court's discretion under s2(2) referred to above, this seems an eminently suitable case for rescission providing Kate acts speedily to avoid the transaction. Although rescission involves restitutio in integrum, the court is concerned to put the parties in broadly, rather than precisely, their pre-contractual positions and can, if necessary, order an account of profits and make allowances for deterioration: *Erlanger v New Sombrero Phosphate Co* (1878).

If Kate is permitted to rescind, she will recover the purchase price paid to Joanna, and the shop will be re-conveyed to the latter. Kate will also be entitled to an indemnity against obligations necessarily incurred by her as a result of having entered into the contract, which would include rates and other burdens imposed on an occupier of property (*Whittington v Seale-Hayne* (1900)), but this is a narrower form of financial relief than the remedy of damages.

In conclusion, Kate has a good claim for negligent misrepresentation for which she should recover damages under s2(1) of the 1967 Act and should also be able to rescind the contract.

4 Misrepresentation, Duress and Undue Influence – Answers

SUGGESTED ANSWER TO QUESTION TWO

General Comment

This problem also concerns the sale of a small business by a sole proprietor. As with similar questions, a successful answer requires a highly structured approach. It is essential to plan the points to be made in the answer before beginning writing and to avoid giving too much detail concerning the facts of the cases cited.

Key Points

- The statements made by Victor may be contractual terms – *Heilbut, Symons & Co v Buckleton* (1913); *Oscar Chess Ltd v Williams* (1957); *Dick Bentley Productions Ltd v Harold Smith (Motors) Ltd* (1965)
- 'Mere puff' does not constitute a misrepresentation – *Dimmock v Hallett* (1866)
- A misleading half-truth is actionable – *Dimmock v Hallett* (1866)
- Failure to correct the misleading impression where a statement true at the time of making has become untrue, may be actionable – *With v Flanagan* (1936)
- The person to whom a statement is made is under no duty to ascertain its accuracy for himself – *Redgrave v Hurd* (1881)
- While a mere statement of opinion is not actionable it is a misrepresentation if the maker implies he had facts to support his opinion or could not possibly have held that opinion – *Bisset v Wilkinson* (1927); *Smith v Land and House Property Corporation* (1884); *Esso Petroleum Co Ltd v Mardon* (1976)
- The misrepresentation must have induced the contract – *Edgington v Fitzmaurie* (1885)
- Damages for fraudulent misrepresentation will only be available if there is actual dishonesty – *Derry v Peek* (1889)
- Damages may be awarded for negligent misrepresentation but only if the maker of the statement cannot show he had reasonable grounds for believing it – s2(1) Misrepresentation Act 1967; *Howard Marine & Dredging Co Ltd v A Ogden & Sons (Excavations) Ltd* (1978)
- Damages are calculated according to tortious principles – *Sharneyford Supplies Ltd v Edge* (1985)
- The court may award rescission or damages in lieu of rescission – s2(1)(b) and (2) Misrepresentation Act 1967

Suggested Answer

Victor has made certain statements to Percy in connection with the purchase of the business. First, it is necessary to discuss whether these statements are terms of the contract or mere representations. The primary consideration is the intention of the parties: *Heilbut, Symons & Co v Buckleton* (1913), *Oscar Chess Ltd v Williams* (1957), *Dick Bentley Productions Ltd v Harold Smith (Motors) Ltd* (1956). The court will have regard to a number of factors; the stage at which the statements were made, whether the statements were followed by a reduction of the terms to writing, whether the person making the statements had special knowledge as compared to the other party.

It is submitted that, in view of the nature of the present statements, the court is more likely to construe them as representations rather than as contractual terms. It is, therefore, necessary to consider whether the statements amount to actionable misrepresentations. It is convenient to analyse the statements into three; the statement that the business was 'in excellent order', the assurance as to profits, and the forecast as to demand. Each statement will be considered in turn.

The statement that the business was 'in excellent order' seems, at first sight, to be what is regarded as a 'mere puff'; a simple laudatory statement made about the business will not be construed as a representation: *Dimmock* v *Hallett* (1866). In the present context, however, this statement might amount to more than a mere puff, particularly in light of the warning Victor had received from his accountant. The statement as to profits is literally correct. Whilst silence of itself does not amount to a representation, the failure to disclose the recent figures would appear to make that statement a misleading half-truth: *Dimmock* v *Hallett*. Furthermore, even if the recent figures only emerged after the statement was made, the failure to disclose the likely downturn in business will make the statement a representation: *With* v *O'Flanagan* (1936). The fact that Percy did not avail himself of the opportunity of inspecting the books does not matter: *Redgrave* v *Hurd* (1881).

The third statement involves a forecast of future demand. Whilst this might be regarded as a mere statement of opinion, which is not construed as a representation (*Bisset* v *Wilkinson* (1927)), an expression of opinion does amount to a representation where the person giving the opinion is in a position to know and could not have reasonably held that opinion: *Smith* v *Land and House Property Corporation* (1884). In *Esso Petroleum Co Ltd* v *Mardon* (1976) the Court of Appeal held that a forecast made by the petrol company was, in view of their special skill and knowledge, a warranty. However, it has been argued here that in the present context the statement will amount to a representation, not a contractual term. It might be suggested that, in view of Victor's illness, which necessitated the business being run by a manager, Victor's statement is only an expression of opinion, as he had at the relevant time no special knowledge. This suggestion cannot be supported; Victor is the proprietor of the firm which had received a warning from the accountant.

Accordingly, though there may be some doubt as to the first statement, it does appear that there have been representations, which are false. Provided that they induced Percy to buy the business, in the sense that they were one reason for his doing so - *Edgington* v *Fitzmaurice* (1885) - an action for misrepresentation will be available to him.

We next must consider the remedies Percy could seek. This depends on whether the misrepresentations were fraudulent, negligent or innocent. There is not sufficient evidence here to establish fraud. The essence of fraud is dishonesty, as the speech of Lord Herschell made clear in *Derry* v *Peek* (1889), and the burden of proving fraud is on Percy. On the facts given it does not appear that he could discharge that burden.

For Percy to be able to claim damages the provisions of s2(1) of the

4 Misrepresentation, Duress and Undue Influence – Answers 73

Misrepresentation Act 1967 must be invoked. Section 2(1) will entitle Percy to damages unless Victor can prove that he not only believed in the truth of the representation, but had reasonable grounds for doing so, up to the time the contract was made. Despite his absence from the business through illness, it seems likely that Victor cannot discharge the burden of proof imposed on him by the Act. In particular, by ignoring, or not making himself aware of the accountant's warning, Victor is deprived of the averment that his belief is based on reasonable grounds. Support for this view can be gained from the majority judgements of the Court of Appeal in *Howard Marine & Dredging Co Ltd v A Ogden & Sons (Excavations) Ltd* (1978). In assessing damages the tortious measure would be employed: *Sharneyford Supplies Ltd v Edge* (1985).

One might add that Percy would be unlikely to maintain a claim in negligence at common law; the special relationship required by *Hedley Byrne & Co Ltd v Heller & Partners* (1964) does not appear to exist between the two parties. But, as it has been submitted that Percy has a claim under s2(1) of the 1967 Act, this is of little concern.

In addition to a claim for damages Percy will be entitled to rescission of the contract, whether the misrepresentations were negligent or innocent. They will be innocent only if Victor has proved his belief on reasonable grounds as required by s2(1). The fact that the contract between the parties has been executed is no bar to rescission, s1(b). The court has a discretion under s2(2) to award damages in lieu of rescission, but nothing here suggests why the court would exercise that discretion. Provided that there are no other bars to rescission, affirmation, delay or the acquisition of third party rights, Percy would succeed in obtaining rescission.

SUGGESTED ANSWER TO QUESTION THREE

General Comment

In this question there are three sets of facts and due weight should be given to each of the possibilities. A common mistake in answering a question of this kind is to write generally about the situation. A good candidate will, as instructed, structure the answer around advice to D and will examine each alternative set of facts in turn.

Key Points

- D may have an action against E for breach of the implied term as to satisfactory quality – s14(2) Sale of Goods Act 1979 as amended by Sale and Supply of Goods Act 1994
- D has no action against E on the basis of the statement made by C since a misrepresentation must be made by a party to the contract
- D may have an action against C for negligent misstatement if he can prove a special relationship – *Hedley Byrne & Co Ltd v Heller and Partners Ltd* (1964)
- If E made the statement, D may have an action for damages for fraudulent misrepresentation against him if he can prove actual dishonesty – *Derry v Peek* (1889)
- Alternatively, the court may order rescission or damages in lieu for negligent

misrepresentation if E cannot show reasonable grounds for believing the statement – s2(1) and (2) Misrepresentation Act 1967
- If E were a private seller (and did not make the statement) then s14 would not apply and D would have no remedy

Suggested Answer

On the first scenario presented in this problem E has not made any statement regarding the piece of china. There can be no question of his liability for misrepresentation. (It is not suggested that C was acting as E's agent). As E was selling in the course of a business, however, he may have incurred liability to D under s14(2) Sale of Goods Act 1979 (as amended by the Sale and Supply of Goods Act 1994). Section 14(2) provides that there is an implied term that the goods are of satisfactory quality. Under s14(2A) of the Act (as amended):

> 'goods are of satisfactory quality if they meet the standard that a reasonable person would regard as satisfactory, taking account of any description of the goods, the price (if relevant) and all the other relevant circumstances.'

In the absence of fuller information it is not possible to say whether there has been a breach of the implied term. Mention should be made of the possibility of C having incurred liability to D for a negligent misstatement under the principle of *Hedley Byrne & Co Ltd* v *Heller and Partners Ltd* (1964). However, there is no suggestion of negligence on C's part, nor of any special relationship between C and D. It may well be that the contract between D and E was concluded as a result of a mistake as to the quality of the china. It is not clear, however, whether the mistake was unilateral or common. Without further information this aspect cannot be usefully discussed.

Two further, alternative, hypotheses remain to be examined. If the statement had been made by E he would have incurred liability for misrepresentation. This would afford D the right of rescission, provided that right had not been barred, as set out above. Even if the misrepresentation were not fraudulent D may be entitled to damages, as it is difficult to see that E, as an antique dealer, could discharge the onus imposed on him by s2(1) Misrepresentation Act 1967. The remedy of damages for misrepresentation has been discussed in part (a) of this question.

If E was a private seller it would appear that D would be without a remedy. Section 14(2) Sale of Goods Act 1979 would not apply. The only avenue that D could explore would be the law relating to mistake. But, as previously suggested, there is insufficient information on this point.

SUGGESTED ANSWER TO QUESTION FOUR

General Comment

This problem question focuses on terms and representations and remedies in relation to either. It deals with a purely private sale so the question of the terms implied under the Sale of Goods Act does not arise. The examiner would be looking for a clear analysis in relation of each of the statements made and an explanation of the remedies available to J.

Key Points

- 'Mere puff' is not actionable – *Dimmock* v *Hallett* (1866)
- Damages may be available for breach of contract if the statements can be shown to be terms of the contract – *Heilbut, Symons & Co* v *Buckleton* (1913); *Oscar Chess Ltd* v *Williams* (1957); *Dick Bentley Productions Ltd* v *Harold Smith (Motors) Ltd* (1965); *Routledge* v *McKay* (1954)
- A statement of opinion may be actionable as misrepresentation if the maker could not reasonably have held such an opinion – *Bisset* v *Wilkinson* (1927); *Smith* v *Land and House Property Corporation* (1884); *Esso Petroleum Co Ltd* v *Mardon* (1976)
- The court may order rescission for negligent misrepresentation or damages in lieu – ss2(1) and 2(2) Misrepresentation Act 967; *Sharneyford Supplies Ltd* v *Edge*
- Damages may be awarded for fraudulent misrepresentation if actual dishonesty can be proved – *Derry* v *Peek* (1889); *Doyle* v *Olby (Ironmongers) Ltd* (1969)
- If there was a special relationship between X and J, damages for negligent misstatement might be awarded – *Hedley Byrne & Co Ltd* v *Heller and Partners Ltd* (1964)

Suggested Answer

X made a number of oral statements to J prior to the sale of the house. The statement that the house was in 'first class condition throughout' appears to be a 'mere puff' and is without legal effect. A vague, eulogistic statement is not actionable: *Dimmock* v *Hallett* (1866).

The further statements with regard to the central heating and that the house was quiet do appear to be more precise statements of fact. It must first be considered whether these statements are contractual terms or 'mere' representations. The question is one of the intention of the parties deduced from all the evidence: *Heilbut, Symons & Co* v *Buckleton* (1913); *Oscar Chess Ltd* v *Williams* (1957); *Dick Bentley Productions Ltd* v *Harold Smith (Motors) Ltd* (1965). The court will employ various criteria in determining whether a statement is a contractual term or a representation. One of these is that if the contract is subsequently reduced to writing, and the statement is not incorporated in the written document, this would indicate that the statement was not intended to be a contractual term: *Routledge* v *McKay* (1954). The contract for the sale of the house would have been in writing. The statements are, moreover, not couched in contractual terms and it is submitted, therefore, that they must be dealt with on the basis that they are, if anything, representations.

For a statement to amount to an actionable misrepresentation it must be:

1   one of fact;
2   false;
3   addressed to the party misled; and
4   a substantial factor in inducing the representee to enter into the contract.

The statement that X had installed a new central heating system that was safe appears to meet all these requirements. It is, therefore, an actionable misrepresentation. The statement that the house was always quiet is perhaps more questionable. It might be considered to be a statement not of fact, but of opinion. But X must be presumed to have known of the conduct of his neighbours and he could not reasonably have held such an opinion. Contrast the case of *Bisset* v *Wilkinson* (1927) with the cases of *Smith* v *Land and House Property Corporation* (1884) and *Esso Petroleum Co Ltd* v *Mardon* (1976). In the former case the particular statement was merely an opinion and did not, therefore, amount to a representation: in the latter two cases, because the parties concerned were deemed to have knowledge of the particular facts, the 'opinions' were regarded as representations. It seems that the statement here would be regarded as a representation in view of X's knowledge. It clearly meets the other requirements for an actionable misrepresentation.

It is not clear what the relevance is of the of the local authority having granted permission for the house next door to be used as described. It is not evident that X was aware that this was going to or might happen. Even if he were so aware, the failure to disclose this would not of itself constitute a misrepresentation. Silence does not amount to a misrepresentation, but X's failure to disclose the eventuality would strengthen the view that his statement that the house was quiet is an actionable misrepresentation.

As there are actionable misrepresentations, what must be now considered are the remedies available to J. Rescission is an available remedy whether the misrepresentation is fraudulent, negligent or innocent. The fact that the contract has been performed is not a bar to rescission – s1(b) Misrepresentation Act 1967. Nor do there appear to be any equitable bars to rescission. Under s2(2) of the Act the court has a discretion to award damages in lieu of rescission (where the misrepresentation is otherwise than fraudulent), but there is nothing to indicate such an exercise of the discretion here.

The further possible remedy is damages. This depends on the nature of the misrepresentation. A remedy in damages is always available for fraudulent misrepresentation. But the onus of proving fraud is on the party alleging it. It is a difficult burden to discharge. In *Derry* v *Peek* (1889) Lord Herschell said that fraud is proved when it is shown that a false representation has been made knowingly, or without belief in its truth, or recklessly, careless whether it be true or false. It is not possible to advise J that he will be able to establish fraud on X's part. If he were able to do so then X would be liable to compensate him for all the losses flowing directly from the misrepresentations. If the decision of the local authority which resulted in the fall in value of the property could be laid at X's door then X would be liable for that loss in addition to his liability for the cost of repairing the central heating: *Doyle* v *Olby (Ironmongers) Ltd* (1969).

However, if J cannot establish fraud, and it is doubtful whether he can do so, he should be advised to pursue a claim for damages under s2(1) of the Act. This sub-section provides that where a party has suffered loss as a result of a misrepresentation and the representor would be liable in damages if the representation had been made fraudulently, then the representor will also be so liable unless he proves that he had reasonable ground to believe and did believe up to the time the contract was made that the facts represented were true. This shifts the burden of proof to X, and it is difficult to see how he could discharge this burden. The measure of damages under s2(1) is the

4 Misrepresentation, Duress and Undue Influence – Answers 77

tortious measure – see the judgment of Mervyn Davies J in *Sharneyford Supplies Ltd* v *Edge* (1985). This means that J would be able to recover his expenses, the cost of the new central heating, but not his loss of bargain, the fall in value of the property.

There does not appear to be any special relationship between X and J which would justify an action for negligent misstatement under *Hedley Byrne & Co Ltd* v *Heller & Partners Ltd* (1964). In any event, as the basis of damages would, in such an action, be the same as that under s2(1), this would not take the matter any further. If X is able to discharge the onus of proof imposed on him by s2(1) then the misrepresentations would be wholly innocent and he would not be liable in damages. But it is submitted that this is unlikely.

SUGGESTED ANSWER TO QUESTION FIVE

General Comment

Here is a question which, again, requires the candidate to discuss the remedies available for misrepresentation although it does not use the word 'remedies'. A sound answer would demonstrate a complete knowledge of the remedies available together with the ability to evaluate them in comparison with one another.

Key Points

Rescission
- Bars to rescission
- Affirmation – *Long* v *Lloyd* (1958); *Peyman* v *Lanjani* (1985)
- Lapse of time – *Leaf* v *International Galleries* (1952)
- Impossibility of restitution – *Clarke* v *Dickson* (1858); *Armstrong* v *Jackson* (1917)
- Third party rights – *Phillips* v *Brooks* (1919); s23 Sale of Goods Act 1979
- Communication of intention to rescind – *Car and International Finance Co Ltd* v *Caldwell* (1965)
- Discretion to award damages in lieu – s2(2) Misrepresentation Act 1967

Damages
- Damages for deceit – *East* v *Maurer* (1991); *Doyle* v *Olby (Ironmongers) Ltd* (1969); *Derry* v *Peek* (1889)
- Damages under s2(1) Misrepresentation Act 1967 – s2(1); *Royscott Trust Ltd* v *Rogerson* (1991); *Whittington* v *Seale-Hayne* (1900)

Suggested Answer

The possible remedies for an actionable misrepresentation are (a) rescission, and (b) damages – though, as will be seen, damages may not always be available and the injured party may be limited to a claim for indemnity.

Rescission
Rescission, setting the contract aside and restoring the parties to their previous position, is a possible remedy for the party who was induced to enter into the contract as a result

of misrepresentation of fact. This would in most instances prove an adequate remedy for the injured party, but certain bars to rescission might deprive him of this remedy. The bars to rescission are: (1) affirmation; (2) lapse of time; (3) impossibility of restitution; and (4) the intervention of third party rights.

1 *Affirmation*
If the injured party has affirmed the contract, that is continued with the contract after he has discovered the falsity of the representation, rescission will be denied him: *Long* v *Lloyd* (1958). However, he will not be deprived of the right to rescind because, knowing of the facts which gave rise to the right to rescind, he proceeded with the contract, unless he also knew that he had the right to rescind: *Peyman* v *Lanjani* (1985).

2 *Lapse of time*
In *Leaf* v *International Galleries* (1952) the plaintiff discovered the falsity of the representation five years after the purchase of a picture. Denning LJ observed that the buyer had accepted the picture, had had ample opportunity for examination of it, and time to see if the representation was fulfilled. Five years having elapsed without notice of rejection, he could not then claim to rescind.

3 *Impossibility of restitution*
When a party exercises his right to rescind he must be in a position to put the parties into their original state before the contract: *Clarke* v *Dickson* (1858). Destruction or alteration of the subject matter would deprive him of the right. The mere fact, however, that the subject matter has decreased in value would not operate as a bar to rescission; that might well be the very reason why the injured party wishes to exercise the right: *Armstrong* v *Jackson* (1917).

4 *Intervention of third-party rights*
This situation most commonly arises where the owner of goods has been induced to part with them as a result of the misrepresentation (usually fraudulent) of the other party to the contract. The contract is voidable at the instance of the original owner of the goods, but he must avoid the transaction before an innocent third party has acquired the goods for value: *Phillips* v *Brooks* (1919). (See also s23 Sale of Goods Act 1979.)

In the normal course of events the party electing to rescind must communicate his intention to do so to the other contracting party. Where he cannot find that other party the taking of all possible steps to regain the goods might constitute effective rescission: *Car and Universal Finance Co Ltd* v *Caldwell* (1965).

Two further bars to rescission have been removed by the Misrepresentation Act (MA) 1967. Under s1 it is not a bar to rescission that the representation has become a term of the contract, or that the contract has been executed. The remedy of rescission might operate harshly against the party guilty of the misrepresentation if such misrepresentation were innocent. Under s2(2) MA 1967 the court has the discretion to award damages in lieu of rescission for a misrepresentation, otherwise than fraudulent, if it considers it equitable to do so.

Damages
The availability of damages depends on the nature of the misrepresentation. Damages would be available if the misrepresentation were fraudulent; the injured party would sue in tort for deceit. The measure of damages is the tortious one: *East* v *Maurer* (1991), but it is not open to the tortfeasor to claim that he could not reasonably have foreseen the the loss incurred: *Doyle* v *Olby (Ironmongers) Ltd* (1969). The burden of proving fraud is a difficult one to discharge - see *Derry* v *Peek* (1889) for the requirements - but the necessity of alleging fraud is obviated by s2(l) MA 1967 (see below).

Prior to the MA 1967 only two categories of misrepresentation were recognised in our law; fraudulent and innocent. For an innocent misrepresentation damages were not available. Section 2(1) introduced the 'fiction of fraud' whereby even if the misrepresentation were not fraudulent, the person induced by it might recover damages, unless the person making the representation proves that he had reasonable ground to believe and did believe up to the time the contract was made that the facts represented were true. This section reverses the onus of proof; if fraud is alleged the onus of proof is on the person alleging it. It has now been established by the Court of Appeal that the measure of damages under s2(1) is the same as that for fraud: *Royscott Trust Ltd* v *Rogerson* (1991).

If the party making the representation discharges the burden imposed on him by s2(1) the misrepresentation might be termed wholly innocent, and the injured party would not then be entitled to damages, but only to an indemnity; that is the expenses he lost which the contract obliged him to incur: *Whittington* v *Seale-Hayne* (1900).

Whilst the MA 1967 has removed some of the anomalies in the remedies available for misrepresentation certain difficulties remain. An innocent party might lose the right to rescind through no fault of his own, and in the event of the person making the misrepresentation proving what is required of him under s2(1), he would not be entitled to damages. Even if he does obtain damages the measure of damages is the one in tort, not in contract, so that he would not recover for loss of expectation.

5

Exclusion Clauses

Introduction

Excluding or limiting clauses in contracts is a very popular area indeed, with examiners tending to favour a problem question approach. Often the effect of a number of clauses is required to be considered within the same question. Candidates should approach this area in a methodical fashion, demonstrating an ability to apply first the common law rules for incorporation of exclusion clauses into a contract and their general construction, then the effect of the relevant clauses when the Unfair Contract Terms Act 1977 is applied, especially when the liability sought to be excluded concerns liability for negligence. Thirdly, the effect (if relevant) of the Unfair Terms in Consumer Contracts Regulations 1994 must be considered.

Questions

INTERROGRAMS

1 What is the situation when the clause upon which the defendant relies to relieve him of liability is an indemnity?
2 What is the significance of an exclusion clause being printed on the back of a ticket?
3 Does a fundamental breach deprive the defendant of the right to rely on clauses which exclude or limit his liability?

QUESTION ONE

Henry, a bus conductor, makes furniture in his spare time. After seeing them advertised in a magazine, he ordered one of Ian's 'Handyman' portable work-benches. Soon afterwards Henry received a letter thanking him for the order and saying that delivery would be made 'subject to our usual conditions'. Two weeks later the workbench was delivered together with a sales note setting out Ian's 'Conditions of Sale'.

The first time Henry used it, the workbench collapsed. Henry fell and suffered serious injuries; an inflammable liquid he was using was spilled and a fire started which caused extensive damage to his house. Ian's conditions of sale state that all conditions and warranties are expressly excluded and that Ian is not to be liable for any loss or damage, however caused.

Advise Henry. Would your answer be different if Henry sold the furniture he makes at a stall in the town's market?

London University LLB Examination
(for external students) Elements of the Law of Contract June 1985 Q3

QUESTION TWO

Tom, a businessman, regularly stayed at the Hotel Splendide whenever he visited London on business. He stayed there last week. As usual there was a notice on the back of his room door stating that 'Neither the Hotel Splendide nor any of its management or other employees will be responsible for any personal injury, loss or other damage to guests or their property howsoever caused.'

The day after he arrived Tom's car was stolen from the hotel car park after a porter who was parking the car had left his key in the ignition and the door unlocked. On hearing of this and going to investigate, Tom slipped on the highly polished corridor outside his room and suffered considerable injury to his back, and his valuable wristwatch struck the floor and was destroyed.

Advise Tom.

London University LLB Examination
(for external students) Elements of the Law of Contract June 1986 Q8

QUESTION THREE

Cecil, a travel agent, ordered a word processor from Beta Ltd for his office. He signed the order form, which provided that Beta Ltd would replace or repair free of charge any goods sold by them which proved to be defective within nine months of purchase but were otherwise not to be under any liability whatsoever for loss or damage caused by defects in the goods.

After Cecil had used the word processor for a month he was so pleased with it that he bought a similar one for his personal use at home. The order form contained the same provision as before concerning Beta Ltd's liability for defective goods.

Shortly afterwards the word processor in Cecil's office developed a fault which caused the loss of the entire records of holiday bookings for July 1989. Cecil had to hire extra staff to do the work of reconfirming the bookings. Soon afterwards the word processor in Cecil's home suffered an electrical breakdown. Cecil received a severe electric shock and was unable to work for six weeks.

Advise Cecil.

London University LLB Examination
(for external students) Elements of the Law of Contract June 1989 Q7

QUESTION FOUR

P who carried on business at Brighton sold a 1969 MG sports car to Q for £5,000. It had been advertised as 'Fully restored'. Q was driving from P's garage to Q's home in Newcastle when eight miles from his home the steering failed and Q crashed into the window of R's shop. The car was a write-off and Q was injured. The sale agreement contained the following clauses:

> '31. It is understood that any statement which is not part of this written agreement is not to be treated as having induced the contract.

32. It is agreed that the vehicle is bought after a thorough examination by the buyer. The vehicle is bought as seen and the seller is not liable for any patent or latent defects.
33. It is agreed that the buyer has not relied on the seller's skill and judgement.
34. In the event of breach the buyer shall have no right to reject the goods or repudiate the contract.
35. It is understood that any damages payable under this contract to the buyer or any other person claiming as a result of the sale to the buyer shall be limited to £500.'

Q is demanding compensation from P. Advise P.

London University LLB Examination
(for external students) Elements of the Law of Contract June 1991 Q3

QUESTION FIVE

Discuss the effect of the Unfair Terms in Consumer Contracts Regulations 1994 on contractual exemption clauses, making particular reference to its relationship with the Unfair Contracts Terms Act 1977.

Written by the Editor June 1998

Answers

ANSWERS TO INTERROGRAMS

1   An indemnity clause is a contractual provision that one party will reimburse the other for any losses sustained by him. Indemnities may be as onerous as exclusions and, in some cases have been used in an attempt to circumvent the law on exclusion clauses by providing that the defendant will be reimbursed costs of action and even damages.

   Section 4 Unfair Contract Terms Act 1977 applies to indemnity clauses. It provides relief where the indemnity is against business liability and the person who provides the indemnity is a consumer. The clause will not be effective in respect of any liability incurred by the other for negligence or breach of contract unless it satisfies the requirement of reasonableness. The section applies whether the liability is that of the person to be indemnified or vicarious or whether it is to the person dealing as a consumer or to someone else.

2   Where an exclusion clause is printed on the back of a ticket, the question is whether or not it has been incorporated into the contract. Reasonable steps must be taken to bring an exclusion to the notice of the other party before the contract is made. It therefore follows that if the ticket in question is issued after the conclusion of the contract, this rule will not have been satisfied.

   There are a number of cases on the point. In *Chapleton* v *Barry UDC* (1940), the plaintiff was injured when a deckchair collapsed. He had paid for the deckchair and had been given a ticket. A clause excluding the Council from liability was printed on the reverse. It was held that the contract had been concluded before the plaintiff received the ticket. Similarly, in *Thornton* v *Shoe Lane Parking Ltd* (1971) the customer at the entrance to an automatic car park put money into a machine which issued a ticket to him. It was held that the contract was concluded at that point and that terms printed on the ticket and displayed at the exit were not part of the contract. In contrast, however, are cases where the taking of a ticket has been held to be acceptance of the offer, for example *Thompson* v *London Midland & Scottish Railway Co* (1930). The explanation of the distinction, given by Lord Denning in the *Thornton* case, is that the contract is concluded when the plaintiff is committed.

3 A fundamental breach is a breach which defeats the main purpose of the contract. It may or may not also be a breach of a fundamental term. At one time, the courts considered that there was a rule of law that an exclusion clause could not protect a party against liability for a fundamental breach. However, the House of Lords in *Suisse Atlantique Société d'Armament Maritime* v *Rotterdamsche Kolen Centrale* (1967) established that this was merely a rule of construction and that an exclusion clause could be effective to cover a fundamental breach, provided that there were clear words.

The later case of *Harbutt's Plasticine Ltd* v *Wayne Tank and Pumps Co Ltd* (1970) took the older viewpoint that a breach of contract by one party accepted by the other as discharging him from further obligation brought the contract to an end including any exclusion clause in it. However, in *Photo Production Ltd* v *Securicor Transport Ltd* (1980), the principle in *Suisse Atlantique* was reaffirmed. In *George Mitchell Ltd* v *Finney Lock Seeds* (1983), Lord Bridge confirmed that this had given '… the final quietus to the doctrine that a "fundamental breach" of contract deprived the party in breach of the benefit of clauses in the contract excluding or limiting his liability.'

SUGGESTED ANSWER TO QUESTION ONE

General Comment

This problem presents two alternatives each requiring different considerations. The first centres on the effect of the Unfair Contracts Terms Act 1977 on exclusions in contracts between a business and a consumer. A successful answer will correctly cite the relevant provisions, accurately summarise the requirements contained in them, and apply these to the facts in the question. The second alternative requires consideration of the case law as to incorporation and construction of the clause followed by application of the 'business liability' provisions of the Act.

Key Points

- Implied conditions as to satisfactory quality and fitness for purpose – ss13 and 14 Sale of Goods Act 1979 as amended by s1 Sale and Supply of Goods Act 1994
- 'Dealing as a consumer' – ss6(2) and 12 UCTA
- Is the transaction on Ian's standard terms of business? – *Partridge* v *Crittenden* (1968); *Butler Machine Tool Co Ltd* v *Ex-cell-o Corp* (1979); *Brogden* v *Metropolitan Railway* (1877); *Parker* v *South Eastern Railway* (1877)
- Does the clause cover the liability in question? – *L'Estrange* v *Graucob Ltd* (1934); *Photo Production Ltd* v *Securicor Transport Ltd* (1980); *George Mitchell Ltd* v *Finney Lock Seeds* (1983); *Joseph Travers & Sons Ltd* v *Cooper* (1915)

- In a business-to-business transaction the clause will be effective if 'reasonable' – s6(3) UCTA
- Definition of 'reasonableness' – s11(1) UCTA
- Matters the court will take into consideration – *R W Green Ltd* v *Cade Bros Farms* (1978); *George Mitchell Ltd* v *Finney Lock Seeds* (1983); Schedule 2 UCTA
- Section 2 UCTA applies to any claims by Henry for negligence

Suggested Answer

In advising Henry as to his rights against Ian, one must consider the effect, if any, in law of the exclusion clause contained in the 'Conditions of Sale' on Ian's sale note. Ordinarily one would consider first whether the clause was incorporated as a term of the contract between Ian and Henry and, secondly, if it was, whether on its true construction it applies to the breach of contract which has occurred, before proceeding to examine the possible application of the Unfair Contract Terms Act 1977. On the unusual facts of this case, it is submitted that the 1977 Act disposes of the matter entirely, for reasons which will be explained. For the same reasons, it is unnecessary to consider the Unfair Terms in Consumer Contracts Regulations 1994, which are complementary to the Unfair Contract Terms Act and apply only where the injured party neither makes the contract in the course of a business nor holds himself out as doing so.

Assuming, against Henry, that the clause was incorporated and on its true construction did apply to protect Ian, one must then consider the 1977 Act. The Act applies to this contract because the liability sought to be excluded by Ian is business liability: s1(3). Further, the contract is one for the sale of goods into which certain conditions are implied by ss13 and 14 of the Sale of Goods Act 1979 (as amended by Sale and Supply of Goods Act 1994), namely that the goods should correspond with their contractual description, be of satisfactory quality, and be reasonably fit for the purpose for which the goods are bought. It is submitted that Ian is in clear breach of s14(2) and (3) of the 1979 Act, and probably s13(1) as well, because the workbench collapsed the first time Henry used it. Such a product cannot possibly be said either to be of satisfactory quality or reasonably fit for the purpose for which it was intended. Henry therefore has a good claim for damages for breach of these implied conditions.

The exclusion or restriction of liability for breach of, inter alia, ss13 and 14 of the 1979 Act is controlled by s6 of the 1977 Act. Section 6(2) renders clauses excluding or restricting such liability totally ineffective as against a person 'dealing as consumer'. This expression is defined in s12 of the 1977 Act and, in the present case, subparagraphs (a)–(c) of s12(1) must be satisfied, namely that:

1 Henry did not make the contract in the course of a business nor held himself out as doing so;
2 Ian did make the contract in the course of a business;
3 the goods were of a type ordinarily supplied for private use or consumption.

The only doubt can arise in relation to (c). It is submitted that workbenches are goods which are ordinarily supplied for private use or consumption: 'do-it-yourself' is a common hobby and workbenches are frequently purchased by such persons. Further, it is likely that the court would construe the word 'ordinarily' as meaning 'commonly', rather than 'on the majority of occasions'; the 1977 Act is a protective statute which would be given a generous rather than a narrow construction, and in any event under s12(3) the burden of proof would be on Ian to show that Henry did not deal as a consumer. Thus, Henry has a claim for damages in respect of his loss.

On the alternative footing that Henry sells the furniture at a market stall different considerations arise and now one must discuss first, the possible incorporation of the clause and, secondly, its construction, before examining again the 1977 Act.

As to incorporation, it is vital to pinpoint the precise moment at which the contract is concluded. The machinery of formation is that Ian's advertisement in the magazine is an invitation to treat only: *Partridge v Crittenden* (1968). Henry's 'order' is a contractual offer, which Ian can accept or reject. By replying in the terms in which he did, Ian did not accept Henry's offer but himself made a counter-offer because his letter introduced new terms into the proposed transaction; namely his standard conditions of business: *Butler Machine Tool Co Ltd v Ex-cell-o Corporation (England) Ltd* (1979).

Although Henry does not expressly accept that counter-offer, in law he will be considered to have done so when the workbench was delivered to him together with a copy of Ian's conditions, and he accepted and used the bench: *Brogden v Metropolitan Railway Co* (1877). Moreover, providing the copy of Ian's terms were delivered to Henry in such a way as to give him reasonable notice of their contents, including the exclusion clause, Henry will be bound by them: *Parker v South Eastern Railway* (1877). In conclusion, on incorporation, whilst the position is not open and shut, it is very likely that the court will regard Ian's terms as forming a part of the contract between him and Henry.

The question of construction can be dealt with very shortly. Ian's exclusion clause is in blanket form and, as such, applies at common law to protect him from liability. A similar clause was upheld in *L'Estrange v Graucob Ltd* (1934). Since *Photo Production Ltd v Securicor Transport Ltd* (1980) and *George Mitchell (Chesterhall) Ltd v Finney Lock Seeds Ltd* (1983) it is settled law that there is a category of fundamental breaches of fundamental terms for which liability can never be excluded. Even if liability in negligence can be established against Ian, the words loss of damage 'however caused' were held in *Joseph Travers & Sons Ltd v Cooper* (1915) to exclude liability for negligence. Thus on the true construction of the clause, Ian is protected.

Turning again to the 1977 Act, on this alternative footing Ian will be able to establish that Henry was not dealing as consumer as defined in s12(1) because Henry bought the workbench for use in his business selling furniture at the market. The prohibition on excluding liability for breach of ss13 and 14 of the 1979 Act imposed by s6(2) of the 1977 Act therefore does not apply; instead s6(3) applies, and the clause will only be effective insofar as it satisfies the requirement of reasonableness set out in s11(1) of the 1977 Act. Before moving to s11(1) one should observe in passing that if Ian was guilty of negligence in the construction of the workbench, then s2 of the 1977 Act will apply to Henry's claim in tort. As to Henry's claim in respect of personal injuries, s2(1) would operate to render Ian's clause totally ineffective; in respect of the damage to the house s2(2) would once more subject the clause to the reasonableness test laid down in s11(1).

Since there is no evidence one way or the other on negligence this point will not be pursued further. The requirement of reasonableness is defined in s11(1) as being that the term shall have been a fair and reasonable one to be included having regard to the circumstances which were, or ought reasonably to have been, known to or in the contemplation of the parties when the contract was made. The language of the subsection is unequivocal: the enquiry is whether it was reasonable to include this clause in this contract, not whether it is reasonable to permit reliance on it.

The burden of proof is on Ian to persuade the court that the clause does satisfy the requirement of reasonableness, s11(1), and s11(2) further informs the court, in this case, to have regard to the guidelines specified in Sch 2 to the Act in considering whether or not the clause is reasonable. The material guidelines here are (a), (c) and (e) of Sch 2: (in short) the parties' respective bargaining strengths, Henry's knowledge or ignorance of the clause and whether it is a common one in the trade, and the fact that the workbench was a standard item and not a 'special order' from Henry. In addition, (*R W Green Ltd* v *Cade Bros Farms* (1978) and the *George Mitchell* case) decided under the Sale of Goods Act 1893 (as amended), indicate that the courts will also look at matters such as the availability of insurance to both parties, the size of their respective commercial concerns, and the scope of the clause; eg does it exclude all liability, including negligence, or merely certain types, or perhaps only restrict rather than exclude it altogether?

Advising on reasonableness under the 1977 Act is not an exact science. As Lord Bridge said in the *George Mitchell* case, what may appear reasonable to one judge may seem unreasonable to another, yet both decisions may be the result of the proper exercise of judicial discretion. As a matter of judgment, it is submitted that Ian's clause would not satisfy the requirement of reasonableness for the following reasons:

1 it is not referred to either in the magazine advertisement, or in the letter sent acknowledging Henry's order;
2 it is quite possible that Henry, although in law bound by the clause, was in fact unaware of it;
3 there was no bargaining between the parties;
4 the clause is too wide-ranging and all-embracing;
5 Ian ought to protect himself against liabilities of this nature by means of insurance.

On the alternative footing that Henry sells his furniture at a market stall, it is submitted that he still has a good claim against Ian because the latter's exclusion clause does not satisfy the requirement of reasonableness prescribed by the 1977 Act.

SUGGESTED ANSWER TO QUESTION TWO

General Comment

Here we are shown a classic approach to the area of exclusion clauses. A detailed analysis is required which will follow a fairly predictable pattern. First it is necessary to consider whether the excluding term has been incorporated into the contract. If it has, then one must next consider whether it covers the breach and satisfies the common law rules as to certainty. Only then does the question of whether the provisions of the Unfair

5 Exclusion Clauses – Answers

Contract Terms Act 1977 apply become relevant. A good knowledge of the case law is therefore of paramount importance.

Key Points

- Whether the notice is effective to incorporate the clause into the contract depends on whether it could be seen prior to or at the time the contract was concluded – *Olley* v *Marlborough Court Ltd* (1949)
- The clause may have been incorporated by a course of dealing between the parties – *Spurling* v *Bradshaw* (1956); *Henry Kendall & Sons* v *William Lillico & Sons* (1969); *McCutcheon* v *David MacBrayne Ltd* (1964); *Hollier* v *Rambler Motors Ltd* (1972)
- The clause will only apply to negligence if this is made clear – *Alderslade* v *Hendon Laundry Ltd* (1945); *Gillespie Bros & Co Ltd* v *Roy Bowles Transport Ltd* (1973); *Joseph Travers & Sons Ltd* v *Cooper* (1915); *White* v *Blackmore* (1972)
- Exclusion of liability for personal injury caused by negligence is wholly ineffective – s2(1) Unfair Contract Terms Act 1977 (UCTA)
- Exclusion of other liability caused by negligence is subject to the reasonableness test – s2(2)UCTA
- The onus of proving reasonableness is on the Hotel – s11(5) UCTA
- Application of the reasonableness test – *George Mitchell (Chesterfield) Ltd* v *Finney Lock Seeds Ltd* (1983); *Photo Production Ltd* v *Securicor Transport Ltd* (1980); *Stag Line Ltd* v *Tyne Shiprepair Group Ltd* (1984)
- Application of the privity rule to the porter's negligent acts – *Adler* v *Dickson* (1955); *Scruttons Ltd* v *Midland Silicones Ltd* (1962); *New Zealand Shipping Co Ltd* v *Satterthwaite (The Eurymedon)* (1975); *Port Jackson Stevedoring Ltd* v *Salmond and Spraggon Ltd (The New York Star)* (1981); *Southern Water Authority* v *Carey* (1985)

Suggested Answer

In order to decide on the effectiveness of the exclusion clause contained in the notice, it is necessary to consider three matters: whether the clause is incorporated into the contract between Tom and the Hotel; whether as a matter of construction the clause covers the incidents that occurred; and the effect, if there is an affirmative answer to both these questions, of the Unfair Contract Terms Act 1977.

Incorporation

Whether a notice displayed in premises has contractual force depends on whether the notice is in a position where it can be seen prior to, or at the time of, the conclusion of the contract. In *Olley* v *Marlborough Court Ltd* (1949) the notice in a hotel bedroom purporting to exclude liability was held to be ineffective because it was only seen after the contract had been concluded. However, notice may be deemed to have been given by virtue of a course of dealings between the parties (*Spurling* v *Bradshaw* (1956), *Henry Kendall & Sons* v *William Lillico & Sons* (1969)), but there must have been a consistent course of dealings: *McCutcheon* v *David MacBrayne Ltd* (1964). In *Hollier* v

Rambler Motors Ltd (1972) Salmon J held that three or four transactions over a period of five years could not be described as a course of dealings.

The question does indicate a consistent course of dealings between the parties and it is, therefore, highly probable that the notice will be regarded as incorporated into the contract by this course of dealings.

It appears that the loss of Tom's car, his personal injury and the damage to his watch were all the result of negligence on the part of the Hotel and its employee. What has to be considered, therefore, is whether the notice is to be construed as excluding liability for negligence. The notice does not expressly refer to negligence, and the courts have held that where liability can arise other than by negligence then, in the absence of clear words, the exclusion clause will be held to apply to those other grounds and not to liability based on negligence: *Alderslade* v *Hendon Laundry Ltd* (1945), *Gillespie Bros & Co Ltd* v *Roy Bowles Transport Ltd* (1973). Liability for negligence may however, be effectively excluded if the clause makes it clear that all damage is to be comprehended within the exclusion, from whatever cause the damage may arise. The clause in question here refers to damage 'however caused'. In *Joseph Travers & Sons Ltd* v *Cooper* (1915) and *White* v *Blackmore* (1972) these words have been held to be effective in excluding liability for negligence.

Having concluded that the notice has been incorporated into the contract and that it does, as a matter of construction, exclude liability for negligence, it remains to consider the effect of the Unfair Contract Terms Act 1977. Under s2(1) of the Act the purported exclusion of liability for personal injury resulting from negligence is rendered totally ineffective. It can be assumed that leaving the corridor in a highly polished state constitutes negligence on the part of the Hotel, and the Hotel will, in consequence, be liable to Tom for the personal injury he has sustained.

The damage caused to Tom's wristwatch falls within the ambit of s2(2) of the Act which requires the notice, to be effective, to satisfy the reasonableness test. (It should be noted that Tom's awareness of the notice does not of itself indicate his voluntary acceptance of any risk - s2(3) of the Act). Under s11(1) of the Act the requirement of reasonableness is that the notice shall be a fair and reasonable one having regard to the circumstances which were, or ought reasonably to have been, known to or in the contemplation of the parties at the time the contract was made. By virtue of s11(5) of the Act the onus of proving that the exclusion clause satisfies the reasonableness test is on the Hotel.

The reasonableness test (imposed by an enactment now superseded by the Unfair Contract Terms Act) was considered by the House of Lords in *George Mitchell (Chesterfield) Ltd* v *Finney Lock Seeds Ltd* (1983) where the limitation clause was held not to be reasonable since the practice of the sellers had been not to rely on the clause in the past but to negotiate settlements of claims. The decision in *George Mitchell* does not provide a great deal of assistance in the present problem. It is submitted that the approach to be adopted here is that indicated by Lord Wilberforce in *Photo Production Ltd* v *Securicor Transport Ltd* (1980) where his Lordship said that in commercial matters, when the parties are not of unequal bargaining power, and when risks are normally borne by insurance, the parties should be left to apportion the risks as they think fit. This approach was adopted by Staughton J in applying the reasonableness test in *Stag Line Ltd* v *Tyne Shiprepair Group Ltd* (1984). The exclusion clause therefore satisfies the reasonableness test so as to exclude the Hotel from liability for the loss of Tom's wristwatch.

With regard to the theft of Tom's car, two matters arise for consideration, the liability of the Hotel itself and the liability of the porter. For the reasons previously given Tom should be advised that the Hotel will be able to rely on the exclusion clause. No distinction can be drawn, in principle, between the loss of the wristwatch and the loss of the car.

The final point to be considered is the liability of the porter for his negligent acts. The clause purports to exclude the liability of employees, and the question is whether the rules of privity of contract will prevent the porter from relying on the clause. It is submitted that the decision in *Adler* v *Dickson* (1955) and the speeches of the majority in *Scruttons Ltd* v *Midland Silicones Ltd* (1962) would preclude the porter from relying on the clause. There are special circumstances in which a third party can rely on the benefit of an exclusion clause as appear from the two Privy Council decisions in *New Zealand Shipping Co Ltd* v *A M Satterthwaite & Co Ltd (The Eurymedon)* (1975) and *Port Jackson Stevedoring Ltd* v *Salmond and Spraggon Ltd (The New York Star)* (1981). The special circumstances were recently considered in *Southern Water Authority* v *Carey* (1985). It would have to be established, inter alia, that the Hotel had authority from the employee that the clause should also apply to him at the time it contracted with Tom and that it could be shown that consideration had moved from the employee. There is no evidence that these requirements have been met.

SUGGESTED ANSWER TO QUESTION THREE

General Comment

Alternative scenarios are here provided by a problem which involves the purchase of one article in the course of a business and another for home use. The student by now should be alerted by this clue that the examiner primarily requires an analysis of the attempt by Beta Ltd to exclude liability with particular reference to both 'business' and 'consumer' liability under the Unfair Contract Terms Act 1977. A good candidate will be able to demonstrate a thorough understanding of the distinction and to cite, summarise and apply the relevant provisions of the Act.

Key Points

- Cecil is bound by signing the order form – *L'Estrange* v *Graucob Ltd* (1934)
- Implied condition as to satisfactory quality – s14(2) Sale of Goods Act 1979
- Liability may be excluded for 'fundamental' breach – *Suisse Atlantique* (1967); *Photo Production Ltd* v *Securicor Transport Ltd* (1980)
- Was Cecil 'dealing as a consumer'? – s12(1) Unfair Contract Terms Act 1977 (UCTA); *R & B Customs Brokers Co Ltd* v *United Dominions Trust Ltd* (1988)
- If he was not a consumer the 'reasonableness test' will apply – ss6(3), 11(1), 11(2)

and Sch 2 UCTA; *George Mitchell (Chesterhall) Ltd* v *Finney Lock Seeds Ltd* (1983); *Smith* v *Eric S Bush* (1990)
- Exclusion of liability for injury due to negligence is wholly ineffective – s2(1) UCTA
- The clause may also be deemed unfair under the Unfair Terms in Consumer Contracts Act 1994

Suggested Answer

This question involves a discussion of the effect of the exclusion clause, and in particular the validity of that exclusion clause under the Unfair Contract Terms Act 1977 and the Unfair Terms in Consumer Contracts Regulations 1994. The two purchases made by Cecil, the one for his office and the one for his home, will be discussed in that order.

The purchase for his office

The exclusion clause is clearly incorporated into Cecil's contract with Beta Ltd. He signed the order form containing the clause: *L'Estrange* v *Graucob Ltd* (1934). This does not require further discussion.

Beta Ltd are in breach of their contract with Cecil. As they have sold the word processor in the course of a business there is the implied condition in the contract under s14(2) Sale of Goods Act 1979 that it is of satisfactory quality. As the word processor developed a fault shortly after its purchase there appears to be a clear breach of this implied condition. What must now be considered is whether, as a matter of construction, the clause covers this breach. As a result of the breach Cecil has suffered considerable loss, but it is now settled that there is no breach of contract so 'fundamental' that liability for its breach cannot be excluded as a matter of law; the question is always one of construction: *Suisse Atlantique Société D'Armament Maritime* v *Rotterdamsche Kolen Centrale* (1967); *Photo Production Ltd* v *Securicor Transport Ltd* (1980). The clause clearly covers the breach and would, at common law, exclude liability for the consequential loss sustained by Cecil.

As to the validity of the clause under the Unfair Contract Terms Act 1977, the Act applies in the present situation by virtue of s1(3)(a) as Beta Ltd's liability for its breach of contract arises 'from things done in the course of a business'. The validity of a clause excluding or restricting liability for breach of a seller's obligations arising from, inter alia, s14(2) Sale of Goods Act 1979 depends on whether or not the purchaser is 'dealing as a consumer'. At first sight, as Cecil has purchased the article for use in his office, s12(1) UCTA would seem definitive that, as he made the contract in the course of a business, he was not dealing as a consumer. However the position is not beyond all doubt in view of the decision of the Court of Appeal in *R & B Customs Brokers Co Ltd* v *United Dominions Trust Ltd* (1988). It was held in that case that where a transaction was only incidental to a business activity, a degree of regularity was required before the transaction could be said to be an integral part of the business, and so carried on in the course of that business. It is, however, highly likely that the purchase of a word processor, now normal office equipment, would be regarded as an integral part of Cecil's business and not merely incidental to that business. Cecil would not therefore be considered to be dealing as a consumer.

Under s6(3) of the Act, as against a person dealing otherwise than as a consumer, liability for Beta Ltd's breach of contract can only be excluded or restricted in so far as the exclusion clause satisfies the requirement of reasonableness. The question is: Does the present clause satisfy this requirement? The requirement is set out in s11(1) of the Act, which provides that the test is that the clause shall have been a fair and reasonable one 'having regard to the circumstances which were, or ought reasonably to have been, known to or in the contemplation of the parties when the contract was made.' Under s11(2) the burden of proving that the clause is a reasonable one is on Beta Ltd. Section 11(2) provides that, in determining whether the clause is a reasonable one for the purposes of s6(3), regard shall be had to the guidelines set out in Sch 2 to the Act. These guidelines refer to such matters as the bargaining strength of the parties, and whether the customer had received an inducement to agree to the clause, or whether, in accepting it, had an opportunity to enter into a similar contract without having to accept a similar term. In *George Mitchell (Chesterhall) Ltd* v *Finney Lock Seeds Ltd* (1983) it was indicated that the courts would also take into account the resources of the parties concerned, and the availability of insurance to the party seeking to rely on the clause. Most recently, in *Smith* v *Eric S Bush* (1990), Lord Griffiths said that in deciding whether an exclusion clause met the requirement of reasonableness these matters should always be taken into account.

Without all the facts before one it is difficult to give Cecil firm advice as to whether or not the present clause would meet the requirement of reasonableness. There does not appear to be any reason to think that the parties were of unequal bargaining strength. It can also, perhaps, be assumed that Cecil could have entered into a similar contract without having to accept a similar clause. On balance, therefore, it can be tentatively concluded that the clause would be effective, as it would meet the reasonableness requirement. Even if it does not, it is submitted that the cost of hiring extra staff would be regarded as too remote, in accordance with the principles relating to remoteness of damage in contract.

The purchase for Cecil's home
It can be assumed that the clause was also incorporated into this contract.

Under s12(1) Cecil would be regarded as 'dealing as a consumer' if:

a   he neither made the contract in the course of a business nor held himself out as doing so;
b   Beta Ltd did make the contract in the course of a business; and
c   the goods in question were of a type ordinarily sold for private use or consumption.

Clearly (b) is satisfied. It appears that subsection (a) would also be satisfied subject to the reservation that, as Cecil had made the previous purchase for his office, there is the possibility that he might be deemed to have held himself out as having made this contract in the course of a business. With regard to subsection (c) it is submitted that in the present day word processors are ordinarily sold for private use or consumption.

If Cecil is dealing as a consumer in the second contract the exclusion clause is totally ineffective under s6(2) of the Act, and Beta Ltd will be liable to him for the damages he has sustained.

Under s2(1) of the Act the exclusion or restriction of liability for death or personal injury resulting from negligence is rendered totally ineffective, and Cecil has suffered personal injury. However, there is no evidence either way as to negligence on the part of Beta Ltd, so this aspect cannot be further pursued.

The exclusions must also be read subject to the Unfair Terms in Consumer Contracts Regulations 1994. The Regulations apply to contracts between 'consumers' and sellers of goods or suppliers of services. They apply only to terms which have not been individually negotiated, ie the seller/supplier's standard terms, but they apply to any kind of term, not just excluding and limiting terms. Such a term will be deemed 'unfair' if it does not satisfy the requirement of good faith and if it causes 'a significant imbalance in the parties' rights and obligations under the contract to the detriment of the consumer'. A consumer is defined as: 'a natural person who, in making a contract to which these Regulations apply is acting for purposes which are outside his business'. The guidelines are, however, much the same as those for determining 'reasonableness' under the Act. If the clause is adjudged unreasonable under the Act, it will also be unfair for the purposes of the Regulations. The only difference is in the definition of 'consumer'. The Act limits the definition to include the proviso that the goods in question are usually bought for the purposes of private use and consumption. The Regulations contain no such proviso and it may therefore be easier for Cecil to claim consumer protection under the Regulations than under the Act. The result, however, could be much the same.

SUGGESTED ANSWER TO QUESTION FOUR

General Comment

Designed to test the candidate's in-depth knowledge of the Unfair Contract Terms Act 1977, the contract here contains multiple exclusions and restrictions. The most important point to notice is that there has been an untrue statement of fact by Q, which means that the candidate is required to consider whether this amounts to a misrepresentation and, if so, the effect of the Unfair Contract Terms Act 1977 in relation to the Misrepresentation Act 1967.

Key Points

- Is the statement 'fully restored' a contractual term? – *Heilbut, Symons & Co* v *Buckleton* (1913); *Dick Bentley Productions Ltd* v *Harold Smith (Motors) Ltd* (1965); *Esso Petroleum Co Ltd* v *Mardon* (1976); *Routledge* v *McKay* (1954)
- Is the statement a misrepresentation, an untrue statement of fact by one party to another which induced the other to enter the contract? – *JEB Fasteners Ltd* v *Marks, Bloom & Co* (1983); *Museprime Properties Ltd* v *Adhill Properties Ltd* (1990)
- A clause purporting to exclude liability for misrepresentation must satisfy the 'reasonableness' test – s3 Misrepresentation Act 1967 as amended by s8 Unfair Contract Terms Act 1977 (UCTA)
- Application of the 'reasonableness' test – ss11(1) and 11(4) UCTA; *Walker* v *Boyle* (1982); *Howard Marine & Dredging Co Ltd* v *A Ogden & Sons (Excavations) Ltd* (1978); *Smith* v *Eric S Bush* (1990)

- P is liable in damages for misrepresentation unless he can prove he believed on reasonable grounds in the truth of the representation – s2(1) UCTA; *Royscott Trust Ltd* v *Rogerson* (1991)
- Breach of implied condition as to satisfactory quality – ss14(2) and 14(6) Sale of Goods Act 1979
- Liability for this breach cannot be excluded against a person dealing as a consumer – ss 2 and 6(2) UCTA
- Measure of damages recoverable – *Hadley* v *Baxendale* (1854); *Victoria Laundry (Windsor) Ltd* v *Newman Industries Ltd* (1949); *The Heron II* (1969)
- Attempted restriction of buyer's remedies as in clause 34 is ineffective – s13(1)(a) UCTA
- Clause 35 may be subject to the contra preferentem rule – *Ailsa Craig Fishing Co Ltd* v *Malvern Fishing Co* (1983)
- Exclusion of liability for personal injury due to negligence is wholly ineffective – s2(1) UCTA
- Privity of contract would prevent extension of clause 35 to third parties

Suggested Answer

The car has been advertised as 'fully restored'. The initial point for decision is whether this statement can be regarded as a contractual term. The question is one of the intention of the parties: *Heilbut, Symons & Co* v *Buckleton* (1913). It could be argued that, because P carries on business (presumably as a car dealer), he has special knowledge, and this would permit the conclusion that the statement was intended to be a contractual term: *Dick Bentley Productions Ltd* v *Harold Smith (Motors) Ltd* (1965); *Esso Petroleum Co Ltd* v *Mardon* (1976). It is submitted, however, that the statement is not sufficiently precise to qualify as a contractual term. Moreover the subsequent reduction of the contract to writing would be a further indication that the statement was not intended to be a term: *Routledge* v *McKay* (1954).

A statement, though not a term, might amount to a representation. In order for it to be a representation it must: (i) be a statement of fact; (ii) be addressed to the party concerned; and (iii) have induced that party to enter into the contract. It is necessary to apply these requirements to the present facts. Though it has been suggested that the statement is too imprecise to be categorised as a contractual term it must have factual content. 'Fully restored' must mean 'restored to working order' to enable the car to be driven more than a few hundred miles without the steering failing. Thus the first requirement is satisfied. It would also appear that the advertisement was addressed to all potential purchasers, including Q. It can also be assumed that it induced Q to enter into the contract. It should be noted, in this context, that the representation need not be the sole inducing factor; it is sufficient that it played a real and substantial part in inducing Q to purchase the car: *JEB Fasteners Ltd* v *Marks, Bloom & Co* (1983). It would also appear that the statement would have induced a reasonable man to contract, therefore the onus of proving that it did not induce Q would fall on P: *Museprime Properties Ltd* v *Adhill Properties Ltd* (1990).

The advertisement therefore amounts to an actionable misrepresentation. However, cl 31 purports to have the effect of excluding liability for any statement inducing the contract. The effectiveness of this exclusion clause must now be considered. It is unnecessary to discuss questions of incorporation or construction of the clause; the sole issue is its validity under the statute. Section 3 of the Misrepresentation Act 1967 as amended by s8 Unfair Contract Terms Act 1977 provides, in effect, that a clause which excludes or restricts liability for misrepresentation, or excludes or restricts any available remedy by reason of such misrepresentation, shall be of no effect unless it satisfies the requirement of reasonableness under s11(1) UCTA.

Section 11(1) provides that in order to determine whether the requirement of reasonableness is satisfied regard is to be had to the circumstances which were, or ought reasonably have been, known to the parties when the contract was made. There is a little case authority on the application of s11(1) to s3 Misrepresentation Act, though a clause excluding liability for misrepresentation has been declared wholly ineffective in *Walker v Boyle* (1982) (cf *Howard Marine & Dredging Co Ltd v A Ogden & Sons (Excavations) Ltd* (1978)). As the contract was between a business and a consumer, and involved (apparently) a standard form of business, the court would take into account the inequality of bargaining strength between the parties and their respective resources: Sch 2 UCTA as read with s11(4); *Smith v Eric S Bush* (1990). A consideration of these factors suggests that the clause would not meet the reasonableness test and would be held wholly ineffective.

Q is claiming compensation from P (not rescission, to which he may also be entitled). Under s2(1) Misrepresentation Act P would be liable in damages to Q unless he (P) proves that he believed in the truth of the representation up until the time the contract was made, and that he had reasonable grounds for doing so. It does not appear that, as a dealer in cars, he could successfully discharge this onus of proof. The Court of Appeal has recently held in *Royscott Trust Ltd v Rogerson* (1991) that the measure of damages under s2(1) is the same as that for deceit, with the result that the innocent party is entitled to recover any loss which flowed from the misrepresentation, even if the loss could not have been foreseen. It would follow, it is submitted, that Q would be entitled to be compensated for his personal injury, the loss of the car and for the damages to which he may be liable to R. (The effect, in this connection, of cl 35 of the sale agreement is considered below.)

The failure of the steering must, it seems, be a breach of the implied condition of the car's satisfactory quality provided for by s14(2) Sale of Goods Act 1979. This subsection can be invoked: P sold the car in the course of business; the exceptions to the implied condition do not apply; the car does not accord with the criteria of merchantability set out in s14(6).

Clause 32 of the sale agreement purports to exclude liability for breach of s14(2). But s6(2) UCTA provides that as against a person dealing as a consumer, liability for breach of the obligations arising from (inter alia) s14 SOGA cannot be excluded or restricted by reference to any contract term. Q did not make the contract in the course of business; P did make the contract in the course of business, and the goods passing under the contract are of a type ordinarily supplied for private use. Accordingly Q dealt as a consumer as provided for by s2 UCTA. It follows that cl 32 is wholly ineffective and P is liable for the damages flowing from his breach of contract. It would also appear that all the loss which Q has sustained is within the reasonable contemplation of the parties, and would therefore be recoverable within the rule of *Hadley* v *Baxendale* (1854) as amplified by *Victoria Laundry (Windsor) Ltd* v *Newman Industries Ltd* (1949) and *The Heron II* (1969).

Clause 33 purports to exclude liability arising from s14(3) SOGA. For the reasons set out above it is also wholly ineffective.

Clause 34 restricts the remedies available to the buyer. This is rendered ineffective by s13(1)(a) UCTA.

Clause 35 appears ambiguous. It is not clear whether it refers only to the terms of the contract or whether it can be interpreted as also covering representations. The application of the contra proferentem rule would indicate the former, and for the reasons previously argued would be wholly ineffective. If it does cover representations then it must satisfy the reasonableness requirement under UCTA to which reference has been made above. Clause 35 is a limitation clause and it is suggested in *Ailsa Craig Fishing Co Ltd* v *Malvern Fishing Co* (1983) that in a limitation clause the contra proferentem rule would be less rigorously applied and that the court might be less prone to declare a clause unreasonable if it merely limits damages, but does not totally exclude liability. There is the possibility, therefore, that the clause might be valid with regard to a claim based on misrepresentation, but this is of academic interest to Q who has clear contractual claims.

Two further points must be noted. It is not clear from the facts presented whether or not there has been negligence on P's part with regard to the failure of the steering. As far as Q's personal injury is concerned s2(l) UCTA would render an exclusion of liability for that injury resulting from negligence totally ineffective. The further point is that clause 35 purports to extend the operation of the clause to third parties. The rule as to privity of contract would not permit this.

SUGGESTED ANSWER TO QUESTION FIVE

General Comment

As this area provides considerable scope for problems on the application of the law, it is rare to find an essay question. This does not, however, mean that the topic does not admit of that type of question and essays might well be set on aspects of both the common law and the Unfair Contract Terms Act 1977. The question selected here seeks to test the candidate's ability not only to learn the provisions of a new piece of legislation but also to assess its likely effect on the existing law.

Key Points

- The purpose and general relationship of the two pieces of legislation
- The scope of the Regulations in relation to contracting parties as compared with the scope of the Act
- Comparison of the test of 'good faith' under the Regulations with 'reasonableness' under the Act

- Comparison of the type of term to which the Act and the Regulations respectively apply
- The effect of the Regulations on a contract
- Types of contract to which the Regulations do not apply

Suggested Answer

The Unfair Contracts Terms Act 1977 ('the Act') was enacted to deal principally with the abuse of standard form contracts in consumer transactions and was part of a general legislative move towards improving the bargaining position of the consumer. The Act is not, however, confined to consumer transactions and deals also with business transactions. The Unfair Terms in Consumer Contracts Regulations 1994 ('the Regulations') were brought into force solely as a consequence of the United Kingdom's need to conform with the harmonisation requirements of the European Community. The Council's directive 93/13/EEC laid down certain obligations to which the legislation of member states was required to conform in relation to contractual terms.

The Regulations have not replaced the Act. They operate alongside the Act and, although there are areas where the two overlap, they are by no means identical. A contractual clause must satisfy the requirements of the Regulations as well as those of the Act, where relevant.

In one sense, the Regulations have a narrower scope. They apply only to terms in contracts between consumers and commercial sellers of goods or suppliers of services and moreover to those terms which have not been individually negotiated, ie standard terms in consumer contracts. If the transaction is solely a business transaction or if the terms have been negotiated, the Regulations do not apply. The terms 'seller' and 'supplier' of goods and services have been given their natural meaning and are further defined as one who:

> 'in making a contract to which these Regulations apply, is acting for purposes relating to his business'.

The term 'consumer' is defined by reg 2(1) as:

> 'a natural person who, in making a contract to which these regulations apply, is acting for purposes which are outside his business'.

Thus a company cannot be a consumer and the regulations do not apply where the plaintiff is a company, unlike the Act. There is, however, no restriction on the nature of the goods or services which are the subject matter of the contract. The 'consumer' provisions of the Act apply only where the goods are 'of a type ordinarily supplied for private use and consumption.'

A term is regarded as not individually negotiated

> 'where it has been drafted in advance and the consumer has not been able to influence the substance of the term': reg 3(3).

This definition is not exhaustive. If one or more terms have been individually negotiated, the regulations will apply to the rest of the terms if the contract viewed as a whole is a 'preformulated standard contract': reg 3(4).

Like the Act, the Regulations strike against 'unfair' terms. Any term which is 'unfair' is not binding on the consumer. However, while 'reasonableness' is the fundamental concept under the Act, in the Regulations it is 'good faith'. To be an 'unfair term' it must be 'contrary to the requirement of good faith' and 'cause a significant imbalance in the parties' rights and obligations under the contract to the detriment of the consumer.'

Despite a difference in terminology, the guidelines in the Regulations are, however, very similar to those in the Act. In determining good faith under the Regulations, the court should take into consideration:

1 strength of bargaining position;
2 whether there was an inducement to the consumer to agree the term;
3 whether the goods were supplied to special order;
4 the extent to which the seller/supplier has dealt fairly and equitably with the consumer and in determining whether a 'significant imbalance' exists;
5 the nature of the goods or services;
6 all the circumstances attending the conclusion of the contract;
7 all the other terms of the contract or other contract on which it is dependent.

Schedule 3 of the Regulations contains a list of example clauses which are prima facie unfair. Clauses which exclude or limit liability for death or personal injury are unfair on the face of it as are those which exclude or hinder the right to take legal action or exercise any other legal remedy. Other exclusion or limitation clauses are unfair if the 'inappropriately' exclude or limit the consumer's rights.

Where a term is adjudged unfair, it is not binding on the consumer but the rest of the contract is unaffected if it is capable of continuing in existence without the unfair term: reg 5(2). This may in future years raise questions of severability and the use of a 'blue pencil' test to strike out unfair parts of a term as in cases on restraint clauses.

There are some exclusions. The Regulations do not apply to terms which (a) define the main subject matter of the contract, or (b) which concern the adequacy of the price or remuneration as against the goods or services supplied. The latter preserves the court's traditional position that it will not act as valuer of goods or services. There is a proviso to both (a) and (b): insofar as the term in question is 'in plain, intelligible language', which does give the courts scope to examine a term which is unclear.

The Regulations also do not apply to contracts relating to employment, contracts relating to succession rights or rights under family law, contracts relating to the incorporation or organisation of companies or partnerships, terms required to be included by statute or other regulatory provision under UK law or which reflect the 'provisions or principles of internal conventions to which member states or the Community are a party'.

While in the area of unfair terms in 'standard form' consumer contracts there is an overlap, the Act is far wider in scope that the Regulations because it applies to terms in any kind of contract, whether or not the terms have been individually negotiated, except those which are specifically excluded (the exclusions being broadly the same, although the Act specifically excludes contracts for the creation, transfer or termination of an interest in land and includes provisions against the employee in contracts of employment). On the other hand, the regulations are wider in scope that the Act since the Act is confined to excluding and limiting terms while the Regulations cover any kind of term except those mentioned above as being excluded. The two should therefore be seen as complementary to one another and it is necessary to look to both to determine whether a contractual term is or is not to be deemed unfair.

6

Capacity

Introduction

This chapter is concerned with categories of persons who are deemed not to have full contractual capacity. The law views them as requiring protection, for consent with full knowledge and understanding is a prerequisite of any contract under English law, and because of specific characteristics, such persons may have entered the contract without sufficient understanding of the obligations which they were incurring.

The most popular topic for examination questions is the incapacity of minors (persons under 18 years of age). However, there are also special rules for persons who drink, mentally disordered persons and corporations.

Questions

INTERROGRAMS

1 How does statute now define 'necessaries' and does that definition differ in any way from earlier common law definitions?
2 What limitations does the law place on the capacity of a corporation to enter into a contract?
3 Why should one beware when making a contract with a person who may be drunk or mentally disordered?

QUESTION ONE

Referring to infants' contracts it has been said that: 'The law on this topic is based on two principles. The first, and more important, is that the law must protect the infant against his own inexperience, ... the second principle is that the law should not cause unnecessary hardship to adults who deal fairly with infants.' (Treitel).

Explain how the law gives effect to these principles.

London University LLB Examination
(for external students) Elements of the Law of Contract June 1986 Q9

QUESTION TWO

Simon is seventeen. He lives in an isolated village and has recently been offered a job as a sales assistant in the nearest town, which is 15 miles from the village. As there is no bus service, he agreed to buy a used car from Finan Motors for £500. Two days later he discovered that he would be able to get a lift to work from a friend. He then told Finan Motors that he no longer needed the car and would not collect it or pay for it.

Simon also bought a personal stereo and a set of golf clubs from General Trading plc.

He has paid for the stereo but not the clubs. Because of a fault the stereo has damaged an irreplaceable tape of great sentimental value.

Consider Simon's rights and liabilities in respect of the car, the stereo and the golf clubs.

London University LLB Examination
(for external students) Elements of the Law of Contract June 1988 Q6

QUESTION THREE

G, aged 16 years, was left an orphan by a car crash which killed his parents. He took an evening job as a delivery boy at his local supermarket to supplement his income. He was owed sixteen weeks' wages amounting to £800 but the supermarket failed to pay. He arranged with Dr Manieri to have weekly piano lessons for six months at £50 per lesson. G was determined to complete his studies as he envisaged becoming a professional piano-player when he completed his education. After two lessons G decided that he did not want any more lessons and wrote to Dr Manieri to this effect. He arranged with his bank manager to borrow £15,000 till his parents' estates had been settled. He was to repay this loan at a rate of £500 per month. After two months he failed to keep up his payments. He had spent £5,000 on a piano. Also, he owed a bookmaker £300. When the estates of his parents were calculated it was found that as a result of debts there was no inheritance for G.

Advise G.

London University LLB Examination
(for external students) Elements of the Law of Contract June 1994 Q3

QUESTION FOUR

Consider the rights and liabilities of Jason, who is 17, in respect of the following transactions:

i he bought a pair of gold cufflinks costing £200 from Harold, but has not paid for them;
ii he has bought an exercise bicycle from Kenneth and paid for it, but has now decided that exercise is a waste of time and wants to have his money back;
iii he agreed to work as an assistant in Simon's shop but left after one week because the hours were too long. The contract with Simon provided that it could only be terminated by six months' notice on either side.

London University LLB Examination
(for external students) Elements of the Law of Contract June 1990 Q7

Answers

ANSWERS TO INTERROGRAMS

1 Earlier definitions in case law were not substantially different. Necessary goods were defined in *Peters v Fleming* (1840) as: 'such articles as are fit to maintain the particular person in the state, station and degree ... in which he is'. The substitution of 'condition' and 'actual requirements' does little to improve the rather vague and feudalistic definition.

There is a paucity of modern authority as to the nature of necessaries. In *Peters v Fleming* itself, jewellery supplied to the son of a wealthy man was found to be necessaries, but in *Ryder v Wombwell* (1869) the court set aside the verdict of a jury that similar items were necessaries. In *Nash v Inman* (1908), 11 fancy waistcoats were considered 'necessaries' in relation to an undergraduate. It is, perhaps, doubtful whether these authorities could provide much guidance in the present day.

It must first be shown that the class into which the goods fall is capable of being 'necessary' and then that the goods supplied were actually necessary at the time of the contract. It is generally considered that services as well as goods are capable of being necessaries (see Treitel, *Law of Contract*).

2 For many decades, the ultra vires rule applied to corporations. This stated that a company could not enter into any contract which was not envisaged in the objects written into its memorandum of association. If it attempted to do so, the contract was void: *Ashbury Railway Carriage and Iron Co v Riche* (1875). The rule also prohibited using a power which the company was given in its memorandum for an object which it was not (eg the borrowing of money (a power) for the purpose of pig farming (an object) in *Re Introductions Ltd* (1970)). The reasoning behind the strict application of the rule is that a company must register its memorandum of association at Companies House and so its contractual capacity is available for everyone to see. The ultra vires rule still exists but its practical effects have been all but extinguished by the provisions of the Companies Act 1985.

Prior to this enactment, companies sought to give themselves greater contractual capacity by drafting the objects clause in their memorandum in the widest possible terms. The court also helped to soften the harshness of the rule as it applied to innocent third parties who might find that they had no redress against a company which reneged on its contractual obligations. (See, for example, *Rolled Steel Products v BSC* (1984)).

Section 35 of the Companies Act 1985 provides that where a company enters into an ultra vires contract the innocent third party is not affected by the lack of capacity and can enforce the contract as if the company had that capacity. Instead the fault shifts to the directors, who may be sued by the company. Section 35 does not, however, protect the company itself.

3 The contractual capacity of both drunken persons and mentally disordered persons is less than for others. This is because their ability to freely consent to their obligations under the contract has been impaired.

If one party was so drunk as not to be able to understand the transaction and the other party knew of this, the court may set the transaction aside. However, the drunken party may ratify the contract when sober. Further, even if the contract falls within this category, the drunken person is still liable to pay a reasonable prices for 'necessaries'.

Section 3(3) Sale of Goods Act 1979 defines necessary goods as goods 'suitable to the condition in life of the ... [person] and to his actual requirements at the time of the sale and delivery'. It is thought that necessary services must also be paid for.

There are two categories of mentally disordered person:

a a person who has been certified under the Mental Health Act 1983, Part IV as being incapable of dealing with his property. Such persons are unable to dispose of their property and the court has control of it, although day-to-day management is usually carried out by a relative.

b a person who has not so been certified.

As regards category ii, the contract may be set aside if the party did not understand the transaction by reason of his disorder and the other party knew of the disorder.

As with drunkards, the mentally disordered person may ratify the contract should the disorder cease temporarily or permanently. Also he will be liable to pay a reasonable price for necessaries.

SUGGESTED ANSWER TO QUESTION ONE

General Comment

Contracts with minors is a popular topic for questions, both problem and essay. Here we have a question directed at the delicate balance which the law attempts to maintain between the parties' interests. A good answer will not only thoroughly explain the law in this area but will give careful consideration to what it achieves and how.

Key Points

- Executed contracts for necessaries are valid – *Peters* v *Fleming* (1840); s3(3) Sale of Goods Act 1979; *Ryder* v *Wombwell* (1869); *Nash* v *Inman* (1908)
- An executory contract for necessaries may or may not be binding on the minor – s3(2) Sale of Goods Act 1979; *Nash* v *Inman* (1908); *Roberts* v *Gray* (1913)
- Loans to purchase necessaries are not valid in law but the loan may be recovered in equity if spent on necessaries – s1 Infants Relief Act (1874); *Marlow* v *Pitfield* (1719)
- Contracts for service, apprenticeship and education are binding on the minor if for his benefit as a whole – *Clements* v *L & NW Railway* (1894); *De Francesco* v *Barnum* (1890); *Doyle* v *White City Stadium* (1935); *Chaplin* v *Leslie Frewin (Publishers) Ltd* (1966); *Denmark Productions* v *Boscobel Productions Ltd* (1969); *Whywall* v *Campion* (1738)
- Some contracts are voidable at the infant's option: contracts concerning real property; contracts involving shares in companies; partnership agreements; marriage settlements
- The infant must repudiate within a reasonable time of attaining majority and remains

liable for obligations which have already arisen - *Steinberg v Scala (Leeds) Ltd* (1923)
- Certain contacts were absolutely void - s1 Infants Relief Act (1874) (repealed by the Minors Contracts Act 1987); *Valentini Canali* (1889); *Pearce v Brain* (1929)
- An infant cannot be sued in tort if the act was within the contemplation of a void contract - *Jennings v Rundall* (1799); *Burnard v Haggis* (1863)
- Equitable restitution may be awarded against the infant - *Stocks v Wilson* (1913)
- Just and equitable transfer by the infant of property obtained - s3 Minors' Contracts Act 1987

Suggested Answer

The first principle which Treitel mentions is given effect by the general common law rule that an infant is not bound by certain contracts. The common law, in this respect, is reinforced by the Infants Relief Act 1874. The second principle finds expression in the rules that certain contracts with infants are valid, others are merely voidable at the instance of the infant, and an infant may incur some liability in tort, quasi-contract and in equity. To reconcile these two principles does create some problems for the law, though perhaps on a smaller scale than prior to 1969, when the Family Reform Act of that year reduced the age of majority from 21 to 18.

Valid contracts

An infant is bound by contracts for necessaries. Necessaries include goods and services which are fit to maintain the infant in the station of life to which he is accustomed: *Peters v Fleming* (1840). Necessary goods are defined by s3(3) Sale of Goods Act 1979 as 'goods suitable to the condition in life of the minor, ... and to his actual requirements at the time of sale and delivery.' The onus of proof is on the supplier to show that the goods are capable of being necessaries (*Ryder v Wombwell* (1869)) and that the goods purchased actually were necessary at the time of purchase: *Nash v Inman* (1908).

It is not entirely clear whether an infant is bound by an executory contract for necessary goods. Section 3(2) of the Sale of Goods Act provides that an infant must pay a reasonable price for 'necessaries sold and delivered'. And necessaries are defined in s3(3) in relation to the time of sale and delivery. Is the infant liable if the goods have been sold, but not yet delivered? The answer depends on whether the infant is liable re, that is because he has been supplied, or consensu, that is because he has contracted. The wording of s3 suggests that the infant is liable re, because he has been supplied. Conflicting views were expressed in *Nash v Inman*. Fletcher Moulton LJ said that the infant was liable because he had been supplied, not because he had contracted. Buckley LJ held, however, that the infant was liable because he had contracted. In *Roberts v Gray* (1913) it was held that an infant was bound by an executory contract for services and education and it is difficult to see how a valid distinction can be drawn between goods and services on this point.

An infant cannot be made liable on a loan to him to purchase necessaries (s1 Infants Relief Act), but if the loan is actually spent on necessaries equity will allow recovery of the money so spent: *Marlow v Pitfield* (1719). Contracts for service, apprenticeship and education are binding on the infant if the contract as a whole is for his benefit, even if certain clauses in it are harsh: *Clements* v *L & NW Railway* (1894). In *De Francesco* v *Barnum* (1890) the infant was not bound because the overriding effect of the contract was held to be oppressive. The binding effect of service contracts has been extended to contracts for the exercise of a profession: *Doyle* v *White City Stadium* (1935), *Chaplin* v *Leslie Frewin (Publishers) Ltd* (1966), *Denmark Productions Ltd* v *Boscobel Productions Ltd* (1969). The law distinguishes between an infant who earns his living by the exercise of a profession and one who earns his living by trading, because in the latter case he risks his capital. 'The law will not suffer him to trade, which may be his undoing': *Whywall* v *Campion* (1738).

Voidable contracts
Certain contracts subsist unless and until avoided. In the case of infants' voidable contracts only the infant may avoid them. The kinds of contract that are voidable at the instance of the infant are:

i   contracts concerning real property;
ii contracts involving shares in companies;
iii partnership agreements; and
iv marriage settlements.

These contracts would not be considered as for necessaries, but to consider them void might well work injustice to the other party, as they involve reciprocal liability extending over a period of time. The rules relating to infants' voidable contracts are (a) that he must repudiate before or within a reasonable time of attaining majority; and (b) the effect of repudiation is that he is relieved of obligations arising after the time of repudiation, but remains bound to meet obligations which have already arisen and cannot recover money paid prior to that time: *Steinberg* v *Scala (Leeds) Ltd* (1923).

Void contracts
Section 1 of the Infants Relief Act provided that contracts entered into by infants for 'the repayment of money lent or to be lent' or for 'goods supplied or to be supplied (other than ... necessaries)' and 'all accounts stated' shall be 'absolutely void'. The effect of the words 'absolutely void' was not entirely clear. Generally speaking, money paid under a void contract can be recovered, but in *Valentini* v *Canali* (1889) an infant was denied recovery and in *Pearce* v *Brain* (1929) it was held that an infant plaintiff could not recover unless there had been a total failure of consideration. Normally, too, property does not pass under a void contract, but in *Stocks* v *Wilson* (1913) Lush J expressed the view, obiter, that property in non-necessary goods obtained by an infant is passed on delivery. Section 1 has now been repealed by the Minors Contracts Act 1987 (see below). Section 2 of the Infants Relief Act also provides that fresh promises made after majority do not render a 'debt' contracted during infancy actionable, nor does any ratification of any promise or contract made during infancy.

Liability of infants in tort
An infant cannot be sued in tort for an act which was within the contemplation of the void contract: *Jennings* v *Rundall* (1799). If, however, the wrongful act is of a kind not

contemplated by the contract, the infant may be exposed to tortious liability: *Burnard* v *Haggis* (1863).

Liability of infants in equity

The court may have power to order restitution against the infant where the infant still has the property in his possession. In *Stocks* v *Wilson* where the infant misrepresented his age to obtain property he was held liable to account for the proceeds of the sale of the property by him to a third party. The infant cannot, however, be held to account for money which he has dissipated.

The position has to some extent been changed by s3 of the Minors' Contracts Act 1987. Section 3(1) gives the court the discretion 'if it is just and equitable' to order the minor to transfer back property he has obtained or property representing it where the contract is unenforceable against the minor or he repudiates it because he was a minor when the contract was made. Treitel makes the point that, while the courts have generally been reluctant to compel the minor to account for money received where there was no fraud, s3(1) appears to extend to the return of money in cases where there was no fraud.

Section 3(2) of the Act provides that nothing in s3 shall taken to prejudice any other remedy available to the other party to the contract. Therefore, even if the court does not exercise its discretion under s3(1), the adult may still look for assistance to equity or the old common law rules.

SUGGESTED ANSWER TO QUESTION TWO

General Comment

This problem clearly concerns the contractual capacity of a minor. A good answer will analyse each of the transactions in turn and consider whether it is binding on Simon.

Key Points

The purchase of a secondhand car
- A minor is bound by a contract for necessaries – *Peters* v *Fleming* (1840); s3(3) Sale of Goods Act 1979; *Nash* v *Inman*
- It may be that he is only bound if he has actually been supplied with the goods – *Roberts* v *Gray* (1913)

The purchase of the stereo
- As it is not a necessary the infant is not bound but the other party is – *Bruce* v *Warwick* (1815)
- Liability under s14 Sale of Goods Act
- Extent of damages – *Hadley* v *Baxendale* (1854); *H Parsons (Livestock) Ltd* v *Uttley Ingham & Co Ltd* (1978); *Bliss* v *South East Thames Regional Health Authority* (1987)

The purchase of the golf clubs
- Not necessaries but Simon may be forced to return them – s3(1) Minors Contract Act 1987

Suggested Answer

This question requires discussion of the contractual capacity of minors.

Simon, a minor, has entered into three contracts: first, for the purchase of a secondhand car; second, for the purchase of a personal stereo; and, third, for a set of golf clubs. It is necessary to examine each of these contracts in turn.

The purchase of a secondhand car

A minor is bound by a contract for necessary goods. Necessary goods were defined in the common law as 'such articles as are fit to maintain the particular person in the state, station and degree ... in which he is': *Peters* v *Fleming* (1840). Section 3(3) of the Sale of Goods Act 1979 defines necessaries as 'goods suitable to the condition in life of the minor ... and to his actual requirements at the time of the sale and delivery.' The onus would be on Finan Motors to prove that the car was not only capable of being a necessary but was so in Simon's particular case: *Nash* v *Inman* (1908).

There seems little doubt, in the circumstances, that the car is a necessary. If the car had actually been delivered to Simon he would be bound by the contract. However, Simon has repudiated the contract before the car has been delivered to him and the question is: can the minor be held to an executory contract? This question has not been finally resolved. In *Nash* v *Inman* Fletcher-Moulton LJ held that the minor was liable re, because he had been supplied, and not consensu, because he had contracted. His Lordship held further that a minor was incapable of contracting, and that the law only imposed an obligation upon him to pay if the necessaries had actually been delivered to him. In the same case, however, Buckley LJ held that a contract for necessaries was one that a minor could make. He held that a minor had a limited capacity to contract. The contention that a minor is only bound if the goods have actually been delivered to him is also supported by the definition of necessaries in the Sale of Goods Act quoted above. Under s3(2) of the same Act the minor is only obliged to pay a reasonable price for the necessaries, which may not be the contract price.

These statutory definitions suggest that a minor is only bound if he has actually been supplied with the necessary goods, and that the minor would not be bound by an executory contract. However, there is authority to the contrary. In *Roberts* v *Gray* (1913) the defendant, who was a minor, desired to become a professional billiard player and made a contract with Roberts under which the parties agreed to accompany each other on a world tour and to play matches together. Roberts expended a great deal of time and trouble and incurred certain liabilities in the course of preparing for the contract. Gray repudiated the contract while it was still largely executory and Roberts obtained damages for breach of contract. In the Court of Appeal Hamilton LJ said:

> 'I am unable to appreciate why a contract which is in itself binding, because it is a contract for necessaries ..., can cease to be binding merely because it is executory ... If the contract is binding at all it must be binding for all such remedies as are appropriate of it.'

In Cheshire, Fifoot & Furmston's *Law of Contract* it is observed that the contract in *Roberts* v *Gray* (1913) was more closely analogous to beneficial contracts of service, which are binding even though not completely executed. It is also observed that all the authorities relied upon by the court in *Roberts* v *Gray* concern beneficial contracts of service. Treitel has the view that it is difficult to justify the distinction between necessary goods and beneficial contracts of service. Treitel considers that the reasons for holding a minor liable and for limiting his liability are the same in both cases.

The position is therefore still open to argument. However it is submitted that Treitel's view is the better one. If that is so, Simon would be bound by the contract and therefore liable in damages to Finan Motors for breach of contract. It is clear that the suppliers could not obtain an order for specific performance against him.

The purchase of the stereo
It seems clear that the stereo is not a necessary. Whilst Simon, therefore, would not be bound by the contract the other party, General Trading plc, is bound by the contract: *Bruce* v *Warwick* (1815). General Trading plc appear to be in breach of contract. More particularly they are in breach of s14(2) of the Sale of Goods Act – the implied condition that the goods supplied under the contract are of satisfactory quality. (The provision in the Infants Relief Act 1874 which made certain contracts with minors 'absolutely void' has now been repealed by the Minors Contract Act 1987.) General Trading plc are therefore liable in damages to Simon. They would therefore be liable for the cost of the tape that has been damaged: such damage would be reasonably foreseeable: see *Hadley* v *Baxendale* (1854). We are informed that the tape was of great sentimental value. Whether this would increase the damages available to Simon is however doubtful. It is not immediately apparent that such increased damages would have been reasonably foreseeable. It could be argued, though, that as General Trading plc could have foreseen the kind of damage, they are not absolved from liability merely because they could not foresee the extent of the damage: *H Parsons (Livestock) Ltd* v *Uttley Ingham & Co Ltd* (1978). It is also possible that Simon's claim for the loss of an article of sentimental value is closely akin to claiming damages for distress. In *Bliss* v *South East Thames Regional Health Authority* (1987) Dillon J stated that damages for distress were limited to cases

> 'where the contract which has been broken was itself a contract to provide peace of mind or freedom from distress.'

A similar view was taken by the Court of Appeal in *Hayes* v *James & Charles Dodd* (1988). It does not appear that the purchase of the stereo was such a contract and that therefore a claim in respect of the sentimental value of the tape could not be supported, as the damages would be too remote.

As the contract for the stereo has already been performed Simon cannot recover the money he paid for it: *Corpe* v *Overston* (1833).

The purchase of the golf clubs
It seems clear that the golf clubs are not necessaries. The supplier cannot therefore claim either the contract price or a reasonable price from Simon. Simon can, however, be held liable to restore the golf clubs to General Trading plc. Such liability was imposed in equity before the Minors Contract Act 1987. Section 3(1) of the Act now gives the court a discretion to order the minor to transfer to the adult party any property acquired by the minor under a contract which was not enforceable against him. There seems to be no reason why the court would not exercise its discretion in favour of General Trading plc and order Simon to transfer the golf clubs back to them.

SUGGESTED ANSWER TO QUESTION THREE

General Comment

A further problem concerning the enforceability of contracts entered into by a minor, this is a fairly complex question and requires separation out into three contracts. Once this has been done, it is quite straightforward and may be tackled with confidence.

Key Points

- Meaning of minor – s1 Family Law Reform Act 1969

The contract with the supermarket
- The supermarket is bound by the contract
- The minor cannot claim specific performance but can claim for an agreed sum – *Flight* v *Boland* (1828)

The contract with Dr Manieri
- Minors are bound by contracts for necessaries
- Definition of 'necessaries' – *Chapple* v *Cooper* (1844); *Peters* v *Fleming* (1840); *Nash* v *Inman* (1908); s3(3) Sale of Goods Act 1979
- The minor may not be bound if the contract is executory only – *Roberts* v *Gray* (1913)

The loan from the bank
- A minor is not liable on a loan contract even if to purchase necessaries – *Darby* v *Boucher* (1694)
- If he has purchased necessaries, the lender may be able to recover the part of the loan used for that purpose – *Marlow* v *Pitfield* (1719); *Re National Permanent Benefit Building Society* (1869)
- The piano could be a necessary – s3(3) Sale of Goods Act 1979
- Even if the loan was obtained by misrepresentation, the bank could not sue – *R Leslie Ltd* v *Sheill* (1914)
- Payments made to the bank cannot be recovered – *Corpe* v *Overston* (1833)

The debt to the bookmaker
- Such debts are unenforceable whether against a minor or adult

Suggested Answer

G, being aged 16 years, is a minor in law: the age of majority is 18 years: s1 Family Law Reform Act 1969. The purpose of the law with regard to minors' contracts is to prevent minors from incurring liability for imprudent bargains because of their inexperience, but also to avoid causing hardship to adults who deal with minors in good faith. Certain contracts are binding on minors; contracts for necessary goods and services; and contracts of service, if for the benefit of the minor as a whole. Certain contracts are voidable at the instance of the minor, but these are not relevant to this problem. Even if a minor is not bound by a contract, the other party may be bound and the contract may have other effects.

The contract with the supermarket

G entered into a service contract with the supermarket. It is not necessary to discuss whether or not G was bound by that contract; in either event the supermarket is bound. Where a contract is not binding on the minor, but is binding on the other party, the minor's remedies are limited in that he cannot claim specific performance: *Flight* v *Boland* (1828). G's claim is, however, for the payment of an agreed sum; whilst it is a claim for the specific performance of the supermarket's obligation to pay the agreed wages, as it is simply a claim for money it is not subject to the restrictions which equity imposes on the enforcement of specific performance. Accordingly, G can claim the £800 owing to him.

The contract with Dr Manieri

Minors are bound by contracts for necessaries. Necessaries consist of necessary goods and necessary services; such services include education of either a liberal or a vocational nature: *Chapple* v *Cooper* (1844). Necessaries are defined in relation to goods as 'such articles as are fit to maintain the particular person in the state, station and degree ... in which he is': *Peters* v *Fleming* (1840). According to Treitel any service can be necessary if it satisfies the test in relation to necessary goods. As G is intent on becoming a professional piano-player it would appear that the piano lessons do fall within the category of necessary services. The question is, however, whether G is bound by an executory contract for these services. It is still a matter for dispute whether a minor is bound by an executory contract for necessary goods: see the differing views of Fletcher Moulton J and Buckley J in *Nash* v *Inman* (1908). The definition of necessary goods in s3(3) Sale of Goods Act 1979 suggests that goods can only be necessaries when they have been actually delivered; a minor would not be bound by an executory contract for such goods. On the authority of *Roberts* v *Gray* (1913), however, it is submitted that so far as necessary services are concerned a minor is bound by the contract for such services even though it is partly executory. G can, therefore, be held liable in damages to Dr Manieri.

The loan from the bank

A minor cannot be made liable on a loan, nor can he be made liable on a loan advanced to enable him to purchase necessaries: *Darby* v *Boucher* (1694). Where the minor has actually used a portion of the loan to discharge his liability for necessaries supplied to him, the lender can in equity recover that portion of the loan used for that purpose: *Marlow* v *Pitfield* (1719); *Re National Permanent Benefit Building Society* (1869). It appears that G has purchased, and paid for, a piano for the sum of £5,000 from the proceeds of the loan. Was the piano a necessary? This question is not without difficulty.

In s53(3) Sale of Goods Act 1979 necessaries are defined as 'goods suitable to the condition in life of the minor ... and to his actual requirements at the time of sale and delivery.' In view of his ambition to become a professional piano-player, a piano might well be regarded as a necessary. What is questionable is whether an apparently expensive instrument, one costing £5,000, could be suitable to G's 'condition in life' and to 'his actual requirements at the time of sale and delivery'. At the time G obtained the loan from the bank, and presumably when he purchased the piano, G apparently believed that he was to receive a substantial inheritance – a belief that proved to be ill-founded. If the piano could be considered a necessary then the bank could recover the £5,000 expended on it. It is, however, arguable that, even if at the time of purchase G was potentially wealthy, a piano costing £5,000 was not suitable to the condition in life of a minor then having to supplement his income by working as a delivery boy; nor, at the commencement of his piano studies, was it suitable to his actual requirements.

There is the possible suggestion in the question that G may have misrepresented the position with regard to his parents' estate to the bank, perhaps fraudulently. Even if this were so the bank would not be able to sue G in tort for recovery of the loan made to him. To allow the bank to do so would be an indirect method of enforcing the invalid contract: *R Leslie Ltd* v *Sheill* (1914).

In conclusion, the bank can probably neither recover the loan, nor can it recover the £5,000 as expenditure made on a necessary. However, the bank is not without a remedy. Under s53(1) Minors' Contracts Act 1987 the court 'may, if it is just and equitable to do so, require (G) to transfer to the (bank) any property acquired by (G) under the contract, or any property representing it'. By virtue of this provision the bank may be able to obtain an order for the transfer of the piano to them.

It remains to note that, although G is not bound by the contract of loan, he cannot recover any payments he has made to the bank: *Corpe* v *Overston* (1833).

The debt to the bookmaker

There is no question of G being held liable for this debt as gambling contracts are unenforceable no matter who the parties are.

SUGGESTED ANSWER TO QUESTION FOUR

General Comment

This problem question on the enforceability of contracts made by a minor is neatly divided into three straightforward parts. It should be easily tackled by any candidate with a good knowledge of the topic.

Key Points

The purchase of the cufflinks
- A minor is bound by a contract for necessary goods – *Peters* v *Fleming* (1840); s3(3) Sale of Goods Act 1979; *Ryder* v *Wombwell* (1869); *Nash* v *Inman* (1908)
- If the cufflinks are not necessaries, the seller may be able to recover the goods – s3(1) Minors' Contracts Act 1987

The purchase of the exercise bicycle from Kenneth
- A bicycle may be a necessary – *Clyde Cycle Co* v *Hargreaves* (1898)
- If not a necessary, Jason will not be able to recover the money paid – *Wilson* v *Kearse* (1800); *Corpe* v *Overston* (1883); *Ex parte Taylor* (1856)

The contract to work for Simon
- A minor is bound by beneficial contracts of service – *Clements* v *L & N W Ry* (1894); *Doyle* v *White City Stadium Ltd* (1935); *De Francesco* v *Barnum* (1890)

- Specific performance may not be awarded against Jason – s16 Trade Union and Labour Relations Act 1974

Suggested Answer

Jason, being under the age of 18, is a minor in law – s1 Family Law Reform Act 1969. This question, therefore, raises the issue of the contractual capacity of minors. Jason has entered into three contracts: (i) the purchase of the cufflinks from Harold; (ii) the purchase of the exercise bicycle from Kenneth; and (iii) the agreement to work as an assistant in Simon's shop. These three transactions will be considered in turn.

The purchase of the cufflinks

A minor is bound by a contract for necessary goods – described in *Peters* v *Fleming* (1842) as:

> 'such goods as are fit to maintain the particular person in the state, station and degree ... in which he is'.

Section 3(3) Sale of Goods Act 1979 defines 'necessaries' as:

> 'goods suitable to the condition in life of the minor ... and to his actual requirements at the time of the sale and delivery'.

There is a paucity of modern authority as to the nature of necessaries. In *Peters* v *Fleming* (1840) jewellery supplied to the son of a wealthy man were found to be necessaries, but in *Ryder* v *Wombwell* (1869) the court set aside the verdict of a jury that similar items were necessaries. It is, perhaps, doubtful whether these two mid-nineteenth-century cases can provide much guidance in the present day.

The onus is on Harold to show that the cufflinks were necessaries. He would have to prove not only that they were capable of being necessaries, but that they actually were necessaries in Jason's case: *Nash* v *Inman* (1908). It seems unlikely that Harold could discharge this onus – it is difficult to conceive that gold cufflinks costing £200 could be regarded as necessaries for a 17-year-old.

If they are not necessaries the contract is unenforceable against Jason. The purchase price cannot be recovered from him. However, Harold is not without a remedy. Equity provides the remedy of restitution where non-necessary goods were sold and transferred to a minor who was guilty of fraud. At common law restitution can also be ordered in certain cases of quasi-contract. This remedy is now also afforded by statute: s3(1) Minors' Contracts Act 1987 gives the court a discretion to order the minor to transfer to the plaintiff any property acquired by the minor under a contract which was not enforceable against him. There does not appear to be any reason why the court should not exercise its discretion in favour of Harold and order Jason to restore the cufflinks to him. The possibility should briefly be considered that, by virtue of Jason's particular circumstances, these articles are considered to be necessaries, although – as has been indicated – this is thought to be unlikely. If they are necessaries s3(2) Sale of Goods Act provides that the minor must pay a reasonable price for them. This may not be the contract price, but there is insufficient information to determine what it might be.

The purchase of the exercise bicycle from Kenneth

The question here again is whether this article can be considered to be a necessary. A helpful authority is, possibly, *Clyde Cycle Co* v *Hargreaves* (1898), which concerned the purchase of a racing bicycle by an apprentice. This was held to be a necessary. However, too much reliance should not be placed on that case. It is not conclusive with regard to the present problem; much depends on the price of the exercise bicycle and on Jason's particular requirements. Both possibilities must be considered: that the bicycle is not a necessary, and that it is. If it is not a necessary the contract would not be enforceable against Jason. But it appears that he has already paid for it. He cannot recover the money paid simply on the ground that he was not bound by the contract because of his minority. Treitel cites three authorities in support of this proposition: *Wilson* v *Kearse* (1800): *Corpe* v *Overston* (1883); and *Ex parte Taylor* (1856). The right to reject the goods and reclaim the purchase price would have to be based on grounds that were also available to an adult.

If the bicycle is a necessary then Jason is bound by the contract, subject to the aforestated provision in the Sale of Goods Act that he would have been required to pay only 'a reasonable price', not necessarily the contract price. But what a reasonable price might have been is of academic interest: he has made the payment and, as indicated by the above three authorities, once the minor has performed the contract, he cannot recover the money.

The contract to work for Simon

This is a contract of service, and the rule in this regard is that a minor is bound by beneficial contracts of service. The test is this: if the contract is to the minor's benefit as a whole, he will be bound by it, notwithstanding that it contains certain provisions that are to his disadvantage: *Clements* v *L & N W Railway* (1894); *Doyle* v *White City Stadium Ltd* (1935). He will not be bound by a service contract if it is on the whole harsh and oppressive: *De Francesco* v *Barnum* (1890). It is difficult to be certain whether or not Jason's contract with Simon would fall into the latter category. No information is given as to the hours of work, the other conditions of the employment and his remuneration. It is conceivable that the mere requirement of six months' notice from a minor performing a menial task would persuade the court that the contract is harsh and oppressive. In that event the contract would not be binding on Jason, and he would not incur any liability by leaving. Even if the contract is binding on Jason the remedy available to Simon is somewhat limited. He could not obtain an order which would have the effect of compelling Jason to return to work. The courts have long refused to order specific performance of contracts involving personal service, and such an order is prohibited by s16 Trade Union and Labour Relations Act 1974. Simon would be confined to a claim for damages for the breach of contract and, in view of the nature of the employment and the plaintiff's duty to mitigate his loss, such claim would only realise an extremely modest amount, and the damages might only be nominal.

7
Mistake

Introduction

Mistake is a topic which provides fertile ground for both problem questions, centring on the practical effects of a mistake, and discussion questions aimed at eliciting an analysis of the legal effects. It also combines well with other topics such as misrepresentation or, more rarely, offer and acceptance. This chapter provides examples of several types of question.

The plethora of material on mistake derives from the classification of mistakes into distinct types and the treatment of the effect of a mistake differently at common law and in equity. This has given rise to abundant case law and fine distinctions.

For obvious reasons, there is no general principle that a mistake will nullify a contract. Candidates wishing to attempt a mistake question should therefore demonstrate a clear knowledge of the types of mistake which the law permits to affect a contract, and their respective effects, ie whether the contract is void or voidable in law and what are the practical effects of that legal distinction on the respective rights of the parties and any third party concerned.

Questions

INTERROGRAMS

1   Explain what is meant by a plea of non est factum.
2   Explain and comment upon the statement that a contract is not made void by a mistake as to the attributes of the other contracting party.
3   How does mistake affect the validity of a contract (if at all) when it leads to the parties being at cross purposes?

QUESTION ONE

'A common mistake, even on a most fundamental matter, does not make a contract void at law: but makes it voidable in equity' (per Lord Denning MR in *Magee* v *Peninne Insurance*).

Explain and comment.

London University LLB Examination
(for external students) Elements of the Law of Contract June 1985 Q5

QUESTION TWO

'If the parties to a contract are labouring under a common mistake of fact when the contract is made the contract is valid but equity may set it aside.'
Explain and comment.

London University LLB Examination
(for external students) Elements of the Law of Contract June 1988 Q4

QUESTION THREE

P and Q are rival art dealers who live in the same town. In August 1988, while P was on holiday in Spain, he acquired what he honestly believed was a valuable painting by Goya. On returning home he offered the painting for sale. Q, after having viewed the painting and also believing it to be a Goya, sent his agent, W, to buy the painting, instructing him to pose as Sir Charles Trevelyan. P sold the painting to W for £250,000, pleased at last that he was attracting wealthy clientele. Q subsequently resold the painting for £300,000 to S who also believed it was a Goya. Last month all the parties discovered that they were mistaken and that the painting is in fact a missing part of Guernica by Picasso and that the art world has been searching for this painting for years. It is worth £2,000,000.

Advise P.

London University LLB Examination
(for external students) Elements of the Law of Contract June 1989 Q5

QUESTION FOUR

D was an antiques dealer specialising in the sale of china. D put cups, saucers and other items in his shop window with lengthy descriptions on the price tags.

a   A cup and saucer were described as early Swansea and the price was £150. D and E, who bought them from D, both believed that they had been accurately described but in fact they proved to be excellent fakes.

b   A teapot was offered for sale at £200. F, believing that it was early Welsh Blue, agreed to purchase it. In fact it was Staffordshire Blue and worth much less. D knew of F's mistake but had said nothing.

c   G walked into the shop and offered D £3,500 for a Nantgarw tea set. D agreed to sell it. G offered to pay by cheque which D refused to accept without some proof of identification. G had pretended to be Sir Robert Slip and G gave his address as Slip Hall. D checked the local trade directory and found that Sir Robert Slip lived at the address given. G also produced a Racing Club membership card containing G's photograph and with the subscription Sir Robert Slip. D allowed G to take the china. G sold the Nantgarw to H, another antique dealer, before D learned that the cheque had 'bounced'.

Advise D.

London University LLB Examination
(for external students) Elements of the Law of Contract June 1991 Q5

QUESTION FIVE

A, who is emigrating to Australia in three months, invites his two work colleagues, B and C, to his house. A offers to sell his favourite painting to B for £1,000 which B accepts. Both A and B believe the painting is by a little known French artist and is probably worth between £1,000 and £2,000.

A also offers to sell his two dining candlesticks to C for £500, which offer C accepts. C believes the candlesticks are gold and worth about £3,000. A knows C believes the candlesticks are gold but he knows that they are only cheap imitations.

A few days later, B and C decide to have their new purchases valued. B took the painting to an art-dealer who identified it as a Manet and offered B £250,000 for it, but B refused to sell. C showed his candlesticks to an expert who informed him that they were made of a very cheap metal and were probably worth about £20 each.

C immediately took the candlesticks around to A's house and demanded his money back which A refused. C also told A about the news that B had received at the art dealer's.

Advise the parties as to their rights and liabilities.

London University LLB Examination
(for external students) Elements of the Law of Contract June 1992 Q5

QUESTION SIX

'A rigid doctrine of mistake in contract at common law is being replaced by excessively flexible principles of equity.'
  Discuss.

London University LLB Examination
(for external students) Elements of the Law of Contract June 1993 Q2

QUESTION SEVEN

On Monday, A wrote to B offering to buy B's picture painted by Augustus John for £25,000. On Tuesday, B replied by leaving a message on A's answerphone stating, 'I assume that you mean the painting of four sisters and I accept.' The painting was worth £20,000. In addition to the painting called 'Four Sisters' B owned another painting by Augustus John called 'Forbidden Fruit' worth £30,000. It was 'Forbidden Fruit' to which A was referring in his letter. On Wednesday, A was told that B owned two paintings by Augustus John, played back his answerphone and sent a message by electronic mail, via internet to B's number saying, 'I accept both at £50,000. Unless I hear from you within two days I will assume that they are mine. You need not bother to reply.' B replied by letter to A stating, 'I may be prepared to sell both.' However, this letter was lost in the post.

Advise the parties. What difference, if any, would it make to your advice if (a) because of a computer fault B had not received A's electronic mail message, or (b) because of a transmission failure the electronic mail message was incomplete and all that B received was, 'I accept'.

London University LLB Examination
(for external students) Elements of the Law of Contract June 1995 Q1

Answers

ANSWERS TO INTERROGRAMS

1   A plea of non est factum (meaning 'not my deed') will enable a party to avoid liability under a contract if he or she can prove that it was signed under a mistake as to the essential nature of the document. The relief is an equitable one and, because of the danger of abuse is construed very strictly.

Some cases illustrate how the plea has evolved since it was first allowed. Originally, the mistake had to be as to the character of the document (ie not as to its contents): *Howatson* v *Webb* (1907). In *Foster* v *Mackinnon* (1869), the plea succeeded when an elderly man was induced to indorse a bill of exchange by being told that it was merely a guarantee. Equally, it was successful in *Lewis* v *Clay* (1898) when the promissory notes were signed under the mistaken impression that the signatory was merely witnessing another's signature.

This distinction was, however, much criticised and was rejected in the leading House of Lords case: *Gallie* v *Lee* (1971). In that case, the plaintiff gave the deeds of her house to her nephew so that he could raise money on the property. L, a friend of P's, induced her to sign a conveyance of the property to him by telling her that it related to the deed of gift to her nephew. The plaintiff was unable to read the document for herself as she had lost her spectacles. L mortgaged the property to a building society who claimed possession for default. The test employed by the House of Lords was that the document must be 'fundamentally', 'radically' or 'totally' different to what the signatory believed it to be. In that case, the plaintiff was not held to have satisfied the test. The new test has also attracted criticism as being likely to lead to uncertainty.

A further restriction on the plea is that it is only available to persons who, for some permanent or temporary reason, are incapable of both reading and sufficiently understanding the document to be signed, and must be unable to understand to the extent that they are unable to detect a fundamental difference between the actual document and the document they had believed it to be: Lord Pearson in *Gallie* v *Lee*. The reason for their inability to comprehend the nature of the document may be due to defective education, illness, innate incapacity, senility or some other cause. Non est factum is not available to someone who grants a power of attorney and then finds that the donee has abused it: *Norwich & Peterborough Building Society* v *Steed* (1992).

2   What falls to be discussed initially here is whether a distinction can be drawn between a mistake as to identity of the contracting party and a mistake as to the attributes of that party. This distinction was made in *King's Norton Metal Co Ltd* v *Edridge, Merrett & Co Ltd* (1897) where the Court of Appeal was constrained to distinguish the facts of that case from those present in the earlier case of *Cundy* v *Lindsay* (1878). In the latter case a party called 'Blenkarn' disguised his letter so as to make it appear to be from a respectable firm called 'Blenkiron & Co' whom the plaintiff knew. It was held by the House of Lords that the mistake was one as to identity which rendered the contract void. In *King's Norton Metal*, on the other

hand, where the rogue fraudulently misrepresented himself as the proprietor of a large business – which did not in fact exist – the mistake was held to be only one as to attributes. This rendered the contract merely voidable, not void.

In *Phillips* v *Brooks* (1919) the rogue obtained goods on credit by fraudulently misrepresenting himself as a well-known titled person. The mistake here was held to be only one as to attributes, that is the creditworthiness of the rogue, and again the contract was voidable only and not void. It is difficult to distinguish this case from that of *Ingram* v *Little* (1961) where the rogue in that instance obtained possession of a car from the sellers having persuaded them to accept a worthless cheque on the strength of his misrepresentation that he was some other person. In *Ingram* v *Little* the sellers were able to recover the car from an innocent third party to whom the rogue had 'sold' the car, the mistake here being regarded as one rendering the contract void.

In *Lewis* v *Averay* (1972) the rogue pretended to be a well-known film actor and gave a worthless cheque in the actor's name in return for the car. The plaintiff seller only allowed the car to be taken away when the rogue produced a special admission card to a film studio to prove that he was the actor. The Court of Appeal followed *Phillips* v *Brooks* and distinguished and disapproved *Ingram* v *Little* and held that the contract was voidable only. It appears therefore that *Ingram* v *Little* is no longer to be relied on although it has not yet been overruled.

Lord Denning stated in *Lewis* v *Avery* that the distinction between a mistake as to identity and a mistake as to attributes was a distinction without a difference. His Lordship also stated that he did not accept the theory that a mistake as to identity renders a contract void. This approach is in conflict with *Cundy* v *Lindsay*, but Lord Denning expressed the view that the case would not be decided in the same way today.

Professor Glanville Williams has also argued that the distinction between attributes and identity is based on a fundamental misconception. He states that what the courts have chosen to call a mistake as to identity is in fact a mistake as to attributes.

It is clear from the authorities cited that, if the distinction between attributes and identity is still valid, a mistake as to attributes does not make the contract void. What is less certain is whether this distinction can validly be made, and, if it can, the extent to which a mistake as to identity will make the contract void.

3   It is submitted that the statement in question refers to three quite different situations, namely:

a   where the effect of the mistake is that offer and acceptance do not coincide and there is therefore no true agreement between the parties;
b   where there is a mistake as to the terms of the offer known to the other party;
c   where there is a mistake as to identity.

These will be considered in turn.

The classic example of (a) is *Raffles* v *Wichelhaus* (1864). Here the parties contracted for the sale and purchase of a cargo of cotton on board the ship Peerless from Bombay. There were two ships of this name, each of which had sailed from Bombay carrying cotton. The contracting parties each intended the contract to deal with a different ship. Since it was impossible for the court to say that the subject matter of the contract was either one cargo or the other, the contract was held to be void for mistake.

A less obvious example is *Scriven Bros & Co* v *Hindley & Co* (1913) where an auctioneer and bidder intended to deal with different subject matter. Here the court concluded the contract was void only because the auction catalogue was somewhat ambiguous: but for this the bidder would probably have been stuck with the lot knocked down to him, whether or not he wanted it.

These two cases are variously treated by commentators as being mistake cases or as being offer and acceptance cases. Their classification is probably not so important as the principle that they illustrate, namely that in exceptional cases where the parties are at cross purposes and it is impossible objectively to impute an agreement to them, consent will be negatived and no contract concluded.

Category (b) derives from the decision of the Court of Queen's Bench in *Smith* v *Hughes* (1871) and is best regarded as an exception to the caveat emptor rule and the general principle that one party is under no duty to correct a misapprehension the other may have (unless the former has caused or contributed to it). The rule in *Smith* v *Hughes* is that where one party makes a mistake as to the terms of the contract, and the other knows of that mistake, the contract is void. The rationale for this principle is that not only are the parties not ad idem, but one of them knows they are not ad idem. Thus in *Hartog* v *Colin and Shields* (1939), where negotiations for skins had been conducted on the basis of a price per piece, it was held that no contract was concluded where one party purported to accept an offer mistakenly made by the other at a price per pound.

Category (c), mistake as to identity, has given rise to a good deal of case law. With some diffidence, it is suggested that the following principles represent the present state of the law.

Where the parties are not physically in each other's presence (eg they are dealing by correspondence), and one party is mistaken as to the identity – not the attributes – of the other and intends instead to deal with some identifiable third party, and the other knows this, then the contract will be void for mistake: *Cundy* v *Lindsay* (1878) and *King's Norton Metal* v *Edridge, Merritt & Co Ltd* (1897).

However, where the parties are inter praesentes, there is a strong presumption which will rarely, if ever, be rebutted, that the parties intend to deal with the person physically present and identifiable by sight and sound, irrespective of the identity which one or other may assume: *Phillips* v *Brooks* (1919) and *Lewis* v *Avery* (1972). Nevertheless, there is some authority (*Lake* v *Simmons* (1927) and *Ingram* v *Little* (1961)) which suggests that in exceptional cases a mistake as to identity inter praesentes can negative consent so as to render a contract void.

SUGGESTED ANSWER TO QUESTION ONE

General Comment

This essay question based on the dictum of Lord Denning is not an easy one to answer. It is often important to decide whether a contract is void or voidable, for this will determine the remedies available to the parties and, in relation to mistake in particular, the rights of any third party who may have innocently acquired the subject matter of the contract. On the question of the effect of common mistake, however, the judgments are not clear and, as the answer below endeavours to explain, Lord Denning's attempt to clarify the matter has not removed the doubt which exists in this area.

Key Points

- Common mistake at common law – *Bell* v *Lever Brothers Ltd* (1932)
- Res extincta – *Couturier* v *Hastie* (1856); *McRae* v *Commonwealth Disposals Commission* (1951)
- Implication of a term that neither party is bound if certain assumed facts are incorrect – *Bell* v *Lever Brothers Ltd* (1932)
- Allocation of risk – *Amalgamated Investment and Property Co Ltd* v *John Walker & Sons Ltd* (1977); *Hitchcock* v *Giddings* (1817); *Cooper* v *Phibbs* (1867); *Gompertz* v *Bartlett* (1853)
- Common mistake in equity – *Solle* v *Butcher* (1950); *Grist* v *Bailey* (1967); *Magee* v *Pennine Insurance* (1969); *Laurence* v *Lexcourt Holdings Ltd* (1978)

Suggested Answer

The extract from Lord Denning's judgment in *Magee* v *Pennine Insurance Co Ltd* (1969) echoes his Lordship's earlier statements of principles on the law of mistake in his judgment in *Solle* v *Butcher* (1950). Properly to analyse this statement requires a discussion of, first, common mistake at law, and secondly, common mistake in equity. In considering common mistake at law, his Lordship has always taken the radical view of the leading House of Lords case on the subject, *Bell* v *Lever Brothers Ltd* (1932). His Lordship has consistently said that, in *Bell*, the House of Lords decided that contracts are never void for common mistake. Whilst it is true that the decision on the facts was that the compensation agreements entered into between Bell and Snelling on the one hand, and Levers on the other, were not void for common mistake, it is respectfully submitted that his Lordship's approach is perhaps a little simplistic. Certainly *Bell* is a difficult case from which to extract a ratio decidendi, but it is suggested that in their speeches the majority were endeavouring to state the circumstances in which a contract would be void for common mistake. The fact that this may not have done so with the clarity one might have desired does no mean that there is no doctrine of common mistake at law.

His Lordship's view is also not one that has attracted widespread judicial or academic support. The normal approach to *Bell*'s case is to seek to derive from it a workable test as to when a contract will be void for common mistake, rather than to deny the possibility altogether. Thus Cheshire and Fifoot have argued that *Bell* decided that a contract will be void for common mistake whether its subject matter is, unknown to the parties, non-existent (res extincta). Whilst this may well be an example of a void contract, it may be doubted whether it is the only type of mistake that will suffice. The learned authors' reasoning is perhaps weakened by their reliance on *Couturier* v *Hastie* (1856) which, as the Australian High Court convincingly demonstrated in *McRae* v *Commonwealth Disposals Commission* (1951), turned on no more than the simple proposition that a seller who is unable to deliver a specific cargo is not entitled to recover the purchase price therefor from the buyer and was not really a case of mistake at all.

Alternatively Slade has argued that a contract will only be void for common mistake where it is possible to imply a term into it that if certain assumed facts are incorrect, neither party is bound by the transaction. Whilst this view derives some support from the speech of Lord Atkin in *Bell*, ultimately it is not a satisfactory basis upon which to found the doctrine of mistake. The supposed term cannot be implied by any of the conventional tests (eg business efficacy, officious bystander, custom or usage, or a necessary incident of the parties' legal relationship) and is artificial since it demands a good deal of judicial creativity to discover such a term in any contract.

Yet another approach, which gives a broader interpretation to *Bell* than that propounded by Lord Denning, is formulated by the editors of *Chitty on Contracts*. They suggest that mistake is all about the allocation of risk. Ordinarily, one or other party will have taken the risk that certain facts which are assumed to be true are not true, and in such a case there is no room for the operation of the doctrine of mistake. Where, however, on the true construction of the contract neither party has taken that risk, so it is said, the contract is void for mistake.

This view commended itself to Sir John Pennycuick in *Amalgamated Investment & Property Co Ltd* v *John Walker & Sons Ltd* (1977) and is to some extent at least consistent with the tenor of the speeches of the majority in *Bell*. It can also be reconciled with some of the older pre-*Bell* mistake cases such as *Hitchcock* v *Giddings* (1817) (res extincta), *Cooper* v *Phibbs* (1867) (mistake as to title), and *Gompertz* v *Bartlett* (1853) (mistake as to quality). Also, *McRae* can be regarded as a case in which the sellers, having warranted the existence of the vessel, took the risk that it did not exist and were therefore liable in damages to the buyers.

Thus, to conclude on the common law, one can say that, with respect to Lord Denning, his statement probably does not accurately reflect the law of England.

Turning next to equity, the first case unequivocally to establish that a contract which is not void at law for common mistake may nevertheless be voidable in equity was *Solle* v *Butcher*, where Denning J (as he then was) said that a contract was liable to be set aside if the parties were under a common misapprehension either as to facts or as to their relative and respective rights, providing the misapprehension was fundamental and the party seeking to set aside the transaction was not at fault. Whilst the authorities from which the court sought to derive this principle perhaps did not justify their radical innovation, since *Solle* this new equitable jurisdiction has become firmly established in *Grist* v *Bailey* (1967), *Magee* v *Pennine Insurance Co Ltd* (1969) and *Laurence* v *Lexcourt Holdings Ltd* (1978). The new jurisdiction holds that a contract may be voidable for common mistake in equity even though it is valid at law and, moreover, that the court can impose terms upon which equitable relief is granted.

Although Lord Denning has suggested that equity has supplanted the common law entirely, it is submitted that unless and until *Bell* is reconsidered by the House of Lords, that case remains authority for the proposition that contracts may be void for common mistake, albeit in limited and uncertain circumstances. The happiest reconciliation of *Bell* on the one hand and *Solle* and the subsequent equity cases on the other may be that suggested by Goff J (as he then was) in *Grist* v *Bailey*. First, his Lordship asked himself whether the contract was void at law and, holding that *Bell* confined mistake at law within very narrow limits, decided it was not. Secondly, his Lordship then asked whether the contract was nevertheless voidable in equity, where the test is less rigorous. On the facts his Lordship concluded that the parties' mistake (as to the security of terms enjoyed by the occupant of a house being offered for sale) was sufficiently fundamental to justify the grant of relief in equity.

Thus, to conclude, in terms of strict legal theory, it is respectfully suggested that Lord Denning's statement in *Magee* is incorrect and that contracts may be void for common mistake, not merely voidable. In practical terms, however, the problems posed by an analysis of *Bell* and the now flourishing equitable doctrine of mistake stemming from *Solle* means that it is to equity rather than the common law that litigants will look in seeking relief from a common mistake.

SUGGESTED ANSWER TO QUESTION TWO

General Comment

One aspect of the law on common mistake which makes it a complex and difficult area for the student is that the common law and equity have historically taken different views. As a complete answer to the question necessitates discussion of all categories of mistake in relation to each of law and equity, the candidate's knowledge of this topic is being extensively tested. It goes without saying that such a question should not be attempted without a thorough knowledge of the case law. In addition, such a complex analysis could easily get out of hand and so it is essential to pre-plan for a well structured answer such as that given below.

Key Points

- Mistake as to the existence of the subject matter - *Couturier* v *Hastie* (1856); *McRae* v *Commonwealth Disposals Commission* (1951); *Associated Japanese Bank (International) Ltd* v *Credit du Nord SA* (1988)
- Mistake as to title - *Cooper* v *Phibbs* (1867); *Bell* v *Lever Brothers Ltd* (1932)
- False and fundamental assumption - *Griffiths* v *Brymer* (1903); *Bell* v *Lever Brothers Ltd* (1932); *Scott* v *Coulson* (1903); *Galloway* v *Galloway* (1914); *Sheik Brothers Ltd* v *Ochsner* (1957)
- Mistake as to quality - *Kennedy* v *Panama Royal Mail Co* (1867); *Smith* v *Hughes* (1871); *Leaf* v *International Galleries* (1950); *Harrison & Jones* v *Bunten and Lancaster Ltd* (1953); *Nicholson and Venn* v *Smith-Marriott* (1947); *Peco Arts Inc* v

Hazlitt Gallery Ltd (1983); *Amalgamated Investment and Property Co Ltd* v *John Walker & Sons Ltd* (1976); *Solle* v *Butcher* (1950); *Grist* v *Bailey* (1967)

Suggested Answer

The assumption behind the quotation in this question is that the landmark decision of the House of Lords in *Bell* v *Lever Brothers Ltd* (1932) has virtually eliminated the possibility of common mistake rendering the contract void at common law. It is submitted that the statement in the quotation is misleading, and in order to support this submission it will be convenient to examine common mistake under four headings.

i Mistake as to the existence of the subject matter.
ii Mistake as to title.
iii Mistake based on a false and fundamental assumption.
iv Mistake as to quality.

Mistake as to the existence of the subject matter

A contract will be void if the subject matter of the contract never existed or had ceased to exist at the time the contract was concluded. With regard to sale of goods, s6 Sale of Goods Act 1979 provides:

> 'Where there is a contract for the sale of specific goods, and the goods without the knowledge of the seller have perished at the time when the contract is made, the contract is void.'

At common law *Couturier* v *Hastie* (1856) is authority for the view that mistake as to the existence of the subject matter makes the contract void. Whilst the concept of the mistake was not the basis of the judgment in that case - indeed the word 'mistake' was not used in the judgments - there are clear indications in the decisions that the contract would be void for mistake. In his speech in the House of Lords, Lord Cranworth LC said that the whole question turned upon the construction of the contract which was entered into between the parties. The Lord Chancellor said that the contract plainly imported that there was something which was to be sold at the time of the contract, and something to be purchased. As no such thing existed, the Lord Chancellor clearly implied that the contract was void.

In *McRae* v *Commonwealth Disposals Commission* (1951) the High Court of Australia was able to distinguish the facts before it from *Couturier* v *Hastie.* There it was held that, as a matter of construction of the contract, there was an implied undertaking that the tanker existed. Whether or not *McRae* can be reconciled with *Couturier* is still a matter for argument. An explanation of the decision in *McCrae* is given by Steyn J in *Associated Japanese Bank (International) Ltd* v *Credit du Nord SA* (1988) where His Lordship suggested that a party should not be able to rely on a common mistake where he had no reasonable grounds for the belief.

Mistake as to title

In *Cooper* v *Phibbs* (1867), A agreed to take a lease of a fishery from B though, contrary to the belief of both parties at the time, A was tenant for life of the fishery and B apparently had no title at all. This mistake rendered the contract void. Lord Atkin in *Bell* thought that mistake as to title corresponded to mistake as to the existence of the subject matter.

False and fundamental assumption
There are circumstances where the parties share a false and fundamental assumption going to the root of the contract, and because of that mistake, the contract will be void. In *Griffiths* v *Brymer* (1903) the parties had entered into an agreement for the hire of a room to view the coronation procession of King Edward VII. However, the decision to operate on the King, which caused the cancellation of the procession, had been taken prior to the conclusion of the contract. It was held that the agreement was made on a missupposition of facts which went to the whole root of the matter of the contract. (It is perhaps doubtful whether this decision can stand with *Bell* v *Lever Brothers Ltd.*) In *Scott* v *Coulson* (1903) a contract for the assignment of a policy of life insurance concluded on the shared mistaken belief that the assured was still alive was held to be void for mistake. In *Galloway* v *Galloway* (1914) a separation deed entered into by the parties on the mistaken assumption they had a valid marriage was also held to be void. The above three cases were heard before *Bell*. However in *Sheik Brothers Ltd* v *Ochsner* (1957) a contract was held to be void for mistake because of an initial commercial impossibility. The case was decided under s20 Indian Contract Act 1872 but the Privy Council expressly applied the principles laid down in *Bell.*

Mistake as to quality
It does appear that mistake as to quality will rarely make the contract void at common law: see the authorities prior to *Bell* of *Kennedy* v *Panama Royal Mail Co* (1867) and *Smith* v *Hughes* (1871).

The decision in *Bell* turned on the question of mistake as to quality, and it is suggested in Cheshire, Fifoot and Furmston's *Law of Contract* that if the mistake in that case did not make the contract void, it would be difficult to envisage circumstances in which a contract would ever be void for mistake as to quality. In *Associated Japanese Bank* Steyn J suggested that this conclusion did not do justice to the speeches in *Bell*. Lord Atkin had held in *Bell* that:

> 'a mistake will not affect assent unless it is the mistake of both parties and is as to the existence of some quality which makes the thing without the quality essentially different from the thing it was believed to be.'

Since the decision in *Bell* it has proved difficult for the courts to find a contract void for mistake as to quality: *Leaf* v *International Galleries* (1950); *Harrison & Jones* v *Bunten and Lancaster Ltd* (1953). In *Nicholson and Venn* v *Smith-Marriott* (1947) and in *Peco Arts Inc* v *Hazlitt Gallery Ltd* (1983) the court would have been prepared to find the contracts in those cases void for mistake as to quality, but in neither case did the decision turn on that point. In *Associated Japanese Bank* Steyn J would also have been prepared to find the contract void for mistake as to quality, but again his Lordship decided the matter on other grounds. In the course of his judgment Steyn J suggested a number of guiding principles:

1 The first imperative was that the law ought to uphold rather than destroy apparent contracts.
2 The common law rules as to a mistake regarding the quality of the subject matter, like the common law rules regarding commercial frustration, are designed to cope with the impact of unexpected and wholly exceptional circumstances on apparent contracts.
3 Such a mistake must be substantially shared by both parties, and must relate to facts as they existed at the time the contract was made.
4 As established by *Bell* v *Lever Brothers Ltd* the mistake must render the subject matter of the contract essentially and radically different from the subject matter which the parties believed to exist.
5 A party cannot be allowed to rely on a common mistake where the mistake consists of a belief which is entertained by him without any reasonable grounds for such a belief. With regard to the latter point Steyn J referred to *McRae* v *Commonwealth Disposals Commission*.

Whilst there are circumstances in which a contract will be held to be void at common law for mistake, such circumstances appear to be limited and somewhat uncertain. Even where the contract is not void at common law, however, equity may be able to provide relief. In *Solle* v *Butcher* (1950) Lord Denning MR said that:

> 'A contract is also liable in equity to be set aside if the parties were under a common misapprehension either as to the facts or as to their relative and respective rights, provided that the misapprehension was fundamental and that the party seeking to set it aside was not himself at fault.'

The correctness of the decision in *Solle* v *Butcher* has been doubted – see for example *Amalgamated Investment & Property Co Ltd* v *John Walker and Sons Ltd* (1976). However, the equitable jurisdiction has become firmly established. The principles of *Solle* v *Butcher* have been considered and applied in the later cases of *Grist* v *Bailey* (1967), *Magee* v *Pennine Insurance Co Ltd* (1969) and *Laurence* v *Lexcourt Holdings Ltd* (1978). According to that jurisdiction a contract may be voidable for common mistake in equity even though it is valid at law. The courts can impose terms on which equitable relief is granted.

Whilst the equitable remedy of rescission is available for common mistake, the remedy is subject to certain bars. The right to rescind may be barred if:

1 the contract has been affirmed;
2 third-party rights have intervened;
3 there has been delay;
4 restitution has become impossible.

SUGGESTED ANSWER TO QUESTION THREE

General Comment

Two areas of mistake are presented for examination in this next question: identity and mutual mistake. In relation to identity mistake, the question is whether a third party has gained property rights in the subject matter of the contract which in turn depends on whether the contract is void or voidable – an area in which there is, as the good candidate will point out – some confusion. In relation to mutual mistake, again the question is whether a mistake as to quality can render the contract void or whether it is merely voidable and, the alternative views which exist concerning the ratio of *Bell* v *Lever Brothers Ltd*.

Key Points

Mistake as to identity
- Presumption in contracts inter praesentes that the seller intended to contract with the person before him – *Lewis* v *Averay* (1972); *King's Norton Metal Co Ltd* v *Edridge, Merrett & Co Ltd* (1897)
- The contract will be void if the identity of the buyer is crucial, voidable if it is not – *Cundy* v *Lindsay* (1878); *Phillips* v *Brooks* (1919); *Lewis* v *Averay* (1972); *Ingram* v *Little* (1961)
- If it is voidable, rather than void, the buyer will have obtained property rights which can be passed to an innocent third party to whom he sells – *Lewis* v *Averay* (1972); *Ingram* v *Little* (1961)

Mutual mistake
- Mistake as to quality rarely makes a contract void at common law – *Bell* v *Lever Brothers Ltd* (1932); *Leaf* v *International Galleries* (1950); *Kennedy* v *Panama Royal Mail Co* (1867); *Smith* v *Hughes* (1871); *Harrison & Jones* v *Bunten and Lancaster* (1953); *F E Rose (London) Ltd* v *W H Pim, Junior & Co Ltd* (1953)
- There are dicta to suggest that in this situation the court might regard the contract as void – *Nicholson and Venn* v *Smith Marriott* (1947); *Peco Arts Inc* v *Hazlitt Gallery Ltd* (1983); *Associated Japanese Bank (International) Ltd* v *Credit du Nord SA* (1988); *Solle* v *Butcher* (1950); *Magee* v *Pennine Insurance Co Ltd* (1969)
- Normally equity might provide a remedy but the remedy for mistake as to quality is barred here – *Solle* v *Butcher* (1950); *Magee* v *Pennine Insurance Co Ltd* (1969); *Grist* v *Bailey* (1967)

Suggested Answer

This question involves discussion of two areas of mistake; mistake as to identity, and mutual mistake.

Mistake as to identity
P sells the painting to W (Q's agent) in the mistaken belief that the buyer is Sir Charles Trevelyan. It seems clear that P has been induced to sell the painting to W by a fraudulent misrepresentation. Whilst the remedy of rescission may be available for such misrepresentation, in this case a third party has acquired rights to the painting, and this is a bar to rescission. Whether P has an action for damages in the tort of deceit against Q or his agent is beyond the scope of this question.

It will not therefore avail P merely to establish that the contract was voidable. P would wish to establish that the contract between himself and W was void at common law for mistake. If he can establish this, then neither W nor S will have acquired rights under the contract and he will be entitled to assert ownership of the painting. The question is: can he be successful in this contention?

In *Lewis* v *Averay* (1972) Lord Denning said that:

> 'When a dealing is had between a seller ... and a person who is actually there present before him, then the presumption in law is that there is a contract, even though there is a fraudulent impersonation by the buyer representing himself as a different man than he is.'

The Court of Appeal derived support from the long-standing decision in *Phillips* v *Brooks Ltd* (1919) where the principle was held to be that the fact that one party is mistaken as to the identity of the other does not mean that there is no contract, or that the contract is a nullity and void from the beginning. This principle appears also to have been accepted by the Court of Appeal in *King's Norton Metal Co Ltd* v *Edridge, Merrett & Co Ltd* (1897).

However there are decisions which appear to be contrary to these authorities, and these must be briefly examined. *Ingram* v *Little* (1961) is difficult to reconcile with either *Phillips* v *Brooks* (1919) or *Lewis* v *Averay* (1972). Although it is a Court of Appeal decision it is submitted that, in view of the criticisms directed against it in *Lewis* and the balance of authority against it, it must be considered of doubtful authority or as turning on its own facts. *Cundy* v *Lindsay* (1878), where the contract was found to be void for mistake can be distinguished. The parties there were not inter praesentes and the decision can be explained on the ground that the offer was made to one person and accepted by another; this is the explanation given by Lord Denning in the Court of Appeal hearing in *Gallie* v *Lee* (1969). The same explanation can be given for the case of *Boulton* v *Jones* (1857).

P must be advised, therefore, that he would be highly unlikely to be able to persuade a court that the contract with W was void for mistake at common law. The equitable remedy of rescission would not avail him for the reason previously given.

Mutual mistake
The actual purchaser of the painting was Q and both he and P were operating under the mistaken belief that the painting was a Goya, whereas it was, in fact, by Picasso. This can be characterised as a mistake as to quality. It appears that this type of mistake rarely makes the contract void at common law. The decision of the House of Lords in *Bell* v *Lever Brothers Ltd* (1932) seems to confine operative mistake as to quality to very narrow limits. In *Bell* Lord Atkin said that:

> 'a mistake will not affect assent unless it is the mistake of both parties and is as to the existence of some quality which makes the thing without the quality essentially different from the thing it was believed to be.'

At first sight the mistake here does seem to meet even this restrictive requirement. But, in his speech, Lord Atkin gave a number of examples of mistake as to quality which his Lordship averred would not affect the validity of the contract. One example is the purchase of a picture which both parties believe to be work of an old master, but which turns out to be a modern copy. This is analogous to the situation here. But this example is cogently criticised by Treitel. He argues that a mistake of this nature stands on a different level from Lord Atkin's other examples. In *Leaf* v *International Galleries* (1950) the purchaser bought a painting under the mistaken belief that it was the work of Constable. There are dicta in that case to the effect that this mistake would not have rendered the contract void. But, as Treitel observes, these dicta are not conclusive; the decision did not turn on that point, the plaintiff only claimed rescission for misrepresentation.

In cases prior to *Bell* the courts, whilst recognising that mistake as to quality could make a contract void, have not been ready to do so: see *Kennedy* v *Panama Royal Mail Co* (1867); *Smith* v *Hughes* (1871). In cases since, *Harrison & Jones* v *Bunten and Lancaster* (1953) and *F E Rose (London) Ltd* v *W H Pim, Junior & Co Ltd* (1953) instance further examples that the courts are not over-ready to find a mistake as to quality to be operative.

In *Nicholson and Venn* v *Smith-Marriott* (1947) the court would have been prepared to find the contract void for mistake, but the decision did not turn on that point. More recently in *Peco Arts Inc* v *Hazlitt Gallery Ltd* (1983) it was a term of the contract that the subject matter was a drawing by a particular artist, but it was, in fact, a copy. The seller conceded that the price was paid 'under a common mistake of fact': however, the only issue before the court was whether the claim was statute-barred.

In the latest reported case on this area of the law, *Associated Japanese Bank (International) Ltd* v *Credit du Nord SA* (1988), Steyn J conducts a searching examination of the authorities and in particular of the facts of and speeches in *Bell*. It has been suggested, most notably by Lord Denning in *Solle* v *Butcher* (1950) and in *Magee* v *Pennine Insurance Co Ltd* (1969), that the effect of the decision in *Bell* was to eliminate the possibility of mutual (common) mistake rendering a contract void at common law. Steyn J concludes that such interpretation does not do justice to the speeches in that case, and that such mistake could have this effect, albeit in wholly exceptional circumstances. Steyn J would have been prepared to find that the contract before him was void for mistake as to quality, but again the matter was decided on other grounds.

In view of the uncertainty of the law in this area one cannot with any degree of confidence advise P that he would be successful in a contention that the contract whereby he sold the painting would be found void for mistake.

Nor will equity come to his assistance. It has been established in *Solle* and *Magee* (above) that even where the contract is valid at law equity may be able to provide relief by granting the remedy of rescission; see also *Grist* v *Bailey* (1967). However, this remedy has been barred as S, a third party, has acquired rights.

Finally, an anomaly has to be noted. Q might be able to have the contract with S set aside by the exercise of the equitable jurisdiction. It would seem less than just for him to obtain the remedy denied to P. But perhaps the court would take cognisance of Q's conduct, and on those grounds refuse him equitable relief.

SUGGESTED ANSWER TO QUESTION FOUR

General Comment

The candidate's knowledge of mistake is here tested by a three-part question, each part focusing on a different area. Although the knowledge required is as extensive as for earlier questions, this approach makes it easier to structure an answer which will fall naturally into three more or less equal parts, respectively discussing mutual mistake as to quality, unilateral mistake and (perhaps the most popular topic in this area) identity mistake. A first-class candidate will not miss the point that the Sale of Goods Act is also applicable.

Key Points

The contract with E
- Mistake as to quality only renders a contract void at common law if the quality is one which makes the thing without the quality essentially different from the thing it was supposed to be – *Bell* v *Lever Brothers Ltd* (1932); *Leaf* v *International Galleries* (1950); *Harrison & Jones Ltd* v *Bunten and Lancaster Ltd* (1953)
- There are dicta to suggest that in this situation the contract could be void – *Peco Arts Inc* v *Hazlitt Gallery Ltd* (1983); *Associated Japanese Bank (International) Ltd* v *Credit du Nord SA* (1988)
- Breach of implied condition under s13 Sale of Goods Act 1979; *Harlingdon & Leinster Enterprise Ltd* v *Christopher Hull Fine Art Ltd* (1990)

The contract with F
- The contract would not be void at common law – *Smith* v *Hughes* (1871)
- Rescission will only be granted if one party had contributed to the other's mistake – *Riverlate Properties Ltd* v *Paul* (1975)
- Breach of implied condition under s13 Sale of Goods Act 1979; *Harlingdon & Leinster Enterprise Ltd* v *Christopher Hull Fine Art Ltd* (1990)

The contract with G
- Where the parties are inter praesentes the presumption is that they intended to contract with one another – *Boulton* v *Jones* (1857); *Lake* v *Simmons* (1927)
- The contract is probably not void for mistake but voidable only – *Phillips* v *Brooks* (1919); *Lewis* v *Averay* (1972)
- Authority to the contrary in *Ingram* v *Little* (1961) is doubtful

Suggested Answer

Each of D's three contracts must be examined in turn.

The contract with E

Both parties conclude the contract in the mistaken belief that the articles are 'Early Swansea' but are in fact fakes. This is an instance of mutual mistake as to quality.

At common law the effect of operative mistake is to render the contract void. Mutual mistake, where it operates, nullifies consent. However, the operation of mistake as to quality has been confined to very narrow limits at common law, particularly by the decision in *Bell* v *Lever Brothers Ltd* (1932). Earlier cases had also set narrow confines within which mistake as to quality was operative: *Kennedy* v *Panama Royal Mail Co* (1867); *Smith* v *Hughes* (1871).

In *Bell*, Lord Atkin said that a mistake as to quality would render a contract void where it was a mistake of both parties which was,

> 'as to the existence of some quality which makes the thing without the quality essentially different from the thing it was supposed to be'.

Lord Atkin gave a number of examples in his speech of contracts that would not be avoided, including the example of the purchase of a painting which both buyer and seller believe to be an old master, but is in reality a copy. This example is closely analogous to the present problem. Treitel believes that this type of case stands on a different level from Lord Atkin's other examples, and that in such a situation the contract should be held void. Some support for this view can be derived from *Peco Arts Inc* v *Hazlitt Gallery Ltd* (1983), though the only issue there was whether the claim was statute-barred. Authority supporting the contention that the contract here would not be held void includes dicta in *Leaf* v *International Galleries* (1950) and the decision in *Harrison & Jones Ltd* v *Bunten and Lancaster Ltd* (1953).

In *Associated Japanese Bank (International) Ltd* v *Credit du Nord SA* (1988), Steyn J reviewed the authorities on the question of mistake as to quality and concluded that, contrary to some of the interpretations of *Bell* v *Lever Bros Ltd*, there was a narrow but perceptible area in which such mistake rendered the contract void. In the present context the balance of authority would suggest that the contract between D and E does not fall within this area and would not therefore be void for mistake at common law.

Equity may provide E with a remedy. Where the mistake is not such as to render the contract void at common law, equity may nevertheless set it aside and thus, in this instance, relieve E of the hardship: *Solle* v *Butcher* (1950); *Magee* v *Pennine Insurance Co Ltd* (1969).

E would have a further remedy. The cup and saucer were described as 'early Swansea' and it appears that there were lengthy descriptions on the price tags. It would seem, therefore, that D is in breach of the condition, implied by s13 Sale of Goods Act 1979, that the goods would correspond with the description. D is an antiques dealer and E, apparently, a private buyer (cf *Harlingdon & Leinster Enterprise Ltd* v *Christopher Hull Fine Art Ltd* (1990) where both parties were dealers).

The contract with F
The contract appears to have been entered into as a result of the unilateral mistake on the part of F. The general rule is that a party is bound, despite his mistake if:

> 'whatever (his) real intentions may be, he so conducts himself that a reasonable man would believe that he was assenting to the terms proposed by the other party, and that other party upon that belief enters into a contract with him ...': *Smith* v *Hughes*, above.

On the authority of that case, it is submitted that the contract would not be void at common law.

Nor can it be said with any certainty that equity would intervene. Rescission for unilateral mistake will only be granted if the one party had contributed to the other party's mistake: *Riverlate Properties Ltd* v *Paul* (1975). The problem does not clearly indicate whether D did so contribute. That he might have done so appears from the information that the articles in question had lengthy descriptions on the price tags attached to them. In this event equity would come to the aid of F, either by granting rescission or by refusing D specific performance.

A further possibility should be mentioned: if the teapot was described as early Welsh Blue, D would be liable for breach of s13 Sale of Goods Act set out above.

The contract with G
This is an instance of mistake as to identity where the parties are inter praesentes. D could not claim that he intended to contract only with a specific named party, Sir Robert Slip, and derive support from the decisions in *Boulton* v *Jones* (1857) or *Lake* v *Simmons* (1927). The facts are closely analogous to those in *Phillips* v *Brooks* (1919) and particularly *Lewis* v *Averay* (1972), in both of which cases the contract was held not to be void for mistake. Authority to the contrary might be found in *Ingram* v *Little* (1961), but this case must be of doubtful authority since the decision in *Lewis* v *Averay*.

Assuming that H was a bona fide purchaser, he acquires good title, and D cannot found a claim against him. D's only remedy is an action in damages against G for fraudulent misrepresentation.

SUGGESTED ANSWER TO QUESTION FIVE

General Comment
Here again we have multiple parties and the best technique to apply in relation to a question such as this is to deal with the transactions separately. The first concerns a common mistake between A and B as to quality and, if you have been following through this series of questions, you will have realised that the salient point is whether the contract is rendered void or voidable. The second contract, between A and C, concerns a unilateral mistake of the 'old oat-new oats' variety.

Key Points

The contract between A and B
- Mistake as to quality only renders a contract void at common law if the quality is one which makes the thing without the quality essentially different from the thing it was supposed to be – *Bell* v *Lever Brothers Ltd* (1932); *Leaf* v *International Galleries* (1950); *Harrison & Jones Ltd* v *Bunten and Lancaster Ltd* (1953)
- There are dicta to suggest that in this situation the contract could be void – *Peco Arts Inc* v *Hazlitt Gallery Ltd* (1983); *Associated Japanese Bank (International) Ltd* v *Credit du Nord SA* (1989)
- Rescission might be ordered but it is unlikely here – *Solle* v *Butcher* (1950); *Grist* v *Bailey* (1967); *Magee* v *Pennine Insurance Co Ltd* (1969); *Riverlate Properties Ltd* v *Paul* (1975)

The contract between B and C
- The mistake is unilateral – *Smith* v *Hughes* (1871)
- Rescission is not available for unilateral mistake – *Riverlate Properties Ltd* v *Paul* (1975)

Suggested Answer

It is most convenient to deal with the contracts between A and B and A and C in turn.

The contract between A and B
In this situation both A and B share the same mistake. It is, therefore, a case of mutual mistake; the expression 'common mistake' is more frequently employed and will be used hereafter.

The common mistake is one as to quality. It is necessary to examine the effect of the mistake at common law and the effect in equity.

The effect of operative mistake at common law is to render the contract void. The decision in *Bell* v *Lever Brothers Ltd* (1932) has confined operative mistake as to quality within very narrow limits. In his speech Lord Atkin said:

> 'a mistake (as to quality) will not affect assent unless it is the mistake of both parties, and is as to the existence of some quality which makes the thing without the quality essentially different from the thing as it was believed to be.'

Lord Atkin gave examples of mistakes as to quality which would not have this effect; one such example was the purchase of a picture which both parties believe to be the work of an old master, and it turns out to be a modern copy. This is the converse of the situation before us.

In *Associated Japanese Bank (International) Ltd* v *Credit du Nord SA* (1988) Steyn J examined the speeches in *Bell* v *Lever Brothers* and concluded that certain commentators were in error in concluding that the decision in that case precluded the possibility of a mistake as to quality ever rendering the contract void at common law; he did say, however, that such a situation would be rare.

Cases in which mistake as to quality did not affect the contract at common law might be mentioned: *Harrison & Jones Ltd* v *Bunten and Lancaster Ltd* (1953); and *Leaf* v *International Galleries* (1950), though that case was not argued on that point. It is significant that in the recent case of *Harlingdon & Leinster Enterprises* v *Christopher Hull Fine Art* (1990), where the paintings which were the subject matter of the sale turned out to be forgeries, the question of mistake was not even mentioned.

In the above cases the mistake made the article less valuable than it was believed to be; here the situation is the converse, but the principle must be the same. Consequently the mistake does not make the contract void at common law.

Nor, it is submitted, would A be able to invoke the assistance of equity. Rescission has been granted in equity in cases of common mistake: *Solle* v *Butcher* (1950); *Grist* v *Bailey* (1967); *Magee* v *Pennine Insurance Co Ltd* (1969). But here there seems no equitable reason why B should be compelled to surrender his good fortune; see the remarks of Russell LJ in *Riverlate Properties Ltd* v *Paul* (1975), to the effect that for equity to compel a man to abandon a good bargain would run counter to the attitudes of much of mankind. His Lordship was speaking in the context of unilateral mistake, but his remarks seem appropriate in the present situation.

The contract between A and C

Here the mistake is unilateral. C believes the candlesticks are gold and valuable. A knows that they are only cheap imitations. We are also informed that A knows of C's belief. The case of *Smith* v *Hughes* (1871) is particularly relevant here. The defendant thought that he was buying old oats; the plaintiff knew that the oats were new. Hannen J said:

> 'In order to relieve the defendant it was necessary that the jury should find not merely that the plaintiff believed the defendant to believe that he was buying old oats, but that he believed the defendant to believe that he, the plaintiff, was contracting to sell old oats ...'

If we apply that statement to the present problem, in order to find for C it would have to be shown that A had the belief that C thought that he (A) was contracting to sell gold candlesticks.

This does not appear to have been the position. C cannot, therefore, claim that the contract is void at common law because of his mistake. Equity here would also prove of no assistance to C. Rescission is not an available remedy for unilateral mistake: *Riverlate Properties Ltd* v *Paul*.

SUGGESTED ANSWER TO QUESTION SIX

General Comment

A further essay question on the distinctions between common law and equity in their approach to mistake, this requires the candidate to evaluate the respective positions adopted by the courts. As with earlier questions on a similar theme a good answer requires careful planning and a coherent internal structure. The answer below shows a different approach to the theme but a comparable design. A good essay answers the specific question posed, contains all the necessary elements and orders them logically and consistently. Beyond this, there is no perfect way to answer a question. Studying different answers to similar questions and practising organising the key points in their own words will assist students to develop their own style.

Key Points

Mistake at common law
- Operates to nullify consent – *Bell* v *Lever Brothers Ltd* (1932)
- Its effect is to render a contract void
- It operates only within narrow limits
- Unilateral mistake – *Smith* v *Hughes* (1871); *Hartog* v *Colin and Shields* (1939); *Raffles* v *Wichelhaus* (1864); *Scriven Bros & Co* v *Hindley & Co* (1913); *Falck* v *Williams* (1900).
- Mistake as to identity – *Cundy* v *Lindsay* (1878); *Ingram* v *Little* (1961); *Lake* v *Simmons* (1927); *Phillips* v *Brooks* (1919); *Lewis* v *Averay* (1972); *Citibank NA* v *Brown Shipley & Co Ltd* (1991)

- Mutual mistake – *Bell* v *Lever Brothers Ltd* (1932); *Magee* v *Pennine Insurance Co Ltd* (1969); *Associated Japanese Bank (International) Ltd* v *Credit du Nord SA* (1988)
- Res extincta – *Couturier* v *Hastie* (1856); *Magee* v *Pennine Insurance Co Ltd* (1969). In *Associated Japanese Bank Ltd* v *Credit du Nord SA* (1988); *Cooper* v *Phibbs* (1867)
- False and fundamental assumption – *Scott* v *Coulson* (1903), *Galloway* v *Galloway* (1914), and *Griffiths* v *Brymer* (1903); *Sheikh Brothers Ltd* v *Ochsner* (1957); *Norwich Union Fire Insurance Society* v *Price* (1934)
- Mistake as to quality – *Kennedy* v *Panama etc Royal Mail Co* (1867); *Leaf* v *International Galleries* (1950); *Harrison & Jones* v *Bunten and Lancaster* (1953); *Bell* v *Lever Brothers* (1932); *Nicholson & Venn* v *Smith-Marriott* (1947); *Associated Japanese Bank (International) Ltd* v *Credit du Nord* (1988)

Mistake in equity
- Even if the contract is not void at common law rescission may be available – *Solle* v *Butcher* (1950); *Magee* v *Pennine Insurance Co Ltd*; *Amalgamated Investment and Property Co Ltd* v *John Walker & Sons Ltd* (1977)
- Rescission is not available for unilateral mistake, unless the one party contributed to the other's mistake: *Riverlate Properties Ltd* v *Paul* (1975); *Malins* v *Freeman* (1837) with *Tamplin* v *James* (1879).

Suggested Answer

Mistake at common law

'If mistake operates at all it operates so as to negative or in some cases to nullify consent': per Lord Atkin in *Bell* v *Lever Brothers Ltd* (1932).

A mistake which negatives consent falls within the category of unilateral mistake. Where unilateral mistake operates the result is to show that there was no true agreement between the parties. Mistake which nullifies consent refers to the category of mutual or common mistake (the terms mutual and common are used interchangeably here). In the case of mutual mistake there has been agreement between the parties, who have shared the mistake, but that mistake relates to so fundamental a matter that the effect of it is to nullify the consent that has been arrived at.

Where mistake does operate at common law the effect of it is to render the contract void. But mistake at common law operates within narrow limits.

Unilateral mistake

The limits within which unilateral mistake operates at common law were expressed by Blackburn J in *Smith* v *Hughes* (1871) as follows:

> 'If, whatever a man's real intention may be, he so conducts himself that a reasonable man would believe that he was assenting to the terms proposed by the other party, and that other party upon that belief enters into the contract with him, the man thus conducting himself would be equally bound as if he had intended to agree to the other party's terms.'

Unilateral mistake has been held to operate so as to render the contract void, but in limited circumstances. In *Hartog* v *Colin and Shields* (1939) the mistake negatived consent where the one party knew from the previous negotiations that the offer in question could not have been intended. Where the parties are at cross-purposes as to the subject matter of the contract this mistake may also negative consent: *Raffles* v *Wichelhaus* (1864); *Scriven Bros & Co* v *Hindley & Co* (1913); *Falck* v *Williams* (1900).

A problematic area has been the one of mistake as to identity. There are cases where the mistake by one party as to the identity of the other has been held to render the contract void: *Cundy* v *Lindsay* (1878); *Ingram* v *Little* (1961); *Lake* v *Simmons* (1927). But these were in special circumstances. The general rule appears to be that mistake as to identity may render the contract voidable, but would not render it void: *Phillips* v *Brooks* (1919); *Lewis* v *Averay* (1972). In a recent case, *Citibank NA* v *Brown Shipley & Co Ltd* (1991), Waller J stated the principle that a mistake as to identity renders the contract void only:

> 'where the findings of fact are: (i) A thinks he has agreed with C because he believes B, with whom he is negotiating, is C; (ii) B is aware that A did not intend to make any agreement with him; and (iii) A has established that the identity of C was a matter of crucial importance.'

Mutual mistake

The decision in *Bell* v *Lever Brothers* (above) has been regarded as having confined the doctrine of mutual (common) mistake within very narrow limits. Lord Denning MR has stated that, as a result of that decision, 'A common mistake, even on a most fundamental matter, does not make a contract void at law: but it makes it voidable in equity.' See *Magee* v *Pennine Insurance Co Ltd* (1969). In *Associated Japanese Bank (International) Ltd* v *Credit du Nord SA* (1988) this view was criticised by Steyn J as not doing justice to the speeches in *Bell*. In those speeches, notably those of Lords Atkin and Thankerton, it was recognised that certain types of mutual mistake could render a contract void, although in very limited circumstances.

The circumstances in which mutual mistake could render a contract void include mistake as to the existence of the subject matter: *Couturier* v *Hastie* (1856) – see also s6 Sale of Goods Act 1979.

A party will not, however, be able to plead mistake where there are no reasonable grounds for his belief: *McRae* v *Commonwealth Disposals Commission* (1951).

Mistake may also render a contract void in the somewhat unusual situation where a party negotiates for the acquisition of rights to property which he already owns: *Cooper* v *Phibbs* (1867).

There are decisions to the effect that a contract will be declared void where the parties shared the same false and fundamental assumption. The earlier cases include; *Scott* v *Coulson* (1903), *Galloway* v *Galloway* (1914), and *Griffiths* v *Brymer* (1903). But these cases are all prior to *Bell* v *Lever Brothers,* and their authority is perhaps doubtful. However, there are also Privy Council decisions post-*Bell* to this effect: *Sheikh Brothers Ltd* v *Ochsner* (1957); *Norwich Union Fire Insurance Society* v *Price* (1934)

It would seem that a mistake as to quality rarely, if ever, renders a contract void at common law. In *Bell* Lord Atkin said that such a mistake 'will not affect assent unless it is the mistake of both parties, and is as to the existence of some quality which makes the thing without the quality essentially different from the thing as it was believed to be.' There are numerous cases where the mutual mistake as to quality did *not* render the contract void: *Kennedy* v *Panama Royal Mail Co* (1867); *Leaf* v *International Galleries* (1950); *Harrison & Jones* v *Bunten and Lancaster* (1953); and, of course, *Bell* v *Lever Brothers* itself. But it is difficult to find a clear and satisfactory decision where the mistake as to quality was of such a nature that the court was able to find that the contract was void ab initio. Such a decision was reached in *Nicholson & Venn* v *Smith-Marriott* (1947), but was said to be wrong by Denning LJ in *Solle* v *Butcher* (below). In *Peco Arts Inc* v *Hazlitt Gallery Ltd* (1983), where a drawing was said to be by a named artist and turned out to be a copy, the seller conceded that the price had been paid under 'a common mistake of fact': but the decision was on the question of limitation of action.

In *Associated Japanese Bank (International) Ltd* v *Credit du Nord SA* (above) Steyn J would have been prepared to find that the mistake as to quality rendered the contract void, but the actual decision turned on another point. Steyn J did state that:

'... the common law rules as to a mistake regarding the quality of the subject matter ... are designed to cope with the impact of unexpected and wholly exceptional circumstances on apparent contracts.'

It is, therefore, apparent that a rigid doctrine of mistake has developed at common law. It remains to consider how this doctrine has been tempered by principles of equity.

Mistake in equity
The leading case is the decision of the Court of Appeal in *Solle* v *Butcher* (1950). The mistake in that case was one as to quality and, in the light of common law doctrine, that mistake could not have been held to render the contract void, but the equitable remedy of rescission was held to be available to the plaintiff. Denning LJ said,

'A contract is ... liable in equity to be set aside if the parties were under a common misapprehension either as to the facts or as to their relative and respective rights, provided that the misapprehension was fundamental and that the party seeking to set it aside was not himself at fault.'

The decision in *Solle* v *Butcher* was followed by Goff J in *Grist* v *Bailey* (1967) and the principle reaffirmed by the Court of Appeal in *Magee* v *Pennine Insurance Co Ltd* (above).

It has been queried whether the decision in *Solle* v *Butcher* is consistent with *Bell* v *Lever Brothers*. See the observations of Buckley LJ and Sir John Pennycuick in *Amalgamated Investment and Property Co Ltd* v *John Walker & Sons Ltd* (1977) and the dissenting judgment of Winn LJ in *Magee* v *Pennine Insurance*.

The equitable principle in relation to mutual mistake is, therefore, an uncertain one. Moreover it appears that rescission is not available for unilateral mistake, unless the one party contributed to the other's mistake: *Riverlate Properties Ltd* v *Paul* (1975). It is not easy to discern the equitable principle behind this distinction. Equity may also intervene by the refusal of the remedy of specific performance. And the courts do not always appear to have been consistent in this regard: contrast *Malins* v *Freeman* (1837) with *Tamplin* v *James* (1879).

It appears, therefore, that the rigidity of the common law doctrine of mistake all but precludes a plaintiff from relying on the mistake in order to avoid the contract. He would be better advised to seek relief in equity, but the flexibility of the equitable principles may lead to an uncertain outcome.

SUGGESTED ANSWER TO QUESTION SEVEN

General Comment

The last question in this section contains traps for the unwary. As the subject matter of the contract is a painting, one is tempted to think immediately of *Leaf* v *International Galleries* (1950) and mistake as to quality, but the good candidate will notice that the paintings are by the same distinguished painter and that the mistake is as to which of the paintings was the subject matter of the contract. The second feature to note is that the question unusually combines mistake with offer and acceptance. To deal with both themes adequately, it is necessary to pre-plan and produce a well-structured analysis.

Key Points

- There is doubt as to which painting the offer relates – *Raffles* v *Wichelhaus* (1864); *Scriven Bros & Co* v *Hindley & Co* (1913);
- Is B's reply acceptance or a counter offer? – *Hyde* v *Wrench* (1840); *Stevenson Jacques & Co* v *McLean* (1880);
- A statement may be an offer although it is expressed to be an 'acceptance': *Bigg* v *Boyd Gibbins Ltd* (1971)
- Acceptance cannot be imposed by silence – *Felthouse* v *Bindley* (1862)
- Postal rules are applicable – *Adams* v *Lindsell* (1818); *Household Fire Insurance Co Ltd* v *Grant* (1879); *Henthorn* v *Fraser* (1892); *Fairline Shipping Corporation* v *Adamson* (1975)

Suggested Answer

It is assumed that the letter sent by A on the Monday constitutes a clear offer. There is an element of doubt on this point as there are two paintings by Augustus John, and it may be difficult to determine, objectively, to which painting the offer can be held to relate.

The reply by B, the message on A's answerphone, is termed an acceptance by B. It cannot, however, be effective as such. The offer was made for the painting 'Forbidden Fruit' and the acceptance relates to the painting 'Four Sisters'. The parties are clearly not ad idem as to the subject matter and the contract would be void for mistake: *Raffles* v *Wicheihaus* (1864); *Scriven Bros & Co* v *Hindley & Co* (1913).

It is, in any event, by no means clear that B's message could be construed as an acceptance. Treitel defines an acceptance as

> 'a final and unqualified expression of assent to the terms of an offer'.

It would not appear that the message falls within this definition. The message could be construed either as a counter-offer, or as a request for information. If it is a counter-offer the effect of it would be to destroy the original offer: *Hyde* v *Wrench* (1840). It may be, however, that the message could be regarded merely as a request for information, which would not amount to a rejection of the offer: *Stevenson Jacques & Co* v *McLean* (1880).

The question of whether a communication is a counter-offer or a request for information depends on the intention of the parties, objectively ascertained. It is submitted that, as the message introduces different subject matter, it must be regarded as a counter-offer, which A is free to accept or reject. Accordingly no contract has been concluded at this point.

On the Wednesday A's message by electronic mail is clearly not an acceptance of B's offer, but a fresh offer to buy both paintings. His use of the words 'I accept' do not contradict the interpretation of the message as an offer; a statement may be an offer although it is expressed to be an 'acceptance': *Bigg* v *Boyd Gibbins Ltd* (1971). The remainder of the message clearly indicates that it was intended as an offer.

In this message A is attempting to impose silence as constituting acceptance. The general rule is that an offeror cannot do so: *Felthouse* v *Bindley* (1862). Whilst the offeree would not be bound by silence, it is possible that the the offeror could be held to have waived communication and to be bound by the offeree's silence – see the discussion by Treitel. This possibility is discussed below.

What has now to be discussed is whether A's fresh offer has been accepted. Two points must be considered: whether B's letter constitutes an acceptance; and, if it does, whether the acceptance can be deemed to have been communicated. B's reply – 'I may be prepared to sell both' – cannot, it is submitted, be regarded as 'a final and unqualified assent' as required by the quotation from Treitel referred to above. That being so, the question whether it has been communicated is an academic one. The problem does, however, require consideration of it.

When an acceptance is sent by post it may be deemed to have been communicated when the letter is posted. This is the effect of the postal rule established in *Adams* v *Lindsell* (1818). It matters not that the letter is lost in the post: *Household Fire Insurance Co Ltd* v *Grant* (1879). The postal rule will apply

> 'where the circumstances are such that it must have been within the contemplation of the parties that, according to the ordinary usages of mankind, the post might be used as a means of communicating the acceptance of an offer': per Lord Herschell in *Henthorn* v *Fraser* (1892).

If B's letter had constituted an acceptance, it could be argued that it was deemed to have been communicated by the application of the postal rule. It would not avail A to maintain that, having made the offer by electronic mail, he did not anticipate an acceptance through the post, but an instantaneous one, as he did not require a reply at all. However, it has been suggested that B's letter was not an unequivocal acceptance of A's offer.

The conclusion thus far is that B is not bound by A's offer transmitted by electronic mail, because the rule is that silence cannot be imposed on the offeree: *Felthouse* v *Bindley*. It is, however, possible to argue – as Treitel does (see previous reference) – that this rule was developed for the protection of the offeree, and that there is no reason in principle why the offeror should not be bound; although, as Treitel concedes, this possibility has been judicially doubted: *Fairline Shipping Corporation* v *Adamson* (1975). In the absence, therefore, of clear supporting authority B could not be advised that he could hold A to the offer to buy both paintings.

At this stage, it is submitted, no contract has been concluded.

There are two further possibilities to be considered: that B had not received A's electronic mail message; and that B received only the incomplete message.

With regard to the first situation, it is well settled that an offer must be actually communicated; an acceptance in ignorance of the offer can have no effect. The position would then be that B's counter offer on A's answerphone to sell the painting 'Four Sisters' had not been accepted by A, and that there had been no further communication between the parties since then. Again, no contract would have been concluded.

The second situation gives rise to more doubt. Here B receives a message which appears to be an acceptance of his counter-offer for the sale of of the painting 'Four Sisters' at £25,000. This clearly was not A's intention, but could it be objectively construed as such? The answer would seem to depend on whether A knew (or had the means of knowing) of the transmission failure. Having chosen to use electronic mail as a method of communication it is arguable that A should bear the risk of imperfect transmission. Moreover his use of the expression 'I accept' would lead a reasonable person to believe that the message was a response to – and therefore an acceptance of – the counter-offer. The conclusion is, that on the assumption that A knew, or should have known of the possibility of the transmission failure, a contract would have been concluded on the terms of B's counter-offer. This conclusion is, however, not without doubt, in the absence of clear authority.

8

Duress and Undue Influence

Introduction

Proof of a contract having been procured by duress or undue influence will vitiate the contract. As duress has historically been confined to threatened or actual violence, it has in practice proved to be a rarer claim than that of undue influence. However, the extension of duress to include 'economic duress' has given it new life. Economic duress is generally to be found in business-to-business contracts, while undue influence will usually nowadays involve some domestic relationship. Questions in this area are perhaps more unusual than in some others. However there is scope for both problem and essay-type questions.

Questions

INTERROGRAMS

1 What is meant by a 'special relationship' in the context of undue influence?
2 '... English law gives relief to one, who, without independent advice, enters into a contract ... when his bargaining power is grievously impaired ...' (Lord Denning in *Lloyds Bank* v *Bundy*). To what extent is this true?
3 To what extent has equity extended the scope of the common law doctrine of duress?

QUESTION ONE

J had lived with his girlfriend K for three years. They each contributed 50 per cent of the council tax and shared the other household expenses equally. J offered to buy for £10,000 K's shares in Big Bank plc, which she had inherited from her father. They were worth £100,000 and J knew this. K agreed because she was afraid that if she did not agree J would leave her. L, J's brother, threatened to tell J that he and K had had an affair before K had started to live with J. L forced K to sign a guarantee for a loan which L was taking from a bank as his business was in difficulty. The guarantee was secured by a charge on the flat in which K and J lived and which K owned.

Advise K. What would be your advice on the following alternative assumptions: (a) J had left K threatening to publish intimate photographs which he had taken when they were living together; or (b) L had become insolvent and the bank were seeking to enforce the guarantee; or (c) when K had agreed to the sale and guarantee she was only 17 years old?

London University LLB Examination
(for external students) Elements of the Law of Contract June 1995 Q5

QUESTION TWO

'The concept of economic duress is built on shaky foundations, since superior bargaining power always coerces.'

Discuss.

London University LLB Examination
(for external students) Elements of the Law of Contract June 1991 Q2

Answers

ANSWERS TO INTERROGRAMS

1 Where a contract has been procured by the undue influence of one of the contracting parties over the other, the contract is voidable in equity at the option of the innocent party.

Such influence is presumed where there is a special relationship between the parties. There are specific categories which have been recognised as 'special relationships': parent and child – *Wright* v *Vanderplank* (1855); solicitor and client – *Wright* v *Carter* (1903); doctor and patient – *Mitchell* v *Homfray* (1881); trustee and beneficiary – *Ellis* v *Barker* (1871); religious adviser and disciple – *Roche* v *Sherrington* (1982). Perhaps surprisingly, there is no presumption of a special relationship between husband and wife (*Midland Bank* v *Shephard* (1988)) unless there are particular circumstances of dependency and mutual trust (*Simpson* v *Simpson* (1988)). Nor is there such presumption of relationship between banker and customer (*Lloyds Bank* v *Bundy* (1975)) or between master and servant (*Mathew* v *Bobbins* (1980)). The categories of special relationship are not closed and it is open to the court to extend the presumption to other kinds of relationship if appropriate.

Where influence is presumed, the party seeking to rely on the doctrine has nothing further to prove and the burden falls on the other party to prove that there has been no undue influence in the circumstances (very often, but not exclusively, by proving that the person relying on the doctrine was independently advised). Where there is no special relationship, to rely on the doctrine the party must prove actual undue influence, which is clearly a greater burden.

2 The extract from Lord Denning's judgment in *Lloyds Bank* v *Bundy* from which this statement is taken has given rise to academic speculation that there is a principle of inequality of bargaining power. In his judgment, Lord Denning appeared to consider that this principle, albeit a limited one, gave a broad relief to anyone who:

> 'without independent advice, enters into a contract on terms which are very unfair or transfers property for a consideration which is grossly inadequate, when his bargaining power is grievously impaired by reason of his own needs or desires, or by his own ignorance or infirmity, coupled with undue influences or pressures brought to bear on him by or for the benefit of another.'

This alternative reason for his judgment in the case was further reiterated in *Clifford Davis* v *WEA Records* (1975) and *Levison* v *Patent Steam Carpet Cleaning Co*

8 Duress and Undue Influence – Answers

(1978) and appeared to receive support from Lord Diplock in *Schroeder Music Publishing Co Ltd* v *Macaulay* (1974).

However, pleas to set aside an agreement purely on the basis of inequality of bargaining power have been rejected in *Burmah Oil* v *Bank of England* (1981) and *Alec Lobb (Garages) Ltd* v *Total Oil (Great Britain) Ltd* (1985). Indeed in that case Dillon LJ said that it was rare in any transaction for the bargaining power of the parties to be equal. In *National Westminster Bank plc* v *Morgan* (1985), Lord Scarman doubted whether '... there is any need in the modern law to erect a general principle of relief against inequality of bargaining power', a view which had been apparent previously in his Lordship's judgment in *Pao On* v *Lau Yiu Long* (1980). The reason is probably that, as Trietel observes, the doctrine of economic duress, upheld in that case, has reduced the need for such a principle in modern law.

3 The common law doctrine of duress required actual or threatened violence to the victim (*Barton* v *Armstrong* (1976). There was some doubt as to whether threats to seize goods could amount to duress (compare *Skeate* v *Beale* (1840) and *Maskell* v *Horner* (1915)). However, it seems that the common law relief is now definitely confined to threatened or actual physical violence: see Kerr J in *Occidental Worldwide Investment Corp* v *Skibs (The Siboen and The Sibotre)* (1976) and Mocatta J in *North Ocean Shipping Co* v *Hyundai (The Atlantic Baron)* (1979). A party who proves duress can avoid the contract. There was an idea at one time that a contract procured by duress was void but this has now been rejected.

Modern law has extended the doctrine to include 'economic duress'. This extension has its roots in the tort of intimidation. This tort was extended to include threat of breach of contract as well as threatened violence: *Rookes* v *Barnard* (1964) and *Morgan* v *Fry* (1968). The thinking of Lord Denning which lay behind this latter decision was also evident in his judgment in *D & C Builders Ltd* v *Rees* (1966), where he compared undue pressure to intimidation, while refusing to extend the doctrine of equitable estoppel to a defendant who had procured the promise to forbear by exerting economic pressure.

However, economic pressure will not of itself constitute duress. In *The Sibeon and The Sibotre*, while upholding the doctrine of 'economic duress', Kerr J expressed the view that the innocent party's will must be '... overborne by compulsion so as to deprive him of any animus contrahendi'.

The relief is an equitable one as is clear from *The Atlantic Baron* where the threat involved was the threat to break a contract which would have had catastrophic dealings on a transaction dependent upon the completion of the contract. Mocatta J found that there had been economic duress but that the contract could not be set aside because the injured party had delayed in taking action.

In a leading case on economic duress in recent times, *Pao On* v *Lau Yiu Long* (1980), the Privy Council upheld Kerr J's view in *The Sibeon and The Sibotre* and laid down a four-part test for whether the doctrine will apply:

a   did the party seeking to rely on the doctrine protest?
b   did he have an adequate legal remedy?

c   was he independently legally advised?
d   did he take steps to avoid the contract?

Further indication of the Lords' views on economic duress came in *The Universe Sentinel* (1983), where the Court of Appeal had made a finding of economic duress. Upholding the Court's finding, the Lords departed from the earlier strict requirements. Lord Scarman spoke of the 'compulsion of the will' of the victim but described it as:

> 'the victim's intentional submission arising from the realisation that there is no other practical choice open to him ...'.

Moreover, while the pressure exerted must be 'illegitimate', ie improper in the legal sense (see *The Evia Luck* (1991)), it is not a requirement that the party exerting it must realise that his victim is acting under it.

SUGGESTED ANSWER TO QUESTION ONE

General Comment

Although questions on undue influence are rare, the topic does provide quite extensive scope and the practical application of this area of law is not so unusual as might be imagined. Based around actual recent cases, this question demonstrates the issues which could arise. A candidate must be able to analyse the relationship(s) between the parties in the question according to the principles which have now been laid down and from this analysis determine whether there is a relationship between the parties which raises a presumption of undue influence or not. If the former, the candidate should be able to indicate whether there is in the problem evidence which would rebut the presumption, and if the latter, whether there is evidence of actual undue influence.

Key Points

- Undue influence has now been judicially classified – *Bank of Credit and Commerce International SA* v *Aboody* (1990); *Barclays Bank plc* v *O'Brien* (1993)
- Class 1 – actual undue influence
- Class 2 – presumed undue influence
- Class 2a – special relationships
- Class 2b – de facto relationships
- Emotional relationship between cohabitees falls within class 2b – *Barclays Bank plc* v *O'Brien* (1993)
- Where someone relies on the guidance or advice of another and the other knows of that reliance, undue influence is presumed – *Lloyds Bank Ltd* v *Bundy* (1975); *National Westminster Bank plc* v *Morgan* (1985)
- Presumption of undue influence may be rebutted by evidence that the complainant had independent advice – *Inche Noriah* v *Shaik Allie Bin Omar* (1929)
- Signing the guarantee falls within Class 1 and K need not show that the transaction was to her disadvantage – *CIBC Mortgages* v *Pitt* (1993)

- The threat to publish the photographs is illegitimate pressure depriving the victim of choice and also blackmail, so is duress – *Universe Tankships of Monrovia v International Transport Workers' Federation (The Universe Sentinel)* (1983)
- Whether the bank can enforce the guarantee or not depends on whether it had constructive notice of the actual influence – *Barclays Bank plc v O'Brien* (1993); *CIBC Mortgages v Pitt* (1994)
- If K was a minor at the time, the transactions would not be binding on her but she could not recover shares transferred to J – *Corpe v Overston* (1833)

Suggested Answer

A person who has been induced to enter into a contract by the undue influence of another (the wrongdoer) is entitled to have that contract set aside as against the wrongdoer. Undue influence is either actual or presumed. The classification of undue influence adopted by the Court of Appeal in *Bank of Credit and Commerce International SA v Aboody* (1990) and by the House of Lords in *Barclays Bank plc v O'Brien* (1994) was on the following lines.

1. *Class 1: actual undue influence.* This involves actual pressure, and it is for the claimant to prove that the wrongdoer exerted the undue influence on the complainant to enter into the particular transaction.
2. *Class 2: presumed undue influence.* Where the complainant shows that there was a particular relationship of trust and confidence between the complainant and the wrongdoer, the presumption will arise that the wrongdoer abused that relationship in inducing the complainant to enter into the transaction. In this class it is not necessary for the complainant to prove undue influence in relation to the particular transaction. Once the confidential relationship is established the burden then passes to the wrongdoer to rebut the presumption by proving that the complainant entered into the transaction voluntarily.
3. *Class 2a: special relationships.* Certain relationships, such as solicitor and client, doctor and patient, will give rise to the presumption of undue influence.
4. *Class 2b: de facto relationships.* The presumption of undue influence will arise even in the absence of a special relationship if the complainant shows that there was a relationship of trust and confidence between the complainant and the wrongdoer. The transactions into which K entered must be examined in the light of the above principles.

The sale of the shares to J

The relationship between J and K is one falling within Class 2b. Where there is an emotional relationship between cohabitees, there is, as Lord Browne-Wilkinson said in *Barclays Bank plc v O'Brien* (1993), an underlying risk of one cohabitee exploiting the emotional involvement and trust of the other. It seems clear, because of K's fear that J would leave her, and her agreeing to sell shares worth £100,000 for £10,000, that a relationship of trust and confidence existed. In *Lloyd's Bank Ltd v Bundy* (1975) Sir Eric Sachs said that the presumption of undue influence arises:

'where someone one relies on the guidance or advice of another, where the other is aware of that reliance and where the person on whom reliance is placed obtains, or may well obtain, a benefit from the transaction ...'.

This approach was approved by the House of Lords in *National Westminster Bank plc v Morgan* (1985). In that case it was also held that, where the presumption of undue influence arose, it was also necessary for the complainant to show that there was 'manifest disadvantage' to the complainant in the transaction. This again is clearly the position here.

The onus now falls on J to prove that K entered into the transaction voluntarily. The most usual way of doing this is to show that the complainant had independent advice. Whilst there is no invariable rule that independent advice is necessary, this may be the only means by which the presumption of undue influence can be rebutted: *Inche Noriah v Shaik Allie Bin Omar* (1929).

It does not appear that K had independent advice, nor are any other circumstances suggested which would enable J to prove that K entered into the transaction voluntarily. Accordingly K would be entitled to set the transaction aside.

The signing of the guarantee on behalf of L
This situation falls within Class 1: actual undue influence. We are told that L forced K to sign the guarantee by his threat. Once actual influence has been established it is not necessary for K to show that the transaction was to her disadvantage: *CIBC Mortgages v Pitt* (1993). K could also have this transaction set aside.

It remains to consider the alternative assumptions.

1   *J's threat to publish the photographs*
    Presumably J uttered this threat in order to induce K to sell him the shares. Although this is not clearly stated, it is difficult to see how it would otherwise be relevant. As the relationship between J and K has terminated, in the circumstances described, the presumption of undue influence cannot arise: there is no longer a relationship of trust and confidence. It would appear, however, that there has been actual influence, with the consequences set out above. Moreover, the threat raises the possibility of invoking the doctrine of duress. Duress involves the application of illegitimate pressure on the victim which gives the victim no real choice but to submit: *Universe Tankships of Monrovia v International Transport Workers' Federation (The Universe Sentinel)* (1983). It is not clear that the threat to publish the photographs constitutes illegitimate pressure, but it is blackmail, and in *The Universe Sentinel* Lord Scarman stated that the doctrine of duress should extend to blackmail. On this assumption, therefore, K would also be entitled to have the transaction set aside.

2   *The enforcement of the guarantee by the bank*
    It has been submitted that the guarantee was executed as a result of the actual influence. The position of the bank depends on whether it had constructive notice of the actual influence. If the bank did, it would have had to take reasonable steps to satisfy itself that K had entered into the obligation freely and with knowledge of the true facts. Otherwise the bank will not be able to enforce the guarantee: *Barclays Bank plc v O'Brien* (above). If the bank could not be held to have had constructive

notice of the actual influence, it would not be tainted by the wrong, and K would not be able to resist enforcement: *CIBC Mortgages* v *Pitt* (1993).

3   *The situation if K was only 17 years old at the relevant times*
As K was a minor at the the time she entered into the sale and the guarantee the transactions would not be binding on her. If, however, the shares had been transferred to J, she could not recover them merely by reason of her minority: *Corpe* v *Overston* (1833).

SUGGESTED ANSWER TO QUESTION TWO

General Comment

The idea of extending duress to cover economic situations is a relatively recent one in the history of Contract law. From a theoretical point of view, its introduction poses a number of interesting questions. It is therefore not unusual to see a problem set on this topic and it has all but supplanted questions on physical duress which do not have substantial practical application in modern times.

Key Points

- Duress is wide enough to encompass economic pressure where the consent of the other party has been overborne by compulsion – Kerr J in *Occidental Worldwide Investment Corp* v *Skibs A/S Avanti (The Sibeon ad the Sibotre)* (1976); Mocatta J in *North Ocean Shipping Co* v *Hyundai Construction Co (The Atlantic Baron)* (1979)
- Duress is distinguishable from mere commercial pressure; an element of coercion is required – Lord Scarman in *Pao On* v *Lau Yiu Long* (1980)
- The factors to consider are: whether the person alleged to be coerced protested; whether he had adequate legal remedy; whether he was independently legally advised; and whether he subsequently took steps to avoid the contract
- Submission arising from realisation that there is no other practical choice – Lord Scarman in *Universe Tankships of Monrovia* v *International Transport Workers' Federation* (1983)
- Uncertainty as to what constitutes illegitimate pressure – Andrew Phang's article 'Whither Economic Duress'
- There is no broad doctrine of inequality of bargaining power as proposed by Lord Denning in *Lloyds Bank* v *Bundy* (1975), *Clifford Davis Management Ltd* v *WEA Records Ltd* (1975) and *Levison* v *Patent Steam Cleaning Co Ltd* (1978), and supported apparently by Lord Diplock in *Schroeder Music Publishing Co Ltd* v *Macaulay* (1974); *Pao On* v *Lau Yiu Long* (1980); *National Westminster Bank plc* v *Morgan* (1985); *Alec Lobb (Garages) Ltd* v *Total Oil (Great Britain) Ltd* (1985)

Suggested Answer

The concept of economic duress is of recent origin, receiving the first clear judicial recognition in *Occidental Worldwide Investment Corp* v *Skibs A/S Avanti (The Sibeon and The Sibotre)* (1976) where Kerr J rejected the earlier narrow confines of duress and held that, in certain circumstances, a contract entered into as a result of economic pressure could be liable to be set aside. Kerr J emphasised, however, that mere commercial pressure, exerted by one party, was not in itself sufficient to constitute duress. He said that the court must 'be satisfied that the consent of the other party was overborne by compulsion so as to deprive him of animus contrahendi'. The concept of economic duress received further recognition in *North Ocean Shipping Co* v *Hyundai Construction Co (The Atlantic Baron)* (1979) where Mocatta J held that a threat to break a contract could amount to duress.

The existence of the doctrine of economic duress has been affirmed by the Court of Appeal in *B & S Contracts and Design Ltd* v *Victor Green Publications Ltd* (1984), by the House of Lords in *Universe Tankships of Monrovia* v *International Transport Workers' Federation* (1983), and by the Judicial Committee of the Privy Council in *Pao On* v *Lau Yiu Long* (1980). In two recent cases the doctrine has been regarded as firmly established. In *Vantage Navigation Corporation* v *Suhail and Saud Bahwan Building Materials LLC (The Alev)* (1989) Hobhouse J stated that the doctrine is 'now well established' and in *Atlas Express Ltd* v *Kafco (Importers and Distributors) Ltd* (1989) Tucker J observed that it was 'a concept recognised by English law'.

There is, it is submitted, still some uncertainty surrounding the operation of the concept. In *The Sibeon and The Sibotre,* as has been noted above, duress was distinguished from mere commercial pressure: it was necessary to show that the will of the party concerned had been overborne by compulsion. In *Pao On* the Judicial Committee of the Privy Council endorsed this approach. Lord Scarman said that there must be the presence of some factor 'which could be regarded as coercion of his will so as to vitiate his consent'. The factors to consider were:

i whether the person alleged to have been coerced did or did not protest;
ii whether he had an adequate legal remedy;
iii whether he was independently legally advised; and
iv whether he subsequently took steps to avoid the contract.

This approach has been subsequently modified. In the *Universe Tankships* case Lord Scarman said that compulsion had been described in the authorities as coercion or the vitiation of consent. But his Lordship went on to say that:

> 'The classic case of duress is, however, not the lack of will to submit but the victim's intentional submission arising from the realisation that there is no other practical choice open to him.'

Lord Scarman emphasised that the lack of choice could be proved in various ways – by protest, by the absence of independent advice, by the steps taken to avoid the contract – but none of these evidentiary matters went to the essence of duress.

> 'The victim's silence will not assist the bully, if the lack of any practicable choice but to submit is proved.'

It has been suggested by Andrew Phang in his article 'Whither Economic Duress' that to regard these matters as merely 'evidentiary' creates considerable uncertainty in applying the doctrine. Moreover, whilst the decisions focus on the illegitimacy of the pressure, there is some doubt as to what constitutes illegitimate pressure. In *Universe Tankships* Lord Scarman suggested that 'illegitimate pressure could include pressure that was not unlawful', but this suggestion was not elaborated on.

The courts have often stressed the distinction between duress and commercial pressure. In *Lloyds Bank Ltd v Bundy* (1975) Lord Denning MR sought to merge the concept of duress with the broader doctrine of 'inequality of bargaining power'. Subsequently Lord Denning reiterated the view that English law recognised the doctrine in *Clifford Davis Management Ltd v WEA Records Ltd* (1975) and in *Levison v Patent Steam Carpet Cleaning Co Ltd* (1978). Some recognition appeared to be afforded to the doctrine by the speech of Lord Diplock in *Schroeder Music Publishing Co Ltd v Macaulay* (1974), but this was in the particular context of a restraint of trade clause in a standard form contract.

This broad doctrine was doubted by the Privy Council in *Pao On* and expressly disapproved by the House of Lords in *National Westminster Bank plc v Morgan* (1985). Lord Scarman observed that the legislature had undertaken the task of enacting restrictions on freedom of contract, and he doubted whether the courts should assume the burden of formulating further restrictions. In the Court of Appeal, in *Alec Lobb (Garages) Ltd v Total Oil (Great Britain) Ltd* (1985), Dillon J, in rejecting the argument based on unequal bargaining power, noted that it was seldom in any negotiation that the bargaining position of the parties was absolutely equal.

Whilst the concept of economic duress does now appear to be firmly recognised in English law doubts remain, both as to the nature of the pressure required and as to the evidence necessary to prove the absence of choice.

9

Privity of Contract and Assignment of Contractual Rights

Introduction

This chapter is concerned principally with the doctrine of privity of contract. The doctrine states that only parties to a contract may have rights and obligations under it. However, to mitigate the harshness which this would sometimes mean to the plaintiff, both the courts and Parliament have devised exceptions to the doctrine. There have been many lawyers, including members of the House of Lords, who have criticised the doctrine and called for its reform or even its abolition. Thus, there is a great deal of scope for both problem and discussion questions in this area.

While someone not a party to a contract can take neither the benefit nor the burden, there is nothing to stop a party assigning his rights to another. This must, however, be done in accordance with the common law and equitable rules which Parliament and the courts have devised.

Questions

INTERROGRAMS

1 While the courts will allow the benefit of a contract to be enforced by and for third parties, it will not allow enforcement of the burdens against third parties. Discuss.
2 Why, despite criticism, does the law still uphold the doctrine of privity of contract?
3 Explain the following legal phrases:

   a chose in action;
   b novation;
   c negotiable instrument.

4 Discuss the role of equity in developing the law relating to contractual assignment.

QUESTION ONE

In January, in preparation for her daughter Bella's wedding in May, Mrs H agreed to hire J's vintage white Rolls-Royce as the bridal car. She engaged K to take the wedding photographs and L to do the catering at the reception.

One week before the wedding J sold the Rolls-Royce to M. M is also a photographer, and although he knew about the arrangements made by Mrs H he would not allow the Rolls-Royce to be used for Bella's wedding unless he (M) was engaged to take the photographs in place of K.

Mrs H refused to employ M as the photographer and had to hire a modern limousine at a greater cost than the vintage Rolls-Royce.

K's flash equipment failed during the service and Bella was heartbroken to find afterwards that there are no pictures of the actual marriage ceremony.

Mrs H, Bella and many more of the guests became ill after eating chicken at the reception which, unknown to L, was contaminated by salmonella.

Advise Mrs H and Bella.

London University LLB Examination
(for external students) Elements of the Law of Contract June 1990 Q6

QUESTION TWO

'English law holds that no stranger to the consideration can take advantage of a contract, although it was made for his benefit.'

Explain and comment. To what extent do you consider that this statement presents an accurate picture of the legal position?

London University LLB Examination
(for external students) Elements of the Law of Contract June 1985 Q7

QUESTION THREE

'The doctrine of privity has in its incidence worked injustice and proved inadequate to modern needs.'

Discuss with particular regard to the extent to which Parliament and the courts have intervened to mitigate the harshness of the doctrine.

Written by the Editor March 1997

QUESTION FOUR

Thomas contracted with Bookit's Tours for his wife, Wanda, and son, Simon, to have a holiday in Spain. When Wanda and Simon arrived in Spain, they found the hotel Thomas had booked did not have room for them and they were obliged to stay in another hotel where instead of two single rooms with en suite bathroom they were forced to share a room with no bathroom facilities. The food was disgusting and some of the guests became ill with food poisoning. The water sports which Simon had particularly looked forward to were unavailable due to staff shortages. Wanda and Simon returned to England a week early.

The day after their return, Thomas died and Wanda discovered the house in which she and Simon had lived with him belonged not to him, as she had thought, but to Tom Brown Ltd, the company in which he was a director. There was no formal tenancy and Thomas had agreed informally with the company that if he should die first, Wanda should live there rent free for the rest of her life, but the company want to evict Wanda and Simon and sell the property. Thomas had also agreed with Greyfriars School that in consideration of services which were rendered to them by Tom Brown Ltd they would educate Simon free of charge until he was 18.

Wanda has become ill and depressed and the school wish to expel Simon for disruptive behaviour. Advise Wanda and Simon of their legal situation.
Written by the Editor June 1998

Answers

ANSWERS TO INTERROGRAMS

1   With regard to the imposition of burdens on third parties the general principle is that a contract cannot do so. This aspect of the doctrine of privity of contract has not led to the controversy which has followed attempts to extend the doctrine in respect of conferring benefits on third parties. There can be little justification for a party having to submit to obligations in a contract to which he was not a party. The only exceptions to this principle are in the law of property. Covenants in leases are binding not only on the original parties, but also on their successors in title. Covenants restricting the use of land may be binding in equity on subsequent purchasers of the land with notice of the covenant: *Tulk* v *Moxhay* (1848). In *Taddy* v *Sterious* (1904) the court refused to extend this principle to goods. The attempted extension of the principle to contracts for the hire of ships by the Privy Council in *Lord Strathcona Steamship Co* v *Dominion Coal Co* (1926) has been disavowed: *Port Line Ltd* v *Ben Line Steamers Ltd* (1958); *Bendall* v *McWhirter* (1952).

   While this represents the state of the law at present, there are ways of imposing a burden on a third party such as the creation of a lien or the creation of an equitable interest or irrevocable licence. Additionally, where there has been interference with contractual rights a cause of action may arise in tort, but not in contract, against the third party guilty of the interference: *Lumley* v *Gye* (1853); *British Motor Trade Association* v *Salvadori* (1949).

2   The doctrine of privity of contract has two aspects: the first is that a person who was not party to a contract cannot acquire rights under it; the second is that a person not party to the contract cannot have obligations imposed on him by that contract. The doctrine has been much criticised, certainly in relation to the first aspect, and Lord Denning made frequent attempts to abandon it, but at the time of writing it remains part of our law. The second aspect of the doctrine can be justified, but it is the refusal of English law to recognise third party rights in the conferring of benefits that is more difficult to justify. Treitel suggests four possible reasons for the retention of the doctrine. The first is that a contract is a personal affair, affecting only the parties to it; the second is that it would not be just to allow a person to sue on a contract when he could not be sued on it; the third is that to allow third party rights would interfere with the rights of the contracting parties to vary or rescind the contract; and the fourth possible reason is that the third party is often a mere donee and that it would be contrary to principle to allow him a contractual right.

   A further feature of the privity of contract doctrine is that the promisee cannot sue for the third party's loss: see *Woodar Investment Development Ltd* v *Wimpey Construction (UK) Ltd* (1980) where the House of Lords disapproved the view of Lord Denning to the contrary in *Jackson* v *Horizon Holidays* (1957). In *Forster* v

Silvermere Golf and Equestrian Centre (1981) Dillon J referred to this rule as 'a blot on our law and most unjust'.

Abolition of the rule that a third party cannot enforce the benefit was recommended by the Law Revision Committee in 1937. And in *Woodar* v *Wimpey* (1980) Lord Scarman remarked that as the legislature had not acted to implement that recommendation the courts might have to. The Law Commission have recently published a consultation paper recommending that a third party should be able to enforce contractual promises subject to the promisor having the same defences and the same rights as to set-off and counter-claim as he would have against the promisee. The Commission recommends that parties to a contract should not be able thereby to impose duties on a third party.

In view of the judicial criticisms and repeated calls for the modification of the doctrine of privity of contract it is difficult to see why English law retains the doctrine.

3 a A chose in action is intangible property which includes not only contractual rights but all kinds of other rights which may only be enforced by legal action. Examples are insurance policies, copyright, patents and rights under trusts or wills. A chose in action may be legal or equitable depending on its nature. In *Torkington* v *Magee* (1902), Channell J defined them as follows:

> 'Chose in action' is a known legal expression used to describe all personal rights of property which can only be claimed or enforced by action, and not by taking possession.'

b One way of transferring contractual benefits and burdens to a third party is by novation. All the parties to the contract and the third party who is to take over the contract must consent to novation. However, novation may be implied where the third party assumes the benefit and burden of the contract and the other party allows him to do so: *Howard* v *Patent Ivory Manufacturing Co* (1888).

c Negotiable instruments are a type of chose in action which have specific characteristics. First, the holder of a negotiable instrument may sue in his or her own name. He may sue all previous parties to the instrument. Second, the instrument is transferred not by assignment but by indorsement or delivery (where payable to order) or mere delivery (where payable to bearer). Third, the transferee takes rights of ownership free of equities (so long as he is a holder in due course).

There are three main types of negotiable instrument in use today. By far the most important of these is the cheque (which is actually a bill of exchange but drawn on a banker and payable on demand - s73 Bills of Exchange Act 1882). There are also other types of bills of exchange, much used in international commercial transactions. The requirements for an instrument to be a bill of exchange are laid down in s3(1) Bills of Exchange Act (1882): it must be an unconditional order in writing addressed by one person to another, signed by the person giving it, and requiring the person to whom it is addressed to pay on demand a sum certain in money to or to the order of a specified person or to bearer.

4 Apart from certain specific exceptions such as negotiable instruments, the common law did not allow transfer of choses in action. Equity not only recognised such assignments but would recognise even the intention to carry out an assignment without any formal execution. The assignment gives the assignee the right to sue in his own name.

Assignments of certain equitable interests do however have to be in writing (s53(1)(c) Law of Property Act 1925).

It is not necessary to give notice to the debtor that the rights have been assigned, but it is desirable from the assignee's point of view, for the rule in *Dearle* v *Hall* (1828) provides that priority of claim is established by the order in which assignees give notice to the debtor.

There are certain principles which stem from an equitable assignment. Firstly, the assignee takes 'subject to the equities', ie any defence which the debtor might have used against the assignor will be available against the assignee. Secondly, the assignee will not be able to enforce the debt unless he has given consideration for the assignment ('Equity will not assist a volunteer'). Thirdly, the assignee must join the assignor in any action against the debtor.

There are some further general limits to assignment. Assignments which are against public policy or which may prejudice the debtor are not enforceable. Examples of the former include the assignment by a wife of her maintenance payments and the assignment of his salary by the holder of a public office. Examples of the latter include personal contracts where the identity of a party is important and contracts to give financial assistance to a party to commence an action.

SUGGESTED ANSWER TO QUESTION ONE

General Comment

This question on the doctrine of privity of contract requires a thorough knowledge of the doctrine and the ability to apply it to the somewhat complex facts given in the problem. It should be noted that the candidate is asked to advise both Mrs H and Bella. Again, this is a question where it is advisable to consider each contract in turn.

Key Points

- A third party cannot acquire rights nor obligations under a contract to which he is not a party - *Dunlop Pneumatic Tyre Co Ltd* v *Selfridge & Co Ltd* (1915); *Forster* v *Golf and Equestrian Centre* (1981); *Woodar Investment Development Ltd* v *Wimpey Construction (UK) Ltd* (1980)

The contract with J for the hire of the Rolls-Royce

- Mrs H has a remedy against J for damages but not specific performance - *Watts* v *Spence* (1976)
- She is entitled to be put in the position she would have been in had the contract been performed
- The doctrine of privity applies to any claim by Mrs H against M - *Dunlop Pneumatic Tyre Co Ltd* v *Selfridge & Co Ltd* (1915)

- It is unlikely that the doctrine in *Tulk* v *Moxhay* would impose equitable liability on M despite the judgment in *Lord Strathcona Steamship Co* v *Dominion Coal Co* (1926); *Port Line Ltd* v *Ben Line Steamers* (1958); *Bendall* v *McWhirter* (1952)
- There may possibly be action against M under the tort of interference with contractual rights – *Lumley* v *Gye* (1853); *British Motor Trade Association* v *Salvadori* (1949)

The contract with K for the wedding photographs
- K may be in breach of duty of skill and care under s13 Supply of Goods and Services Act 1982
- Damages for distress have been awarded but only in certain classes of cases – *Jackson* v *Horizon Holidays Ltd* (1975); *Jarvis* v *Swans Tours Ltd* (1973); *Bliss* v *South East Thames Regional Health Authority* (1987); *Hayes and Another* v *James & Charles Dodd* (1988)
- The doctrine of privity applies to any claim by Bella against K – *Tweddle* v *Atkinson* (1861); *Beswick* v *Beswick* (1968)

The contract with L for the catering
- L may be in breach of the implied term in s14(2) Sale of Goods Act 1979 and Mrs H can sue him
- The doctrine of privity applies to any claim by Bella but Mrs H may be able to claim damages for her – *Jackson* v *Horizon Holidays* (1975); *Woodar Investment Development Ltd* v *Wimpey Construction (UK) Ltd* (1980)
- The doctrine of privity also applies to the guests

Suggested Answer

The main issues raised here are those arising out of the doctrine of privity of contract. The question also requires some discussion of the availability of damages for distress for breach of contract.

The basic rule of privity was expressed in the following terms by Viscount Haldane in *Dunlop Pneumatic Tyre Co Ltd* v *Selfridge & Co Ltd* (1915):

> '... in the law of England certain principles are fundamental. One is that only a person who is a party to a contract can sue on it. Our law knows nothing of a jus quaesitum tertio arising by way of contract.'

The consequence of the doctrine of privity of contract is that a third party cannot acquire benefits under a contract to which he was not a party, nor can a third party have obligations imposed on him by such contract. The doctrine has been characterised as 'a blot on our law and most unjust' by Dillon J in *Forster* v *Golf and Equestrian Centre* (1981). Lord Scarman appeared to call for its abolition in *Woodar Investment Development Ltd* v *Wimpey Construction (UK) Ltd* (1980). As long ago as 1937 the Law Revision Committee recommended that where a contract expressly conferred a benefit on a third party it should be directly enforceable by the third party. However, these reforms have not as yet been implemented, though there are statutory exceptions to the privity rule and it may be possible to circumvent it.

Adverting to the particular problem, it is necessary to examine each of the contracts in turn.

The contract with J for the hire of the Rolls-Royce
J is clearly in breach of contract by selling the car to M. Mrs H can sustain an action against him for the breach. The remedy of specific performance is not, of course, available as performance is impossible: *Watts v Spence* (1976). Her remedy against J is a claim for damages. In accordance with the general principle that the purpose of an award of damages is to put her in the position she would have been in if the contract had been performed, she would be entitled to the difference between the contract price and the price she has to pay for the other vehicle. It is possible that she might have suffered distress at not being able to obtain the vintage Rolls-Royce. The question of damages for distress is dealt with below.

M, to whom the Rolls-Royce has been sold, knows of Mrs H's contractual rights, but refuses to allow her to exercise them unless he is engaged as the photographer. Because of the rules of privity of contract, this does not afford Mrs H any contractual claim against M: *Dunlop v Selfridge* (above). M is not a party to the contract between Mrs H and J and the obligations of that contract cannot be imposed on him at common law. Nor would equity impose any liability on him. The rule in *Tulk v Moxhay* (1848) appears to be confined to interests in land: the purported extension of that rule by the Judicial Committee of the Privy Council in *Lord Strathcona Steamship Co v Dominion Coal Co* (1926) has never been followed in the English courts and that decision must be regarded as doubtful authority; see the judgments of Diplock J in *Port Line Ltd v Ben Line Steamers Ltd* (1958) and Denning J in *Bendall v McWhirter* (1952).

The one possibility of circumventing the privity rule and fixing M with liability is in the law of Tort which recognises liability for interfering with contractual rights: *Lumley v Gye* (1853); *British Motor Trade Association v Salvadori* (1949). There are a number of trade union cases in this area of the law, but citation of them is beyond the scope of this question. It is an essential ingredient of the tort that the wrongdoer knew of the contractual rights, but M possessed that knowledge and could not, it appears, escape liability.

The contract with K for the wedding photographs
It is assumed that the failure to take the photographs constitutes a breach of contract on K's part. Section 13 Supply of Goods and Services Act 1982 imposes a duty on the supplier of a service to carry out that service with reasonable skill and care. The question is: to whom, and to what extent, is he liable for that breach?

The question suggests that it is Bella, and not Mrs H, who has suffered distress as a result of the breach. Two points emerge for discussion: first, the extent to which a court will award damages for distress; second, who can sue for such distress. Damages for distress have been awarded in cases involving contracts for a holiday: *Jackson v Horizon Holidays Ltd* (1975); *Jarvis v Swans Tours Ltd* (1973). But an award of damages for distress is limited to certain classes of cases. In *Bliss v South East Thames Regional Health Authority* (1987) Dillon LJ held that such an award should be confined to cases 'where the contract which has been broken was itself a contract to provide peace of

9 Privity of Contract and Assignment of Contractual Rights – Answers 155

mind or freedom from distress'. In *Hayes and Another v James & Charles Dodd* (1988) Staughton J was of the opinion that the class might be somewhat wider than that, 'but it should not include any case where the object of the contract was not comfort or pleasure or the relief of discomfort, but simply view to profit'. A claim for damages for distress would, it is submitted, fall at least within the limits set by Staughton J. By the same token Mrs H might well have a claim for damages for distress against J for his failure to supply the Rolls-Royce.

The question of who can sustain a claim for the distress against K must next be addressed. The privity rule is the clear difficulty in the way of an action by Bella. The rule that a benefit cannot be conferred on a third party was established in *Tweddle v Atkinson* (1861) and affirmed by the House of Lords in *Beswick v Beswick* (1968). There is no evidence on the facts presented to indicate that Mrs H acted as Bella's agent, or that Bella was in any sense a party to the contract.

Nor can Mrs H sue for Bella's loss. In *Jackson v Horizon Holidays* (1975) Lord Denning held that the promisee could always sue for the third party's loss, but this view was expressly disapproved by the House of Lords in *Woodar v Wimpey* (1980). It must be concluded, therefore, that no claim will lie against K.

The contract with L for the catering
The question suggests that there has been no negligence on L's part, so no action in tort will lie. So far as a contractual claim is concerned, L appears to be in breach of the implied term in s14(2) Sale of Goods Act 1979 in that he has failed to supply goods of a merchantable quality. Clearly Mrs H, as a party to the contract, can sue for damages for the illness she has suffered. What of Bella's illness? In *Woodar v Wimpey* Lord Wilberforce 'explained' the decision in *Jackson v Horizon Holidays*. Although he rejected the view that the promisee can sue for the third party's loss, he was not prepared to part from the actual decision in that case. He said that it could be supported as a special type of contract, examples of which are persons contracting for family holidays or ordering meals in a restaurant, calling for special treatment. All the members of the family would be regarded as parties to the contract. Lord Russell appeared to hold that he did not criticise the outcome in *Jackson* because there the third party's loss was also the promisee's loss.

The strict application of the privity rule would debar Bella from a claim against L, and would also prevent Mrs H from suing for Bella's loss. However, the decision in *Jackson*, as justified by the House of Lords in *Wimpey*, permits the possibility that Bella can sustain an action on the basis that she too was a party to the contract with L, or that Mrs H can claim that Bella's loss was also her own. Whether this can be extended to the guests is extremely doubtful.

SUGGESTED ANSWER TO QUESTION TWO

General Comment
This wide-ranging question on the doctrine of privity of contract requires the candidate to take a critical view of the topic. A well-structured answer and a coherent logical argument are required whichever viewpoint the writer chooses to adopt.

Key Points

- The doctrine of privity of contract - *Tweddle* v *Atkinson* (1861); *Dunlop Pneumatic Tyre Co Ltd* v *Selfridge & Co Ltd* (1915); *Scruttons Ltd* v *Midland Silicones Ltd* (1962); *Beswick* v *Beswick* (1968)
- A party cannot recover damages for a third party unless a trust or agency relationship exists - *Jackson* v *Horizon Holidays Ltd* (1975); *Lloyds* v *Harper* (1880); *Woodar Investment Development Ltd* v *Wimpey Construction (UK) Ltd* (1980); *Forster* v *Silvermere Golf and Equestrian Centre* (1981); *Beswick* v *Beswick* (1968)
- Statutory exceptions to the doctrine - s14(2) Marine Insurance Act 1906; ss47(1), 56(1) Law of Property Act 1925; s148(4) Road Traffic Act 1972
- A promise for the benefit of a third party - *Tomlinson* v *Gill* (1756); *Les Affreteurs Reunis* v *Leopold Walford (London) Ltd* (1919); *Re Flavell* (1883); *Re Schebsman* (1944)
- Agency is an exception to the doctrine
- Collateral contracts - *Shanklin Pier Ltd* v *Detel Products Ltd* (1951); *Hamzeh Malas & Sons* v *British Imex Industries Ltd* (1958)

Suggested Answer

The statement refers to the doctrine of privity of contract and in considering it the following will be discussed:

a the general rule;
b exceptions to it; and
c how the law may be developed in future cases.

The general rule

The rule that a person cannot acquire enforceable rights under a contract to which he is not a party, even though it may have been made for his benefit, is considered to have been conclusively established in 1861 in the case of *Tweddle* v *Atkinson*, where the fathers of a bride and groom agreed with each other to pay certain sums to the groom, adding that the groom should have the power to recover those sums by action if either failed to pay. The bride's father defaulted and the groom sued, but his action failed on the grounds (inter alia) that he was not a party to the contract.

The rule in *Tweddle* v *Atkinson* has been affirmed by the House of Lords on three separate occasions this century, namely *Dunlop Pneumatic Tyre Co Ltd* v *Selfridge & Co Ltd* (1915), *Scruttons Ltd* v *Midland Silicones Ltd* (1962) and *Beswick* v *Beswick* (1968). In the latter case their Lordships disagreed with the conclusion of the Court of Appeal that s56(1) of the Law of Property Act 1925 had abolished the doctrine of privity, and expressed the view that the subsection created only a limited exception in the law of real property. Although in *Woodar Investment Development Co Ltd* v *Wimpey Construction (UK) Ltd* (1980) certain remarks were made by their Lordships about the desirability of overruling *Tweddle* v *Atkinson*, unless and until this is done by the House, or the legislature chooses to amend the law by statute, *Tweddle* is binding authority on all inferior courts that a stranger cannot sue on a contract to which he is not a party.

9 Privity of Contract and Assignment of Contractual Rights – Answers

The practical consequences of the rule can often be that a considerable injustice is suffered. Not only can the third party not sue, but the promisee also cannot sue to recover damages on behalf of the third party unless a relationship of trust or agency exists. In *Jackson* v *Horizon Holidays Ltd* (1975) Lord Denning held that *Lloyds* v *Harper* (1880) established the principle that a promisee who made a contract for the benefit of a third party can recover damages on the latter's behalf. This judgment was strongly disapproved by all five members of the House in *Woodar* v *Wimpey* and although *Jackson* was technically not overruled, it seems inconceivable that it would be followed in future cases. Henceforth *Lloyds* v *Harper* is to be regarded as dealing with relationships of trust or agency only and, in consequence, the third party's loss will be uncompensated. In *Forster* v *Silvermere Golf and Equestrian Centre* (1981) Dillon J said this result was a blot on the law and most unjust; it remains, nevertheless, the law.

A means of avoiding this injustice and preventing the third party's loss not being remedied was utilised in *Beswick* v *Beswick* where the plaintiff, the promisee's widow, was able as his administratrix to obtain specific performance against the defendant, the promisor, in her own favour as third party beneficiary, thereby preventing the defendant from breaking his contract with impunity. However, specific performance is a discretionary remedy and not automatically granted, and although the court might be strongly minded to order it so as to prevent injustice occurring, it will not always be possible eg as in *Woodar* v *Wimpey*, where the contract had been terminated and was not capable of being specifically enforced.

Exceptions

Because of the injustice that may flow from a strict application of the rule in *Tweddle* v *Atkinson*, there are many exceptions to it, statutory, equitable and at common law. Some are true exceptions and others are devices adopted by the courts to circumvent the rule.

Of the statutory exceptions, reference has already been made to s56(1) of the 1925 Act. Whilst their Lordships in *Beswick* did not speak with one voice as to the true construction of that sub-section, the predominant view was that it only applied in the law of real property where there is a purported grant to or covenant with a named person who is not a party to the instrument. Other important statutory exceptions are contained in the law of insurance, in particular the Married Women's Property Act 1882, s148(4) Road Traffic Act 1972, s14(2) Marine Insurance Act 1906 and s83 Fires Prevention (Metropolis) Act 1774. These, in one field of insurance or another, allow an action to be maintained on an insurance policy by a person who is not a party to it.

The most important equitable exception is that of a trust: where A makes a promise to B for the benefit of C, C can enforce the promise if B has been instituted trustee of the promise for C: *Tomlinson* v *Gill* (1756) and *Les Affreteurs Reunis* v *Leopold Walford (London) Ltd* (1919). Whilst the concept of a trust of a contractual right is straightforward and comprehensible, determining in any particular case whether one has been created can be a question of considerable difficulty and leave much room for judicial ingenuity.

For a trust to be instituted the 'three certainties' must be present, ie of intention, subject matter and objects. In contract, it is the first that gives rise to the most difficulty, since it is rare for the promisor and promisee to make their intention clear in the terms of their agreement. Accordingly the question is often one of inference: whether one can impute to them an irrevocable intention to benefit the third party. Irrevocability is vital, since once a trust is created it is enforceable by the beneficiary and cannot be dissolved or determined by the settlor or the trustee or both. The difficulty of deducing the parties' intentions has led to different conclusions being reached in cases involving broadly similar facts eg *Re Flavell* (1883) and *Re Schebsman* (1944). Taking a broad view of the trust cases, it is probably fair to say that at one time the trust of a contractual right was a device commonly used to circumvent the doctrine of privity, but that often it was no more than device, and it involved attributing to the parties an intention they almost certainly never possessed. Now, by contrast, it seems no longer to be in favour.

Other exceptions, apparent or real, are the doctrine of agency, including the rules relating to undisclosed principals; collateral contracts, which may be used to 'construct' a contract (eg *Shanklin Pier Ltd* v *Detel Products Ltd* (1951)); and established commercial practices which the courts are reluctant to upset, particularly the proposition that the bank is liable to pay on presentation by the seller of the proper shipping documents, although it is doubtful whether in terms of strict legal analysis a contract exists between them (eg *Hamzeh Malas & Sons* v *British Imex Industries Ltd* (1958)).

Reform
As long ago as 1937, the Law Revision Committee in its 6th Interim Report recommended the abolition of the rule in *Tweddle* v *Atkinson*, and that third parties should be entitled to enforce contracts made for their benefit, providing certain conditions were satisfied. Since then, two decisions of the House of Lords, *Scruttons* and *Beswick*, have spurned this opportunity. However, in the House of Lords case of *Woodar* v *Wimpey*, there was a significant shift in judicial thinking. Although the point did not fall squarely for consideration, Lords Salmon, Keith and Scarman all said, obiter, that the time had come to reconsider and probably reverse the rule in *Tweddle* v *Atkinson*, and that if the legislature did not soon take this step then their Lordships' House should consider doing so. It seems, therefore, that the days of that rule may now be numbered.

Conclusion
It is submitted that the statement is broadly correct, though it is a general rule subject to exceptions rather than being an absolute one. Further, it is a rule which, it appears, may now be retaining only a precarious foothold in English law.

SUGGESTED ANSWER TO QUESTION THREE

General Comment
This essay question requires the candidate to evaluate the effect of the doctrine of privity. It requires a sound knowledge of the doctrine and its exceptions and of the relevant case law.

9 Privity of Contract and Assignment of Contractual Rights – Answers

Key Points

- Reasons for the doctrine – *Tweddle* v *Atkinson* (1861); *Re Burgess' Policy* (1915)
- Formulation of the present doctrine – *Tweddle* v *Atkinson* (1861); *Dunlop Pneumatic Tyre Co Ltd* v *Selfridge & Co Ltd* (1915)
- Judicial disapproval of the doctrine – *Smith and Snipes Hall Farm* v *River Douglas Catchment Board* (1949); *Drive Yourself Hire Co (London) Ltd* v *Strutt* (1954); *Scruttons Ltd* v *Midland Silicones Ltd* (1962); *Beswick* v *Beswick* (1968); *Woodar Investment Development Ltd* v *Wimpey Construction (UK) Ltd* (1980); *Swain* v *Law Society* (1983); *Forster* v *Silvermere Golf and Equestrian Centre* (1981)
- Parliamentary intervention – Law Commission Report 1937; s14(2) Marine Insurance Act 1906; ss47(1), 56(1) Law of Property Act 1925; s148(4) Road Traffic Act 1972
- Exceptions to the doctrine: agency
- Exceptions to the doctrine: trust – *Tomlinson* v *Gill* (1756); *Gregory and Parker* v *Williams* (1817); *Walford's* case (1919); *Re Schebsman, ex parte Official Receiver Trustee* v *Cargo Superintendents (London) Ltd* (1944); *Beswick* v *Beswick* (1968)
- The Court of Appeal and the House of Lords have interpreted the doctrine differently – *Jackson* v *Horizon Holidays Ltd* (1975); *Woodar Investment Development Ltd* v *Wimpey Construction (UK) Ltd* (1980); *Linden Gardens Trust* v *Lenesta Sludge Disposals Ltd* (1993)
- Exceptions to the doctrine: collateral contracts – *Shanklin Pier Ltd* v *Detel Products Ltd* (1951); *IBA* v *EMI Electronics* (1980)
- Miscellaneous exceptions – *Hybart* v *Parker* (1858); *The Satanita* (1895)

Suggested Answer

The doctrine of privity of contract states simply that one who is not a party to a contract can neither claim rights under it nor be subject to any of its obligations. While it would clearly be unreasonable to enforce contracts imposing liability on strangers, the courts have had more difficulty rationalising the corollary and various reasons have been proposed from time to time. Possibly it is no more than a corollary and it would be unfair to allow a party to acquire rights under an instrument under which he has no liabilities: *Tweddle* v *Atkinson* (1861). However, other possibilities have been proposed, particularly that to allow enforcement would affect the rescission and variation rights of the parties (*Re Burgess' Policy* (1915)), and that it is simply an aspect of the rule that the law does not enforce gratuitous promises (Treitel, *The Law of Contract*).

Whatever the reason for the doctrine, it has had a long and varied history. The present formulation was established in *Tweddle* v *Atkinson*. Prior to that, there had been no consistency in its enforcement. The doctrine was approved by the House of Lords in *Dunlop Pneumatic Tyre Co Ltd* v *Selfridge & Co Ltd* (1915) but, as the quotation (from Cheshire & Fifoot, *Law of Contract*) suggests, it has never received universal approval. Its existence has even been doubted in the Court of Appeal (Denning LJ in *Smith and Snipes Hall Farm* v *River Douglas Catchment Board* (1949), and *Drive Yourself Hire Co (London) Ltd* v *Strutt* (1954)), although in *Scruttons Ltd* v *Midland Silicones Ltd* (1962) a majority of the House of Lords disagreed with Lord Denning (as he was by then) and reaffirmed the doctrine. Lord Denning MR returned to consider the doctrine in the Court of Appeal in *Beswick* v *Beswick* (1968), this time stating that it was:

'at bottom ... only a rule of procedure'.

And this time the House of Lords did not contradict him when they came in their turn to consider the case, expressing no particularly firm view on the subject. The attitude of the House of Lords has appeared to soften even further in later cases, notably *Woodar Investment Development Ltd* v *Wimpey Construction (UK) Ltd* (1980) and *Swain* v *Law Society* (1983).

So far as parliamentary intervention is concerned, while the Law Commission recommended reform as early as 1937, no substantial overhaul of the doctrine has been undertaken to date. Instead, Parliament has acted only in piecemeal fashion in response to particular problems. Examples include permitting husband and wife to enter insurance contracts benefitting each other or their children and allowing third parties to sue on road traffic accident insurance policies.

Of necessity, of course, the courts have had to act on a case-by-case basis and by developing exceptions to the doctrine, although judicial dicta have stated that the doctrine of privity is: 'a blot on the law and most unjust' (*Forster* v *Silvermere Golf and Equestrian Centre* (1981)) and that it was most unsatisfactory and in need of consideration by the legislature or the House of Lords: *Woodar* v *Wimpey*.

The first major exception to the doctrine, agency, was established almost at the same time as the doctrine itself was becoming entrenched in the law. Where a contract is made by one person (the agent) on behalf of another (the principal) the contract is enforceable against and by the principal but the agent is not personally liable under it. Agency is of such fundamental necessity to the commercial world – without it, companies would be unable to operate and contracts could not be made overseas to name just two implications – that it is a formidable exception which has formed a body of law in its own right.

The second important exception, which again has a long-standing body of law and stretches in its application far beyond the doctrine of privity, is the constructive trust. This concept is taken from equity. A constructive trust has none of the formalities of other trusts but is discovered by the courts in the intentions of the parties. The constructive trust has on a number of occasions been used to circumvent the doctrine of privity but never, it must be pointed out, to enable the non-contracting party who is to benefit from the contract to sue in his own name. The trust device merely enables a contracting party to sue on his behalf.

The possibility of a constructive trust where parties have made a contract in which a benefit is conferred on a third party was first established in *Tomlinson* v *Gill* (1756). It was developed in *Gregory and Parker* v *Williams* (1817) and recognised by the House of Lords in *Walford*'s case (1919).

However, even though as mentioned above, the courts have sometimes doubted the doctrine, it should not be thought that they will always find a constructive trust in order to avoid it. In *Re Schebsman, ex parte Official Receiver Trustee* v *Cargo Superintendents (London) Ltd* (1944) Du Parcq LJ said:

'unless an intention to create a trust is clearly to be collected from the language used and the circumstances of the case, I think that the court ought not to be too astute to discover indications of such an intention.'

And in more recent decades, there have been few cases where a claim on the basis of constructive trust has succeeded.

The most recent leading case is *Beswick* v *Beswick* (1968). Here, the deceased and the defendant had agreed that the deceased's widow was to receive an annuity from the defendant. The defendant failed to maintain the payments and the widow sued both in her capacity as administratrix of her husband's estate and in her personal capacity. It was held by the House of Lords that she could succeed as administratrix but not in her personal capacity. In that case, the House had to decide on the proper interpretation of s56(1) Law of Property Act 1925, which says:

'a person may take an immediate or other interest in land or other property, or the benefit of any condition, right of entry, covenant or agreement over or respecting land or other property, although he may not be named as a party to the conveyance or other instrument.'

It was this section which, Lord Denning claimed, had extinguished the doctrine of privity altogether, but the judges in the House of Lords were reluctant to accept that Parliament had intended to so fundamentally affect the common law in this way.

The difference between the House of Lords interpretation of the doctrine and that of the Court of Appeal can be seen in two other cases. In *Jackson* v *Horizon Holidays Ltd* (1975) the plaintiff contracted for a holiday for himself, his wife and children in Ceylon. The holiday was a disaster and the plaintiff sued for damages for all three of them. The Court of Appeal held that the plaintiff could claim not just for the disappointment suffered by himself but for that of his wife and children also. In 1980 the question came before the House of Lords in *Woodar Investment Development Ltd* v *Wimpey Construction (UK) Ltd*. Here the House upheld the decision in *Jackson* but stated that the Court of Appeal had arrived at their decision for the wrong reasons. The plaintiff was claiming for his own loss which was increased by the disappointment of his wife and children. This is not necessarily the end of the matter, however, for it has already been mentioned that the House of Lords in *Woodar* considered that the law on this point was unsatisfactory.

Perhaps in consequence, in a more recent case, the House has widened a formerly narrow exception to include all contracts. In *Linden Gardens Trust* v *Lenesta Sludge Disposals Ltd* (1993), they had another opportunity to consider the doctrine of privity. The case concerned a building contract between an 'employer' and a 'contractor' providing for development work to be done by the contractor on a particular site owned by the employer. The employer then transferred the site (but not the benefit of the contract) to a third party. The employer brought an action for breach of the contract and the contractor argued that the employer had suffered no loss. The House upheld the plaintiff's claim on two grounds: firstly, the employer had in fact suffered a financial loss because he had had to spend money to obtain the benefit of the bargain (Lord Griffiths); secondly, because there was a long established exception to the doctrine of privity that a shipper of goods can claim damages against a carrier under a contract of carriage where property and risk in the goods have passed to a third party and the goods are lost or damaged, on the basis that the shipper is treated as making the contract for the benefit of all persons who may subsequently acquire an interest in the goods. The remainder of the court thought this exception could be extended to contracts generally although only those which concerned the transfer of an interest in property where there was loss or damage to the property.

A further exception to the doctrine has been the collateral contract, which can sometimes be seen as a device. A second contract, connected with the first, is found between one of the contracting parties and the third party, enabling the third party to sue in his own right: *Shanklin Pier Ltd* v *Detel Products Ltd* (1951). This has mainly enabled an injured third party to sue on warranties given not to him but to the person with whom he contracted. To enforce the contract, however, the third party must have given consideration, although the consideration may be no more than the entering into the main contract. There must also be a contractual intention: *IBA* v *EMI Electronics* (1980).

There are other miscellaneous exceptions, for example where a person becomes a member of a club, his contract being with other members with whom he has had no dealings (*Hybart* v *Parker* (1858)), or where a number of people agreed to enter into competition, subject to the rules of the organiser their contract is with one another: *The Satanita* (1895). Covenants in a lease may be enforced by successors in title. Assignment by which the rights and liabilities of a contracting party are transferred to another is also clearly an important exception. Finally, Trietel (*The Law of Contract*) has identified another modern situation where a third party may be able to sue an independent valuer employed by a building society or other organisation providing him with a mortgage. However, this situation is likely to be dealt with under the rules of tort, as in *Smith* v *Eric S Bush* (1990), which are outside the scope of this answer.

In conclusion, the doctrine is clearly in an unsatisfactory state and any intervention has been of a piecemeal and exceptional kind. Undoubtedly there has been injustice, as in *Forster* v *Silvermere* (above), where the plaintiff could only recover damages for her own loss and not the loss to her children.

SUGGESTED ANSWER TO QUESTION FOUR

General Comment

A problem question which revolves around the doctrine of privity of contract, this demands a thorough knowledge of the area and ability to apply that knowledge. In particular, the candidate needs to be able to discuss whether the relevant situation might be seen by the court as an exception to the doctrine.

Key Points

- The doctrine of privity will generally prevent any contractual claim by a person who was not a party to the contract - *Tweddle* v *Atkinson* (1861); *Dunlop Pneumatic Tyre Co Ltd* v *Selfridge & Co Ltd* (1915); *Beswick* v *Beswick* (1968)

9 Privity of Contract and Assignment of Contractual Rights – Answers 163

- There are exceptions to the doctrine, the scope of which may be enlarging – *Woodar Investment Development Ltd* v *Wimpey Construction (UK) Ltd* (1980); *Linden Gardens Trust* v *Lenesta Sludge Disposals Ltd* (1993); *Shanklin Pier* v *Detal Products Ltd* (1951)

The contract with the travel company
- Damages may be claimed for distress or disappointment arising from a ruined holiday – *Jarvis* v *Swans Tours* (1973); *Jackson* v *Horizon Holidays Ltd* (1975); *Williams* v *Travel Promotions Ltd* (1998)
- There is some doubt as to whether damages may be claimed by the contracting party on behalf of members of his family – *Jackson* v *Horizon Holidays Ltd* (1975); *Woodar Investment Development Ltd* v *Wimpey Construction (UK) Ltd* (1980); *Forster* v *Silvermere Golf and Equestrian Centre* (1981)
- If Wanda is administratrix of Thomas's estate, she may be able to sue in that capacity – *Beswick* v *Beswick* (1968)
- Wanda and Simon may have an action in tort

Right of Wanda to remain in the marital home
- The court might find a constructive trust in her favour
- She would not be able to sue on her own behalf
- Thomas's personal representative could sue on her behalf and she could herself sue as Thomas's administratrix – *Beswick* v *Beswick* (1968)
- She may have registrable equitable rights to remain

Simon remaining at his school
- The court might find a constructive trust in his favour as the contract was made for his benefit
- Simon will not be able to sue in his own right but Thomas's personal representatives may be able to sue on his behalf
- He would probably not be awarded specific performance and his remedy would be damages

Suggested Answer

The issues here revolve around the problem of privity of contract. The doctrine of privity, which states that only those who are parties to a contract may sue and be sued on it, is long established in English law. Prior to the case of *Tweddle* v *Atkinson* (1861) there was considerable disagreement in the cases over the application of the doctrine. Here the defendant contracted with another that he would pay a sum of money to the other's son on his marriage to the defendant's daughter. It was held that the son could not enforce the contract. The doctrine was given House of Lords approval in *Dunlop Pneumatic Tyre Co Ltd* v *Selfridge & Co Ltd* (1915). As neither Wanda nor Simon were contracting parties to any of the contracts, although they were clearly intended to benefit under them, they will have to bring themselves within one of the exceptions to the doctrine in order to be able to obtain the benefit.

The basis of the exceptions is not always clear. For a period, Lord Denning's view that the doctrine had been abolished by s56(1) Law of Property Act 1925, which says:

'a person may take an immediate or other interest in land or other property, or the benefit of any condition right of entry, covenant or agreement over or respecting land or other property, although he may not be named as a party to the conveyance or other instrument',

was in the ascendant. But, in *Beswick* v *Beswick* (1968) the House of Lords made it clear that the doctrine was still in existence. Their Lordships have, however, expressed dissatisfaction with the doctrine (*Woodar Investment Development Ltd* v *Wimpey Construction (UK) Ltd* (1980), with Lord Scarman apparently calling for its abolition, and another more recent House of Lords case (*Linden Gardens Trust* v *Lenesta Sludge Disposals Ltd* (1993)) may be interpreted to show a softening of the court's attitude towards the doctrine by enlarging the scope of exceptions to it.

A number of exceptions have long been identified. First there are contracts made by an agent. Where the situation is one of agency, a person who makes a contract on behalf of another (the agent) is not personally liable but that other (the principal) can sue and be sued on the contract. Second, there are constructive trusts. These are not trusts in the precise meaning of the word as having been formally set up but are inferred by the court from the intention of the parties. The purpose of the contract being to confer a benefit on a non-contracting party, the contracting parties hold the benefit on trust for that other. Third, there are collateral contracts. One of the main parties to a contract may make a subsidiary contract with another person. If that other person gives a warranty, the non-contracting main party who is not directly in contractual relationship with him, may sue on it: *Shanklin Pier Ltd* v *Detel Products Ltd* (1951).

The fourth exception has until recently been considered as confined to a particular situation. Where a shipper of goods enters a contract of carriage, the carrier is liable to a third party to whom the shipper has meantime transferred property and risk in the goods for loss or damage subsequent to the sale. In the *Linden Gardens Trust* case the majority in the House of Lords extended this exception to a situation involving a building contract and the transfer of an interest in land, and considered that it applied to all kinds of contract. The broader implications of this are still to be seen.

There are other minor exceptions, which are not specifically relevant here, but it should be noted that, except in the case of agency, the rights are not directly enforceable by the third party on whom the benefit is conferred and it is the contracting party who holds those rights, who must bring the action.

The contract with the travel company
It has been established that damages for distress or disappointment arising out of a ruined holiday can be claimed (*Jarvis* v *Swans Tours* (1973); *Jackson* v *Horizon Holidays Ltd* (1975)). A recent case which concerned a change of hotel was *Williams* v *Travel Promotions Ltd* (1998) where under the booking conditions the travel company reserved the right to vary flights, hotels and itinerary without prior notice or compensation. The travel company changed the plaintiff's hotel at short notice to avoid an early morning return journey. It was held, on a construction of the contract, that the company had only the right to make necessary changes and change the hotel only if it was overbooked. They had no right to make changes simply where it was required or sensible. However, in the former case, the plaintiff was suing on his own behalf and, while in the latter case the plaintiff was able to claim damages in respect of the distress

suffered by his family, the ground for the decision has been criticised in the House of Lords (*Woodar* v *Wimpey* above), and it may be that it was no more than compensation for the extension of his own loss, although Lord Wilberforce's explanation of *Jackson* was that a family holiday contract was in a category of its own and all the family members would be regarded as parties. However, even he was not prepared to go as far as saying that the plaintiff could sue for the third party's loss. Further, in *Forster* v *Silvermere Golf and Equestrian Centre* (1981) Dillon J held that the plaintiff could recover only her own loss and not that of her children even though he considered it 'a blot on the law and most unjust'. Thus, at first sight it seems that any action by Wanda or Simon against the travel company will fail due to the death of Thomas, and even if the rights under the contract were held by Thomas on behalf of Wanda and Simon, they are unable to bring an action in their own right.

However there are possibilities which may avail them. Firstly, it may be argued that Thomas made the contract as agent for his wife and son. It is not clear who paid for the holiday but it is certainly a possibility that Thomas was authorised to act on his wife's behalf in booking the holiday. The marital relationship often gives rise to implied agency, eg in respect of the pledging of a spouse's credit. If this is the case, the contract will in fact be with Wanda and Simon and they can sue on it.

The second possibility is that, assuming Wanda is administratrix of Thomas's estate, she may be able to sue in that capacity. In *Beswick* v *Beswick* (1968) a widow, whose deceased husband had contracted with the defendant for her to be paid an annuity after his death, was permitted to enforce the contract not as a beneficiary in her own right but as the administratrix of his estate.

Failing that, Wanda and Simon might be able to bring an action in tort on the basis of the travel company's negligence, but discussion of such an action is outside the scope of this answer.

The right of Wanda to remain in the marital home
Certainly here the sole purpose of the contract was to confer a benefit on Wanda and the court would be likely to find a constructive trust in her favour. However, applying *Beswick* v *Beswick*, she would, again, not be able to sue on her own behalf and would have to sue as personal representative, or, if she was not Thomas's personal representative, persuade his personal representative to sue for her.

It may also be mentioned that Wanda may have registrable equitable rights to remain in the home as a result of having contributed to the marriage. However, this would depend on precisely what rights Thomas had in the property and a full discussion is outside the scope of this answer.

Simon remaining at his school
Again, the contract was made by Thomas for the benefit of his son. His personal representatives may be able to enforce the contract but Simon will not be able to sue in his own right. Even if the personal representatives are prepared to sue the school, their award is likely to be restricted to damages compensating for the loss of school fees for the remainder of the period until Simon reaches 18. It is highly unlikely that the court would order specific performance of the contract and insist that Simon be reinstated.

10
Illegality

Introduction

The court will not enforce a contract which is void for illegality. If the contract is not void, however, some rights and obligations may be enforceable. Contracts may be illegal as formed or illegal in performance, and the candidate must be able to explain the different effects of each. Both may appear in the same question. The candidate must also be aware of the situations in which the court will refuse to enforce a contract on grounds of public policy. Principal among these are contracts in restraint of trade. Restraint clauses have long been held to be void if too wide to protect the interests of the party who inserted the clauses. Although a restraint clause may appear in any kind of contract, there are two particular kinds of contract which have attracted a large body of case law: contracts of employment and contracts for the sale of a business. A successful candidate will be required to show familiarity with the cases in question, as well as more recent cases involving 'solus agreements', tying the tenant of a petrol station to a particular petrol company.

Questions

INTERROGRAMS

1 There are several kinds of contract which the courts refuse to enforce on the grounds of public policy. A contract in restraint of trade is one example. Explain and illustrate some of the others.
2 Explain, illustrating with examples from case law, how the doctrine of restraint of trade has been applied to many diverse factual situations.
3 'Neither party to an illegal contract can enforce it.' Discuss

QUESTION ONE

'The unsatisfactory nature of the doctrine of restraint of trade is due to the inherent contradiction between it and the idea of freedom of contract.'
  Discuss.

London University LLB Examination
(for external students) Elements of the Law of Contract June 1989 Q6

QUESTION TWO

'Even if a person has entered into a contract which is unenforceable because of illegality the courts can provide him with redress so long as he comes with clean hands.'
Discuss.

London University LLB Examination
(for external students) Elements of the Law of Contract June 1990 Q5

QUESTION THREE

S was registered as a licensed plant and seed dealer under legislation which made it an offence to deal in such materials without an appropriate licence. Also, the relevant legislation required each delivery of seeds to be accompanied by a delivery note accurately describing the seeds.

In January, S agreed to deliver 20lb of special spring cabbage seed to T for £200. By mistake the delivery note incorrectly described the seeds. T failed to pay for them but nevertheless went on to use them, which caused a failure in three fields causing losses of £44,000, since the seed delivered was ordinary spring cabbage seed.

In February, S delivered 3lb of seed to U without any delivery note after U had said that 'Between friends we do not need to worry about such things.' U failed to pay.

In March, S provided rare plants to W to decorate her house. Unknown to S, W was notorious as a keeper of a well-known brothel and wanted the plants to create a more relaxing atmosphere for her customers. W failed to pay the £14,000 price for the plants.

In April, after S's licence had run out, he agreed to supply 39lb of seed to V for which V had paid £1,250. When S discovered that his licence had expired, he refused to deliver the seed or return the money paid because, he alleged, it would be an offence to do so.

Advise S. What difference, if any, would it make to your advice if S knew, when the agreement with V was made, that the licence had expired?

London University LLB Examination
(for external students) Elements of the Law of Contract June 1991 Q4

QUESTION FOUR

a 'Contracts illegal as formed and illegal as performed are treated differently but there is no reason why they should be.'
   Discuss.
b P was a registered supplier of electrical goods. The Supply of Electronic Goods Act 1992 which set up a registration system required all designated goods to be supplied by a registered supplier and accompanied by a statutory note of delivery.

   Q received 200 designated goods without a statutory note after Q had persuaded P that as they knew each other well it was unnecessary.

   R ordered a massage machine for R's brothel from P. The statutory note was provided.

P supplied 100 designated goods to S when unknown to P his statutory registration had expired because he had failed to renew it.

P has not been paid for any of these goods.

Advise P.

London University LLB Examination
(for external students) Elements of the Law of Contract June 1993 Q6

Answers

ANSWERS TO INTERROGRAMS

1   The categories of case which the courts refuse to enforce on grounds of public policy are as follows:

Contracts which pervert the course of justice
Agreements to conceal or compound a crime are unenforceable. Compounding a criminal offence is defined by s5 Criminal Law Act 1967. While concealing evidence would fall within this definition, it appears that the court is not prepared to extend this to an agreement not to give evidence in a civil hearing, see *Fulham Football Club Ltd* v *Cabra Estates plc* (1992) which concerned an agreement by plaintiffs with a development company that they would not give evidence to support the local authority's application for planning permission rather than the development company's.

Agreements not to appear in court and give evidence in criminal proceedings are unenforceable as is an agreement to indemnify someone who has stood surety for bail.

In the area of bankruptcy and liquidation, statute makes voidable agreements to transfer property which would amount to a fraudulent conveyance or the fraudulent preference of a creditor over others.

Champterty and maintenance
Both of these grounds concern civil rather than criminal litigation. Maintenance is interference in litigation by a person who has no concern or interest in it. Champerty is where one party agrees to finance another's action in return for a share in the winnings. Both were formerly torts and crimes but under ss13 and 14 Criminal Law Act 1967 they are no longer. However, contracts made for these purposes are still unenforceable. Examples of cases are *Martell* v *Consett Iron Co Ltd* (1955) where an association for the protection of rivers from pollution supports an action by one of its members and *Picton-Jones & Co* v *Arcadia Developments* (1989) where surveyors agreed to act for defendants on terms that fees would only be payable if the action were successful.

Interference with government or foreign relations
The common law offence of accepting a bribe or showing favour as a public officer has now been replaced by s117 Local Government Act 1972, but any contract by a public officer to do so is unenforceable. Equally unenforceable is a contract to

procure an honour or public office in return for payment: *Parkinson* v *Royal College of Ambulance* (1925).

There are a number of examples of cases where a contract to mislead a public authority by concealing or misrepresenting facts has been held void. One is *Alexander* v *Rayson* (1936) which concerned a contract to deceive the rating authority as to the rates payable in respect of a service flat.

The principle that contracts to trade with the enemy are unenforceable has, of course, only been relevant when the country has been at war. A contract to interfere with foreign relations can, however, be relevant at any time. Where a contract aids a party to circumvent the law in their own country, it will be illegal and unenforceable, as illustrated by *Regazzoni* v *KC Sethia* (1958), which concerned an agreement to export Indian goods to South Africa via Italy to avoid sanctions. A recent example is *Howard* v *Shirlstar Container Transport Ltd* (1990), where the defendants agreed to pay the plaintiff a sum of money to fly an aircraft belonging to them out of Nigeria without obtaining the necessary clearance. The court, however, allowed the plaintiff to claim the money because, although the contract was illegal, the purpose had been to save his own and his crew's lives.

Family contracts

Marriage brokerage contracts are void (*Hermann* v *Charlesworth* (1905)) and also contracts to restrain or prevent a marriage (*Lowe* v *Peers* (1768)). A contract by parties to divorce proceedings is void if made with a corrupt intention. For example, in *Brodie* v *Brodie* (1917), a contract between a couple who had felt obliged to marry because the woman was pregnant, that they would not live together after the marriage, was held to be void.

Contracts to promote sexual immorality

These are contracts which promote extra-marital sexual intercourse. A contract between lovers is not now generally illegal even if the purpose is to provide a mistress with a home: see, for example, *Tanner* v *Tanner* (1975). However, contracts concerning prostitution are invalid (*Pearce* v *Brooks* (1866)), although it is not illegal of itself to contract with a prostitute: *Appleton* v *Campbell* (1826).

Contracts interfering with personal liberty

This last category is concerned with contracts which restrict an individual's liberty without due cause. An example is *Howard* v *Millar's Timber and Trading Co* (1917), where the contract to lend money imposed restrictions on the disposal of the plaintiff's house, his leaving his job, borrowing more money or leaving home. Due cause was found in *Denny* v *Denny* (1919), where a father imposed restrictions in return for paying his son's debts. It was held that this was for the son's moral benefit.

2   In *Petrofina (Great Britain) Ltd* v *Martin* (1966) Diplock J (as he then was) defined a contract in restraint of trade as being one in which a party (the covenantor) agrees with the other (the covenantee) to restrict his liberty in future to trade with others in such manner as he chooses. The restraint of trade doctrine can operate in an infinite variety of situations. This answer will consider some of the more notable ones and the application principles in each case.

However, before looking at particular examples of the application of the doctrine, some general principles which apply in all cases can be briefly stated. In *Nordenfelt* v *Maxim Nordenfelt Guns & Ammunition Co Ltd* (1894), the starting point for any analysis of the modern law of restraint of trade, the House of Lords held that all contracts in restraint of trade are prima facie unenforceable, that there is no difference between a partial and a total restraint, and that it is a question of law whether in any given case the circumstances justify the restraint which is sought to be imposed, judged at the time the contract was concluded. Further, their Lordships held that for a restraint to be justified it had to be both reasonable as between the parties (as to which the burden of proof is on the covenantee) and also reasonable in the interests of the public (where the burden of proof is on the covenantor).

To these principles may be added certain propositions derived from a late House of Lords decision, *Esso Petroleum Co Ltd* v *Harper's Garage (Stourport) Ltd* (1968), where their Lordships stressed that the categories of contracts to which the doctrine applies are not closed and that it can apply as well to the use of land as to the activities of an individual. Now some examples of contracts in restraint of trade can be considered. The most common example is that of a covenant contained in a contract of employment whereby an employer seeks to restrict his employee's activities after termination of the employment.

Employer–employee covenants are of broadly three types:

a Covenants restraining the use of confidential information. Even in the absence of an express obligation, an employee will usually be under an implied duty not to disclose or make use of confidential information: *Faccenda Chicken* v *Fowler* (1986). However, an express covenant has the advantage of drawing the employee's attention to this duty, and providing the information can properly be regarded as confidential and being the property of the employer (*Printers & Finishers* v *Holloway* (1965)), the covenant will usually be enforced.

b Non-solicitation covenants. These too are normally regarded as unobjectionable by the courts providing (a) the employee has had contact with and acquired influences over customers and (b) it is limited to soliciting persons who were customers of the employer whilst the employee worked for him: *Konski* v *Peet* (1915). Although such covenants are often defined as to area and direction, consideration of time and space are not usually considered crucial: *Plowman* v *Ash* (1964).

c Covenants against doing business. These are the most drastic and wide ranging types of covenant because they effectively prevent the employee from earning his living in the same field as his employer. Because of this sterilising effect, the courts scrutinise them with particular care. Matters to which the courts especially have regard are the areas to which the covenant extends, its duration, the activity restrained and the seniority or otherwise of the position held by the employee. Essentially the courts have to embark on a balancing exercise, considering on the one hand the necessity of preventing the employer from obtaining an unfair advantage over his employee, and on the other the desirability of allowing every man to earn his living as he chooses.

Consequently each case turns on its particular facts and reported decisions can only be a guide to future cases. Thus in *Mason* v *Provident Clothing & Supply Co Ltd* (1913) an area within 25 miles of Islington was regarded as being too wide, whereas in *Forster & Sons Ltd* v *Suggett* (1918) a nationwide, and in *Nordenfelt* a worldwide, restraint was upheld. Similarly in *Fitch* v *Dewes* (1921) a lifelong restraint was considered reasonable, yet in *M & S Drapers* v *Reynolds* (1957) a five-year restraint was unenforceable. In each of these cases the court struck the balance between the parties' and the public interest in a different way.

Finally on employer–employee covenants, it should be noted that in certain cases the doctrine of severance has been applied such that it may be possible to delete the offending, excessive part and leave behind a reasonable and enforceable covenant: *Goldsoll* v *Goldman* (1915). However, severance must not remove the bulk of the contractual consideration supplied by one party (*Alec Lobb* v *Total Oil* (1985)), nor can the court rewrite the covenant: *Attwood* v *Lamont* (1920).

Not dissimilar principles to those discussed above apply to covenants in contracts for the sale of a business (*Vancouver Malt* v *Vancouver Breweries* (1934)) or in partnership agreements: *Bridge* v *Deacons* (1984). Here, though, the courts take a less strict line, since generally in such cases the parties will have been in more equal bargaining positions than in employer-employee cases. A relatively recent example of a contract to which the doctrine applies is that of solus petrol agreements. A succession of cases from the mid-1960s show that the doctrine may apply to an exclusive dealing agreement between a petrol station and an oil company. The courts have enumerated the following distinction. The doctrine will apply to a solus tie whereby a person in occupation of land restricts his freedom to trade; it will not apply where the solus tie is contained in a conveyance or lease whereby a person acquires the right to occupy land, albeit subject to that restriction: *Esso Petroleum Co Ltd* v *Harper's Garage (Stourport) Ltd* (1968).

Although the validity of this distinction has been questioned by some commentators, it has been adopted and applied in later cases, eg *Cleveland Petroleum Co Ltd* v *Dartstone Ltd* (1969) and *Texaco* v *Mulberry Filling Station* (1972). The courts have, however, been astute to prevent oil companies taking advantage of this distinction by devising elaborate schematic transactions such as a lease and lease-back (*Amoco* v *Rocca Bros* (1975)) or a lease and lease-back to a company specifically incorporated for this purpose *(Alec Lobb)*.

Lastly, simply to show the wide variety of situations to which the doctrine has been applied, one might refer to *Eastham* v *Newcastle United Football Club* (1964) (Football Association's player transfer system held unenforceable), *Greig* v *Insole* (1978) (ban on cricketers who joined Mr Packer's 'circus' likewise), and *Schroeder Music Publishing Co Ltd* v *Macaulay* (1974) (grossly disadvantageous contract between a music publisher and a songwriter struck down). Thus although the doctrine applies to certain commonly encountered types of contract, it can apply to unusual and one-off instances as well.

3   In discussing the enforceability of illegal contracts it is necessary to consider the respective positions of the guilty and the innocent parties.

The guilty party
The general rule is that the guilty party, that is one who knew of the illegality, cannot enforce an illegal contract: *Pearce* v *Brooks* (1866).

Whilst the guilty party cannot enforce an illegal contract, he is not debarred from bringing an action on a wrong independent of the illegal contract. Thus in *Edler* v *Auerbach* (1950) the landlord succeeded in a claim in tort in respect of a bath wrongfully removed by the tenant of premises let under an illegal lease.

Where the illegality lies in the method of performance, the guilty party may be able to enforce it. The shipowner in *St John Shipping Corporation* v *Joseph Rank Ltd* (1957) successfully claimed his freight charges although he had overloaded his ship, contrary to statute. In *Howard* v *Shirlstar Container Transport Ltd* (1990) the defendants engaged the plaintiff to fly aircraft, which they owned, out of Nigeria for a fee. The plaintiff in doing so committed breaches of Nigerian air traffic control regulations. It was held that this did not debar him from claiming his fee. The basis of that decision was that 'it would not amount to an affront to the public conscience to afford the plaintiff the relief he sought'. This 'public conscience' test was, however, rejected by the House of Lords in *Tinsley* v *Milligan* (1994). The House of Lords held that the purpose of the legislation in *Howard* as in *St John Shipping* was not to invalidate contracts but only to prohibit conduct. The contract would not be enforceable where the intention that one party should do an illegal act existed at the time of contracting: *Ashmore, Benson, Pease & Co Ltd* v *A V Dawson Ltd* (1973).

The innocent party
A party to an illegal contract may be innocent, because he is mistaken either as to the law or as to the facts. The general rule is that mistake of law does not give the innocent party the right to enforce the contract: *Nash* v *Stevenson Transport Ltd* (1936). Where a party is mistaken as to the facts he may be able to enforce it. There are cases where a claim by an innocent party has been upheld, and cases where the claim has been rejected. In *Archbolds (Freightage) Ltd* v *S Spanglett Ltd* (1961) the defendants contracted to carry the plaintiffs' whisky in a van which was not licensed to carry goods belonging to third parties, thus committing a statutory offence. The whisky was stolen, and the plaintiffs, who did not know that the van was not properly licensed, were able to recover damages for breach of contract. A leading case where the claim of the innocent party was rejected is that of *Re Mahmoud and Ispahani* (1921). A contract was made to sell linseed oil. At that time it was an offence, by legislation, to buy or sell linseed oil without a licence. The seller had a licence to sell and was induced to enter into the contract by the buyer's fraudulent misrepresentation that he also had a licence. The buyer later refused to accept the oil and it was held that the seller could not claim damages for non-acceptance.

The tests upon which to decide whether an illegal contract should or should not be enforceable are not entirely clear. One suggestion is that the innocent party can sue if the contract is illegal as performed, but not where it is illegal in its formation. This appears to be the approach in Cheshire, Fifoot and Furmston's *Law of Contract*, but Treitel observes that this does not fit all the cases.

With regard to statutory prohibitions, the principles on which it should be decided whether an innocent party's claim should be accepted or rejected were set out by Kerr LJ in *Phoenix General Insurance Co of Greece SA* v *Adas* (1988). His Lordship held that where a statute prohibits both parties from concluding or performing a contract when both or either of them have no authority to do so, the contract is impliedly prohibited. But where a statute merely prohibits one party from entering into a contract and/or imposes a penalty on him if he does so, it does not follow that the contract itself is impliedly prohibited. Whether or not the statute has this effect depends on considerations of public policy.

Even if the innocent party is not able to enforce the contract he may have alternative remedies. He may have an action on a collateral contract or a claim based on misrepresentation. In *Strongman (1945) Ltd* v *Sincock* (1955) the defendant employed a firm of builders to effect work on his house. He promised to obtain the necessary licences, without which it was illegal to do the work. He only got licences for part of the work. The builders could not sue on the building contract, which was illegal, but recovered damages for breach of the collateral undertaking to obtain the necessary licences.

In *Shelley* v *Paddock* (1980) the plaintiff was induced by the fraudulent misrepresentation of the defendant to enter into a contract to buy a house in Spain. This involved a violation of exchange control regulations. As the plaintiff's breach of the law was innocent, she was entitled to damages for the fraud.

SUGGESTED ANSWER TO QUESTION ONE

General Comment

This essay question on the doctrine of restraint of trade requires an analytical approach to the case law. In an discussion of the doctrine, it is important to remember that at different times in the history of the doctrine, the courts have regarded freedom of contract as paramount and at others have favoured the rights of the individual to trade.

Key Points

- Definition of a contract in restraint of trade - Diplock LJ in *Petrofina (Great Britain) Ltd* v *Martin* (1966)
- Requirement to balance freedom to contract and freedom to trade - *Colgate* v *Bachelor* (1569); *Schroeder Music Publishing Co Ltd* v *Macaulay* (1974)
- The principles of the doctrine - Lord Macnaghten in *Nordenfelt* v *Maxim Nordenfelt Guns & Ammunition Co Ltd* (1894)
- Protection of a legitimate interest - *NW Salt Co* v *Electrolytic Alkali Co Ltd* (1914)
- Public interests - *Att-Gen for Australia* v *Adelaide Steamship Co* (1913); *Esso Petroleum Co Ltd* v *Harper's Garage (Stourport) Ltd* (1968)
- Application of the doctrine in relation to contracts of employment - *Herbert Morris Ltd* v *Saxelby* (1916); *Faccenda Chicken* v *Fowler* (1986); *Mason* v *Provident Clothing & Supply Co Ltd* (1913); *Forster & Sons Ltd* v *Suggett* (1918); *M & S Drapers* v *Reynolds* (1957); *Fitch* v *Dewes* (1921)
- Application of the doctrine in relation to business sales

- Application of the doctrine to exclusive distributorship agreements – *Esso Petroleum v Harper's Garage (Stourport) Ltd* (1968); *Cleveland Petroleum Co Ltd v Dartstone Ltd* (1969)
- Other contracts – *Pharmaceutical Society of Great Britain v Dickson* (1970); *Eastham v Newcastle United FC* (1964); *Nagle v Fielden* (1966); *Greig v Insole* (1978)

Suggested Answer

An agreement in restraint of trade has been judicially defined as 'one in which a party (the covenantor) agrees with any other party (the covenantee) to restrict his liberty in the future to carry on trade with other persons not parties to the contract in such manner as he chooses': per Diplock LJ (as he then was) in *Petrofina (Great Britain) Ltd v Martin* (1966).

It must be conceded that there is a contradiction between the doctrine of restraint of trade and the idea of freedom of contract. The courts are required to balance the competing principles of freedom of contract and freedom of trade. A person is entitled to carry on any lawful trade or occupation that he chooses, but he should also be free to limit that right by a contract into which he freely enters. The doctrine has been justified in different ways. In the earliest cases the restriction on an individual's right to trade was regarded as being 'against the benefit of the Commonwealth': *Colgate v Bachelor* (1569). More recently, in *Schroeder Music Publishing Co Ltd v Macaulay* (1974) the justification was said, in the House of Lords, to be that it protected the weaker party against the stronger.

The modern law on restraint of trade derives from the House of Lords' decision in *Nordenfelt v Maxim Nordenfelt Guns & Ammunition Co Ltd* (1894). The policy of the law was formulated by Lord Macnaghten in the following propositions:

a all restraints of trade, if there is nothing more, are contrary to public policy, and therefore void;
b but there are exceptions: restraints of trade may be justified by the special circumstances;
c it is a sufficient justification, indeed it is the only justification, if the restriction is reasonable – reasonable in the interests of the parties and reasonable in the interests of the public.

It is for the party in whose interest the restriction is imposed (the covenantee) to show that it is in the interests of the parties; the onus of showing that it is against the public interest is on the party subject to the restriction (the covenantor).

For the restraint to be reasonable in the interests of the parties, the covenantee must show that he is protecting a legitimate interest, and that the restraint goes no further than is necessary for the protection of that interest. It has been said – and this is an expression of the inherent contradiction – that a restraint cannot be unreasonable if the parties have agreed to it: *North West Salt Co v Electrolytic Alkali Co Ltd* (1914). But the courts, in their role of custodians of public policy and protectors of the weak against the strong, do make these findings.

It is not common for the courts to find that a restraint that is reasonable in the interests of the parties is nevertheless unreasonable in the interests of the public. In *Attorney-General for Australia* v *Adelaide Steamship Co* (1913) the Privy Council found that they were not aware of any such case. More recently, however, the importance of recognising the public interest has been recognised: *Esso Petroleum Co Ltd* v *Harper's Garage (Stourport) Ltd* (1968).

It is necessary to examine various types of contract in which the doctrine operates.

Employment contracts
In such contracts the employee covenants that he will restrict his work and trading activities after the termination of the contract. But the employer is not entitled to protect himself merely from competition: an employee must, as a matter of public policy, be allowed to use the skills and experience he has gained in the employment even if he then competes with his former employer: *Herbert Morris Ltd* v *Saxelby* (1916) *Faccenda Chicken* v *Fowler* (1986). The employer must show that he is protecting a legitimate interest; trade secrets or customer connections. Trade secrets consist of the knowledge of some secret process, formula or design. An employer is also entitled to protect his customer connections. But he must show that the employee had a direct, influential relationship with the customers: in this regard the status of the employee will be an important feature; the more senior an employee the more likely it will be that he will have had this kind of relationship.

Having established that there is a legitimate interest to protect, the employer must then satisfy the court that the restraint goes no further than is necessary for the protection of that interest. This involves an examination of the area of the restraint, its duration and the activities which it covers. Much depends on the particular facts. In *Mason* v *Provident Clothing & Supply Co Ltd* (1913) a restraint which operated within twenty-five miles of London was held to be unreasonable, whereas in *Foster & Sons Ltd* v *Suggett* (1918) a restraint operating throughout the United Kingdom was upheld. In *M & S Drapers* v *Reynolds* (1957) a term of five years was held to be unreasonably long; in *Fitch* v *Dewes* (1921) a life-long restraint was upheld.

Contracts between the seller and purchaser of a business
In these contracts it is legitimate for the purchaser to protect himself from competition from the former owner of the business. Without such protection the value of the goodwill he has purchased might be rendered nugatory. Whilst similar considerations apply with regard to the reasonableness of the restraint as will be invoked in employment contracts, the courts will subject it to much less scrutiny. The livelihood of the covenantor is not primarily in issue, and the parties will be regarded as being of equal bargaining strength. The courts here will have more regard to the concept of freedom of contract.

Exclusive distributorship agreements
This is a comparatively recent development. The doctrine has been held to apply to an exclusive dealing agreement between a petrol company and a petrol station - a so-called solus agreement - whereby the petrol station undertakes to keep and supply only the company's products. In *Esso Petroleum* v *Harper's Garage* (above) the House of Lords

held that the doctrine applies where a person in occupation of land restricts his freedom to trade; it will not apply where a person who had no prior right of occupation acquires land subject to a restriction. This distinction has been adopted in, inter alia, *Cleveland Petroleum Co Ltd* v *Dartstone Ltd* (1969).

In *Pharmaceutical Society of Great Britain* v *Dickson* (1970) Lord Denning said that the doctrine of restraint of trade was not confined to particular kinds of contracts. Thus it has been applied to the Football Association's player transfer system (*Eastham* v *Newcastle United Football Club* (1964)); to the refusal of the Jockey Club to grant a woman a trainer's licence (*Nagle* v *Fielden* (1966)); and to a ban on cricketers who joined Mr Kerry Packer's 'circus': *Greig* v *Insole* (1978).

SUGGESTED ANSWER TO QUESTION TWO

General Comment

Illegal contracts are unenforceable at law. The use of the term 'clean hands' in this question, however, indicates that the candidate is required to discuss the situations in which equity may come to the aid of an innocent party disadvantaged by the harsh common law rule.

Key Points

- An innocent party, though he cannot enforce an illegal contract, may recover money or property passing under it
- Parties not in pari delicto - *Kiriri Cotton Co Ltd* v *Dewani* (1960); *Kasumu* v *Baba-Egbe* (1956); *Smith* v *Cuff* (1817); *Hughes* v *Liverpool Victoria Legal Friendly Society* (1916)
- Contract entered into under a mistake - *Re Mahmoud and Ispahani* (1921); *Archbolds (Freightage) Ltd* v *S Spanglett Ltd* (1961); *Phoenix General Insurance Co of Greece* v *Adas* (1988); *Oom* v *Bruce* (1810); *Harse* v *Pearl Assurance Co* (1904)
- Repudiation of the illegal contract - *Kearley* v *Thomson* (1890); *Taylor* v *Bowers* (1876); *Bigos* v *Bousted* (1951)
- Independent right to the property - *Bowmakers Ltd* v *Barnet Instruments Ltd* (1945); *Belvoir Finance Co* v *Stapleton* (1971); *Taylor* v *Chester* (1869)

Suggested Answer

This question requires discussion of the circumstances in which a party to an illegal contract, although he cannot enforce the contract, may be able to recover money or property passing under it. The general rule is expressed in the maxim in pari delicto potior est conditio possidentis. This means that where the parties are equally culpable with regard to the illegality, recovery of money or property is not permitted, with the consequence that the person in possession is in the stronger position.

However, there are exceptions to the rule. The broad principle behind the exceptions is that a court will decide whether or not to permit recovery depending on which option would give better effect to the prohibition of the contract. The exceptions can be grouped under four headings: (i) where the parties are not in pari delicto; (ii) the contract has been entered into under a mistake; (iii) the person seeking recovery has repudiated the illegal contract; and (iv) where the plaintiff does not rely on the illegal contract to claim recovery. These will be considered in turn.

The parties not in pari delicto
Where a statute has been enacted for the protection of a particular class of persons it is in the interests of public policy that a plaintiff within that class should be permitted recovery. Thus in *Kiriri Cotton Co Ltd v Dewani* (1960) where the prohibition was against the payment of premiums exacted by landlords for the granting of a lease, the tenant was allowed to recover the premium he had paid: see also *Kasumu v Baba-Egbe* (1956). If a plaintiff has been coerced into entering into an illegal contract by duress, recovery may be allowed: *Smith v Cuff* (1817). Recovery will also be possible where the plaintiff enters into an illegal contract, being induced to do so by a fraudulent misrepresentation which concealed the illegality: *Hughes v Liverpool Victoria Legal Friendly Society* (1916).

The contract entered into under a mistake
Where a party enters into an illegal contract under a mistake of fact he may not be without a remedy where he is innocent of the facts which render the contract illegal. Indeed the innocent party may in some circumstance be able to enforce the contract. Whether he is able to do so depends on the nature of the prohibition. If the statute prohibits both parties from concluding the contract neither the innocent nor the guilty party may enforce it: *Re Mahmoud and Ispahani* (1921). Where the prohibition is directed against one party, coupled with a sanction, the innocent party may be permitted to enforce the contract, depending on public policy considerations: *Archbolds (Freightage) Ltd v S Spanglett Ltd* (1961); *Phoenix General Insurance Co of Greece SA v Adas* (1988). Even if the innocent party is not able to enforce the contract, which he entered into under a mistake of fact, he may be able to recover money or property: *Oom v Bruce* (1810). There can be no recovery where the mistake is one of law: *Harse v Pearl Assurance Co* (1904).

Repudiation of the illegal contract
It is in the interests of public policy that people should be encouraged to repudiate illegal contracts into which they may have entered. A party is therefore afforded a locus poenitentiae and may withdraw from the illegal contract and recover his payment. But the repudiation must be in time. In *Kearley v Thomson* (1890) recovery of a payment was not allowed because the illegal purpose had been substantially carried out when the plaintiff sought to withdraw from the transaction. In contrast, where there was an illegal scheme to defraud creditors, the plaintiff had repudiated the scheme before the purpose had been carried out, and was permitted to recover the payment: *Taylor v Bowers* (1876). Furthermore the repudiation must be voluntary. It will not avail a plaintiff if his repudiation of the illegal contract is occasioned by a third party or by the other party's breach of that contract: *Bigos v Bousted* (1951). A plaintiff cannot be said to have come with clean hands if the repudiation has been forced on him by external pressures.

No reliance on the illegal contract
A plaintiff may be able to recover property (but not generally money) if he can establish a right to that property independent of the illegal contract. In *Bowmakers Ltd* v *Barnet Instruments Ltd* (1945) the plaintiffs delivered certain machine tools to the defendants under illegal hire-purchase agreements. The defendants, in breach of the agreements, failed to pay the due instalments, sold some of the machine tools and refused to return the remainder. The defendants, by virtue of their breaches of contract, no longer had any right to possess the goods. The plaintiffs were successful in an action for damages for the tort of conversion: they were able to establish their right to the goods without relying on the illegal transactions. See also *Belvoir Finance Co* v *Stapleton* (1971). Recovery will not be permitted under this heading where the plaintiff is compelled to plead the illegality in order to found his claim: see *Taylor* v *Chester* (1869).

SUGGESTED ANSWER TO QUESTION THREE

General Comment

This problem on illegal contracts has a complicated set of facts which must be considered carefully before attempting the question. What is required here is a well-planned answer which separately approaches each of the three contracts in the question following a suitable introductory paragraph.

Key Points

- The general rule is that illegal contracts are unenforceable as a matter of public policy and money or property passing under the contract cannot be recovered, but there are exceptions

The contract between S and T
- Contracts illegal in formation are unenforceable - *Pearce* v *Brooks* (1866)
- With contracts illegal in performance, the court must consider whether the law intends to prohibit the contract or penalise conduct - *St John Shipping Corp* v *Joseph Rank Ltd* (1957)
- The innocent party may bring an action for breach - *Archbolds (Freightage) Ltd* v *S Spanglett Ltd* (1961)

The contract between S and U
- Where parties collude they are both denied enforcement - *Ashmore, Benson, Pease & Co Ltd* v *A V Dawson Ltd* (1973); *Pearce* v *Brooks* (1866)

The contract between S and V
- The contract is not necessarily void because it is an offence for one party to enter into it - *Re Mahmoud and Ispahani* (1921); *Bloxsome* v *Williams* (1824); *Phoenix General Insurance Co of Greece SA* v *Adas* (1988)
- Implied collateral warranty - *Strongman (1945) Ltd* v *Sincock* (1955)
- Misrepresentation - *Shelley* v *Paddock* (1980); *Hughes* v *Liverpool Victoria Friendly Society* (1916)

Suggested Answer

The general rule is that illegal contracts are not, as a matter of public policy, enforceable: this finds expression in the maxim ex turpi causa non oritur actio. Public policy also, as a general rule, prohibits the recovery of money or property passing under an illegal contract: this is reflected in the maxim in pari delicto potior est conditio defendentis. There are, however, exceptions to both these rules, or rather situations in which they do not apply. The relevant principles must now be applied to each of the contracts which S has concluded.

The contract between S and T

The illegality here lies in the incorrect description of the seeds in the delivery note. The contract is therefore illegal in its performance and not in its formation. The rights and liabilities of both parties must be considered in light of this. S, having been responsible for the inaccurate delivery note, is the guilty party with regard to the illegality. Whilst the general rule is that the guilty party may not enforce a contract illegal in its formation (*Pearce* v *Brooks* (1866)), the law adopts a more flexible attitude where the illegality relates merely to its performance. The question that will then be considered is whether the legislation intended to prohibit the contract or merely to penalise conduct: *St John Shipping Corporation* v *Joseph Rank Ltd* (1957). It is clear that the legislation prohibits dealing in the relevant materials without the appropriate licence, but the requirement with regard to the accuracy of the delivery note may relate only to conduct in the performance of the contract and the legislation may provide an adequate penalty for failure to comply with this requirement. In this event S would be entitled to enforce the contract and claim the purchase price of £200. This is subject to any claim T may have against him.

T is the innocent party in the transaction. *Archbolds (Freightage) Ltd* v *S Spanglett Ltd* (1961) is authority for the proposition that the innocent party may bring an action on the contract in the event of breach. However, it is not entirely clear whether or not S has been in breach of contract. The problem presented does not make explicit whether particular cabbage seed was agreed upon and delivered, though incorrectly described in the delivery note, or whether the contract was for the seed described in the delivery note, which was not in fact delivered. In the latter event S was in breach of contract and T would be entitled to bring an action for the loss he has sustained.

The contract between S and U

In this situation the parties agree to contravene the requirement of the delivery note. Where the parties collude in the method of performance which they both know is illegal then both parties are denied enforcement: *Ashmore, Benson, Pease & Co Ltd* v *A V Dawson Ltd* (1973). It follows that S cannot recover the purchase price.

The contract between S and W

In this situation there does not appear to have been any infringement of the legislation relating to dealing in the relevant materials. The illegality relates to the use to which W put the materials. It is clear that, if S had provided the plants knowing that they were to used for an immoral purpose, he would be denied enforcement: *Pearce* v *Brooks* (above). However, S is innocent of W's intention and there is no public policy rule that would prevent recovery of the purchase price.

The contract between S and V

When S entered into the agreement to sell the seeds to V he had no authority to do so. The position of the innocent party in this situation is not without difficulty. The leading case of *Re Mahmoud and Ispahani* (1921) held that where a statute prohibits both parties from concluding a contract, when one or either of them has no authority to do so, the contract is impliedly prohibited. But it does not follow that because it is an offence for one party to enter into a contract, the contract itself is void: *Bloxsome* v *Williams* (1824); and see the analysis of these two cases by Pearce J in the *Archbolds* case (above). 'Whether or not the statute has this effect depends on considerations of public policy in the light of the mischief which the statute is designed to prevent, its language, scope and purpose, the consequences for the innocent party, and any other relevant considerations': per Kerr LJ in *Phoenix General Insurance Co of Greece SA* v *Adas* (1988).

On the present information it is not possible to say with certainty whether considerations of public policy would allow enforcement of the contract by V, who is an innocent party. Arguably the decision in the *Phoenix Insurance* case would prohibit such enforcement. In this event no claim would lie against S by V for the failure to deliver the seed or return the money. V might not be without a remedy, however, if S knew that the licence had expired at the time the agreement was made. He may be able to rely on an implied collateral warranty that S had the requisite licence: *Strongman (1945) Ltd* v *Sincock* (1955) – though the warranty was express in that case. V might also be able to recover damages for misrepresentation (*Shelley* v *Paddock* (1980)) and he might be able to rescind the contract. A further possibility is that V could recover the money he has paid in reliance on S's fraudulent misrepresentation that the contract was legal: *Hughes* v *Liverpool Victoria Legal Friendly Society* (1916).

SUGGESTED ANSWER TO QUESTION FOUR

General Comment

A stiff test of the candidate's knowledge and abilities is provided by this two-part examination question on illegal contracts. For the first part, the candidate is required to write a discussion essay on the different approaches of the courts to contracts illegal as formed and illegal as performed. In the second part, the principles discussed must be applied to a set of problematical facts.

Key Points

The essay
- The position of the guilty party
  - The guilty party cannot enforce a contract illegal as formed – *Alexander* v *Rayson* (1936); *Pearce* v *Brooks* (1866)
  - The contract may be enforced if illegal in performance – *St John Shipping Corp* v *Joseph Rank Ltd* (1957); *Howard* v *Shirlstar Container Transport Ltd* (1990)

- The position of the innocent party
  - Innocent means mistaken as to the law or the facts
  - Mistake as a law does not allow the innocent party to enforce - *Nash* v *Stevenson Transport Ltd* (1936);
  - Where the mistake is as to facts, the innocent party may be able to enforce - *Archbolds (Freightage) Ltd* v *S Spanglett Ltd* (1961); *Re Mahmoud and Ispahani (1921); Phoenix General Insurance Co of Greece SA* v *Adas* (1988)
  - A party is not innocent if he intends the other to perform an illegal act - *Ashmore, Benson, Pease & Co Ltd* v *A V Dawson Ltd* (1973)

The problem
- The contract with Q - payment may not be enforced by P - *St John Shipping Corp* v *Joseph Rank Ltd* (1957); *Ashmore, Benson, Pease & Co Ltd* v *A V Dawson Ltd* (1973)
- The contract with R - it is not clear whether or not P can enforce payment - *Pearce* v *Brooks* (1866); *Appleton* v *Campbell* (1826)
- The contract with S
- P cannot enforce the contract - *St John Shipping Corp* v *Joseph Rank Ltd* (1957);

Suggested Answer

a The different treatment of contracts illegal as formed and illegal as performed is in respect of the right to enforce such contracts. It is convenient, in discussing this question, to look in turn at the positions of the guilty party and the innocent party.

The position of the guilty party
The guilty party cannot enforce a contract which is concluded for an illegal purpose. A landlord who drew up a lease in a manner designed to deceive the local authority in respect of rates could not sue for the rent: *Alexander* v *Rayson* (1936). The owner of a brougham who knowingly let it to a prostitute for the purpose of her profession could not sue for the hire: *Pearce* v *Brooks* (1866).

The courts take a different view, however, where the illegality is merely in the method of performance. In *St John Shipping Corporation* v *Joseph Rank Ltd* (1957) the shipowner was held entitled to his freight even though he had overloaded his ship, in contravention of the statute. Devlin J found that, the offender having been deprived of the fruits of his crime by the penalty imposed by the statute, it would be curious if he were also to be deprived of his freight charges. In *Howard* v *Shirlstar Container Transport Ltd* (1990) the illegality was in the performance of the contract. The offender was engaged to remove an aircraft from Nigeria, and did so in breach of Nigerian air traffic control regulations. His criminal conduct was designed to free himself from danger. The Court of Appeal held that this was an instance where it would not be an affront to the public conscience to permit enforcement of the contract.

The position of the innocent party
'Innocent' in this context means that the party is mistaken as to the law or as to the

facts. Mistake as to the law does not generally give the innocent party the right to enforce a contract affected by illegality: *Nash v Stevenson Transport Ltd* (1936). Where he is mistaken as to the facts, the innocent party may be able to enforce the contract, depending on the nature of the prohibition which engenders the illegality: contrasting cases are: *Archbolds (Freightage) Ltd v S Spanglett Ltd* (1961) and *Re Mahmoud and Ispahani* (1921). The distinction between these cases, and the position with regard to the statutory prohibition on contracts, was analysed by Kerr LJ in *Phoenix General Insurance Co of Greece SA v Adas* (1988). This may be summarised as follows:

i   Where a statute prohibits both parties from concluding or performing a contract, the contract is prohibited and neither party can enforce it - as in *Re Mahmoud and Ispahani*.

ii But where a statute merely prohibits one party from entering into a contract and/or imposes a sanction on him if he does so, this does not necessarily render the contract unenforceable: (the unilateral prohibition in *Archbolds (Freightage) Ltd* on the carrier did not debar his innocent customer from bringing an action on the contract). Whether or not the statute has this effect depends on considerations of public policy.

A party to an illegal contract is not 'innocent' if he enters into a contract with the intention that the other party should perform an illegal act: *Ashmore, Benson, Pease & Co Ltd v A V Dawson Ltd* (1973). It appears that, with regard to both the guilty and the innocent party, the paramount question is one of public policy. In the case of the guilty party the court will not assist him to gain the fruits of his crime, but if the illegality is merely in the performance of the contract, and there is a criminal sanction attached to the illegal performance, public policy does not necessarily require the further imposition of a civil penalty. As far as the innocent party is concerned the effect of a statutory prohibition is construed in the light of the mischief which the statute was designed to prevent.

b This part of the question involves an application of the principles discussed above to the three contracts into which P has entered. These contracts will be dealt with in turn.

The contract with Q
Here the illegality consists in the failure to provide the required statutory note. If that were all it might well be that P could enforce payment as in the *St John Shipping* case (above). But in that case Devlin J said that 'a contract which is entered into with the object of committing an illegal act is unenforceable'. Where an intention that one party should do an unlawful act exists at the time of contracting neither party can enforce the contract: *Ashmore, Benson* (above) There appears to have been such intention here; accordingly P cannot enforce payment.

The contract with R
The statute is not relevant to this contract. It is not stated whether or not the massage machine is one of the 'designated goods' so it is not clear if the statute applies. In any

event P has complied with the statutory requirements. The illegality lies in the fact that the machine has been ordered for an immoral purpose. If P knew the purpose for which the machine was intended, it is clear that he could not enforce payment: *Pearce v Brooks* (above). If P knew neither the purpose for which the machine was intended, nor that R kept a brothel, it is equally clear that he could enforce payment. What is less certain is the situation – possibly unlikely – if he knew that R kept a brothel, but did not know that R intended to use the machine in the brothel. There is authority which supports the view that this limited knowledge would not deprive P of enforcement: *Appleton v Campbell* (1826). As P's state of knowledge is not known it is not possible to give a more definite answer for this particular contract.

The contract with S

The position here is that P is no longer a 'registered supplier' but that P is ignorant of this. What has to be investigated is the purpose of the statute. Does it intend merely to impose an obligation on suppliers of designated goods, possibly coupled with a penalty for non-compliance, or does it mean to prohibit the contract? In *St John Shipping* (referred to previously) Devlin J gave this example:

> '... a person is forbidden by statute from using an unlicensed vehicle on the highway. If one asks oneself whether there is in such an enactment an implied prohibition of all contracts for the use of unlicensed vehicles, the answer may well be that there is.'

Applying that example to the present facts it seems that there is an implied prohibition on the supply of designated goods by unregistered suppliers, and that the contract with S falls within the prohibition. P cannot therefore enforce payment.

11

Frustration, Discharge and Breach

Introduction

This chapter is concerned with the performance of contractual obligations or, perhaps more accurately, non-performance giving rise to an action for breach of contract or a claim that the contract has become frustrated due to supervening events and no further performance is due.

Frustration is one of the most popular topics in examinations and may be the basis of either problem or discussion questions. However, the topic is complex. The courts have over the decades shifted their view of the theoretical basis on which the doctrine is founded and the cases are sometimes subject to fine distinctions. However simple a question may seem on the face of it, the unprepared candidate faces considerable danger when entering these waters.

The questions below give a good indication of the complexities involved and how these may be dealt with in a competent answer. Questions on repudiatory breaches of contract and the likely outcome of an action for breach have been included. This topic is, however, closely allied with the importance which the court attaches to the contractual term broken.

Questions

INTERROGRAMS

1 Explain the 'radical change in obligations test'.
2 What effect did the Law Reform (Frustrated Contracts) Act 1943 have on the common law relating to frustration?

QUESTION ONE

Lord Blessers, who wishes to celebrate his daughter's wedding in style, arranges an open air pop concert in Blessers Park, in the county of Loamshire. On 1 February he engages a famous group 'The Wild Things' to appear for £5,000. He is obliged to pay them £1,000 immediately, the balance to be payable on 1 July, the day of the concert. On 1 March he engages a catering firm 'Eatwell' to provide 500 lunches in a marquee in Blessers Park for £10,000 payable on 1 July. On 1 June foot and mouth disease, which has been affecting neighbouring counties for the previous six months, breaks out in Loamshire. The disease cannot be contracted by human beings but can be spread by them. The Minister of Agriculture appeals to residents of Loamshire, on a 'voluntary basis', to cancel any outdoor events.

Lord Blessers immediately cancels the celebrations and informs the group and the caterers that their services are no longer required. The group has spent considerable sums of money setting up an elaborate stage whilst the caterers have incurred considerable expense in preparations.

Advise 'The Wild Things' and 'Eatwell'.

How would your advice differ, if at all, if the bride had been killed in an accident a week before her wedding day?

London University LLB Examination
(for external students) Elements of the Law of Contract June 1987 Q7

QUESTION TWO

'It is not hardship or inconvenience or material loss itself which calls the principle of frustration into play. There must be as well such a change in the significance of the obligation that the thing undertaken would, if performed, be a different thing than that contracted for.'

Explain and comment.

London University LLB Examination
(for external students) Elements of the Law of Contract June 1988 Q2

QUESTION THREE

M was a famous singer who on 1 November 1992 had been engaged by Aber Opera to sing the leading role in their performance on 1 March. M was to receive £5,000 as a fee. Aber Opera were able to charge much higher ticket prices because of the participation of M. By 1 January the tickets were sold out. On 20 January M told Aber Opera that he had accepted an engagement elsewhere where they were prepared to pay a £10,000 fee. Eventually, Aber Opera agreed to raise the fee to £12,500 and paid £2,500 by 28 January as M had demanded. On 1 February, M wrote to say that he was going to the USA to make records and might not be back in time for the Aber Opera performance. In fact, M did not go to the USA but fell ill on 27 February and was unable to perform on 1 March because of ill health. Aber Opera were in difficulties as customers were demanding the return of their payments made for the scheduled performance.

Advise Aber Opera.

London University LLB Examination
(for external students) Elements of the Law of Contract June 1993 Q5

QUESTION FOUR

Alan is a well-known actor. He was booked for six months by the Totally Useless Theatre Company to appear in a West End play but, following bad reviews, he walked out of the production and disappeared for two weeks. The company had to engage a substitute, who has proved more popular with audiences. Alan has now returned saying that he had to go away because he was ill and demanding to be allowed to continue with the contract. Advise the company.

Written by the Editor June 1998

QUESTION FIVE

Bryan rents Cecil's cottage for £50 per week. Lately, he got behind and owes Cecil £250. He saw Cecil last week to offer him a part payment of £100 and a promise of the rest this week. Cecil, however, believed he had just won a fortune on the lottery and said to Bryan, 'Forget it, mate. I'm in the money now!' Cecil then discovered he had lost his lottery ticket and now wants to claim the outstanding rent. Bryan has, however, spent the money. Advise Bryan.

How would your answer differ if Bryan had offered Cecil a gold watch worth £100 in settlement of the debt and Cecil had accepted it?

Written by the Editor June 1998

Answers

ANSWERS TO INTERROGRAMS

1 The given quotation requires an analysis of the test employed to determine whether or not a contract has been frustrated. Prior to 1863 contractual obligations were regarded as absolute, irrespective of the change in circumstances: *Paradine* v *Jane* (1647). At that date the doctrine of frustration was introduced into English law by the decision in *Taylor* v *Caldwell* (1863), where it was held that a contract for the use of a music hall was frustrated when the building was destroyed by fire. This was said to rest on there being an implied term of the contract that the building should continue to exist, and on its destruction the parties were discharged of further obligations.

The courts have subsequently discarded the implied term approach in favour of the radical change in obligations tests, first propounded in the speech of Lord Radcliffe in *Davis Contractors Ltd* v *Fareham Urban District Council* (1956). His Lordship said that

> 'frustration occurs whenever the law recognises that without default of either party a contractual obligation has become incapable of being performed because the circumstances in which performance is called for would render it a thing radically different from that which was undertaken by the contract. Non haec in foedera veni. It was not this that I promised to do.'

The principle enunciated by Viscount Radcliffe has been approved by two further decisions of the House of Lords: *National Carriers Panalpina (Northern) Ltd* (1981) and *The Nema* (1982).

Two further points emerge from Viscount Radcliffe's speech. The first is that it is not hardship or inconvenience or material loss itself which calls the principle of frustration into play. The second is that although his Lordship referred to a contractual obligation being 'incapable of being performed' he did not mean that frustration occurs only when the contract is physically impossible of performance. Elsewhere in his speech he refers to such a change in the significance of the obligation that the thing undertaken would, if performed, be a different thing from that contracted for.

Davis v *Fareham* is itself an illustration of the first point. Delay caused by bad weather and the shortage of labour rendered the contract unprofitable for the appellants, but this did not constitute a frustrating event. Further illustration is afforded by *The Eugenia* (1964) where the closure of the Suez Canal caused delay and considerable additional expense. Lord Denning emphasised the point, saying: 'The fact that it has become more onerous or more expensive for one party than he thought is not sufficient to bring about a frustration. It must be more than merely more onerous or more expensive. It must be positively unjust to hold the parties bound.'

The second point, that it is not only physical impossibility that causes frustration, is illustrated by cases such as *Jackson* v *Union Marine Insurance Co* (1873) and *Krell* v *Henry* (1903). In both these cases physical performance was still possible but the supervening events had rendered the nature of the contractual obligations fundamentally different.

The question is, therefore, not simply whether there has been a radical change in the circumstances, but whether there has been a radical change in the obligation. Was 'performance ... fundamentally different in a commercial sense?': *Tsakiroglou & Co Ltd* v *Noblee Thorl GmbH* (1962).

2 The effect of frustration is to excuse the parties from further performance but this common law principle has been partially modified by the Law Reform (Frustrated Contracts) Act 1943.

Under s1(2) of the Act all sums paid or payable in pursuance of a frustrated contract shall be recoverable or cease to be payable. This is subject to the proviso that if the payee has incurred expense in or for the purpose of the performance of the contract, the payee may retain all or part of such sums as the court considers just, up to the amount of the expenses incurred. However, if a party had not stipulated for pre-payment he will not be able to recover.

Section 1(3) provides that where a party to the contract has, by reason of anything done by another party in or for the purpose of the performance of the contract, obtained a valuable benefit before discharge, the other party may recover from him such sum not exceeding the value of the benefit as the court considers just, having regard to all the circumstances of the case. There is some academic controversy about how the meaning of 'valuable benefit' should be construed.

The relationship between the subsections was considered by Robert Goff J in *BP Exploration* v *Hunt (No 2)* (1982) and the following principles emerge from his judgment:

a The Act was designed to prevent unjust enrichment.
b Under s1(3) the court is concerned with doing justice between the parties.
c The court should endeavour to achieve consistency between the sections because they both stem from principle (a).
d The purpose of the Act is not to do such things as apportion loss, put the parties into the position they would have been in had the contract been performed, or restore the parties to the position they were in before the contract was made.
e The valuable benefit should be the end product of services rendered not just the service itself.

f   The benefit is to be valued at the date of frustration.
g   Money paid is recoverable but if the benefit is not money it is the reasonable value of the plaintiff's performance, ie reasonable remuneration for services or a reasonable price for goods.

Finally, it should be noted that the Act does not apply to four types of contract: voyage charterparties; contracts for carriage of goods by sea; insurance contracts and contracts for the sale of specific goods which perish.

SUGGESTED ANSWER TO QUESTION ONE

General Comment
A problem question on the doctrine of frustration, the trap here is that the unwary candidate might lose marks by advising the wrong party.

Key Points
- The doctrine of frustration may apply to the contracts – *Taylor* v *Caldwell* (1863); *Davis Contractors* v *Fareham UDC* (1956); *National Carriers* v *Panalpina* (1981)
- Neither contract is incapable of performance and the courts do not readily find frustration – *Davis* v *Fareham UDC* (1956); *Tsakiroglou* v *Noblee Thorl* (1952); *The Eugenia* (1964)
- Frustration could be self-induced – *Maritime National Fish* v *Ocean Trawlers* (1935);
- 'The Wild Things' and 'Eatwell' can recover damages either for loss of profit or for expenses – *CCC Films* v *Impact Quadrant Films* (1984)
- The death of the bride would be a frustrating event – *Krell* v *Henry* (1903)
- The contract would then be automatically discharged immediately – *Hirji Mulji* v *Cheong Yue SS* (1926)
- At common law the parties would be discharged from their obligations – *Appleby* v *Myers* (1867)
- Advance payments may be recovered unless expenses have been incurred but excess expenses cannot be recovered – ss1(2) and 1(3) Law Reform (Frustrated Contracts) Act 1943; *BP Exploration* v *Hunt (No 2)* (1979)

Suggested Answer
One must advise 'The Wild Things' and 'Eatwell' whether their contracts with Lord Blessers were frustrated, and if so what the parties' respective rights and liabilities are. The doctrine of frustration was introduced into English law by the Court of Queen's Bench in *Taylor* v *Caldwell* (1863). In that case, which concerned the hire of a music hall, the court held that it was an implied term of the contract that since the performance of the contract depended upon the continued existence of the music hall, its destruction by fire automatically discharged both parties from their outstanding obligations.

It was for many years considered that the juridical basis of the doctrine of frustration was that stated in *Taylor* v *Caldwell*, namely by implying the appropriate term into a particular contract. Recent decisions of the House of Lords have, however, restated the juridical basis in (it is submitted) a more satisfactory way. In *Davis Contractors Ltd* v *Fareham Urban District Council* (1956) Viscount Radcliffe formulated the 'radical change in the obligation theory'. His Lordship formulated the test in the following way: 'Non haec in foedera veri, it was not this that I promised to do.' His Lordship's test has been subsequently adopted and applied in *National Carriers* v *Panalpina (Northern) Ltd* (1981) and *The Nema* (1982) and is now generally accepted as correctly stating the law of frustration.

This test must therefore be applied to see if the two contracts in question have been frustrated. It should be noted that there is no legal or physical impossibility preventing either contract being performed. The Ministry of Agriculture has appealed to residents on a 'voluntary basis'; it has not taken any legal steps to prevent outdoor events taking place.

No doubt it is very public spirited of Lord Blessers to respond to the Ministry's appeal. That, however, does not amount to frustration of either contract. It is not correct to say that either contract is incapable of performance (per Viscount Radcliffe in *Davis* v *Fareham*); both are still well capable of being performed. Cases such as *Tsakiroglou & Co Ltd* v *Noblee Thorl* (1962), *The Eugenia* (1964) and *Davis* v *Fareham* itself indicate that the courts do not readily accede to a plea of frustration. It is submitted that a court would not do so here. Alternatively, as it was Lord Blessers who cancelled the contracts, the case could be regarded as one of self-induced frustration: *Maritime National Fish Ltd* v *Ocean Trawlers Ltd* (1935). Accordingly Lord Blessers was not entitled to cancel the contracts and both the group and 'Eatwell' can recover damages from him for breach of contract, either for loss of profit or in respect of expenses thrown away: *CCC Films (London) Ltd* v *Impact Quadrant Films Ltd* (1984).

The alternative set of facts postulates that the bride has been killed a week before the wedding. In these circumstances it is submitted that both contracts would be frustrated. The concert and the meals are part of the intended celebration of the wedding. If the bride is killed, no wedding can take place. The facts as varied are similar to *Krell* v *Henry* (1903), where a contract to hire rooms overlooking the route of the coronation procession was held to be frustrated when the coronation was cancelled.

Thus next one must consider the consequences which flow from the contracts being frustrated.

Taking first the group, it is settled law that a frustrating event discharges a contract automatically and immediately: *Hirji Mulji V Cheong Yue SS* (1926). At common law, the position was that whilst the parties were discharged from any outstanding future obligations, accrued rights and liabilities subsisted and remained enforceable: *Appleby* v *Myers* (1867). The common law principles have been modified, though not entirely replaced, by the Law Reform (Frustrated Contracts) Act 1943, the provisions of which must now be considered in relation to the pop group's concert.

Lord Blessers has paid £1,000 in advance of the due date for performance and prior to the frustrating event. Section 1(2) of the 1943 Act renders this sum recoverable, subject however to the court having a discretion to allow the group to retain all or part of it if it has incurred expense in performance of the contract. In *BP Exploration* v *Hunt (No 2)* (1979) Robert Goff J explained this subsection as giving statutory recognition to the defence of change of position. The facts disclose that the pop group has spent considerable sums in setting up a stage, so it is possible that the court will allow it to keep all (or certainly part) of the £1,000 paid by Lord Blessers in advance. On the other hand if the group has incurred expenses in excess of this sum, it cannot recover such excess from Lord Blessers under sl(3) of the 1943 Act. Thus the best it can do is to persuade the court to allow it to retain the whole of the £1,000.

The position of 'Eatwell' is even weaker. In this case there have been no advance payments forthcoming or due from but not paid by Lord Blessers, so sl(2) can have no application. Further, again sl(3) as construed in *BP* v *Hunt* does not apply either since Lord Blessers has not received any valuable benefit within the terms of the sub-section.

SUGGESTED ANSWER TO QUESTION TWO

General Comment

The aim of this question is to establish the candidate's understanding of the test the courts use to determine whether or not a contract is frustrated and knowledge of the topic in general.

Key Points

- Contracts were originally regarded as absolute – *Paradine* v *Jane* (1647)
- Breach of implied term of existence of subject matter was later held to discharge the contract – *Taylor* v *Caldwell* (1863); *Blackburn Bobbin Co Ltd* v *T W Allen & Sons Ltd* (1918)
- The courts have now substituted the 'radical change in obligations' test – *Davis Contractors Ltd* v *Fareham UDC* (1956); *National Carriers Ltd* v *Panalpina (Northern) Ltd* (1981); *The Nema* (1981)
- A contract will not be frustrated merely because it becomes more difficult or expensive to perform – *The Eugenia* (1964)
- Supervening legal impossibility – *Taylor* v *Caldwell* (1863); *Metropolitan Water Board* v *Dick, Kerr & Co Ltd* (1918); *Denny, Mott & Dickson Ltd* v *James B Fraser & Co Ltd* (1944)
- Performance has become fundamentally different in the commercial sense – *Tsakiroglou & Co Ltd* v *Noblee Thorl* (1962); *Jackson* v *Union Marine Insurance Co* (1873); *Krell* v *Henry* (1903); *Herne Bay Steam Boat Company* v *Hutton* (1903)
- The frustrating event must have arisen without the fault of either party – *Maritime National Fish Ltd* v *Ocean Trawlers Ltd* (1935); *Paal Wilson* v *Blumenthal* (1983)

Suggested Answer

This question requires a discussion of the test that the courts will employ to determine whether or not a contract is frustrated. Prior to 1863, contractual obligations were regarded as absolute. In *Paradine* v *Jane* (1647) a tenant was held liable to pay the rental notwithstanding that he had been expelled from the premises by enemy invasion. In English law the concept of frustration was first recognised in the case of *Taylor* v

Caldwell (1863) where the defendants had agreed to let the plaintiffs have the use of a music hall. After the conclusion of the agreement and before the performance of the contract the hall was destroyed by fire. Blackburn J held that because the music hall had ceased to exist without fault of either party both parties were discharged from their further obligations.

The basis of the decision in *Taylor v Caldwell* was the implied term theory; the parties had contracted on the basis of the continued existence of the music hall.

The implied term theory was adopted in later cases; see, for example; *Blackburn Bobbin Co Ltd v T W Allen & Sons Ltd* (1918). Here the defendants had agreed to sell to the plaintiffs a certain quantity of Finland birch timber. It was the custom of the defendants to import that timber direct from Finland and this became impossible because of the outbreak of war. This practice was, however, unknown to the plaintiffs and it was held by the Court of Appeal that there was nothing to show that the plaintiffs contemplated that the sellers were adopting this practice. Accordingly the contract was not frustrated.

The implied term theory has now largely been discarded in favour of the 'radical change in obligations' test. This test was first enunciated by Lord Radcliffe in *Davis Contractors Ltd v Fareham Urban District Council* (1956) where his Lordship said that 'frustration occurs whenever the law recognises that without default of either party a contractual obligation has become incapable of being performed because the circumstances in which performance is called for would render it a thing radically different from that which was undertaken by the contract. Non haec in foedera veni. It was not this that I promised to do'. This test has been approved by two further decisions of the House of Lords: *National Carriers Ltd v Panalpina (Northern) Ltd* (1981) and *The Nema* (1981).

It has been repeatedly emphasised that a contract will not be frustrated merely because it becomes more difficult or expensive to perform. In *Davis* the contractors had entered into a contract with the council to build 78 houses for the sum of £92,425 within a period of eight months. Owing to unexpected circumstances and without the fault of either party there was a serious shortage of skilled labour and of building materials and the work took 22 months to complete, with the result that the contractors unavoidably incurred considerable additional expense. The delay and consequent further expense was not, however, sufficient to frustrate the contract. In *The Eugenia* (1964) Lord Denning MR said:

> 'The fact that it has become more onerous or more expensive for one party than he thought is not sufficient to bring about a frustration. It must be more than merely more onerous or more expensive. It must be positively unjust to hold the parties bound.'

Lord Denning also observed that the implied term theory had been discarded by nearly everyone for the simple reason that it did not represent the truth. In that case if the parties had contemplated the occurrence of the event they would not have said 'it is all over between us'. They would have differed about what was to happen, so that there was no room for an implied term. There will be a frustrating event if the subject matter of the contract is physically destroyed as in *Taylor v Caldwell* (above) or if there is a supervening legal impossibility: *Metropolitan Water Board* v *Dick, Kerr & Co Ltd* (1918); *Denny, Mott & Dickson Ltd* v *James B Fraser & Co Ltd* (1944).

Frustration is not, however, confined to physical or legal impossibility. The contract will also be frustrated if performance has become fundamentally different in a commercial sense: *Tsakiroglou & Co Ltd* v *Noblee Thorl* (1962). In *Jackson* v *Union Marine Insurance Co* (1873) a ship, the subject matter of the contract, ran aground and the consequent repairs took over six months to complete. It was held that the delay was so long as to put an end in a commercial sense to the commercial speculation entered upon by the parties. In *Krell* v *Henry* (1903) the defendant had hired a room to witness the coronation procession of King Edward VII. Owing to the King's illness the coronation was postponed. The contract was held to be frustrated on the grounds that the state of things which the parties contemplated was no longer in existence. A contrasting case, also arising out of the postponed coronation of King Edward VII, was that of *Herne Bay Steam Boat Company* v *Hutton* (1903). In that case the defendant hired a board in order to witness a royal naval review. Owing to the postponement of the coronation the review was cancelled. However the fleet was still there and it was held that the doctrine of frustration did not apply in these circumstances.

Finally it must be noted that the event in question must have arisen without the fault of either party. The doctrine cannot be relied on if the frustration is self-induced: *Maritime National Fish Ltd* v *Ocean Trawlers Ltd* (1935): *Paal Wilson* v *Blumenthal* (1983).

SUGGESTED ANSWER TO QUESTION THREE

General Comment

While the question of frustration is perhaps the first to come to mind when reading this problem, there are also questions of consideration, duress and repudiatory breach to be tackled. Students should consider the facts carefully to determine how these diverse strands may be combined and, in studying the answer, note how they have been separated out to provide a clear and well-structured analysis of the situation.

Key Points

- The only consideration for the increased fee was the performance of an existing duty which may be good consideration if there was no duress - *Williams* v *Roffey Bros & Nicholls (Contractors) Ltd* (1991)
- Economic pressure can amount to duress if it amounts to illegitimate pressure which compels the will of the victim - *Occidental Worldwide Investment Corp* v *Skibs A/S Avanti (The Sibeon and The Sibotre)* (1976); *North Ocean Shipping Co Ltd* v *Hyundai Construction Co Ltd (The Atlantic Baron)* (1979); *Pao On* v *Lau Yiu Long* (1980); *Universe Tankships* v *ITWF (The Universe Sentinel)* (1982)
- The effect of duress is to render the transaction voidable - *Atlas Express Ltd* v *Kafco Ltd* (1989); *Vantage Navigation* v *Suhail & Saud Bahwan* (1989); *Dimskal Shipping Co SA* v *ITWF (The Evia Luck)* (1991)
- M's letter of 1 February may be a repudiatory breach - *Mersey Steel and Iron Co* v

11 Frustration, Discharge and Breach – Answers

Naylor Benzon & Co (1884); *Federal Commerce & Navigation Co Ltd v Molena Alpha Inc* (1979); *Woodar Investment Development Ltd v Wimpey Construction (UK) Ltd* (1980)
- Active steps are necessary to accept a repudiatory breach – *State Trading Corp of India v M Golodetz Ltd* (1989); *Fercometal Sarl v Mediterranean Shipping Co SA* (1988)
- A party unable to perform his obligations through illness may be a frustrating event – *Condor v The Barron Knights Ltd* (1966); *Davis Contractors Ltd v Fareham UDC* (1956)
- The effect at common law is to discharge the parties from further obligations – *Taylor v Caldwell* (1863)
- The rights of the parties to payment and recovery are determined under ss1(2) and 1(3) Law Reform (Frustrated Contracts) Act 1943

Suggested Answer

The consideration for the increased fee

Brief mention should be made of this aspect. It seems that the only consideration furnished by M for the promise to pay the increased fee, and for the advance payment, is the performance of an existing duty to Aber Opera. The performance, or the promise to perform, an existing duty can be good consideration, provided that the promise to pay the increased fee was not given as a result of duress on the part of M: *Williams v Roffey Bros & Nicholls (Contractors) Ltd* (1991). In view of the conclusion as to duress, this point is not proceeded with further.

The question of duress

The contract between Aber Opera and M is for him to provide his services on 1 March for the fee of £5,000. It is not stated when this fee was to be paid, but it can be assumed that the fee was payable on conclusion of the performance. This assumption is made because the advance of £2,500, referred to below, was only paid as a result of M's subsequent demand.

The statement by M of 20 January that he had accepted an engagement elsewhere at a higher fee, coupled with his demand for the payment of £2,500, constitutes a threat that he would break his contract with Aber Opera, unless he received a higher fee and the advance payment. This threat, if not express, is clearly implied: no other inference can be drawn from his conduct.

It has been recognised since *Occidental Worldwide Investment Corp v Skibs A/S Avanti (The Sibeon and The Sibotre)* (1976) that economic pressure can in law amount to duress. Further recognition of this concept was afforded shortly thereafter in *North Ocean Shipping Co Ltd v Hyundai Construction Co Ltd (The Atlantic Baron)* (1979). The elements of economic duress are illegitimate pressure which amounts to compulsion of the will of the victim: see the judgments of Lord Scarman in *Pao On v Lau Yiu Long* (1980) and *Universe Tankships v ITWF (The Universe Sentinel)* (1982). The effect of duress is to render voidable the transaction into which the victim has entered. The doctrine of economic duress has been applied in a number of recent cases, including:

Atlas Express Ltd v *Kafco Ltd* (1989); *Vantage Navigation* v *Suhail & Saud Bahwan* (1989); and *Dimskal Shipping Co SA* v *ITWF (The Evia Luck)* (1991).

A threat to break a contract constitutes illegitimate pressure – see the cases cited above. M, it has been argued, has made this threat. Compulsion of the will of the victim can be inferred where the victim has no real choice but to submit to the threat. The tickets for the performance having been sold out, it is submitted that Aber Opera are in this position. On this aspect of the matter, therefore, it can be concluded that the promise to pay the increased fee can be set aside, and the advance payment recovered.

The effect of M's letter of 1 February
In this letter M states that he might not be back in time for the Aber Opera performance. As he raises this as only a possibility it is not clear that this amounts to a repudiatory breach. In *Mersey Steel and Iron Co* v *Naylor Benzon & Co* (1884) Lord Selborne said that:

> 'you must examine what (the) conduct is to see whether it amounts to a renunciation, to an absolute refusal to perform the contract ...'.

It cannot be said with complete assurance that M's letter constitutes an 'absolute refusal'. It is not always easy to decide whether the conduct in question constitutes a repudiatory breach: compare the two decisions of the House of Lords in *Federal Commerce & Navigation Co Ltd* v *Molena Alpha Inc* (1979) *and Woodar Investment Development Ltd* v *Wimpey Construction UK Ltd* (1980).

Even if, however, M has committed a repudiatory breach (which is doubtful), the breach does not appear to have been accepted by Aber Opera. It appears that active steps are necessary to indicate acceptance of the breach: *State Trading Corp of India* v *M Golodetz Ltd* (1989). There is nothing to suggest such steps, so that Aber Opera must be taken to have affirmed the contract. Both parties accordingly remain bound by it: *Fercometal Sarl V Mediterranean Shipping Co SA (1988)*.

At this juncture the contract still subsists, but on its original terms; the promise to pay the increased fee and the advance payment having been set aside on the grounds of duress. It remains to consider whether the contract has been frustrated by M's illness.

Frustration
M fell ill a few days beforehand and was unable to perform on 1 March. It is unnecessary within the confines of this answer to give a detailed exposition of the law relating to the doctrine of frustration. It is sufficient to note that, if a party is unable to perform his obligations through illness, this can be a frustrating event: *Condor* v *The Barron Knights Ltd* (1966). This falls within the test propounded by Lord Radcliffe in *Davis Contractors Ltd* v *Fareham Urban District Council* (1956).

The contract between Aber Opera and M being frustrated it is necessary to examine the effect of this at common law and by statute.

At common law the effect of frustration is to discharge the parties from any further obligations: *Taylor* v *Caldwell* (1863). Thus Aber Opera are discharged from the obligation to make any further payment and M, obviously, is discharged from the obligation to perform.

Further adjustment of the rights of the parties is provided by the Law Reform

(Frustrated Contracts) Act 1943. Under sl(2) of the Act Aber Opera can recover the advance payment of £2,500 made to M. (It has been suggested, above, that Aber Opera could in any event have recovered this on the grounds of duress). There is a proviso to sl(2) to the effect that, where a party to whom a sum was paid has incurred expenses in the performance of the contract, the court may allow him to retain from the sum paid an amount not exceeding his expenses. But there is nothing to indicate that M has incurred such expenses.

Under sl(3) of the Act provision is made for the situation where one party has obtained a valuable benefit, other than a payment of money, for the recovery from that party of a just sum not exceeding the value of the benefit. But at the date of the discharge of the contract by frustration neither party has received such benefit, so this sub-section does not apply.

Summary
1. There may have been good consideration for the promise to pay the increased fee and for the advance payment, but for the duress.
2. Aber Opera can set aside the promise to pay the increased fee and recover the advance payment on the grounds of duress.
3. It is not certain that M has repudiated the contract, but in any event Aber Opera has affirmed the contract.
4. Aber Opera can recover the advance payment under s1(2) Law Reform (Frustrated Contracts) Act 1943, even if they could not have done so on the grounds of duress, and the parties are discharged from further obligations.

SUGGESTED ANSWER TO QUESTION FOUR

General Comment
The thrust of this question is whether or not there has been a repudiatory breach of the contract and, if so, whether the injured party is entitled to rescind or is confined to a claim in damages.

Key Points
- If Alan has no lawful excuse there is a repudiatory breach
- The breach must have been accepted by the company
- If it is not so serious as to entitle the company to rescission they themselves may be in breach – *Cehave* v *Bremer* (1976)
- Factors to be taken into consideration – *Bettini* v *Gye* (1876); *Poussard* v *Spiers* (1876)

Suggested Answer
The question here is whether Alan has broken the contract and, if so, what is the effect of such a breach. On the face of it, there has been a repudiatory breach of contract by Alan. However, there is no breach where the non-performance is justified by some lawful excuse. Alan claims that he walked out and disappeared because he was ill. If this

could be proved, with suitable medical evidence, it may be that Alan would be taken not to have broken the contract since he could not help himself, although he would have to explain why he did not inform the theatre company of his illness before walking out and overcome the suspicion that his doing so might have been as a result of pique at the bad reviews rather than actual incapacitating illness. If Alan has committed a repudiatory breach, then that breach to be effective must have been accepted by the company. Employing a substitute may appear to be an act of acceptance, but if the company employed the substitute merely as a stand-in until Alan's return, this may not be the case.

Even if Alan has broken the contract, there remains the question of whether the company is entitled to rescind the contract or whether they are merely entitled to damages. If the breach is not so serious as to afford a right to rescission, the defendants may find themselves in breach. There are two cases which are particularly relevant to this situation. In *Bettini* v *Gye* (1876) the plaintiff, an opera singer, was engaged by the defendant to sing for the Covent Garden Opera season. The contract provided inter alia that the plaintiff was to be in London at least six days before the commencement of the engagement so as to take part in rehearsals. The plaintiff was prevented by temporary illness from fulfilling this obligation, giving no advance notice of delay to the defendant, and when he finally arrived, the defendant refused to accept the plaintiff's services. It was held that this refusal was unjustified, the relevant factors being that the plaintiff, having been engaged for 15 weeks, the delay only affected a small part of the period; secondly that he had been deprived of his earning power (as the contract prevented him from singing elsewhere) for the period of the delay.

The second case is *Poussard* v *Spiers* (1876) which, being heard in the same year, also concerned a plaintiff opera singer, engaged by the defendants for six months to play a leading part in a new opera. A week before the production was due to open the plaintiff became ill, and two days later the defendants entered into a contract with a substitute performer for the first night if the plaintiff could not appear and, should she so have to substitute, for a four week period thereafter. The plaintiff did not appear on the first night but recovered within a few days. However, the defendants refused to take her back. The court held that the defendants' refusal was justified. The material factors in this case were that the illness was serious and of uncertain duration and that no substitute capable of performing could be engaged except under a permanent contract. The court rejected the idea, without giving clear reasons, that the plaintiff could be re-engaged after the substitute's four-week contract had terminated.

The material factors in the instant question therefore would appear to be the seriousness of Alan's illness, the proportion of the contract for which it continued, and the terms on which the substitute was engaged. We are not given sufficient information in the question to judge these factors but it is submitted that, if Alan can establish that his illness was genuine, the fact that he was away for two weeks would not justify the company in refusing to continue with a contract which has more than five months left to run. The company is therefore to be advised that they may be forced to take Alan back or to pay him for the remainder of the contractual term, and that they may have a remedy against him in damages for walking out on the production without notice. However, since they appear to have suffered little damage due to the popularity of the substitute, any award of damages would be likely to be merely nominal.

11 Frustration, Discharge and Breach – Answers

SUGGESTED ANSWER TO QUESTION FIVE

General Comment

This question concerns the waiver of rights under a contract. If any party makes a clear and unequivocal waiver of his rights, then he cannot later pursue them. The question is whether Cecil has in fact waived his rights.

Key Points

- Bryan has broken the contract which would enable Cecil to rescind
- Cecil may have waived his rights if there has been a clear and unequivocal representation to that effect – *David Blackstone Ltd* v *Burnetts (West End) Ltd* (1973); *Peyman* v *Lanjani* (1985)
- The right to rescind is not normally lost by mere failure to exercise it unless the delay is unreasonable – *Tyrer & Co* v *Hessler & Co* (1902); *The Laconia* (1977)
- There is no consideration for Cecil's forbearance
- If Cecil accepted part payment in full settlement, equitable estoppel will prevent him suing for the balance – *Central London Property Trust Ltd* v *High Trees House Ltd* (1947)
- This will not be the case if there was economic pressure on him to accept it – *D & C Builders Ltd* v *Rees* (1966); *Foakes* v *Beer* (1884)
- Cecil may or may not be able to sue for future payments – *Central London Property Trust Ltd* v *High Trees House Ltd* (1947); *Brikom Investments Ltd* v *Carr* (1979)
- A requested gift may be good satisfaction – *Pinnel's Case* (1702)

Suggested Answer

This question concerns the waiver of contractual rights. Bryan initially broke the contract by failing to pay the rent which may have enabled Cecil (subject to any statutory rights Bryan may have) to rescind the contract and bring the tenancy to an end However, Cecil does not appear to have exercised those rights and by failing to do so, may have waived them and affirmed the contract: *David Blackstone Ltd* v *Burnetts (West End) Ltd* (1973). However, waiver requires a 'clear and unequivocal representation': *Peyman* v *Lanjani* (1985). The right to rescind is not normally lost by mere failure to exercise it, however (*Tyrer & Co* v *Hessler & Co* (1902)) unless the delay is unreasonable: *The Laconia* (1977). In any event, even if he has elected to waive his right to rescind, Cecil has not abandoned his claim for the rent.

Later Bryan offers Cecil a part payment. It is not clear from the question whether Cecil accepted that part payment or whether his injunction to 'forget it, mate' applies to the whole of the back rent. Nor is it clear that those words, which may be used in a colloquial sense to mean 'don't worry about it', can be taken literally. Cecil may simply have meant that he was giving Bryan further time to pay. In any event, there appears to be no consideration for Cecil's forbearance.

If Cecil intended to abandon the whole debt, then he must show a clear and unequivocal intention to do so. Furthermore, that representation must have been acted upon by Bryan. Bryan has in fact changed his position by spending the money.

If Cecil accepted the part payment in full settlement of the outstanding debt, the doctrine of equitable estoppel will prevent him from suing for the balance: *Central London Property Trust Ltd* v *High Trees House Ltd* (1947). This is an equitable remedy only and, had Cecil been under economic pressure to accept the part payment, the doctrine would not have applied (*D & C Builders Ltd* v *Rees* (1966)) and the usual common law rule in *Pinnel's Case* (1602) (affirmed in *Foakes* v *Beer* (1884)) will apply. However, the reverse seems to have been the case. Promissory estoppel probably acts merely as a suspension of the creditor's rights so he would be able to enforce future payments. However, see *Brikom Investments Ltd* v *Carr* (1979) where the creditor's rights were wholly extinguished.

If Cecil's intention was merely to give Bryan time to pay the full debt, then the forbearance is as to time and may amount to a variation of the contract rather than an abandonment of his rights.

If Cecil had requested the gold watch in payment, he will be unable to claim the balance:

> 'The gift of a horse, hawk or robe, etc, in satisfaction is good, for it shall be intended that a horse, hawk or robe, etc, might be more beneficial than the money': *Pinnel's Case.*

If the watch was offered and accepted without Cecil having requested it, it is submitted that the doctrine of equitable estoppel would apply. The court would not in any event be prepared to act as valuer of the watch.

12

Remedies and Quasi-Contract

Introduction

This chapter concerns itself solely with remedies available to a plaintiff in contract. The principal remedy sought is damages, that is to say, pecuniary compensation for loss or damage. Damages are the only available remedy at common law. They are available as of right and a plaintiff who has proved his case is entitled to an award of damages, even if these are only nominal. The measure of damages is subject to the principle first laid down in *Hadley* v *Baxendale* (1854), which has consistently been affirmed but has been restated and refined in a large number of cases since. These cases are covered in the solutions below and the student should be able to discuss them in a competent manner.

While the common law provides only one remedy, equity provides a number. These remedies, chief among which are rescission, specific performance and injunctions, are designed to mitigate the hardship which an award of damages only might cause the successful plaintiff. An award of damages is not entirely ruled out by an equitable remedy and the plaintiff may sometimes have both.

Equitable remedies are only available at the court's discretion and are subject to general equitable principles. In addition, each remedy has its own distinct rules as to when the remedy will or will not be awarded.

While a whole chapter has been devoted to the topic of remedies, it should never be forgotten that consideration of the appropriate remedy forms part of the answer to any contractual problem question. Students will therefore find this topic referred to elsewhere throughout the book and study of the principles contained in this section is vital to success in relation to other topics.

Questions

INTERROGRAMS

1. 'The aim of the court in assessing damages is that the party to be compensated is, so far as money can do it, to be placed in the same position as if the contract had been performed.' Discuss this statement.
2. Explain what is meant by quantum meruit.
3. When will the court refuse to grant specific performance of a contract?

QUESTION ONE

In January Olive, a successful business executive living and working in London, was appointed manager of a firm in Manchester, commencing on 1 April 1985. Having found a house she liked in Manchester, Olive engaged Paul, a builder, to do some renovation to it, the contract providing that the work would be completed by 31 March at the latest.

In breach of contract Paul did not complete the renovation until 31 May and Olive was unable to move into the house until June. During April and May Olive continued to live in London at the weekends, flying to Manchester and back each week, and stayed in a five-star hotel in Manchester during the week. She also engaged a nanny to look after her two small children during her absence.

Olive is now claiming that Paul should pay her air fares between London and Manchester, the hotel bills, the cost of the nanny and a 'substantial sum' to compensate her for the emotional distress of being separated from her family.

Advise Paul.

London University LLB Examination
(for external students) Elements of the Law of Contract June 1985 Q9

QUESTION TWO

Equity has provided a plethora of reliefs and remedies where the common law has provided only one. Discuss.

Written by the Editor June 1998

QUESTION THREE

a   Peter is a minor part actor in a television soap opera and has unexpectedly gained immense popularity. When he asked the television company for whom he works under a 12-month fixed contract for more money, the company refused to pay and Peter walked out. The company now wants to enforce the contract which still has six months to run.

b   Michael agreed with Byegones Antiques to buy a set of chairs for £500 because he secretly believed them to be Hepplewhite. He paid a deposit of £100 and promised to return next day with the balance. When he did so, he found the chairs had been sold for £1,000 to another buyer. Byegones has offered him his deposit back but Michael wants the chairs as he believes them to be worth £20,000.

c   Brian, a famous film actor, known for family entertainment, agreed that Ben should write his biography and allowed Ben access to his private papers on condition that Ben agreed to write nothing about Brian's extra-marital relationships. Ben's biography contains a lot of details about these relationships which Ben's publishers believe will help to sell the book but Brian naturally wishes to prevent publication.

Discuss the legal implications of the above situations.

Written by the Editor March 1998

QUESTION FOUR

A Ltd employed B Ltd to build a multi-purpose sports complex. B Ltd engage subcontractors, C Ltd, who use cement which turns out to be highly unsuitable for the purpose for which it is used. Soon after completion and occupation of the building cracks begin to appear. The complex has to close for expensive repairs and a lot of revenue is lost. A Ltd had also put in a bid, which has to be withdrawn, to host the

World Badminton Championships which would have produced large amounts of revenue.

Advise A Ltd.

London University LLB Examination
(for external students) Elements of the Law of Contract June 1987 Q

Answers

ANSWERS TO INTERROGRAMS

1   The principle followed by the courts in assessing damages for breach of contract is that the purpose of the award is to compensate the plaintiff for the loss of bargain he has suffered as a consequence of the breach. The plaintiff must prove his loss and if he cannot do so he will be awarded only nominal damages. An alternative measure of damages to loss of bargain is to compensate the plaintiff for the wasted expenditure he has incurred as a result of the defendant's breach, see *Anglian Television Ltd v Reed* (1972). The plaintiff has the right to choose to claim either for loss of bargain or for wasted expenditure - *CCC Films (London) Ltd v Impact Quadrant Films Ltd* (1984), subject to the overriding requirement that the plaintiff is not to be put in a better position than he would have been if the contract had been fully performed - *C & P Haulage v Middleton* (1983).

The award of damages for loss of bargain is subject to the limitation that the damages must not be too remote. The purpose of putting the plaintiff in the position he would have been in if the contract had been performed would, if logically pursued, give the plaintiff a complete indemnity for all loss resulting from a breach however unpredictable or improbable. It is recognised that this would be too harsh. Accordingly rules have been developed to limit the liability of the defendant to loss which the law regards as sufficiently proximate.

The modern law stems from the judgement of Alderson B in *Hadley v Baxendale* (1854) where the rule was said to consist of two limbs. To be recoverable the damages should be such as may fairly and reasonably be considered either arising naturally, ie according to the usual course of things, from such breach of contract itself, or such as may reasonably be supposed to have been in the contemplation of both parties, at the time they made the contract, as the probable result of the breach of it.

The rule in *Hadley v Baxendale* was reformulated by Asquith J in *Victoria Laundry (Windsor) Ltd v Newman Industries Ltd* (1949) in the following propositions:

a   The aggrieved party is only entitled to recover loss which was at the time of the contract reasonably foreseeable as liable to result from the breach.
b   What was reasonably foreseeable depends on the knowledge then possessed by the parties.
c   Knowledge is of two types, imputed and actual. Imputed knowledge is the knowledge that everyone, as a reasonable person, is taken to have of the ordinary

course of things. Actual knowledge is knowledge which the contract-breaker actually possesses, of special circumstances outside the ordinary course of things, which make additional loss liable to result.

d   The contract-breaker need not have actually asked himself what loss was liable to result, it is sufficient that as a reasonable man he would have done so.

e   The plaintiff need not prove that it would be foreseen that the loss would necessarily result from the breach; it was sufficient that it was a 'serious possibility' or a 'real danger'. This could be expressed as 'liable to result' or 'on the cards'.

These propositions were considered by the House of Lords in *The Heron II* (1969). Whilst they were generally approved, their Lordships held that the test was not one of 'reasonable foreseeability' but one of 'reasonable contemplation', a term denoting a higher degree of probability. Their Lordships also disapproved of the colloquialism 'on the cards', and used a variety of expressions to indicate the degree of probability, including 'not unlikely', 'liable to result', 'a real danger' and 'a serious possibility'. No single formulation was adopted.

In *H Parsons (Livestock) Ltd* v *Uttley Ingham & Co Ltd* (1978) Lord Denning said that different tests applied to physical (damage to person or property) and economic (deprivation of profit) loss. In the former it was sufficient if the loss was a slight possibility, in the latter it had to be shown that the loss was a serious possibility. Scarman J (with whom Orr J agreed) rejected Lord Denning's distinction and adopted the 'serious possibility' test.

Two further points must be noted. Firstly, difficulty of assessment is no bar to an award of damages: *Chaplin* v *Hicks* (1911). Secondly, damages may be awarded for distress, vexation and disappointment occasioned by a breach of contract, provided they are not too remote: see, for example, *Jarvis* v *Swans Tours* (1973), *Jackson* v *Horizon Holidays* (1975).

2   An order of specific performance decrees that the defendant be obliged to perform his part of the contract. An award of specific performance is subject to a number of provisos:

a   It will not be awarded where damages would be an adequate remedy. In *Flint* v *Brandon* (1803) it was said that:

> 'This court does not profess to decree a specific performance of contracts of every description. It is only where the legal remedy is inadequate or defective that it becomes necessary for courts of equity to interfere ...'.

For example, a plaintiff may have contracted to buy a unique item which is not readily available in the market. The court may order specific performance rather than damages and the defendant is obliged to transfer property in that item to him. There are many cases where the courts have been prepared to order specific performance where the property in question is a house.

b   Where the contract is for personal services, specific performance is not available: *Ryan* v *Mutual Tontine Association* (1893).

c   Specific performance is not available where performance would require constant supervision: *Ryan v Mutual Tontine Association* (1893).
d   It will not be awarded against one party where it could not be awarded against the other eg where the other's contract was one for personal services or where the other is a minor.
e   The court is unwilling to grant specific performance to a party who has breached an essential condition as to time, even if the delay is slight: *Union Eagle Ltd v Golden Achievement Ltd* (1997).

3   Where the injured party has partly performed the contract, he may recover reasonable remuneration for work done or services provided on a quantum meruit basis: eg *De Bernardy v Harding* (1853). This may also be possible if the contract does not make full provision for payment: *Sir Lindsay Parkinson & Co Ltd v Commissioners of Works* (1949).

Another possible basis for a claim is where the party has rendered services under a contract which he believes to be valid but which is in fact void: *Craven-Ellis v Canons Ltd* (1936).

The amount which the court will award – if no contractual provision has been made – is determined by reasonableness in relation to the goods delivered or services rendered. This is now provided for in the Sale of Goods Act 1979 and the Supply of Goods and Services Act 1982 respectively.

SUGGESTED ANSWER TO QUESTION ONE

General Comment

While it should be noted that Paul is the party the candidate is asked to advise, it is Olive's claim that we must consider. It is not sufficient that the liability of one party to a contract be established. One must then ascertain what remedy the court will award and to what extent the losses suffered by the innocent party are compensatable by damages. To succeed in this question, the candidate must understand the heads of loss which are compensatable and be able to apply the rules so as to establish whether the hypothetical party can claim for all or part of his or her loss.

Key Points

- The heads of loss which Olive is attempting to recover are: air fares; hotel bills; cost of nanny; emotional distress

Air fares

- The loss must have been in the reasonable contemplation of the parties at the time they entered into the contract as having been the probable result of its breach – *Hadley v Baxendale* (1854); *Victoria Laundry Ltd v Newman Industries Ltd* (1949)
- The importance of the parties' knowledge – *The Heron II* (1969); *Parsons (Livestock) Ltd v Uttley Ingham & Co Ltd* (1978)
- The duty to mitigate – *British Westinghouse Electric Co Ltd v Underground Electric Railways* (1912)

Hotel bills
- It must be a serious possibility that the loss will occur in the ordinary course of things – *Hadley* v *Baxendale* (1854)
- If the loss might have been contemplated, it is irrelevant that it was not – *Wroth* v *Tyler* (1974)
- The duty to mitigate – *British Westinghouse Electric Co Ltd* v *Underground Electric Railways* (1912)

Cost of nanny
- Problem of causation and remoteness of damage
- If Paul knew of Olive's circumstances when the contract was concluded the second limb of *Hadley* v *Baxendale* will apply

Distress
- Damages for distress used not to be recoverable – *Addis* v *Gramphone Co* (1909)
- In recent years it has been established that the court has jurisdiction to award damages for distress if not too remote – *Jarvis* v *Swans Tours* (1973); *Jackson* v *Horizon Holidays* (1975); *Heywood* v *Wellers* (1976); *Cox* v *Phillips Industries* (1976); *Perry* v *Sidney Phillips & Son* (1982)

Suggested Answer

Olive is claiming to recover damages from Paul in respect of four heads of loss, namely:

a air fares;
b hotel bills;
c cost of a nanny;
d emotional distress.

The validity of each of these claims will be discussed in turn.

Air fares

Plainly this head of loss was caused by Paul's breach of contract. That, however, is not sufficient to render the expense recoverable from Paul. In addition, Olive must show that the loss falls within the rule in *Hadley* v *Baxendale* (1854) as explained in later cases and is not too remote; also, questions of mitigation may arise. In considering principles of remoteness, the important question to ask is whether Paul knew, at the time he entered into the contract with Olive, that she had a house and family in London but had been appointed to a position in Manchester and required the new house for that purpose. The state of Paul's knowledge is important because for loss to be recoverable as damages for breach of contract it must have been in the reasonable contemplation of the parties at the time they entered into the contract as having been the probable result of its breach: *Hadley* v *Baxendale*. As explained by the Court of Appeal in *Victoria Laundry (Windsor) Ltd* v *Newman Industries Ltd* (1949), the parties' knowledge is all-important and is of two types, imputed and actual. Everybody is taken to possess the former and to know the usual course of things (the first limb of the rule in *Hadley* v *Baxendale*), the latter is knowledge of special circumstances which makes additional loss likely. This part of the Court's judgment was not disapproved in *The Heron II* (1969) and is accordingly still good law. Moreover, it is sufficient that, given the knowledge of the parties, the head of loss is a 'serious possibility', a phrase used by a number of their Lordships in *The Heron II* and subsequently adopted as the test for remoteness of damage in contract by Orr and Scarman LJJ in *Parsons (Livestock Ltd) v Uttley Ingham & Co Ltd* (1978).

It is submitted that the expense of air fares incurred by Olive cannot be regarded as being in the ordinary course of things, because it is quite possible that a person purchasing a property in Manchester already lives nearby and not in London (cf the possibility in *Hadley v Baxendale* that the plaintiffs might have had another mill shaft). However, if Paul did know of Olive's personal circumstances then he must be advised he did have actual knowledge of special circumstances that made additional loss likely; there must have been a serious possibility that Olive would feel it necessary to commute from London to Manchester and back. However, it cannot sensibly be argued that she was acting unreasonably and failing in her duty to mitigate by flying rather than using some other form of transport, or in doing so every weekend. The duty to mitigate requires a plaintiff to act reasonably (*British Westinghouse Electric Co Ltd v Underground Electric Railways* (1912)), and in all the circumstances there is little prospect of persuading the court that Olive acted unreasonably.

Hotel bills
Where, due to a builder's breach of contract, a purchaser of a house is unable to occupy the property by the contractual completion date, it must be a serious possibility that in the ordinary course of things (the first limb of the rule in *Hadley v Baxendale*) the purchaser will incur expense in obtaining alternative accommodation for the interim. Further, so long as the type of loss is one that might have been contemplated by the parties, it is irrelevant that the extent of it could not: *Wroth v Tyler* (1974). Thus in principle it is clear that the cost of alternative accommodation is a head of loss recoverable by Olive from Paul. The position is a fortiori if Paul in fact knew that Olive's former home was in London.

On the other hand there is a substantial argument that can be raised on Paul's behalf that in staying at a five-star hotel Olive has not acted reasonably in mitigating her loss: *British Westinghouse*. Unless Olive can demonstrate that there was no other suitable accommodation available, it is submitted that the court would conclude that Olive acted with unreasonable extravagance in staying at a five-star hotel and will award her a lesser sum than that in fact expended by her, assessed by reference to a more reasonable and less luxurious style of accommodation.

Cost of nanny
Olive may run into difficulties on the question of causation in respect of sums paid by her to a nanny. As she was a working woman with children she would, presumably, have engaged a nanny to care for them during the day whether she was based in London or Manchester. This therefore was an item of expenditure which she would have incurred in any event and is therefore not recoverable from Paul. She may, however, have a good claim in respect of monies paid to the nanny on those evenings when she was in Manchester, or alternatively in transit to or from London, since this additional

expenditure would plainly be caused by Paul's breach of contract. The considerations as to remoteness which arise are the same as those discussed in connection with the air fares above. If Paul had knowledge of Olive's personal circumstances at the time the contract was concluded, then the loss would fall within the second limb of the rule in *Hadley* v *Baxendale* and be recoverable from him. If he was unaware of the relevant facts, again it is submitted that the court would regard the loss as being too remote.

Distress
Until relatively recently the decision of the House of Lords in *Addis* v *Gramphone Co Ltd* (1909) was considered to lay down the rule that distress or disappointment was not a head of loss for which damages could be awarded in contract. However, in a succession of recent cases the application of the *Addis* principle has been considerably narrowed and it is now widely regarded as dealing only with claims for damages for distress consequent upon an employee being wrongfully dismissed and not laying down a general rule which applies throughout the law of contract.

The cases which have established that damages for distress may be awarded, providing the normal test as to remoteness is satisfied, are, in chronological order: *Jarvis* v *Swans Tours* (1973); *Jackson* v *Horizon Holidays* (1975); *Heywood* v *Wellers* (1976); *Cox* v *Phillips Industries* (1976) *and Perry* v *Sidney Phillips & Son* (1982). Taken together, they establish that the courts have a general jurisdiction to award damages for distress caused by a breach of contract if it is not too remote.

Here the distress suffered by Olive is due to her being separated from her family and not due to the delay itself. Again issues of remoteness arise. Depending upon whether or not Paul was aware that Olive had a family living in London, the distress might be regarded as being either a serious possibility which could have been contemplated, or conversely, too remote. Though if Olive were to establish that Paul knew she had a family in London, he should not be too concerned by her claim to recover a 'substantial sum'. Although damages are now awarded for distress, the sums awarded are not extravagant and tend to be in hundreds rather than thousands.

SUGGESTED ANSWER TO QUESTION TWO

General Comment

The requirement for a good mark in this question is the ability to summarise the main remedies available in equity and their effectiveness as an alternative to damages. It is not necessary to discuss the rules applicable to an award for damages since the focus is on the equitable remedies. The pitfall with this type of question is a tendency to 'ramble' and write everything one knows about the topic without really answering the question. Students should remember that, in an examination, the inclusion of a good deal of irrelevant material wastes time and gains no marks. The ability to produce a well-structured summary of the law under examination conditions usually denotes an outstanding candidate.

Key Points

- Monetary compensation for loss or damage ('damages') is available as of right for the plaintiff who has won his case but the measure of damages may not be sufficient to compensate him in the circumstances
- Equitable remedies are more flexible but are only discretionary
- The plaintiff who seeks equity must come with 'clean hands' and without unreasonable delay
- Specific performance – where the plaintiff has good reason to want the contract performed rather than monetary compensation – is not always available
- Injunctions (prohibitory, mandatory and interlocutory) may force the defendant to do something or prevent him from doing something
- Rescission – puts the parties back in the position that they would have been in had the contract not been made – is subject to a number of 'bars' (restitution impossible; affirmation; third party rights; unreasonable delay)
- Restitution – the return of money paid – there must have been a 'total failure of consideration'
- Rectification – amending a contract to reflect what the parties actually agreed
- Equitable estoppel – preventing a party from enforcing his legal rights where he has forgone them
- Non est factum – signature of a deed while mistaken as to the nature of the transaction – the rules for granting this relief are very restrictive.

Suggested Answer

The common law remedy is damages which means monetary compensation for the loss or damage suffered by the plaintiff. However, there are many situations where the common law remedy will be harsh or inadequate. In a number of these instances, equity will provide relief of its own. As equity and the common law have been administered by the courts since the Judicature Acts 1893-95, equitable remedies are available to the plaintiff in appropriate situations. The important thing to remember that damages are available as of right. The plaintiff who has proved his case is always entitled to damages, even if these should be nominal only. Equitable remedies are available only in the court's discretion.

Equitable remedies may be categorised as follows:

Specific performance

An order of specific performance decrees that the defendant be obliged to perform his part of the contract. The order is available where damages would be an inadequate remedy. For example, a plaintiff may have contracted to buy a unique item which is not readily available in the market. The court may order specific performance rather than damages and the defendant is obliged to transfer property in that item to him. The courts are usually prepared to order specific performance where the property in question is a house.

The court will not order specific performance of a contract for personal services for that would interfere with personal liberty. Nor will an order be made in respect of a contract which requires constant supervision.

Injunctions

There are three types of injunction which the court may order: prohibitory, which prevents the defendant from doing something; mandatory, which compels the defendant to perform his contractual obligations; and interlocutory, which maintains the balance between the parties until full trial of the action.

A mandatory injunction is very similar to an order of specific performance but the court will not grant a mandatory injunction if it would be tantamount to an order for specific performance in a situation where specific performance would not be ordered (see above).

The court will not grant an injunction of unlimited duration where it might be used oppressively. In *Phonographic Performance Ltd* v *Maitra* (1997), which concerned a licence to play certain records, when the plaintiffs sought an unlimited injunction against the defendants it was held to be unnecessary. The plaintiffs had been accustomed to using injunctions to force payment for past unlicensed playing of records and the court found that this was oppressive.

Rescission

Rescission is the commonest equitable remedy. The injured party is entitled to avoid the contract and any further liability under it, and the court will attempt to put the parties back into the position they would have been in had the contract not been made. Rescission will generally be granted where a party has broken a condition of the contract. It will also be available in cases of misrepresentation and common mistake.

There are a number of restrictions on the grant of rescission:

a   Restitution in integrum must be possible – ie it must be possible to put the parties back into the position that they were before the contract was made.
b   The injured party must not have affirmed (evidenced an intention to continue with) the contract.
c   Third parties should not have gained rights to any property which is the subject matter of the contract.
d   The injured party should not have delayed unreasonably in enforcing his rights.

These restrictions are known as 'bars to rescission'.

While a right to rescind may be expressly provided for in the contract, it has been held that this right is not exhaustive. In *Stocznia Gdanska SA* v *Latvian Shipping Co* (1998) which concerned a contract to design and build two ships, the court held that there was a presumption that the party did not intend to abandon any remedies unless there were clear words in the contract to say so.

Restitution

Where a party has wholly or partly performed his side of the bargain, the court may award restitution, ie the return of money paid or recompense for benefits he has provided under the contract.

The rule with the former is that money paid can only be recovered if there has been a 'total failure of consideration'. There is no right if there has been only a partial failure, although this may give rise to a claim for rescission. There may be a total failure of consideration if the benefit received by the plaintiff is different in kind from that bargained for: *Rowland* v *Divall* (1923). For a modern discussion: see *Lipkin Gorman* v *Karpnale Ltd* (1991). Where the injured party has partly performed the contract, he may have a claim for his payment in respect of the services rendered. The amount which the court will award – if no contractual provision has been made – is determined by reasonableness in relation to the goods delivered or services rendered. This is now provided for in the Sale of Goods Act 1979 and the Supply of Goods and Services Act 1982 respectively. Equally, he may recover if the contract does not make full provision for payment: *Sir Lindsay Parkinson & Co Ltd* v *Commissioners of Works* (1949). Another possible basis for a claim is where the party has rendered services under a contract which he believes to be valid but which is in fact void: *Craven-Ellis* v *Canons Ltd* (1936).

Rectification
Where the contract does not reflect the exact terms agreed by the parties, rectification will be available. That is to say the court will order that the written contract be amended in accordance with the true agreement made by the parties. This may happen in the case of mistake.

While remedies are awarded to the plaintiff, reliefs are afforded to a defendant against whom equity decrees that it would be inequitable to allow an action. The two principal reliefs in contract are equitable or promissory estoppel and non est factum.

Equitable (or promissory) estoppel
This operates where a creditor has accepted part payment of a debt and then attempts to sue the debtor for the balance. The court will prevent the creditor from enforcing the action. It is generally thought that this relief acts as a suspension of the creditor's rights and does not extinguish them totally. Relief will not be granted where the debtor has used the creditor's economic position to force the creditor to accept a lesser payment: *D & C Builders* v *Rees*.

Non est factum
Equity will give relief to someone who has signed a deed while mistaken as to the nature of the transaction.

All remedies and reliefs are subject to equitable principles. It has already been mentioned that they are not available as of right and are discretionary only. The principle mentioned under the heading of rescission above, that the plaintiff should not unreasonably delay enforcing his claim (the doctrine of laches), applies to all equitable remedies. Further, equity demands that the plaintiff must come to equity 'with clean hands' and that 'he who seeks equity must do equity', so that anyone seeking an equitable remedy or relief must have behaved equitably himself – the basis of the *D & C Builders* decision (above).

Equity, therefore has remained flexible and responsive to the needs of those who come before the courts and, while in most cases damages will provide sufficient remedy, more appropriate remedies are available where they are needed.

SUGGESTED ANSWER TO QUESTION THREE

General Comment
While this three-part problem raises questions of performance and breach, the main thrust is as to the remedies available to the injured parties and whether those remedies will be sufficient to compensate them for the breach of contract. It is designed to test the candidate's ability to apply rules relating both to damages and equitable remedies to practical situations, and requires very careful analysis and consideration of the parties' requirements. The candidate should be able to appreciate why damages would not in these different situations compensate the injured parties and why an equitable remedy might not be available as an alternative.

Key Points

a
- Is Peter's walking out a repudiatory breach? If so, the seriousness of the breach would justify rescission
- It would not automatically terminate the contract: the injured party may rescind or affirm - *Michael* v *Hart & Co* (1902)
- The television company would like Peter to return but the court will not usually award specific performance of an employment contract - *Johnson* v *Shrewsbury and Birmingham Railway* (1853)
- Nor will the court grant a mandatory injunction if the effect would be a grant of specific performance - *Whitwood Chemical Co* v *Hardman* (1926)
- If there is a restriction in Peter's contract on his working for someone else, the court may grant an injunction to restrain him from breaching it - *Lumley* v *Wagner* (1852); *Warner Bros Pictures Inc* v *Nelson* (1937); *Page One Records Ltd* v *Britton* (1968)

b
- If Byegones had accepted Michael's offer they are in breach of contract by selling to someone else and liable in damages
- The measure of damages would be the return of Michael's deposit
- Specific performance will not be awarded where damages would be adequate
- It may be that damages would not be adequate if the chairs were rare and of specific importance - s52 Sale of Goods Act 1979; *Cohen* v *Roche* (1927)

c
- Ben has broken a condition of the contract and Brian would probably be able to claim damages for loss of reputation and loss of work - *Hadley* v *Baxendale* (1854); *Victoria Laundry* v *Newman Industries* (1949)
- Damages will not compensate Brian sufficiently and an injunction against publication would be sought
- Injunctions are discretionary and subject to equitable principles, one of which is that the plaintiff must come 'with clean hands'

Suggested Answer

Peter
By walking out of the production, Peter appears to have evidenced an intention not to be

bound by the contract. If he does not intend to return unless he is paid more money, this is a repudiatory breach which goes to the substance or root of the contract, since it is fundamental to the contract that Peter performs in the television production. This is on the assumption that Peter had no lawful excuse, such as illness.

The seriousness of the breach means that it would justify rescission by the injured party, the television company. However, a breach, even though it justifies rescission, does not automatically terminate the contract: *Michael* v *Hart & Co* (1902). The injured party may elect either to rescind or to affirm the contract.

The company, however, does not want to rescind but wishes to affirm the contract. The implication is that they want Peter to return to the production. If Peter insists on failing to perform, the question is whether the company can compel him. Specific performance – compelling a party to perform his obligations under a contract – is an equitable remedy and, like all equitable remedies, available only at the court's discretion. The court generally will not grant specific performance of a contract for personal services on the ground that it interferes with an employee's personal liberty: *Johnson* v *Shrewsbury and Birmingham Railway* (1853). There are what Treitel refers to as 'a growing list of exceptions' but these generally concern the situation where it is the employee who is seeking reinstatement. An order of specific performance will be refused where the defendant is entitled to terminate the contract by notice as the order would then serve no purpose.

A mandatory injunction may compel a party to a contract to perform his positive obligations. However, the court will not grant this if the indirect effect would be a grant of specific performance: *Whitwood Chemical Co* v *Hardman* (1926). We are not told whether and to what extent Peter's contract prevents him working for anyone else. The court may grant an injunction to restrain the employee from acting in breach of such a restraint: *Lumley* v *Wagner* (1852). Where the restraint is wide, this may put economic pressure on the employee so that he has no choice but to work for the plaintiff: *Warner Bros Pictures Inc* v *Nelson* (1937). It is said, however, that such an injunction will not be granted except where it leaves the employee some other reasonable means of earning a living: *Page One Records Ltd* v *Britton* (1968).

On the facts given in the question, it seems unlikely that the court will compel Peter to return to the production and the company's remedy will be in damages.

The contract between Michael and Byegones Antiques
Assuming that Byegones has accepted Michael's offer to buy the chairs, they have broken the contract by selling to someone else. They would therefore be liable in damages to Michael. However, the damages would be no more than the return of the deposit as Michael appears to have suffered no economic loss. He would, however, prefer an order of specific performance since he believes the chairs to be worth £20,000.

Specific performance will not be awarded where damages are an adequate remedy. This may be the case where the plaintiff cannot obtain a satisfactory substitute and specific performance in cases concerning the sale of land has often been awarded on this ground. However, here we are concerned not with land but with goods. Section 52 Sale of Goods Act 1979 gives the court a discretion to award specific performance where the contract goods are 'specific or ascertained'. This was based on s2 Mercantile Law

Amendment Act 1856 and while the courts were often restrictive in their application of that section, confining it to unique goods such as heirlooms and great works of art, it is generally considered that s52 has a much wider scope. In *Cohen* v *Roche* (1927), the court refused specific performance of a set of Hepplewhite chairs saying that they were 'ordinary articles of commerce and of no specific value or interest'. It is submitted that, given the antiques revival which makes such articles rare and sought after in this decade, the court would revise the view taken in that case and would perhaps grant Michael specific performance of the contract.

Brian's contract with Ben

First it is necessary to mention that this question concerns a possible breach of confidentiality, discussion of which is outside the scope of this book.

As regards the contractual aspects of the situation, there is no doubt that Ben has broken the condition on which he was permitted to write the book and to view Brian's private papers. Brian would probably be able to claim damages for loss of reputation and loss of work stemming from that: *Hadley* v *Baxendale* (1854); *Victoria Laundry (Windsor) Ltd* v *Newman Industries Ltd* (1949). However, in order to prevent the book being published, Brian will have to obtain a prohibitory injunction. This is an order that the defendant refrains from doing what he has promised not to do and, on the face of it, Brian may be entitled to such an order. Injunctions are, however, an equitable remedy, are only available at the court's discretion, and are subject to equitable principles. One principle is expressed in the form of a maxim: equity will only assist those who come with clean hands. Generally this refers to the case where the plaintiff has taken advantage of the defendant in some way. However, if the court were to take a moral stance over Brian's marital infidelities, they could well refuse him the protection of equity to hide them from public view.

SUGGESTED ANSWER TO QUESTION FOUR

General Comment

The candidate is required to consider here the respective heads of damage suffered by the plaintiff. The question tests the candidate's ability to apply the rule in *Hadley* v *Baxendale*, as subsequently developed by the courts, to a practical situation. Note, too, the minor additional points on privity of contract and strict liability.

Key Points

- Incorrect construction of a building falls within the first limb of *Hadley* v *Baxendale* (1854)
- Loss of revenue is also within the first limb – *Victoria Laundry* v *Newman Industries* (1949); *Parsons* v *Uttley Ingham* (1978)
- Where possible, the courts will put a value on the loss of a chance: *Chaplin* v *Hicks* (1911)
- Is the loss of the chance to host the championships within the second limb in *Hadley* v *Baxendale*? – *Victoria Laundry* v *Newman Industries* (1949); *The Heron II* (1969)

12 Remedies and Quasi-Contract – Answers

Suggested Answer

In advising A Ltd one must consider whether it can recover damages in respect of i) the cost of repairs; ii) loss of revenue while the complex is closed; and iii) loss of revenue from hosting the world championships.

First, two preliminary points must be made. The contract for the construction of the complex was made between A Ltd and B Ltd. It was the latter who employed the sub-contractors, C Ltd, who used the unsuitable cement. No contractual relationship existed between A Ltd and C Ltd and C Ltd therefore cannot have incurred any liability in contract to A Ltd, since priority of contract did not exist between them. On the other hand it matters not that B Ltd may have acted reasonably in engaging C Ltd and may have believed them to be competent sub-contractors. Liability in contract is strict and if B Ltd have not built or caused the complex to be built in a proper manner, they are in breach of their contract with A Ltd.

Turning now to the items of loss listed (i) to (iii) above, item (i) causes little difficulty. If a building, be it a sports complex or anything else, is incorrectly constructed, it is plain and obvious that the owner is going to incur expense in correcting the fault. Such a head of loss is within the first limb of the rule in *Hadley* v *Baxendale* (1854) – loss occurring in the usual course of things – and A Ltd can therefore recover the cost of repair from B Ltd. Item (ii) is also relatively straightforward. B Ltd must have known that A Ltd wished to have the complex built in order to use it. So long as it is undergoing repairs, it will clearly be out of commission and incapable of being used. The loss of revenue which results is again within the first limb of the rule in *Hadley* v *Baxendale*. Indeed, their head of claim is very similar to the general loss of profits claim which succeeded in *Victoria Laundry (Windsor) Ltd* v *Newman Industries Ltd* (1949), where knowledge of the likely use of the subject matter of the contract to earn revenue was imputed to the contract breaker. Alternatively, adopting the test used by the majority of the Court of Appeal in *H Parsons (Livestock) Ltd* v *Uttley Ingham & Co Ltd* (1978), loss of revenue during repair was a serious possibility if the complex was not properly built.

It is the third head of loss, the loss of revenue from possibly holding the World Badminton Championships, which raises most difficulties. In this regard, first it should be noted that although there was no certainty that the complex would play host to the championships, that of itself is no bar to A Ltd recovering damages. Where possible, the courts will put a value on the loss of a chance: *Chaplin* v *Hicks* (1911).

The problem regarding this item is that of remoteness. Hosting a world sports championship is something far out of the ordinary for any sports complex. There is a real danger the court would regard this head of loss as being too remote. *Hadley* v *Baxendale* is the source of the modern law of remoteness. Clearly this head of loss is not within the first limb of the rule, so is it within the second limb, viz something the parties could have contemplated as being the probable result of the breach? As explained in *Victoria Laundry,* a part of the case approved by the House of Lords in *The Heron II* (1969), remoteness depends on knowledge, and the second limb of the rule is concerned with actual knowledge of special circumstances which make additional loss, over and above loss arising in the ordinary course of things, likely.

It is submitted that the possibility of A Ltd hosting the world championships was so unlikely that unless B Ltd had actual knowledge of this possibility, the lost revenue is irrecoverable (by analogy with the lucrative dyeing contracts in *Victoria Laundry*). Alternatively, to apply the test of Orr and Scarman LJJ in *Parsons*, it was not something both parties could have contemplated at the time the contract was concluded as being a serious possibility in the event that B Ltd was in breach. This third head of loss is, therefore, irrecoverable.

13

Agency and Sale of Goods

Introduction

One of the major exceptions to the doctrine of privity is agency, which grew up whilst the doctrine was being formulated and has a long and venerable history of its own. An agent can make a contract which binds his principal (the person who appointed him) rather than himself. Agents must however act within the scope of their authority and the question of whether or not an agent has authority in a particular situation forms the basis of many problem questions. The contract of agency itself - that between the principal and agent - gives rise to specific rights and obligations, some of which are implied in law. Questions on this area usually involve no more than a good knowledge and ability to describe the consequences of such a contract, although the implied duties may sometimes give rise to a problem question.

The implied terms under the sale of goods legislation are an important topic for the student to grasp but the norm in degree examinations is to combine the topic with another such as exemption clauses. The questions below demonstrate such an intermingling of topics.

Questions

INTERROGRAMS

1 It is settled that for the principal to be bound his agent must act within the limits of the agent's authority. What kinds of authority can an agent have?
2 What is meant by the 'exceptions to the nemo dat rule'?
3 What remedies are available to the unpaid seller of goods?
4 What is the 'doctrine of the undisclosed principal'?

QUESTION ONE

Lovejoy, an antiques dealer, has recently been abroad for an extended visit. Before leaving, he asked Eric to 'mind the business for me and keep things ticking over'.

At Lovejoy's express request, Eric attended an auction to bid on Lovejoy's behalf for a George I silver epergne. Lovejoy's precise instructions to Eric were: 'Go up to £3,000 if you have to.' In the event, Eric secured the epergne for £5,000.

Lovejoy also asked Eric to buy a painting for him from another dealer, Gimbert. Lovejoy told Eric: 'Get the painting whatever it costs but don't tell Gimbert you are buying for me or he won't sell.' Eric told Gimbert he was buying the painting for a relative of his and Gimbert agreed to sell it to him for £8,000.

From abroad, Lovejoy wrote to Tinker, a fellow dealer saying: 'Eric will be minding the shop while I am away. Give him any help he asks for.' Eric went into Tinker's shop and selected a number of items, saying to Tinker: 'As you know, I'm running Lovejoy's business while he's away. He will pay you for these when he gets back.'

Lovejoy has now returned and discovered that the epergne is worth only £500 and he does not want to buy it. He also considers that the items Eric purported to buy on his behalf from Tinker are worthless and that he should not be liable to pay for them as Eric had no instructions to buy from Tinker. Meanwhile, Gimbert has discovered that the painting was intended for Lovejoy and refuses to part with it, even on payment of £8,000 cash.

Advise Lovejoy of his contractual rights and liabilities.

Written by the Editor March 1997

QUESTION TWO

T, a pilot, agreed to sell his second-hand estate car to U, a self-employed plumber, for £6,000. T assumed that U was going to use the car in the course of U's plumbing business, although he knew that U had a number of convictions for burglary. In fact U bought it as a get-away car. Whilst U and his wife, V, were on a shopping trip, a wheel came off and U and V were injured. As a result of the accident U was unable to work for six weeks. He lost £4,000 from his plumbing business and £5,000 which he would have earned from burglary. The sale agreement in respect of the car contained the following clauses:

> '46. The Vehicle is sold as seen with no undertaking about suitability or condition.'
> '47. There is no liability in respect of any damage, harm or injury which arises from the use of the vehicle.'

Advise U. What difference, if any, would it make to your advice if T had sold the vehicle in the course of T's business?

London University LLB Examination
(for external students) Elements of the Law of Contract June 1992 Q1

QUESTION THREE

H saw a 1936 Flying Standard car for sale on a Lom's Garage forecourt for £4,000. He stopped and examined it thoroughly before taking it out for a test drive. The sales manager stated that the car, 'was restored but not in concourse condition. You will have to buy it as found'. H agreed to take the car and drove it from the garage having arranged to buy it from Fortin Finance Co Ltd to whom Lom's Garage was going to sell it. H was to make monthly instalments of £200 per month for two years. Three months after he agreed to buy the car the brakes failed and H ran into a car driven by J. Both were seriously injured.

The agreement between H and Fortin Finance Co Ltd stated:

> '44 It is understood that any statements made by the supplier have no contractual effect between us and the purchaser from us.
> 45 Fortin Finance Co Ltd accepts no responsibility for the condition of the vehicle and shall not be liable for any consequential losses resulting from the condition, use or safety of the vehicle.

46 H agrees to indemnify Fortin Finance Co Ltd for any damages which are or may become payable under this contract in the event of any judgment that they are in breach of contract or any other legal duty.'

Advise H.

*London University LLB Examination
(for external students) Elements of the Law of Contract June 1994 Q4*

Answers

ANSWERS TO INTERROGRAMS

1 If the agent is to escape personal liability under a contract which he purports to make on behalf of his principal, he must act within the scope of his authority. There are a number of different kinds of authority:

   a Express authority is the authority which has clearly been given to him by the principal. Where the authority given is capable of more than one interpretation, the principal may be bound even if the agent incorrectly interprets his authority (*Weigall* v *Runciman* (1916)), unless it is reasonable for the agent to seek clarification and he fails to do so: *European Asian Bank* v *Punjab & Sind Bank* (1983). If the agent exceeds his express authority, the principal may not be liable unless the other contracting party can show that the agent had some other kind of authority.

   b Incidental authority is the authority to do all those things which are not specifically referred to in the appointment but which are incidental to carrying out the purpose for which the agent was appointed. For example, if P goes abroad and asks A to sell his car for him, A probably has incidental authority to advertise the car and show it to prospective buyers. If a solicitor is asked to form a company for a client, he has incidental authority to do all the things necessary to the formation of the company even though these may not be specifically mentioned. This type of authority is interpreted fairly strictly. For example, an agent employed to sell has no incidental authority to receive payment: *Mynn* v *Joliffe* (1834).

   c Usual authority is the authority which an agent of a particular type usually has. For example in *Watteau* v *Fenwick* (1893) the manager of a public house contracted to buy cigars in his own name and the seller was permitted to sue the owner of the public house since this was within the usual authority of a public house manager. However this type of authority only applies where the agent belongs to a well known class of agents: *Jerome* v *Bentley & Co* (1952). Otherwise the plaintiff must rely on establishing customary or apparent authority (see below).

   d Customary authority is authority to act in accordance with the custom of the market in which he is operating (*Graves* v *Legg* (1857)), but this only applies where the custom is not inconsistent with the principal's express instructions: *Perry* v *Barnett* (1885).

e   Apparent authority (sometimes referred to as ostensible authority) is the authority which third parties are entitled to assume that the agent has because the principal has placed him in a particular position or otherwise made a representation to the third party that the agent is entitled to act in the transaction. It appears that there is some overlap with usual authority but, as stated above, usual authority only applies where the agent belongs to a clearly-defined class of agents who have clearly understood authority. Some examples of apparent authority include *Summers* v *Solomon* (1857) where the manager of a jewellery shop who bought jewellery from a supplier which was paid for by the owner of the shop continued to buy jewellery on this basis after he had left his employment. It was held that the owner was liable. In *Freeman & Lockyer* v *Buckhurst Park Properties Ltd*, K was permitted to act as managing director of the defendant company, even though he had not been appointed as such. He made contracts with the plaintiff architects which the company later sought to avoid on the ground that he had no authority to make them. The court held that he had apparent authority and the company was bound. A more recent case is *Panorama Developments (Guildford) Ltd* v *Fidelis Furnishing Fabrics Ltd* (1971) where the properly appointed secretary of a company entered into contracts which the company later sought to avoid on the ground that he had no authority. It was held that the modern company secretary has implied authority (usual or apparent) to enter into contracts concerning the administration of the company and the plaintiffs were entitled to assume from his position that he had the authority to make the relevant contracts.

The rules for determining apparent authority, which were set out in *Freeman & Lockyer,* are that:

a   there must have been a representation of authority;
b   the representation must have been made to the other contracting party;
c   the representation must have been made by the principal; and
d   the contracting party must have relied on that representation.

It is therefore not express authority alone which determines the principal's liability and regard will be had to the circumstances of the case to establish whether the agent did or did not have sufficient authority to make the contract.

2   The rule stems from the Latin phrase nemo dat quod non habet which means that a person who does not have good title to goods, eg a thief or a receiver of stolen property, cannot pass good title to a third party. There are a number of exceptions to that rule. The exceptions were determined under the case law but have been codified into statute law by the Sale of Goods Act 1979. These are as follows:

a   The owner is estopped from denying the seller's authority to sell the goods, eg by holding out a person as his agent: s21(1).
b   Where goods are sold by a factor to a person taking in good faith without notice of lack of authority: s21(2)(a).
c   Where goods are sold under a common law or statutory power of sale or a court order, eg by a bailiff or pawnbroker: s21(2)(b).

- d Where goods are held under a voidable contract (see identity mistake, Chapter 7), a person taking in good faith without notice of lack of title before the seller has avoided, may obtain good title: s23.
- e Where a buyer or seller is, with the other party's consent, in possession of the goods or documents to title, he or she may pass good title to a buyer who takes the goods in good faith without notice of the other's claim: s25.
- f Where the hirer of a motor vehicle sells it to a third party who takes in good faith without notice of the hire-purchase or conditional sale agreement, the third party will obtain good title: ss27–29 Hire Purchase Act 1965.

One common law exception which was abolished by statute was a sale in a market ouvert.

3 The unpaid seller has a wide range of remedies. These can be categorised into remedies against the goods and remedies against the buyer.

Remedies against goods

- a A lien on the goods, which is a limited equitable right to retain and to sell the goods if payment is not made. The seller must be in possession of the goods although property has passed to the buyer, but if he has extended credit, the lien does not arise until the credit period has ended: s41 SOGA 1979.
- b Stoppage in transit, which allows the seller to take possession of the goods while they are in the possession of a carrier if the buyer becomes insolvent. The goods are still in transit if the buyer rejects them but not if he takes delivery, if the carrier agrees to hold on behalf of the buyer, or if he wrongfully refuses to deliver the goods to the buyer. Sale or disposition by the buyer does not affect this right unless the seller has agreed or the document of title has been transferred to the buyer who passes it to a person taking in good faith and for value.
- c The right to withhold delivery if property has not passed to the buyer: s39(2) SOGA 1979.
- d The seller who has exercised any of the above rights only has a right to resell them if:
    - i the goods are perishable; or
    - ii he gives notice of his intention to resell and the buyer does not tender the price within a reasonable time;
    - iii a right of resale is expressly reserved in the contract.

Remedies against the buyer

- a Action for the price may be brought if property has passed or a date for payment has been agreed: s49 SOGA.
- b Action for damages for non-acceptance. The measure of damages is estimated as the loss directly and naturally resulting in the ordinary course of events from the breach. Where there is an available market in the goods, this will usually be the difference between the contract price and the market price at the date of the breach: s50 SOGA. Otherwise the seller will be entitled to loss of bargain damages (see remedies in Chapter 12): *W L Thompson Ltd v Robinson (Gunmakers) Ltd* (1955); *Charter v Sullivan* (1957).

4   The doctrine of the undisclosed principal is applied in the situation where an agent apparently negotiates a contract for himself alone. There is a distinction between non-disclosure of the principal's name and non-disclosure of the existence of an agency. In the former case, whether or not the principal is bound by the contract is determined by the understanding between the parties. If the other contracting party accepts that there is an agency then the principal will be bound. If, however, the agent signs the contract without disclosing the existence of any agency at all, both he and the principal are bound by it and it may be enforced against either of them at the option of the other contracting party.

Equally, the doctrine of the undisclosed principal states that, generally, either the agent or the principal may take the benefit of the contract. However, there are established situations where the principal will not be able to take the benefit. These are:

a   it would be inconsistent with the terms of the contract to permit it: *Siu Yin Kwan* v *Eastern Insurance Co* (1994);
b   the third party wished to deal only with the agent: *Collins* v *Associated Greyhound Racecourses Ltd* (1930); *Greer* v *Downs Supply Co* (1927).

With regard to the first of these, the courts are often reluctant to allow the principal to be deprived of his rights: *Humble* v *Hunter* (1848); *F Drughorn Ltd* v *Rederiaktiebologat Transatlantic* (1919). Concerning the second, the other contracting party must demonstrate sufficient reason for not wishing to deal with the principal: *Nash* v *Dix* (1898); *Said* v *Butt* (1920). If he is unable to do so, in the last resort the other contracting party may be able to have the contract set aside for fraud or misrepresentation: *Archer* v *Stone* (1898).

SUGGESTED ANSWER TO QUESTION ONE

General Comment

The agency principle is a substantial exception to the doctrine of privity of contract, without which business would be unworkable. Stated simply, the principle is that one may enter into a contract for and on behalf of another and bind that other to the terms of the contract if the relationship of agent and principal exists between them. There are, however, many kinds of agency and the plethora of situations in which it can exist makes it a fertile topic for questions. The problem question here is fairly typical and requires the candidate to distinguish between different types of agency relationship within the same situation and analyse the transactions accordingly.

Key Points

- Where someone enters into a contract as agent for another, he is not bound by the contract but the other is
- There must be an express or implied appointment – *Heard* v *Pilley* (1869)
- The principal will only be bound if the contract was within the agent's authority
- Types of authority: express, incidental, usual, customary, apparent – *Weigall* v

Runciman (1916); *European Asian Bank* v *Punjab & Sind Bank* (1983); *Mynn* v *Joliffe* (1834); *Watteau* v *Fenwick* (1893); *Jerome* v *Bentley & Co* (1952); *Graves* v *Legg* (1857); *Perry* v *Barnett* (1885)

The purchase at the auction
- Eric's actual authority was limited
- If the auctioneer did not know of the limitation Eric's apparent authority was unlimited
- Lovejoy is bound by the contract and must seek repayment from Eric

The painting bought from Gimbert
- If Eric failed to disclose the agency, both Lovejoy and Eric are bound
- The undisclosed principal (Lovejoy) cannot take the benefit if it would be inconsistent with the terms of the contract – *Siu Yin Kwan* v *Eastern Insurance Co* (1994); *Humble* v *Hunter* (1848); *F Drughorn Ltd* v *Rederiaktiebolagat Transatlantic* (1919)
- The undisclosed principal cannot take the benefit if the third party wanted to deal only with the agent – *Collins* v *Associated Greyhound Racecourses Ltd* (1930); *Greer* v *Downs Supply Co* (1927)
- Misrepresentation could have vitiated the contract – *Archer* v *Stone* (1898)
- Gimbert may be able to avoid the contract if he had sufficient reason for not wanting to deal with Lovejoy – *Nash* v *Dix* (1898); *Said* v *Butt* (1920); *Dyster* v *Randall & Sons* (1926)

The items purchased from Tinker
- Where the principal holds out to a third party that another is representing him that other is his agent with ostensible authority
- Such a representation can be implied by putting the agent in a particular position – *Summers* v *Solomon* (1857)
- Merely leaving Eric in charge of the shop probably does not give him the necessary authority
- There may be sufficient authority in Lovejoy's express instructions to Eric
- Lovejoy is probably not bound to pay Tinker, who must claim against Eric

Suggested Answer

This question involves the topic of agency. Agency is an important exception to the doctrine of privity of contract which states that one who is not a party to a contract can neither enforce rights nor acquire liabilities under it. One who makes a contract on behalf of another (an agent) is not bound by the contract and acquires no rights under it, but the other (the principal) can claim the rights and incurs the liabilities. If Eric has acted as Lovejoy's agent in the relevant transactions, Lovejoy will be bound by them.

The first question is whether Eric has been appointed agent. Such appointment may be express or implied and may be made orally even though the contract which the agent is appointed to make must be in writing: *Heard* v *Pilley* (1869). Whether or not an agency has been created is a matter of interpreting the words used. An agent is one who acts on behalf of another, and Lovejoy's words to Eric: 'Mind the business for me and keep things ticking over', strongly suggest that Lovejoy intended to create a general agency with regard to his business. It also seems he expressly asked Eric to be his agent in regard to two specific transactions: bidding for him at the auction and purchasing the painting from Gimbert.

Having established that an agency has been created, it is then necessary to consider the extent of the agent's authority for, where an agent acts beyond the scope of his authority, his principal (the person on whose behalf he acts) is not bound. An agent may have different kinds of authority:

1. Express authority is the authority which has clearly been given to him by the principal. Where the authority given is capable of more than one interpretation, the principal may be bound even if the agent incorrectly interprets his authority (*Weigall v Runciman* (1916)), unless it is reasonable for the agent to seek clarification and he fails to do so: *European Asian Bank v Punjab & Sind Bank* (1983).
2. Incidental authority is the authority to do all those things which are not specifically referred to in the appointment but which are incidental to carrying out the purpose for which the agent was appointed. This type of authority is interpreted fairly strictly. For example, an agent employed to sell has no incidental authority to receive payment: *Mynn v Joliffe* (1834).
3. Usual authority is the authority which an agent of a particular type usually has (*Watteau v Fenwick* (1893)) and this only applies where the agent belongs to a well known class of agents: *Jerome v Bentley & Co* (1952).
4. Customary authority is authority to act in accordance with the custom of the market in which he is operating (*Graves v Legg* 1857)), but this only applies where the custom is not inconsistent with the principal's express instructions: *Perry v Barnett* (1885).
5. Apparent authority (sometimes referred to as ostensible authority) is the authority which third parties are entitled to assume that the agent has, because the principal has placed in him a particular position or otherwise made a representation to the third party that the agent is entitled to act in the transaction.

In the light of the above definitions, it is now necessary to consider each of the transactions in turn.

The purchase at the auction
As already stated above, Eric appeared to have express authority to bid on Lovejoy's behalf for the epergne. However, that authority was apparently limited by Lovejoy's express instruction: 'Go up to £3,000 if you have to.' While Eric was not expressly forbidden to bid higher, it is submitted that this was implicit in the instruction. It is, however, not necessary to decide this point if the auctioneer did not know of the limitation on Eric's authority. So far as he is concerned, Eric has been held out as Lovejoy's agent and he is entitled to assume that Eric had unlimited authority. Therefore, whatever Eric's express authority was, he had apparent authority to bid as high as he chose on Lovejoy's behalf. Lovejoy will therefore be bound by the contract and will have to seek repayment of the additional £2,000 from Eric.

13 Agency and Sale of Goods – Answers

The purchase bought from Gimbert

The situation here is a little different for, although Eric is clearly Lovejoy's agent with express authority to buy the painting on Lovejoy's behalf, Eric's statement to Gimbert that he is buying for a relative is rather ambiguous, in that it is not clear whether he has disclosed the agency but failed to reveal the name of his principal, or failed altogether to disclose the agency. An agent is not obliged to disclose the name of his principal and, where he does not do so, whether he acted as agent or principal in the transaction depends on the intention of the parties: *Southwell v Bowditch* (1876). Eric clearly intended to act as agent and it will therefore depend on how Gimbert interpreted his words. If both agreed that there was an agency, the usual rules will apply and Lovejoy will be both bound and entitled under the contract.

If, however, Eric failed to disclose the agency at all and led Gimbert to believe he was buying on his own behalf, the rule is slightly different. Both he and Lovejoy will be bound under the contract and either may enforce it or have it enforced against him.

The situation here is that Lovejoy wishes to enforce rights under the contract but Gimbert does not wish to sell to him. There are two situations where an undisclosed principal cannot take the benefit of a contract made on his behalf. Firstly, if it would be inconsistent with its terms (*Siu Yin Kwan v Eastern Insurance Co* (1994)), which would depend on an interpretation of the contract and how Eric had signed it. However, the courts generally show a marked reluctance to exclude the principal's rights in this situation (cf the contrasting cases of *Humble v Hunter* (1848) and *F Drughorn Ltd v Rederiaktiebolagat Transatlantic* (1919). Secondly, if the third party can show that he wanted to deal with the agent and no one else, eg because of the agent's reputation, (*Collins v Associated Greyhound Racecourses Ltd* (1930)), or because the agent owed money to the third party which was to be set off under the contract: *Greer v Downs Supply Co* (1927). This may be the case here but there is nothing in the question to indicate it.

Where the third party simply does not wish to deal with the principal there are a number of additional considerations. Firstly, if the agent expressly states that he is not acting for the principal, the contract can be avoided for fraud or misrepresentation, if this representation induced the contract: *Archer v Stone* (1898). However, it may be that Eric has not misrepresented the situation and he and Lovejoy are in fact related. The situation is then less clear. There are three relevant cases: *Nash v Dix* (1898). In the first, D, a vendor of land, disapproving of the proposed user, refused to sell to P. A then bought from D and sold to P but D repudiated his contract with A. It was held that A was not an agent but a reseller and P was entitled to take the benefit of the contract. It appears that, had A been an agent, P would not have been entitled to do so. The second case is *Said v Butt* (1920) where a theatre critic who was refused tickets by a theatre company had a friend purchase one on his behalf. It was held that the company were entitled to refuse him entry because the personality of the members of the audience was (in this case) a material consideration. In the third case, *Dyster v Randall & Sons* (1926), a somewhat different conclusion was reached. This too concerned the purchase of land by an agent where the vendor did not wish to sell to the principal. This time the principal was permitted to enforce the contract on the ground that refusal would be futile since the agent could assign his rights to the principal.

While this decision has been criticised by, inter alia, Trietel on legal grounds, it seems a sensible, pragmatic approach. However, even if one accepts that given the nature of land, the vendor has a right to be concerned about its ownership, it is submitted that this does not hold true for a painting, and the personality of the principal, in this case Lovejoy, is not a material consideration.

It is therefore submitted that Lovejoy can enforce the contract.

The items purchased from Tinker

In this situation, Eric has no express authority to buy the items in question and his own representation to Tinker that he is running the business for Lovejoy is irrelevant except insofar as it may give Tinker an action against Eric himself or enable him to avoid the contract for breach of warrant of authority or misrepresentation.

To enforce his claim against Lovejoy, Tinker would have to establish that Eric had apparent (ostensible) authority to buy the items on Lovejoy's behalf. If a principal represents to a third party that someone has authority then he is bound and the representation does not need to be express. It can be implied simply by placing the agent in a particular position. For example, in *Summers* v *Solomon* (1857) the owner of a jewellery shop employed a manager to run the shop and regularly paid suppliers for jewellery which the manager purchased for the shop. When the manager continued to make purchases from the suppliers after he had left the defendant's employment, the defendant was held liable to pay for them. Lovejoy's letter to Tinker merely states that Eric will be 'minding the shop' while he is away and it is submitted that, unless it is customary in the trade, or unless Lovejoy is accustomed to allow his shop assistants to make purchases for the shop, this does not represent that Eric has the necessary authority.

It is left only to consider the general terms of Eric's appointment and whether the transaction in question falls within those terms. Initially Lovejoy asked Eric to 'mind the business' and 'keep things ticking over'. It is submitted that there may be more authority implicit in these words than in the phrase used in correspondence with Tinker and that it could be interpreted to mean that Eric had authority to make purchases for the shop. However, the expressions used are very vague and it is submitted that Lovejoy's letter to Tinker may provide clarification of Eric's actual authority and may be interpreted as notifying Tinker of a restriction. While the expressions are vague and Eric may be taken to interpret them as he chooses, it would be up to him to seek clarification from Lovejoy before acting on them.

It is therefore submitted, in conclusion, that Lovejoy is not bound to pay Tinker and Tinker must seek payment from Eric himself.

SUGGESTED ANSWER TO QUESTION TWO

General Comment

This unusual set of facts provides two alternative possibilities: a private sale or a sale in the course of a business. Note that it is the seller's position that is relevant here. The first alternative can be dealt with quite simply as can the question of illegality of the buyer's

13 Agency and Sale of Goods – Answers

intention. The majority of the marks available would be gained by applying the Unfair Contract Terms Act 1977 to a sale in the course of a business.

Key Points

- The implied condition as to satisfactory quality applies to sales in the course of a business – s14(2) Sale of Goods Act (1979) SOGA as amended by s1 Sale and Supply of Goods Act 1994
- Was the car of satisfactory quality within the meaning of the Act? – s14(2A) and (2B) SOGA; *Bartlett* v *Sydney Marcus* (1965); *Crowther* v *Shannon Motor Co* (1975)
- Exclusion of liability under the implied condition is subject to the 'reasonableness' test – s6(3) Unfair Contract Terms Act 1977 (UCTA)
- Factors the court will take into consideration in applying the test – s11(1) and Sch 2 UCTA; *George Mitchell Ltd* v *Finney Lock Seeds Ltd* (1983); *R W Green Ltd* v *Cade Bros Farms* (1978)
- The onus of proving reasonableness is on T – s1(5) UCTA
- The clause will not cover negligence unless clearly stated – *Alderslade* v *Hendon Laundry Ltd* (1945); *Smith* v *South Wales Switchgear* (1978)
- Exclusion of liability for personal injury due to negligence is wholly ineffective – s2(1) UCTA
- 'Unfairness' under the Unfair Terms in Consumer Contracts Regulations 1994
- If the sale were a private one s14(2) SOGA does not apply
- Where a party has the intention of committing an unlawful act at the time of contracting, it may be against public policy to allow him to enforce the contract – *Coral Leisure Group* v *Barnet* (1981)

Suggested Answer

The situation if the sale were a private one

On the assumption that the accident was caused by a defect which existed in the vehicle at the time of the sale, it must be considered whether such defect constitutes a breach of contract by T. The statutory implied term as to satisfactory quality imposed by s14(2) Sale of Goods Act 1979 as amended by the Sale and Supply of Goods Act 1994 does not apply in these circumstances as such term is implied only where the seller sells goods in the course of a business.

It appears that the exclusion clauses were incorporated into the contract, as it is stated that the sales agreement contained the clauses. As a matter of construction the clauses also appear to have covered the defect. The breach does appear to have been 'fundamental', but it is now settled law that the question as to whether or not an exclusion clause covers the breach is a matter of construction of the clause: *Suisse Atlantique* (1976); *Photo Production Ltd* v *Securicor Transport Ltd* (1980).

U is accordingly advised that, if the sale were a private one, he has no cause of action against T.

The situation if T had sold the vehicle in the course of his business

In this event the implied condition as to satisfactory quality provided for in s14(2) Sale of Goods Act would apply. Satisfactory quality is defined as being of a standard that a reasonable person would regard as satisfactory having regard to description, price and all other relevant circumstances: s14(2A) and (2B). A purchaser of a second hand car should expect defects to develop sooner or later: *Bartlett* v *Sydney Marcus* (1965), but it is submitted that the nature of the incident indicates that the car was not usable at the time it was sold: see for example *Crowther* v *Shannon Motor Co* (1975). A car that is not usable is clearly not of satisfactory quality. Clauses 46 and 47 purport to exclude the statutory liability. The effectiveness of these clauses must be now examined in the light of the Unfair Contracts Act (UCTA) 1977. It appears that U made the contract in the course of a business and was accordingly not dealing as a consumer: s12 UCTA. Under s6(3) UCTA the relevant liability can only be excluded in so far as the clauses satisfy the requirement of reasonableness. Under s11(1) regard must be had 'to the circumstances which were, or ought reasonably to have been, in the contemplation of the parties when the contract was made'. Regard must also be had to the matters specified in Sch 2 to the Act. The 'Guidelines' set out in Sch 2 do not assist in the present problem in the absence of further information as to the matters to be considered. In *George Mitchell (Chesterhall) Ltd* v *Finney Lock Seeds Ltd* (1983) the limitation clause was held not to be reasonable because it was the practice of the seller not to rely on such a clause; in a contrasting case the clause was held to be reasonable in view of the quality and price of the goods concerned: *R W Green Ltd* v *Cade Bros Farms* (1978). We do not have any information here as to the business practice of T or the price of the vehicle. The seriousness of the defect, however, would suggest that the clauses would not meet the reasonableness requirement. It must be noted that the onus of proving that the clauses meet the reasonableness requirement is on T: s11(5) UCTA. It is submitted, therefore, that T would be liable for breach of the implied condition of merchantibility. Whether or not he could be sued on this account is considered below.

It is not clear whether T was negligent in selling the car with the defect in question. If he were, then a court might well decide that the clauses in the sale agreement do not cover negligence: *Alderslade* v *Hendon Laundry Ltd* (1945); *Smith* v *South Wales Switchgear* (1978). Even if they do, as far as the personal injuries are concerned, s2(1) UCTA would render the clauses totally ineffective. It must be noted that U's wife, V, was not a party to the contract and therefore the clauses cannot be imposed on her.

While UCTA is probably sufficient to deal with the matter and defeat the clause, it is necessary for the sake of completeness to mention the Unfair Terms in Consumer Contracts Regulations 1994. The Regulations apply to contracts between 'consumers' and sellers of goods or suppliers of services. They apply only to terms which have not been individually negotiated, ie the seller/supplier's standard terms, but they apply to any kind of term, not just excluding and limiting terms. Such a term will be deemed 'unfair' if it does not satisfy the requirement of good faith and if it causes 'a significant imbalance in the parties' rights and obligations under the contract to the detriment of the consumer'. A consumer is defined as: 'a natural person who, in making a contract to which these Regulations apply is acting for purposes which are outside his business'. The guidelines are, however, much the same as those for determining 'reasonableness' under the Act. If the clause is adjudged unreasonable under the Act, it will also be unfair for the purposes of the Regulations.

13 Agency and Sale of Goods – Answers   227

The relevance of U's intention to use the car for an illegal purpose

T assumed that U was going to use the vehicle for a legitimate business; the mere fact that he knew that T had criminal convictions does not make him a party to the illegality. U intended to use the vehicle for an illegal purpose, and bought it for that purpose. Where a party has the intention of committing an unlawful act at the time of contracting it is submitted that it would be against public policy to permit him to enforce the contract: see *Coral Leisure Group* v *Barnet* (1981). Even if T were liable for negligence in selling the car it is contended that to allow U to frame his action in tort would constitute an evasion of the illegality rule and thus would similarly be against public policy.

In conclusion it would appear that U has no cause of action against T. It is, in consequence, unnecessary to consider whether he could recover for his financial loss. If T were negligent V, U's wife, would have a claim in tort against him.

SUGGESTED ANSWER TO QUESTION THREE

General Comment

This problem is relatively straightforward and concerns the application of the Sale of Goods Act 1979 to a 'consumer' contract and the effect of the Unfair Contract Terms Act 1977 on attempts by the seller to exclude or restrict liability under the Sale of Goods Act.

Key Points

- There may be an implied condition as to satisfactory quality – s14(2) Sale of Goods Act 1979 (SOGA) as amended by s1 Sale and Supply of Goods Act 1994
- The meaning of 'satisfactory quality' in this context – s14(2A) and (2B) SOGA; *Bartlett* v *Sydney Marcus* (1965); *Lee* v *York Coach and Marine* (1977)
- The statement as to restoration may be a misrepresentation, exclusion of liability for which under cl 44 is subject to the 'reasonableness' test – s3 Misrepresentation Act 1967 as amended by s8 Unfair Contract Terms Act 1977(UCTA)
- Clause 44 may also be void under s56(3) Consumer Credit Act 1974
- Clause 45 is totally void as H was dealing as a consumer – ss 12 and 6(2) UCTA
- Clause 46 is also subject to the 'reasonableness' test
- Liability of Lom's Garage – s75(1) Consumer Credit Act 1974; *Shanklin Pier* v *Detel Products Ltd* (1951); *Andrews* v *Hopkinson* (1957)
- Application of the Unfair Terms in Consumer Contracts Regulations 1994

Suggested Answer

It is firstly necessary to determine what, if any, is the breach of contract as between Fortin Finance and H.

The contract between H and Fortin Finance is one of sale of goods (it is, apparently, a credit sale, and not a hire-purchase agreement) and one must examine whether there has been a breach of the implied condition in s14(2) Sale of Goods Act 1979 as amended by s1 Sale and Supply of Goods Act 1994. This subsection provides that: 'Where the seller sells goods in the course of business, there is an implied condition that the goods supplied are of satisfactory quality, except that there is no such condition:

a   as regards defects specifically drawn to the buyer's attention before the contract is made; or
b   if the buyer examines the goods before the contract is made, as regards defects which that examination ought to reveal.'

Fortin Finance clearly sell in the course of a business. It does not appear that any defects were specifically drawn to H's attention, so that proviso (a) does not apply. H examined the car thoroughly before taking it out for a test drive, which suggests that proviso (b) may be relevant. However, one can assume that H's examination would not have revealed a defect in the brakes. Section 14(2) probably applies and the question is whether the car was of 'satisfactory quality'. Satisfactory quality is defined as being of a standard that a reasonable person would regard as satisfactory having regard to description, price and all other relevant circumstances: s14(2A) and (2B).

The car in question is a second-hand 1936 model. A second-hand car 'is satisfactory if it is in usable condition, even if it is not perfect' (per Lord Denning MR in *Bartlett* v *Sidney Marcus* (1965)); but a car which is unsafe to drive is clearly unsatisfactory: *Lee* v *York Coach and Marine* (1977). A car whose brakes fail is patently unsafe to drive. The definition of 'satisfactory' in s14(2)A and B requires that regard be had to the price - £4,000 is a not an inconsiderable price. The definition also requires reference to 'all other relevant circumstances'. In this context one must examine the statement of the sales manager of Lom's Garage. He said that the car was not in concours (the word is misspelt in the question) condition. This means that the car was not in superb condition, fit for exhibition. He added that H would 'have to buy it as found'. But he also said that the car was 'restored'. This can only mean that it was restored so as to be able to function safely as a car. Fortin Finance are, it is submitted, liable for this statement. It is safe to assume that Lom's Garage was acting as agent for Fortin Finance. (There might be deemed to be this agency relationship by s56(2) Consumer Credit Act 1974.)

In conclusion, therefore, Fortin Finance are liable for the breach of the implied condition as to satisfactory quality. What now falls for discussion is the effect of the exclusion clauses on this liability.

The clauses are stated to be incorporated in the contract. This does not have to be further discussed. Nor is it necessary to discuss whether, as a matter of construction, the clauses cover the breach and are otherwise effective at common law. This is clearly so. What requires examination is the validity of the clauses under the Unfair Contract Terms Act 1977 (UCTA).

Clause 44
This clause purports to exclude liability for the statement made by the sales manager of Lom's Garage that the car was restored. If this statement was a misrepresentation, then the provisions of s3 Misrepresentation Act 1967 (as amended by s8 UCTA) would make this clause subject to the requirement of reasonableness. If the statement was a contractual term then, paradoxically s3 would not apply (3). But arguably Fortin Finance are in breach of the implied condition as to merchantibility even in the absence of this

statement. In any event cl 44 of the agreement might be rendered void by s56(3) Consumer Credit Act 1974.

Clause 45

H was 'dealing as a consumer' within the provisions of s12 UCTA. Accordingly s6(2) of UCTA applies. This renders the clause totally void.

Clause 46

This clause falls within s4 UCTA which makes such an indemnity clause subject to the requirement of reasonableness as set out in s11. In *Smith* v *Eric S Bush* (1993) Lord Griffiths refers to factors which should always be taken into account in determining whether a clause satisfies the requirement. Among the factors he mentions are the bargaining strength of the parties and their respective financial resources. It can be assumed that H was confronted with a standard form contract with little or no opportunity of negotiating its terms. The parties were, consequently, of unequal bargaining strength. It seems to me also that it is indisputable that Fortin Finance have the greater financial resources, including the greater facility to cover themselves by insurance.

It is therefore submitted that Fortin Finance are liable to H for the loss he has suffered and cannot rely on the indemnity clause in the event of J, the other driver, pursuing a claim against them.

Finally, as to whether Lom's Garage have incurred liability to H at common law. By statute, under s75(1) Consumer Credit Act 1974 Fortin Finance and Lom's Garage might have incurred joint and several liability. At common law it appears that Lom's Garage would be liable on a collateral contract for the statement of the sales manager that the car had been restored, on the principle in *Shanklin Pier Ltd* v *Detel Products Ltd* (1951). This principle was applied in *Andrews* v *Hopkinson* (1957), a case particularly relevant to the situation under discussion.

While the Unfair Contract Terms Act disposes of the problem in this instance, it is necessary for the sake of completeness to mention the Unfair Terms in Consumer Contracts Regulations 1994. The Regulations apply to contracts between 'consumers' and sellers of goods or suppliers of services. They apply only to terms which have not been individually negotiated, ie the seller/supplier's standard terms, but they apply to any kind of term, not just excluding and limiting terms. Such a term will be deemed 'unfair' if it does not satisfy the requirement of good faith and if it causes 'a significant imbalance in the parties' rights and obligations under the contract to the detriment of the consumer'. A consumer is defined as: 'a natural person who, in making a contract to which these Regulations apply is acting for purposes which are outside his business'. The guidelines are, however, much the same as those for determining 'reasonableness' under the Act. If the clause is adjudged unreasonable under the Act, it will probably also be unfair for the purposes of the Regulations.

Old Bailey Press

The Old Bailey Press integrated law library is planned and written to help students at every stage of their studies. Each of our range of Textbooks, Casebooks, Revision WorkBooks and Statutes are all designed to work together and are regularly revised and updated.

We are also able to offer Suggested Solutions which provide students with past examination questions and solutions for most of the subject areas listed below.

Old Bailey Press books can be purchased from University or local bookshops, or in case of difficulty, orders can be placed directly using this form.

Here is the selection of modules covered by our series:

Administrative Law; Commercial Law; Company Law; Conflict of Laws (no Suggested Solutions Pack); Constitutional Law: The Machinery of Government; Obligations: Contract Law; Conveyancing (no Revision Workbook); Criminology (no Casebook or Revision WorkBook); Criminal Law; English Legal System; Equity and Trusts; Law of The European Union; Evidence; Family Law; Jurisprudence: The Philosophy of Law (Sourcebook in place of a Casebook); Land: The Law of Real Property; Law of International Trade; Legal Skills and System; Public International Law; Revenue Law (no Casebook); Succession: The Law of Wills and Estates; Obligations: The Law of Tort.

Mail order prices:

Textbook £10

Casebook £10

Revision WorkBook £7

Statutes £8

Suggested Solutions Pack (1991–1995) £7

Single Paper 1996 £3

Single Paper 1997 £3.

Note: Prices held until 1 August 1999

Students placing orders after 1 August 1999 are advised to confirm prices with Old Bailey Press before ordering

To complete your order, please fill in the form below:

Module	Books required	Quantity	Price	Cost
		Postage		
		TOTAL		

For UK, add 10% postage and packing (£10 maximum).
For Europe, add 15% postage and packing (£20 maximum).
For the rest of the world, add 40% for airmail.

ORDERING

By telephone to Mail Order at 0171 385 3377, with your credit card to hand

By fax to 0171 381 3377 (giving your credit card details).

By post to Old Bailey Press, 200 Greyhound Road, London W14 9RY.

When ordering by post, please enclose full payment by cheque or banker's draft, or complete the credit card details below.

We aim to despatch your books within 3 working days of receiving your order.

Name

Address

Postcode   **Telephone**

Total value of order, including postage: £

I enclose a cheque/banker's draft for the above sum, or

charge my   ☐ Access/Mastercard   ☐ Visa   ☐ American Express
Card number

☐☐☐☐ ☐☐☐☐ ☐☐☐☐ ☐☐☐☐

Expiry date   ☐☐☐☐

Signature: .... Date: ....